SPORT ADMINISTRATION

SPORT ADMINISTRATION

Learning Designs for Administrators of Sport, Physical Education, and Recreation

By

JOHN J. JACKSON, Ph.D.

Director
School of Physical Education
University of Victoria
Victoria, British Columbia, Canada

CHARLES C THOMAS • PUBLISHER
Springfield • Illinois • U.S.A.

Published and Distributed Throughout the World by
CHARLES C THOMAS • PUBLISHER
2600 South First Street
Springfield, Illinois, U.S.A.

© *1981, by* CHARLES C THOMAS • PUBLISHER
ISBN 0-398-04440-6
Library of Congress Catalog Card Number: 80-29290

*With THOMAS BOOKS careful attention is given to all details of
manufacturing and design. It is the Publisher's desire to present books that are
satisfactory as to their physical qualities and artistic possibilities and appropriate for their particular use. THOMAS BOOKS will be true to those laws of
quality that assure a good name and good will.*

Library of Congress Cataloging in Publication Data

Jackson, John J.
   Sport administration

     Bibliography: p.
     Includes index.
     1. Sports—Organization and administration—Study and teaching.
   I. Title
   GV713.J33   796'.06   80-29290
   ISBN 0-398-04440-6

Printed in the United States of America
PS-R-1

For Enid, Debbie, and Richard

PREFACE

V AST AMOUNTS OF PUBLIC and private money are spent on programs to provide physical educational, recreational, and sports opportunities for a wide variety of populations. Thus, many organizational structures exist to facilitate these programs and there is a very great need for skilled administrators. Of course, it is not only for financial reasons that skilled administrators are needed; in today's complex organizations, administrators' nature gives them the potential to enrich or destroy people's lives.

Students of physical education, recreation, and sport, together with their teachers in colleges and universities, typically have respectively found learning about, and teaching, administration to be a frustrating experience. Students often argue lack of relevance for them and, consequently, teachers find students' attention hard to capture and retain. A major cause of this problem has been that material presented to students has had no theoretical basis because the subject has often been taught by teachers who have not studied administration but merely been given the task because of long experience in the field.

Thus the purpose of this book is to enhance the administration teaching-learning process by presenting a theoretical base and then linking it with very specific situations from the fields of physical education, recreation, and sport. All in such a way that successful students will be capable of inquiring, analyzing, discriminating, and deciding. This is not suggesting that an administrator can be totally trained in college; however, he can be taught many fundamentals which will be a sound base from which to build practical capabilities.

The book, then, is principally designed as an undergraduate

class text and has more than enough content for the usual course. By careful selection, the teacher can choose topics that best suit his students' likely needs. Alternatively, a teacher, graduate student, or practicing administrator may use the book for self-tuition; in such situations it would be necessary to delve more deeply into the readings and activities suggested in the designs.

Chapter One explains what is meant by a *learning design* and describes how it may be treated to provide a learning experience. After defining the nature of administration and related terms, Chapter Two considers philosophical issues. The remainder of the book begins by dealing with the structure of organizations and progresses through a range of topics concerned with the management of organizations; paying particular attention to the behavior of the people who constitute the organizations.

Though the intent is to train students to leave university capable of *doing* a job, the content is not of the basic "how to organize a volleyball tournament" type. Rather, the emphasis is on general theories linked with actual cases which have occurred in many parts of the world. Thus, the approach reflects that there are some general statements which can be made about administration and that these generalities apply in the organizational worlds of physical education, recreation, and sport.

J. J. J.

ACKNOWLEDGMENTS

T HE PERMISSION OF the following publishers is gratefully acknowledged for their allowing copyright material to be reproduced: Basil Blackwell Publisher Limited for the Christopher Hodgkinson citations from *Towards a Philosophy of Administration*; Hancock House Publishers Ltd., for adaptation of my chapter in *Safety in Gymnastics*; Macmillan Publishing Co., Inc., for Amitai Etzioni's "Typology of Compliance Relations" and his definitions of power and involvement from *A Comparative Analysis of Complex Organizations*; Macmillan Administration (Basingstoke) Ltd., for Martin Albrow's quotations from *Bureaucracy*; McGraw-Hill Book Company for Douglas McGregor's Theory X and Theory Y reproduced from *The Human Side of Enterprise*; Prentice-Hall, Inc. for the Cutlip and Center citations from *Effective Public Relations*; and Van Nostrand Reinhold Ltd. for the planning figures taken from Thomas L. Burton's *Leisure: Making Man's Environment*.

Several former teachers, colleagues, and supervisors have contributed directly or indirectly to my development, and to this book's, so I sincerely appreciate their help and friendship: Stan Beaumont, Jim Biddle, Jack Boddington, "Chella" Chelladurai, Hobie Clarke, Tim Collins, Ann Hall, Jack Harrison, Peter Heron, Christopher Hodgkinson, Jay Jones, George Little, Larry Locke, Ben Lowe, Gordon McIntosh, Peter McIntosh, Herb McLachlin, John McLeish, Ray Nystrand, Larry Oliver, Bill Orban, Gerry Redmond, Rolf Rogers, Doug Scott, Daryl Siedentop, Gilbert Swift, Gerry Strickland, Jim Thoden, Maria and Gus Vanderpolder, Frank Wellock, John Wheatley, Trevor Williams, and Earle Zeigler.

A number of my former students helped to develop cases and I thank them all for their cooperativeness and their ideas: Blair Boland, Ann Greenwood, Kelley Holgate, Dave Killick, John Lutz, Steven Martin, and Doug Richardson.

I am forever grateful for the fine opportunities to work on satisfying projects which the University of Victoria provides and for the friendships of my School of Physical Education and Faculty of Education colleagues. Certainly my own immediate supervisors, Norma Mickelson, Bruce Howe, and Arthur Kratzmann have done whatever was necessary to provide a setting for my job satisfaction!

Finally, a very special thanks to my graphics expert Lesley Davies and to those amazing, long-suffering typists Betty Christensen, Marion Saunders and Norine Young.

CONTENTS

xi

SPORT ADMINISTRATION

Chapter 1

INTRODUCTION

LEARNING DESIGNS

A *learning design* is an accumulation of information relating to a topic which is intended to be learned by a student. It is called a learning design because the content is presented in an ordered fashion which intends to ensure that the learner fully understands the topic when the learner activities have been completed. Subsequent chapters contain one or more learning designs; the number of designs being dependent on the variety of topics to be dealt with in the chapter.

Learning Design Characteristics

Each design has the following subdivisions:
1. The purpose the design is intended to serve.
2. An essay which presents the concepts, issues, theories, principles, and generalizations which need to be understood for intelligent application.
3. Required (or strongly recommended) related readings.
4. Related supplementary readings.
5. A case study or studies.
6. Suggested learner activities which stem from the issues in the case.

Numbers one through four in the list are easily understood, but the case study and related learning activities need further elaboration.

CASE STUDIES

Those who cannot remember the past
are condemned to repeat it.
                                    Santayana

3

General Considerations

Historical Background

As long ago as 1870, the "case method" was introduced at Harvard in teaching law and used the body of offical opinions which had been collected from the generally authoritative character of legal decisions. It was at Harvard, also, that the Graduate School of Business Administration started to collect and use real cases from the business world in 1919. Of course, these were not of the same nature as legal cases but generally were descriptive of the behavior of people in business organizations who had problems and were required to make decisions (Stein, 1962:28-33).

A "case" to a medical doctor usually means the case history of a patient: it records symptoms, treatments, and results. Similarly is the situation with social workers, counsellors, political scientists, public administrators, and others. Their common ground is the "examination of particulars prior to, or as part of, generalization" (Stein, 1962:16).

Problems requiring decisions are not new in the broad field of sport and nor is the case method of teaching. Writing in 1959, Zeigler expressed the view that physical education and athletics administrators could be best prepared by using the case method. Further that they would be unlikely to be adequate if chosen solely on the basis of previous unrelated scholarly records.

DEFINITION OF A SPORT ADMINISTRATION CASE. Adapting Stein's (1962:25) definition to this context: a sport administration case is a narrative of the events that constitute or lead to a decision, or group of related decisions, by a sport administrator or a group of sport administrators.

Purposes And Advantages Of The Case Method In Sport Administration

The cases presented in the learning designs of this book vary in content to cover a wide range of situations: some are concerned with broad policy decisions which administrators have to make, while others are more mundane. An important feature of all of them is that they deal with issues that existed or still exist. Sometimes, separate incidents have been linked so that a particular point could be made. They all either describe the decisions that were made at the time or leave the decision for the reader to make.

Names of people, places, and dates of events have been changed and disguised. However, this has been done carefully so as not to deviate from the cases' major thrusts.

The cases have been carefully chosen from my own and others' experiences to take into account a variety of purposes which the case method has. The purposes and advantages may be summarized as:

1. To convey vicarious experience of the pressures, complexity, humbling, and numbing reality of actual sport administration problems. This is learning by empathy as the learners place themselves in various role situations.
2. To demonstrate the difficulties of applying textbook principles in actual situations.
3. To develop an understanding of the interdependence in real life of what is usually learned separately in the social sciences in the universities.
4. To develop the ability to suspend judgement before making decisions based on, perhaps, incomplete knowledge. This requires intellectual and emotional poise: the mental toughness to isolate, assimilate, and integrate the multiple cues which lead to deciding from among possible alternative actions.
5. To use empirical findings from sport situations for a better understanding of existing general theories. Conversely, it is a way in which existing theories may be tested by empirical data; thus, the method may contribute to the development of social science theories.
6. To convey substantive knowledge.
7. To make the student be an active participant in the learning process. Experience shows that the case method heightens students' interest in the topics, creates involvement, develops awareness, and leads to a feeling of accomplishment or mastery (cf. Bock 1962:95, and Golembiewski and White, 1976:vii-xxix).

Some Limitations Of The Case Method
In Sport Administration

Whilst largely favoring the case method, Waldo (1952) speculated that it might prove to be a road that "leads nowhere in particular even though it has six lanes and landscaped shoulders." Let's consider briefly how much can be inferred from past experience.

Bertrand Russell (1978:33-36) has provided graphic analogies. We have a firm belief that the sun will rise every day because it has risen in the past. However, some happening in space could conceivably change this occurrence in the future; therefore, the only reason for the belief that the sun will rise again is that it has done so in the past. Similarly, a chicken is fed every day by the same person, then one day, unexpectedly for the chicken, the person wrings its neck instead of feeding it. Thus expectations such as the above are only probable and we should not seek proof that they must be fulfilled; only for reasons in favour of the view that they are likely to be fulfilled.

The principle Russell (1978:37) was examining is called the *principle of induction* and he stated it in general law terms as follows:

(a) The greater the number of cases in which a thing A has been found associated with a thing of sort B, the more probable it is (if no causes of failure of association are known) that A is always associated with B;

(b) Under the same circumstances, a sufficient number of cases of the association of A with B will make it nearly certain that A is always associated with B and will make this general law approach certainty without limit.

But Russell cautions here there may be other data that could seriously alter the probability. For example, a man who has seen only white swans might argue, on this principle, that it is probable that all swans are white. Thus, we base our conduct on associations that have worked in the past and we think are likely to work in the future; this likelihood is dependent for its validity on the inductive principle which has been shown to have flaws.

Later, in the learning designs, various "laws," theories, generalizations, and principles will be identified as propagated by their originators. By applying administration case material to the type of "law" test that Russell described, bearing in mind the likely confounding factors, it can readily be seen that certainty of outcome cannot be forecast. Thus, when trying to relate the theories to the cases' problems, this limitation should always be borne in mind.

Furthermore, the theories should be looked at as carefully as possible to see how they were derived. In administration, generally, there is a paucity of theories which have been derived from scientific methods. In sport, in particular, there are few administrative theories that have been scientifically tested or derived. Zeigler and Spaeth (1975:xiv) described much administration of physical education and athletics research as little more than "utilitarian principles" which dissolve in "value-laden declarative statements" under close scrutiny and have little "predictive strength."

This section serves as a cautionary note but ends more optimistically. Ten years down the elegant six-lane road that leads to nowhere in particular, Waldo (1962:63) had this to say of the case method: "It is a tool with limitations, but is also one of demonstrated usefulness. There is no responsible alternative to using it." That, too, is my opinion.

Methods of Analyzing Cases

The teacher has a vital role to play in preliminary and ongoing analyses of cases. There is no substitute for the teacher's experience and theoretical knowledge of the case content. Of course the analysis is enhanced if the students also have experience; they will have theoretical knowledge from what they have been required to do in the earlier part of the design.

All the methods listed below can be used as oral or written exercises. Oral treatment is mostly favored because discussion with peers and experienced, knowledgeable people tends to reveal more of the complexities and so enhance analytical skills.

As well as prediscussion reading of the theoretical component of the designs, students should also read the case before the class when the analysis is to take place. This helps to ensure that the main issues in the case are identified and the combined wisdom is likely to uncover related problems. It is useful to reveal all the related problems because they make the situation realistic. However, care should be taken to deal mainly with very important points and not trivia.

Having clarified case facts and told the students to focus on given detail, the teacher should allow the students to have free discussion for awhile. In big classes, this is usefully done by dividing the class into small groups of three students. Whichever method is used for free discussion, the teacher should later lead the way to the desired outcome by skillful questioning of the entire class. In this way the students begin to understand how the particulars of the case can be related to generalizations, and they also have the experience of making difficult decisions from possible alternative choices.

A number of specific case analysis methods are described below. Usually, it is best to use one per case in class; however, cross-combinations of parts of the separate methods become possible and appropriate as students' expertise grows. Alternatively, a case may be analyzed in two separate ways; for example, Case Analysis Methods A and E (see immediately below). Finally, groups of three or four students may be required to present a case analysis to the whole class as a term assignment.

Case Analysis Method A (CAM A)

The numbered stages should be dealt with in the order they are listed.

1. Identification of the problem(s)/issue(s).
    (a) The nature of the problem—fundamental pathology?
                                   —basically healthy?
    (b) Place the problems in priority order.
2. Identify the goals for administrative action.
    (a) Short-term.
    (b) Long-term.
3. Using all relevant theory concepts and/or experience/intuition, weigh the plausible alternatives and their likely consequences.
4. Develop a strategy for administrative action.
5. Compare what actually happened with the proposal for action. Obviously this can only be done when the actual outcome is known.
6. Identify the principles that evolve. This is closely linked with number three above.

Case Analysis Method B (CAM B)

The analysis should answer the following questions.
1. What is going on? (The symptoms.)
2. Why is it happening? (The causes.)
3. What are the alternatives for correcting the causes?
4. Considering all the relevant variables, what is your optimum solution and why is it optimum? The optimum solution should include the contingency plans for action that would be used if the main strategy proved to be wrong.

Case Analysis Method C (CAM C)

Write a case study that relates to a specified administrative topic and then analyze the case using CAM A, CAM B, or CAM E (see below). The case narrative should include:
1. A description of the people involved which includes details of their social background and psychological characteristics.
2. A description of the social setting.
3. A series of events which clearly pinpoints a specified administrative topic.
4. The clear need for a sport administrator to make a decision.
5. The actual outcome of the case in the form of an appendix.

Case Analysis Method D (CAM D)

Use CAM E (see below) with CAM A or CAM B to produce a more sophisticated analysis and decision. See the example of this approach later in the chapter.

Case Analysis Method E (CAM E)

This method has rarely (probably never) been used in sport administration classes outside of my own. Its rarity makes necessary a rather longer explanation than has been given to the other methods. However, once the concepts are understood, the analysis can be done quite quickly.

A statement made by John Gronouski, former Dean of the Lyndon Baines Johnson School of Public Affairs at the University of Texas, serves as an introduction: "I haven't done my job if I graduate a kid who doesn't understand that no policy change is possible in any public entity without political realities being taken into account. It's not in the catalogue but the most important course I teach is the fine art of compromise." Similarly, Butler's (1971) *The Art of the Possible* was about national and international political life and recognized that many fine ideas were held by theorists but, frequently, the ideas were not practical in the real world. What perceptive, intelligent politicians should do is strive for "the art of the possible."

There follows here a brief description of the work developed from social anthropology for modern organization theory by Rogers (1971). Traditionally, when analyzing organizations in Western society, the approach has been through structural and functional components of organization; that is, through the planning, organizing, staffing, directing, and controlling functions. On the other hand, behavioral aspects have usually dealt with personality, group interaction, motivation, leadership, intergroup conflict, and other similar issues. Rogers' (1971) point is that these approaches are fine but that insufficient emphasis has been directed towards the aspects of human organization which are political in nature.

Rogers (1971:139) argues that organizations "are small societies—be they a convent, an industrial firm, or a tribe of Bushmen in the Kalahari." As such they are subject to certain basic influences (in a relative sense) that originate within them and from the environment. Thus, all organizations have "an idealogic (religious) system, a social system (status and role relationships), a technological (economic) system, a judicial system, and a political system." These systems are only distinguishable for analytical purposes and may be present in very varying degrees; but they are always present.

FIELD-ENVIRONMENT. Rogers (1971:46-47, 131) used the field-environment construct as the empirical configuration within which the analysis of the political process can be carried out. Making organization-oriented goals the focus of investigation, his definitions were:

> The political *field* encompasses the individuals and groups, together with their repertories of resources, values, and rules directly involved in the process or processes centering on these goals. . . . Its social and territorial scope and the areas of behavior it involves change as additional actors enter into the process or as former participants

withdraw as they bring new types of activities into their interaction and abandon old types.

The *environment* incorporates the field and is made up of those individuals and groups with their repertories who are directly involved with the actors in the field but not in the process under investigation.

It is seen, then, that the distinction between the field and the environment is purely analytical and requires the analyst to define his operational distinction.

THE POLITICAL PROCESS. Rogers (1971:47) adapted his understanding of political activity from Swartz (1968) and Turner's (1957) "political phase development" which represents the types of related processes that occur over time in "fields." The phases in the political process are:

1. *The mobilization of political capital* in which individuals or groups build up support for themselves and those with whom they identify.
2. *Breach of the peace.*
3. The *crisis* is a "momentous juncture or turning point in the relations between components of a political field." It is when "apparent peace becomes overt conflict and covert antagonisms become visible."
4. Other variables moderate what has happened and constitute *counterveiling tendencies.* These inhibit complete cleavage in organizations where there is widespread agreement on basic values. Rogers (1971:47) points out that this phase is particularly characteristic of organizations in which subgroups are multifunctional and most relations are multiplex. Multiplex refers to those relationships where the network of interaction between individuals is multiple rather than single. A sport administrator often has multiplex relationships in his organization and his instructor has a simplex relationship with a client; that is, the interaction between the squash instructor and a student is confined to advice on squash (Rogers, 1971:19-24 citing Gluckman, 1955:18-20.)
5. Closely related with number four above is *deployment of adjustive or redressive mechanisms.* It works in the same direction as number four and, if successful, leads to phase six.
6. *Restoration of the peace* involves the reestablishment of

relations between the parties and changes in field-environment boundaries. As well, the organizational groups may change together with different allocations of power, prestige, and other resources.

In summary Rogers (1971:135) stated: "Thus Turner's phases constitute, essentially, the basic modes of political activity in most—if not all—groups when examined over time." He was careful to point out, however, that all the phases do not always occur and that they do not necessarily happen in the order described above. Nevertheless, it is a most useful analytical device.

My own view is that when students become familiar with the process, they can understand what is "going on" in an organizational setting and it sometimes helps them to predict what will happen next. To comprehend this more fully the related readings are recommended and, also, an example of a case being analyzed by CAM E is given later in this chapter. To test this process outside of sport, students are advised to analyze C. P. Snow's (1951) *The Masters.*

Finally, Rogers' (1971) purpose is to suggest that organizations are becoming more multiplex so that their administration becomes more political. If not handled properly by skilled administrators, then conflict and confrontation occurs. Handled well, there will be few dysfunctional consequences.

An Example of Case Analysis Method B

This example is briefly stated here with the reminder that it would best be analyzed by guided discussion and skillful questioning.

Case Narrative

Penny Wheeler, a young physical education teacher, was disturbed that no racquet sports could be offered in her school's program because of inadequate facilities. Finally, after much persuasion, her principle agreed that two badminton courts could be marked out in the lunch room, which had an adequately high ceiling. The room was used for lunches and as a study hall so that the only time it could be used for badminton was 4:00 P.M.

There was a good turnout of students on the first day of badminton and many had hardly had any playing time when the janitor walked onto the court with his broom at 5:00 P.M.

Wheeler: You can't clean now. We'll be here until 6:00 P.M.

Janitor: This is the only time I have. You give me one order, the drama teacher wants the stage set up, Mr. Davies has told me to clean out his chemistry storeroom, and I have to lock all the doors and windows.

Wheeler: You just can't do it now. I have all these students waiting to play.

Janitor: This is the last straw. I'm leaving this madhouse.

With that, he threw his broom down and stormed out of the room.

Analysis

WHAT IS GOING ON? (THE SYMPTOMS.) A teacher who is trying to improve her program gives an order to a janitor, which causes a dispute between the two and leads to the janitor walking off his job.

WHY IS IT HAPPENING? (THE CAUSES.) There are three major reasons:

1. The principle of authority has been violated. It states, (a) that there should be a clear line of authority that is known and recognized by all employees, and (b) that each worker should only report to one supervisor.
2. The principle of definition has been violated. It states that the duties, authority, responsibilities of each position, and relations between positions should be defined and made known to everyone.
3. The principle of correspondence was violated. It states that authority should be commensurate with responsibility.

WHAT ARE THE ALTERNATIVES? There are no good alternatives that would correct the causes other than those described in the optimum solution.

WHAT IS YOUR OPTIMUM SOLUTION? The principal must establish within his school's structure the principles of authority, definition, and correspondence. Given all of these, an incident such as the one described would not occur. Penny Wheeler should be advised to build "political support" for herself within the school by being "nice" to people, and she should not just give harsh orders to any employee.

Additional Comments

The above is a brief, but very much to the point, written analysis. It is one way this case could be analyzed. A more usual way would be to analyze by discussion and questioning. Without training, students do not isolate the issues and they do not relate cases to general principles. It is very important that general principles be linked to the cases. If there are no general theories, see if the case may be leading to some new ones.

Quite often, then, cases in this book do not describe all that happened so that the student has to make decisions without any guidance or hindsight.

An Example of Case Analysis Method D

Because the original case here is very lengthy, only a summary is provided. Also, the analysis is an example of the type of treatment it may receive. The analysis does not claim to deal comprehensively with all the issues. Again, a case analysis *may* be written as an assignment but discussion and questioning would probably be more efficient.

Summary of the Facts in the Case

The Wukari Company was a foreign owned sporting goods company which operated branches in Ibadan, Benin City, and Kano from its Lagos headquarters. Established in 1935, it originally imported goods from Britain but recently started manufacturing in Nigeria in the hope that profits would rise. All middle and top executives were foreign whilst supervisors and workers were Nigerian.

Joseph Oyo, a diploma-accountant, had worked very successfully as a sales supervisor at the Ibadan Branch for ten years despite repeated requests to move to Lagos as assistant accountant. He wanted to move because he did not like the considerable travelling his job entailed, and, also, he wanted to work in a better position for which he was qualified. Further, Oyo wanted to be near his family. Finally, Ibadan manager, Brian Smith, arranged

Oyo's transfer to Lagos as assistant accountant where he soon excelled and was given more work and responsibility by the chief accountant. After awhile Oyo had to delegate some of his tasks to subordinates who resented the action and felt he was becoming despotic. However, the chief accountant was pleased because overall efficiency had increased and he recommended Oyo for a new position as associate accountant.

The Executive Board's policy was to advertise new positions within the organization and select purely on merit but, nevertheless, asked Lagos to submit another name in addition to Oyo. The chief accountant reluctantly recommended Benjamin Warri, a highly rated business administration graduate who had been with the company for two-and-one-half years. The Selection Committee interviewed all and chose Warri.

Oyo and the chief accountant were shocked and management was in an awkward situation because Warri, who had been working for Oyo, would in the future be his supervisor. Two days later Oyo resigned.

Analysis

IDENTIFICATION AND DISCUSSION OF SYMPTOMS. The symptoms indicating that all was not well in the Wukari Company revolved primarily around the area of unsatisfactory superior-subordinate relations. These relations will be analyzed in the next section but, briefly, they included the "colonial" attitudes of the board and of Brian Smith, which must have annoyed Oyo. For example, the board employed *no* Nigerians in higher positions, and Smith showed no understanding of Oyo's personal wishes. The lines of authority and job descriptions were not clear (see Oyo passing extra work to subordinates who resented it). The final symptoms were Oyo's resignation coupled with the chief accountant's being "upset."

IDENTIFICATION AND DISCUSSION OF CAUSES. It is proposed here to analyze the "process" (of Oyo's resignation) using the conceptual framework described by Rogers (1971). He drew principally on the work of Swartz (1968) and Turner (1957) for his model and wrote: ". . . we have made organization-oriented goals the focus of investigation and have defined the political field as encompassing the individuals and groups, together with their repertories of the process or processes centering on these goals. The environment incorporates the field and is made up of those individuals and groups with their repertories who are directly involved with the actors in the field but not in the process under investigation."

Following this conception, Rogers used Turner's *Political Phase Development* to analyze the political activity. The components will be identified below with reference to this case.

The field consists of the people contributing to Wukari's goals who were directly involved in the lead-up to Oyo's resignation (the political process being studied); that is, Oyo, Warri, the chief accountant, the Executive Board, and the Executive Board's Selection Committee. The contents of the field include the values, meanings, resources, and relationships perceived and employed by these principal participants in the process. These are particularly significant for they relate to the cultural differences between the colonial foreign capitalists and the hardworking Nigerian who had strong family ties, a very different cultural background, and the seemingly impossible task of improving his life's situation.

The environment, which incorporates the field, includes the religious, economic, social values, meanings, and resources of the Wukari Company. Also, the executives, the supervisors, the workers, the top management teams, Brian Smith, Oyo's Lagos subordinates, and Oyo's family. These values, meanings, and resources may be employed or *not* employed to have an effect on a process. For example, the colonial attitude of the board is its value; the chief accountant is a resource whose recommendation is not accepted (i.e. not employed). Some of the meanings are difficult to interpret in this case; for instance, the board promotes on "merit" but what is meant by "merit?" It must be assumed that either it considers a management graduate to have more potential than a diploma-accountant or else it fears the possibility of a hardworking Nigerian being able to rise on his ability in the company—thus ultimately threatening the board's own position.

To explain the general sequence of events in this case, Turner's "Political Phase Development" will be used. First, mobilization of political capital in which the "actors" build up support for themselves, is represented by Oyo's hard work within the company and by the way he was able to satisfy the chief accountant. The board members appointed a Selection Committee and made arbitrary rules so that they could do what they liked.

The second phase, breach of the peace, occurred when the chief accountant was requested to submit another name in addition to Oyo's and this soon led to the third phase, crisis, which was Warri's appointment.

Countervailing tendencies, the fourth phase, are represented by the chief accountant being upset at Warri's appointment and the predicament management is in when trying to handle the new situation in practice.

The fifth phase, deployment of adjustive or redressing mechanisms immediately follows the fourth in that Oyo resigns and this leads to the final phase, restoration of the peace. Rogers (1971:72) carefully pointed out that though "peace" carries the connotation of reconciliation and reconciliation does not occur in this case, for analytical purposes, the termination of the episode can be regarded as "peace."

ALTERNATIVE SOLUTIONS. 1. *Continue from where the case ends.* Most likely the same type of situation would occur again at a later date. Such autocratic management is likely to produce an unhappy work force so that eventually profits will go down. Alternatively, if Warri *really* was chosen on objective merit, the situation may improve. For instance, his greater book knowledge may enable him to get subordinates to work without resentment and hence company profits may rise.

2. *Ask Oyo to withdraw his resignation* and Warri to resume as assistant accountant. If this occurred it would seem that profits would continue to rise. However, it is unlikely that the "colonial" board would be willing to reverse its decision though it may if the chief accountant was able to give good reasons (economic and social). Oyo may still have difficulties with his subordinates unless better job descriptions and lines of communication were established. Such improvement would be an Executive Board responsibility in the first place and would have to be implemented at headquarters. There is no indication that the Executive Board has either the knowledge or intention to take such actions and, in practice, they would not be likely to change suddenly. Therefore, the probable outcome of Oyo being reinstated remains

problematical. Further it must be recognized that Oyo may not be willing to rejoin the company because he has had long experience of his rulers and may rightly feel they will never change to his advantage.

OPTIMUM SOLUTION. The writer assumes himself to be in the position of consultant to the Executive Board *after* Oyo has resigned. Bearing in mind the political process that has taken place, and the reasons for it, it is not recommended that Oyo be asked to return. The board would be advised to take the following actions in order to achieve its future profit goals:

1. Invite some Nigerian businessmen to join the Executive Board so that the cultural difference between the employees and the board could be better "bridged." The Nigerian board members would understand the workers' cultural background, would not be likely to be so brutal, and the workers would not have cause to feel too dominated by colonialists.

2. For the same reasons as those stated in number one above, a procedure for selecting Nigerians for middle and top executive positions should be established.

It may seem to the Executive Board members that one and two may eventually lead to their personal downfall but it need not do so if numbers are controlled. The Nigerians may become powerful but still the company would profit and a genuine partnership of cultures could arise. Otherwise it is felt the company would eventually die because Nigerians do not want to be subservient—particularly as they become more wealthy, educated, and possess more skills.

3. The lines of authority between all employees and the Executive Board must be clearly defined and made known to all. Additionally, job descriptions must be given to all and discussed. This would help to alleviate the sort of dissatisfaction that arose between Oyo and his subordinates and would lead to each individual having some say in his working functions.

4. It is recommended that trained personnel officers be appointed to headquarters and branches (the number depending on the number of staff). Or, that managers be given training in personnel supervision. This would enable individuals' personal desires to be considered and accounted for in a way that would ultimately contribute to the goals of the company.

Summary

The structure of the book, which is made up of sport administration learning designs was explained. A learning design is an accumulation of information relating to an administrative topic which is intended to be learned by the student.

Each design contains an explanation of its purpose and an essay which presents the concepts, issues, theories, principles, and generalizations which need to be understood by the student for intelligent application. Recommended readings are given and supplementary readings listed.

The final part of each design contains a case study and may be used in a variety of ways. After briefly outlining the case method's history, a sport administration case was defined as a narrative of the events that constitute or lead to a decision, or a group of related decisions, by a sport administrator or a group of sport administrators.

The purposes, strengths, and limitations of the case method were discussed and the conclusion was reached that it has demonstrated usefulness and that there is no responsible alternative to using it if skilled administrators are to be trained. This is particularly so if some decisions are left to the learner and the analysis is always related to theory.

Five methods of analyzing cases were described and examples of two analyses were presented for students' guidance in carrying out the learner activities in subsequent chapters.

References

Bock, Edwin A.: Case studies about government: Achieving realism and significance. In Bock, Edwin A. (Ed.): *Essays on the Case Method in Public Administration.* New York, International Institute of Administrative Sciences, 1962.

Butler, Lord R.A.: *The Art of the Possible.* London, Hamish Hamilton, 1971.

Gluckman, Max: *The Judicial Process Among the Barotse of Northern Rhodesia.* Manchester, England, Manchester University Press, 1955.

Golembiewski, Robert T., and White, Michael (Eds.): *Cases in Public Management,* 2nd ed. Chicago, Rand McNally, 1976.

Rogers, Rolf E.: *The Political Process in Modern Organizations.* New York, Exposition Press, 1971.

Russell, Bertrand: *The Problems of Philosophy.* Oxford, Oxford University

Press, 1978 (Eighth impression). First published in Home University Library, 1912.

Snow, Charles Percy: *The Masters*. London, Macmillan, 1951.

Stein, Harold: On public administration and public administration cases. In Bock, Edwin A. (Ed.): *Essays on the Case Method in Public Administration*. New York, International Institute of Administrative Sciences, 1962.

Swartz, Marc J. (Ed.): *Local-Level Politics*. Chicago, Aldine, 1968.

Turner, V. W.: *Schism and Continuity in an African Society*. Manchester, England, Manchester University Press, 1957.

Waldo, Dwight: Review of Stein, Harold (Ed.): *Public Administration and Policy Development: A Case Book*. New York, Harcourt, Brace and Co., 1952. In *American Political Science Review, XLVI*:876, 1952.

Waldo, Dwight: Five perspectives on the cases of the inter-university case program. In Bock, Edwin A. (Ed.): *Essays on the Case Method in Public Administration*. New York, International Institute of Administrative Sciences, 1962.

Zeigler, Earle F.: *Administration of Physical Education and Athletics: The Case Method Approach*. Englewood Cliffs, New Jersey, Prentice-Hall, 1959.

Zeigler, Earle F., and Spaeth, Marcia J. (Eds.): *Administrative Theory and Practice in Physical Education and Athletics*. Englewood Cliffs, New Jersey, Prentice-Hall, 1975.

Chapter 2

ADMINISTRATION AND PHILOSOPHY

LEARNING DESIGN 2.1

THE NATURE OF ADMINISTRATION

The purpose of this learning design is to establish what is meant by the word "administration" and some closely related terms. This will be done by making reference to the past, by stating some current definitions, and by defining the interpretation of the word as it is used later in this book.

Historical Perspective

As long ago as 3,000 B.C., the Sumerians, famous for their development of a written language, kept business, legal, and historical records on clay tablets. "Thus, some of the earliest writings in existence provide illustrations of managerial control" (Hodgetts, 1975:6). The Babylonians' (2,350 B.C.) most significant contribution in this area of interest was their Code of Hammurabi, which contained 285 laws dealing with various concerns; among them some on managerial guidelines covering such topics as control, responsibility, and minimum wage. For example, a hired farmhand stealing seeds or crops would have his fingers cut off (Harper, 1904:37 cited by Hodgetts, 1975:7).

In what is believed to be the world's oldest military treatise, the ancient Chinese (500 B.C.) made contributions to administrative thought with Sun Tzu's *The Art of War*. In it he outlined what should be a general's strategy, tactics, and ways to outmaneuver the enemy (Phillips, 1941:26 cited by Hodgetts, 1975:8-9).

The Romans provided many illustrations of efficient management techniques; consider, for example, their roads which can

21

still be seen in England. However, the most famous example is in the administrative work of Diocletian (A.D. 284) who designed a new structure for the whole empire. Instead of having many people reporting directly to him, he divided the empire into one hundred provinces and placed each province in one of thirteen dioceses. The dioceses were further divided into four geographical areas; each with one administrator. Diocletian administered one diocese himself so only had three people reporting to him. With two levels between himself and the provincial governors, who only had civil power (opposed to military power), it was very difficult for anyone to defy his imperial authority (Hodgetts, 1975:9).

Though the Roman Empire has not survived to the present day, one of its formal organizations has. That is, of course, the Roman Catholic Church which has made some important contributions to administrative theory in terms of hierarchy of authority, functional specialization, and the staff concept (Koontz and O'Donnell, 1972:20 cited by Hodgetts, 1975:9-11).

In looking for advanced pioneers of "scientific management" (see Chapter 5), an instance is found in the Arsenal of Venice. It was probably the largest industrial establishment of the fifteenth century; covering sixty acres of land and water it employed two thousand workers engaged in shipbuilding. It has been said to anticipate modern meat packing and automobile assembly plants (Lane, 1934:129-175 cited by Albers, 1969:11-12).

Though more is written about Machiavelli in Chapter Five, he is important in this historical perspective. Born in 1469 in Florence, he later made careful analyses of the prince's (administrator's) job and derived some practical principles which many find useful today (Machiavelli, 1961).

The Industrial Revolution occurred between 1700 and 1785 and its effects were most notable in Great Britain where major changes took place in the basic organization of production. The stages are not very important here but basically progressed from home industries (domestic system) to the "factory system" in which the management controlled the new division of labor, coordination, and the work flow. Thus, management of this period became interested in the mechanical aspect of jobs; higher production by having one man do the work of many (Smith, 1937:7 cited by Hodgetts, 1975:15).

Ancient Sport Administration

Just as administration was traced to the Sumerian civilization (3,000-1,500 B.C.), so can be the first real evidence of sports and games. Archaeological artifacts show drawings of boxers and wrestlers engraved on clay tablets (Howell and Howell, 1979:5). Some historians think the drawings may be representing dancers but, nevertheless, on this evidence, and on what follows in this chapter, it is reasonable proof that some form of sport administration existed in the earliest river valley civilization.

For further indication of ancient sport administration it must be remembered that the Olympic Games were set against a background of athletic interest which was already prevalent in Homeric Greece. The ancient Olympic Games began in 776 B.C. and were held every fourth year until A.D. 393 when they were abolished by the Roman Emperor Theodosius (Howell and Howell, 1979:33-34).

Thus, it can be seen that administration in general, and sport administration in particular, are as ancient as man himself. Terms used to describe the practice may have been different, and certainly the need for good administrators and managers has grown as society has become more complex.

Recent Definitions

A review of recent interpretations of "administration" and "management" reveals that the words are often used synonymously or as meaning different things to different people.

General

Hodgetts (1975:5) points to the popular definition of *management* as, "getting things done through people." A similar view, but with reference to administration, is "cooperative group behavior." (Simon, Smithburg, and Thompson, 1950:4). Or, as Simon (1976:72) stated elsewhere, administration is "the art of getting things done," and administrative organizations are "systems of cooperative behavior."

According to Haimann and Scott (1974:6), management may refer to executive personnel, processes, or "a body of knowledge, a practice, a discipline." They took this last aspect from Lilienthal's statement, "In creating the Tennessee Valley Authority, Congress adopted and carefully wrote into law the basic principles of modern management." (Lilienthal, 1944:167). Incidentally, here, Lilienthal's diaries provide most interesting reading for anyone keen to see behind the scenes of administration. However, Haimann and Scott's (1974:6) definition stresses "process" and is: "Management is a social and technical process that utilizes resources, influences human action, and facilitates changes in order to accomplish an organization's goals."

Having pointed out that "management" is commonly used as a noun, verb, and adjective, Sikula (1973:17) uses it only to refer to the process. He maintains a good definition should identify the managerial processes, the human element, and a statement on the overall purpose of the process. Thus, for Sikula: "Management includes the processes of planning, organizing, controlling, leading, staffing, motivating, decision making, and communication, in an attempt to coordinate human and nonhuman resources for the purpose of efficiently and systematically achieving the stated objectives of any organization." He, further, views "management" as a discipline.

Penultimately, as representative of general definitions, Albers (1969:vii) regards the basic elements of managerial action to be "planning, communication, and motivation within an organized managerial structure." He believes the skills involved have *universal* properties which can be applied in various functional areas, at any level of an organizational hierarchy. 'Finally, Drucker (1973:x) describes management as "the alternative to tyranny."

Sport Administration

Here some views of "administration" by sport writers are investigated. Zeigler (1959:9), in the educational field, sees "administration" associated with such terms as "superintendence, direction, management, planning, supervision, organization, regulation, guidance, and control." In common usage it is "the process of directing people in an endeavor." Later, Zeigler (1977:217) wrote a chapter with the title, "The Role of Administration (Management)," which seems to indicate that he views the words as synonymous. Voltmer and Esslinger (1967:v) stated the words were synonymous in common usage and described the crux of either to be "managing human behavior."

Resick, Seidel, and Mason (1970:21) also see the concept as a process with their definition, "The function of administration is the process by which the job gets done." Frost and Marshall (1977:1-2) were more explicit with: "Administration consists of the leadership and guidance of individuals, the procuring and manipulating of resources, and the coordinating of many diverse efforts—to the end that effective progress be made toward the achievement of the goals and purposes of the organization."

In a general critique of definitions, Dale (1973:4) has made some useful observations. Those definitions concerned only with managing people assume that all the manager needs to know is how to get people to do what he wants them to do, but that is no good if he does not know what they should be doing. Also, the definitions that emphasize "processes" ignore the important administrative function of *setting* objectives.

Administration-Management Definition

In this section a distinction is made between administration and management. First, a list of dictionary (*Webster's New Collegiate Dictionary*, 8th ed.) definitions is presented so as to identify various classes of meanings. Administration is:

1. The act or process of administering;
2. The performance of executive duties (management);
3. (a) A body of persons who administer;
   (b) A group constituting the political executive in a presidential government;
4. The term of office of an administrative officer or body;
5. The execution of public affairs as distinguished from policy-making.

This list helps to clarify the classes of administration but it still suggests in one place (number 2) that it is synonymous with management. Number five is one which requires most explanation and the dictionary definition is at odds with the most distinguished writers on the topic!

To clarify what I mean by administration and management, Hodgkinson's (1978:4) definition is employed (Figure 1).

Art	———————	Science
Policy	———————	Execution
Values	———————	Facts
Upper Echelons	———————	Lower Echelons
Strategy	———————	Tactics
Qualitative	———————	Quantitative
Human	———————	Material
Reflective	———————	Active
Generalism	———————	Specialism

ADMINISTRATION   **MANAGEMENT**

Figure 1. Conceptual continua for the definition of administration (Courtesy of Basil Blackwell Publisher Ltd.)

Pointing out that tight definitions cannot be given for such complex concepts, Hodgkinson (1978:4-5) expands:

> Without by any means exhausting the dimensions associated with these sets of activities it can be seen that any definition would have to allow for a continuum from the highest level of administration to the lowest level of management, the more so since, as Barnard points out (1972:6), these functions are pervasive across organizations and across persons in organizations regardless of title or ostensible rank. In general then we mean by administration those aspects dealing more with the formulation of purpose, the value laden issues, and the human component of organizations. By management we mean those aspects which are more routine, definitive, programmatic, and susceptible to quantitative methods. Curiously, the two terms have differing transatlantic usages; the interpretation given here controverts, for example, that of Keeling (1972), *The Administrative Process in Britain* (Methuen, 1972). It does, however, conform to the American authorities most relevant to this text (Simon, Barnard) and indeed with the nomenclature of the Royal Institute of Public Administration [in Britain]. By and large, administrators in our terms will tend to be located high in the organizational status hierarchy while managers will tend to the middle and lower levels of supervision and responsibility. Loosely, we can consider administration to be the art of influencing men to accomplish organizational goals while management is the ancillary and subordinate science of specifying and implementing means to accomplish the same ends. Administration is ends-oriented, management is means-oriented. The pure administrator is a philosopher, the pure manager— a technologist. But there is no approximation to purity at either end of the spectrum in the fact and practice of administration or management.

Two points are of incidental interest here when Hodgkinson acknowledges the influences on him of Simon and Barnard. In the case of Simon, however, he points to Simon's "rather unsuccessful" attempt "to disentangle administrative from policy decisions." (Simon, 1976:53-54). And Barnard did not like the terms administration or management but preferred instead the usage "executive." As with Hodgkinson, in this book, executive is used synonymously with administrator or administrative (Hodgkinson, 1978:6).

Hodgkinson (1978:6) reiterates that both categories of activity pervade any organization: "And in the hard world outside of academic distinctions managers will persist in intrusion into the administrative ambit while administrators will persist in withdrawing from responsibilities by 'a retreat into management.'"

Administration's General Nature

Business administration, hospital administration, public administration, educational administration, sport administration, and others have the common aspect of administration. It is the contention here that administration in-general incorporates a "form of human behavior which defines and achieves ends through organizations" (Hodgkinson, 1978:7). As Barnard (1976: xxviii) has reasoned: "Clergymen, military men, government officials, businessmen, and university officials have common problems and adopt similar strategies to meet them. They understand each other easily outside of technical discussion."

Zeigler (1979:4-5) tried to identify which skills and competencies a manager should have. He reviewed 700 "management science" papers written between 1960 and 1975 and ended with what seemed like "more than one hundred discrete competencies and/or skills" and he had "only scratched the surface." Thus, he decided to group them under the "Three-skill approach" made famous by Katz (1974:90-102). Katz's three skills were *technical*, *human*, and *conceptual*, but Zeigler, from his research, found it necessary to add a "mixed skill category" (conjoined skills) and one in which "self-development skills" (personal skills) could be placed. Zeigler's purpose, it should be noted, was to develop a competency-based approach for management development in sport and physical education.

Characteristics Of Administrative-Managerial Work

It has been pointed out that administration has general

qualities no matter what field the endeavor and, also, that administration and management occur to some degree at all levels of organizational hierarchies. Furthermore some people's time will be almost entirely devoted to administrative-managerial tasks. What is life like for such people and what are they like themselves?

A number of studies have been done to investigate these issues but one by Mintzberg (1973) provides ample information for the purpose here. The administrator or manager is always extremely busy, works long hours, and has little free or private time relative to other organizational members. His work is characterized by brevity, variety, and fragmentation. He is forced to superficiality and gravitates to the more active aspects of his work which are current, specific, well-defined, and non-routine. His time is consumed with his preferred non-written communication, informal contact, unscheduled meetings, scheduled meetings, and he lives continuously aware of what else he might be doing or must be done (Mintzberg, 1973:51-52).

Based on empirical investigation of five chief executives, Mintzberg (1973:166-167) describes the manager [administrator] as vested with formal authority over his organizational unit and having two basic purposes: (1) he must ensure that his organization produces its specific goods or services efficiently, and (2) he must ensure that his organization serves the ends of the persons who control it.

To operationalize these purposes, Mintzberg identifies ten interrelated working roles that are performed by all managers (administrators). The ten may be grouped under three headings:
1. Interpersonal (Figurehead, leader, liaison).
2. Informational (monitor and disseminate internal flow of intelligence and act externally as spokesman).
3. Decisional (Entrepreneur, disturbance handler, resource allocator, and negotiator).

These roles have more precision but are quite similar to Barnard's (1976:215-234) executive functions, which were (1) maintenance of the organizational communication system, (2) securing the essential organizational services from individuals, and (3) formulating the organization's purposes and objectives.

Anyone who has been a conscientious sport administrator will know how true Mintzberg's analysis is. It applies in varying degrees to physical education teachers, coaches, recreation directors, university professors, athletic directors, department chairmen, or deans.

CHARACTERISTICS OF ADMINISTRATORS. There is an extensive literature on this topic and more aspects will be discussed in Chapter Four, "Leadership." For the purpose here, a quote from Simon, Smithburg, and Thompson (1950:395) links the likely characteristics with the roles described above:

> Highly mobile individuals—individuals with very strong personal ambitions—gravitate into positions of power. In order to mount the ladder of hierarchical success it is often necessary to take actions or make decisions of a somewhat cold-blooded kind. One must "go to lunch with the right people." Sometimes friends must be bypassed. Occasionally someone must be fired who badly needs his job. Yearnings and aspirations in incapable people must sometimes be disregarded. Most persons, except those who have strong personal ambitions or unusually strong attachments to a goal, find such behavior difficult. Consequently, many highly mobile people climb upward in organizational hierarchies by a kind of self-selection.

Summary

This learning design has included a description of the nature of administration-management from an historical perspective and up to many current definitions which are imprecise. Hodgkinson's distinctions were adopted to give more precision to an area of interest which is not a science (even though some of its methods may be). In fact, administration is carried out in organizations by people who have values that are bound to influence their decisions. Thus, quoting Hodgkinson (1978:3), "Administration is philosophy in action."

References

Albers, Henry H.: *Principles of Management*, 3rd ed. New York, Wiley, 1969.

Barnard, Chester I.: *The Functions of the Executive*, 30th ann. ed. Cambridge, Massachusetts, Harvard University Press, 1976.

Dale, Ernest: *Management: Theory and Practice*, 3rd ed. New York, McGraw-Hill, 1973.

Drucker, Peter F.: *Management: Tasks, Responsibilities, Practices*. New York, Harper and Row, 1973.

Frost, Reuben B., and Marshall, Stanley J.: *Administration of Physical Education and Athletics*. Dubuque, Iowa, Brown, 1977.

Harper, Robert F.: *The Code of Hammurabi, King of Babylon*. Chicago, University of Chicago Press, 1904, cited by Hodgetts *Management* 1975:7.

Haimann, T., and Scott, William G.: *Management in the Modern Organization*, 2nd ed. Boston, Houghton Mifflin, 1974.

Hodgetts, Richard M.: *Management: Theory, Process, and Practice*. Philadelphia, W. B. Saunders, 1975.

Hodgkinson, Christopher: *Towards a Philosophy of Administration*. Oxford, Basil Blackwell, 1978.

Howell, Maxwell L., and Howell, Reet: Physical activities and sport in early societies. In Zeigler, Earle F. (Ed.): *History of Physical Education and Sport*. Englewood Cliffs, New Jersey, Prentice-Hall, 1979.

Katz, Robert L.: Skills of an effective administrator. *Harvard Business Review*, 52:90, 1974.

Koontz, H., and O'Donnell, C.: *Principles of Management: An Analysis of Managerial Functions*, 5th ed. New York, McGraw Hill, 1972, cited by Hodgetts, *Management* 1975:9-11.

Lane, Frederic C.: *Venetian Ships and Shipbuilders of the Renaissance*. Baltimore, The Johns Hopkins University Press, 1934, cited by Albers, *Principles of Management*, 1969:11-12.

Machiavelli, N.: *The Prince*. Translated by George Bull. 39. Harmondsworth, England, Penguin, 1961.

Lilienthal, David, E.: *TVA: Democracy on the March*. New York, Harper and Row, 1944.

Mintzberg, Henry: *The Nature of Managerial Work*. New York, Harper and Row, 1973.

Phillips, Thomas R.: *Roots of Strategy*. Harrisburg, Pennsylvania, Military Service Publishing Company, 1941, cited by Hodgetts, *Management*, 1975:8-P.

Resick, Matthew C., Seidel, Beverly L., and Mason, James G.: *Modern Administrative Practices in Physical Education and Athletics*. Reading, Massachusetts, Addison-Wesley, 1970.

Sikula, Andrew F.: *Management and Administration*. Columbus, Ohio, Merrill, 1973.

Simon, Herbert A.: *Administrative Behavior*, 3rd ed. New York, Free Press, 1976.

Simon, Herbert A., Smithburg, Donald W., Thompson, Victor A.: *Public Administration*. New York, Knopf, 1950.

Smith, Adam: *The Wealth of Nations*. New York, The Modern Library, 1937, cited by Hodgetts, *Management*, 1975:15.

Voltmer, Edward F., and Esslinger, Arthur A.: *The Organization and Administration of Physical Education*, 4th ed. New York, Appleton-Century-Crofts, 1967.

Zeigler, Earle F.: *Administration of Physical Education and Athletics: The Case Method Approach*. Englewood Cliffs, New Jersey, Prentice-Hall, 1959.

Zeigler, Earle F.: *Physical Education and Sport Philosophy*. Englewood

Cliffs, New Jersey, Prentice-Hall, 1977.
Zeigler, Earle F.: "Elements of a competency-based approach to management development: a preliminary analysis." Paper read at the CAHPER Convention, Winnipeg, June, 1979.

Important Related Reading

Hodgkinson, *Towards a Philosophy*, 1978, ch. 1.

Supplementary Readings

Barnard, *The Functions of the Executive*, 1976.
Dunsire, Andrew: *Administration: The Word and the Science*. London; Martin Robertson, 1973. (An exceptionally good book for graduate students. By "science" Dunshire means "the study of" and he presents a study of "administration." In doing so, he identifies fifteen meanings of administration.)
Katz, *Effective Administrator*, 1974.
Mintzberg, *Managerial Work*, 1973.
Simon, *Administrative Behavior*, 1976.
Simon, Smithburg, and Thompson, *Public Administration*, 1950.

Case 2.11

The Donkey

Henry York's early experience was as a horticulturalist and he began his professional career in a city parks department. Over the years he moved through a succession of positions until he became commissioner (head professional administrator) of parks and recreation in a large city in Ontario. This gave him a wider exposure to other aspects of city government because of his contacts with the heads of other city departments. After three years as commissioner he was appointed city manager of Rufton, a western U.S. city with a population of 500,000.

Rufton was a progressive city in which York had overall responsibility for twenty departments. One of the departments was that for recreation and the director was George Orton, a World War II veteran who had worked for the department for twenty years. Prior to York's arrival in Rufton, Orton had been director for five years and had developed a fine system for the delivery of programs; one part of this system with the city zoo.

York worked very hard at his job, arriving in the office at 7 A.M. and often remaining there until 8 P.M. He opened mail himself, supervised all departments closely, and often demanded his approval of routine department decisions. He overruled department heads to such an extent that department employees started going straight to him for decisions.

One place of particular interest to York was the city zoo, which had extensive gardens and a variety of wild life; he often dropped in on his way home from work and on weekends. The zoo manager, Sid Bean, was relatively young but keen to develop the zoo and introduce more exotic exhibits. He was particularly interested in the zoological aspects of his work. York, by contrast, seemed more interested in having the gardens and walkways look attractive. With this in mind he constantly gave direct orders to the zoo maintenance men or to the zoo manager.

Early one Sunday morning York let himself into the zoo, waved to the security guard, and set off towards the cougar cage. Along the way he noticed a trail of donkey manure down the center of the major walkway. He yelled to the security guard to fetch him a shovel and wheelbarrow; then he cleaned it up himself.

Next day he called Bean and shouted at him about his incompetence after explaining what he had had to do the previous day. He warned Bean that he was close to losing his job. Bean was very upset and went immediately to see his boss, Orton. What was Orton to do now?

Case Analysis Method
CAM A or CAM B (see Chapter 1).

Case 2.12

The Tail Wags The Dog

Miss Pitt was fifty and had held an important secretarial position in a Boston law firm. She began to suffer increasingly from arthritis, so the doctor advised her to move to Arizona where the dry climate would be more suitable for her. On arrival in Arizona she had some difficulty finding an adequate position so she took a job as secretary III in a state college physical education department. It was a busy office with a secretary II, a secretary I, and herself to serve the faculty members. A particular aspect of her work was to be a confidential secretary to the chairperson of the department.

Thirty-five-year-old Dr. Zeitouni was very active as a research physiologist and busy as an administrator with a U.S. national sport team, in addition to overseeing the work of fifteen professors and ten coaches. To complicate her busy life still further she had a husband who worked as a social worker and two teenaged children.

During her first year in Arizona, Miss Pitt found the procedures of the office somewhat inefficient but gradually developed things more to her liking. By the end of her second year she knew more of the "details" of the department's operations than anyone else. She asked Dr. Zeitouni if she may prepare the timetable for the upcoming year and Dr. Zeitouni readily agreed. Miss Pitt kept very careful control of department expenditures and could increasingly advise Dr. Zeitouni how much remained in various accounts.

Professors were allowed up to $200 per year for "local travel and professional development." Some occasionally spent more if others asked for less. One particular faculty member, Dr. Watts, had a reputation for not doing much work but he had tenure and led a comfortable life. He always used his $200.

In preparation for the 1980 Olympic Games, Dr. Zeitouni was off campus for two weeks during the previous fall with her team. Dr. Watts asked Miss Pitt to get him a travel advance cheque for $75. Miss Pitt knew of his work habits, decided it would be a waste of public money, so sent him a memorandum saying all the money in the account had been used. It was not true. Later, the disgruntled Dr. Watts complained to Dr. Zeitouni saying he had only spent $100 of his allowance and had missed an important workshop in which a new technique was demonstrated. What should Dr. Zeitouni do?

Case Analysis Method
CAM A or CAM B (see Chapter 1).

Case 2.13

Soccer Sacrifices

John Bosanquet was owner of Watbridge United, a First Division professional soccer team in England. Three years ago the team ended the season third from the bottom of the twenty-two team league and just avoided relegation to the Second Division. The club was also in serious financial difficulties.

Bosanquet then hired Jock Yolan as manager (coach), and the team's performance began to improve. In Yolan's first year they finished fourteenth and then fifth the next year. Just beyond the halfway stage of the third season, Watbridge were in second place and still in the cup competition. Furthermore, the club was in a sound financial situation, the players respected Yolan, and the fans admired him. Yolan had a fiery temper, however, and hated taking orders from anyone.

Whenever a transfer (trade) was in the offing, Bosanquet and Yolan always discussed the situation carefully because large sums of money were involved; but, Yolan had final say.

That February the two men had a number of disagreements about players needed for the future; after one particularly fierce argument Bosanquet took off for two weeks in the Bahamas. While he was away, Yolan, without consulting Bosanquet, sold the services of Dennis Duggan (considered one of the most promising strikers in the league) to a new Canadian club that had just been admitted to the North American Soccer League. Yolan's reason being that he wanted the money for two other needed players. When Bosanquet found out, he immediately fired Yolan.

Case Analysis Method
CAM B (see Chapter 1).

LEARNING DESIGN 2.2.

ADMINISTRATION: PHILOSOPHY IN ACTION

Most high officials leave office with the perceptions and insights with which they entered; they learn how to make decisions but not what decisions to make.

Henry Kissinger (1979)

Kissinger's quote brings into focus the purpose of this learning design. Which decisions should administrators make? If, as has been demonstrated, administration is philosophy in action, then a sport* administrator is better if he knows how to answer this question. Indeed, he ought to be able to answer it better than "the man on the street" or Henry Kissinger.

The Nature Of Value

The issues under discussion here have been debated by philosophers for centuries and many books on the topic are available for students who wish to delve more deeply. However, careful study of this design will be adequate for sport administrators. The work of Hodgkinson (1978:103-121) is referred to extensively because his analytical model of the value concept takes into account other theories and philosophical stances. In describing his model, other related examples are given and discussed.

Fact and Value

Though not precisely so (cf. Russell, 1978), for the purpose here the world of fact "is given" (objective) and the world of value "is made" (subjective). Facts "refer to propositions which are ostensible, publicly verifiable, and in some way possessing the quality of being true," and, as Hodgkinson (1978:105-106) states, "values can never be true or false . . . they occur only in the head . . . are concepts of the desirable with motivating force." A value refers to a "preferred state of affairs, or to a condition which ought to be." Nothing has value but it may be given value by us. To take the position that something has value is to commit the naturalistic fallacy (Moore, 1903:10-20).

A unitary self has motives which provide a source for values which, in turn, are a source of attitudes and behaviors. The last two mentioned qualities are the only aspects which are publicly verifiable by observation (Hodgkinson, 1978:106-109). They

---

*By "sport" is meant free, spontaneous, physical activity engaged in during leisure time for the purposes of amusement, relaxation, and development. This is the European definition taken from the Council of Europe's concept "Sport For All." Further, where it does not in the above, it is meant to include what is usually understood by "physical education," "physical recreation," "athletics," and North American "sport." Thus, in this book, it is used as an "umbrella" term for convenience to describe the administrators whose tasks are being discussed. Also, it should be noted, some tasks of recreation administrators are concerned with recreations which are not "sport."

make values "public"; sometimes as ideals, social norms, cultural standards, laws, systematized philosophies, and so on.

Hodgkinson's Value Model

The understanding of values in sport administration is complex and this model is helpful in developing a common language and in resolving value conflicts.

"GOOD"-"RIGHT." It is necessary first to distinguish between the values "good" and "right." Hodgkinson (1978:110) uses the Kantian difference between the "desired" and the "desirable" or the axiological (good) and the deontological (right). "Good" refers to what is "enjoyable, likeable, pleasurable" while "right" refers to what is "proper, moral, dutybound, or simply what ought to be." "Good" is known directly as a matter of preference while "right" comes from a moral sense, conscience, sense of collective responsibility, or "superego." Fairly obviously, this causes internal personal conflict; why should a person forego self-indulgent desires in favour of moral nomothetic demands? Hodgkinson (1978:111-115) distinguishes three value types.

1. *Type III values.* These are "grounded in individual affect and constitute the individual's preference structure." Why is boxing good? Because I like it. Why do I like it? I like it because I like it. A fact of nature. Such a value is "justifiable only because the world is what it is and not some other thing" (p. 112).

The psychological correspondences for Type III values are "rooted in the emotional structure; they are affective, ideosyncratic, idiographic, and direct. They are basically asocial and hedonistic" (p. 113).

Type III philosophical correspondences "are those which lend themselves to the reductions of logical positivism and behaviorism." These positions should not be underestimated in administrative philosophy for the logical positivist position is exemplified by Simon (1976:249-50) who says: "The terms 'good' and 'bad' when they occur in a study on administration are seldom employed in a purely ethical sense. Procedures are termed 'good' when they are conducive to the attainment of specified objectives, 'bad' when they are not conducive to such attainment." Simon stated there would be no science of administration if it was otherwise (p. 249) and thus attempted to separate means from ends.

To give a sport example from McIntosh (1979a:109), it may be said, "you did wrong to punch your opponent," (in soccer) is no more than saying, "you punched your opponent," for the logical positivist A. J. Ayer would maintain that since a moral judgement has no literal meaning it cannot be true or false and, therefore, cannot be argued about. To take Ayer's extreme position that *all* values are mere expressions of emotive preference is to elevate, unjustifiably, logic and science above ethics and values (Hodgkinson, 1978:114). Finally, Hodgkinson describes Type III values as "subrational" (p. 111).

2. *Type II values*. In Hodgkinson's hierarchy, and moving upwards from "good," there are three ways in which a value can be adjudged as "right" (p. 112). Two of the ways come under this head as Type II*b* (consensus) and Type II*a* (consequences).

The grounding for Type II values is in the will of the majority of a given collectivity. If the consensus judges it right, a Type II*b* value is yielded. If upon reasonable analysis of the likely consequences entailed by the pending value judgment, the majority holds the resultant state of affairs to be desirable, then a Type II*a* value is yielded (p. 112).

The psychological correspondences for Type II values may be broadly described as cognitive. They engage the reasoning faculty; they are preeminently rational, collective, and social. In the extent they override "individual indulgence, they are disciplinary and nomothetic" (p. 113).

Type II values correspond to the philosophical positions of humanism, utilitarianism, and pragmatism. Supported by the social and cultural status quo, reason and compromise are venerated so that administrators, who subscribe to prudence and expediency, find such philosophical orientations to be particularly attractive (p. 114).

Classical utilitarians Bentham and Mill thought good and bad consequences could be defined in terms of happiness; the greatest good for the greatest number. Unfortunately, as soon as calculations are begun, it is found that happiness is not a common currency and some majorities favor acts which are immoral (McIntosh, 1979a:97). Hume's rule utilitarians, by contrast, believe that ethical actions and judgments should conform to firm and publicly advocated moral rules which determine correct behavior. As McIntosh points out, such a philosophy explains much of the ethical basis of sport where the ordinary rules of life are suspended for the duration of the contest. For example, it is all right to punch an opponent on the nose in boxing but not in hockey (according to the rules). Without adherence to rules, sport becomes impossible.

3. *Type I values.* The grounding of Type I values is metaphysical. Hodgkinson calls them "grounds of principle" (p. 112) which take the form of "ethical codes, injunctions, or commandments, such as the Kantian categorical imperative or the Mosaic 'Thou shalt not kill'" (p. 113). However, as Hodgkinson further points out, whether they derive from moral insight, religious revelation, or aesthetics "they are unverifiable by the techniques of science and cannot be justified by merely logical argument." In fact, "the farthest argument can lead is to an ethic of enlightened self-interest." And that, of course, is Type IIa in grounding. So, Type I values are "absolute" and this distinguishes them from the "more relative Type II values and the entirely relative Type III values" (p. 113). Type I values are also transrational in that "they need not conflict with rationality" but may do so if looked at from a Type II standpoint; for example, a human sacrifice of the Kamikaze variety is grounded in extreme patriotism.

Type I values "are based on the will rather than upon the reasoning faculty; their adoption implies some kind of act of faith, belief, commitment." The psychological correspondence is conative. Such acts can only be done on an individual basis so are idiographic but they may be nomothetically endorsed (p. 113). For example, a hockey team is dedicated to winning and the players are expected to adopt Type I values. Some do not make such a commitment and, if they are to stay in the team, they will have to accept values at the level of consensus; that is, Type IIb. The quality of the commitment is not so great and the coach would prefer it to be Type I. Similarly is the case with other administrators and their subordinates.

The philosophical correspondence of Type I values, because of their metaphysical or transrational grounds, "are often codified in religious systems" (p. 115). The positivists reject this higher dimension as literally nonsense or as disguised expressions of affect. Hodgkinson (1978:115) concludes his description of the model with the observation that, "adherents of Type II values must walk a razor's edge between the chasms of positivistic nihilism on the one side and metaphysical commitment on the other."

Values In Sport

In his book *Fair Play*, McIntosh (1979a:119) points to three kinds of "ought" statements which may be applied to answering the question "what should I do?"

1. Action X is required in order to conform to the standard which people accept (statement of sociological fact). [Type II.]
2. I have a feeling that I ought to do X (statement of psychological fact). [Type III.]
3. I ought to do X (value judgment). [Type I.]

Thus, McIntosh's numbers one and two do not imply imperatives but he points out how "psychological facts" are often confused with moral judgments: "A football player may have a strong feeling that he ought to obey his captain, but he may question whether he really ought to deliberately disable an opponent if told to do so."

From the point of view of a Kantian* categorical imperative, clearly the player ought not to injure his opponent even if he could somehow "get away" with it in the rules of the game. Thus, rules can only take us so far then morals ought to be applied. McIntosh (1979b:29) stated: "My final conclusion is, then, that the future of fair play will be determined in part by our cultural environment and in part by our psychological needs but above all by our own moral decisions. *It is a heavy responsibility that we carry*" (emphasis added).

Hodgkinson's Postulates

Clearly Hodgkinson's model has far reaching implications for sport administrators. As he says, everyone except "saints, supermen, and psychopaths" experiences the decision tension that there is between lower level values' indulgence and the higher level values' denial; that is, the saint has no tension "because he

---

*A categorical imperative commands us unconditionally. When we act according to a principle which we could not wish to be generally applied, Kant thinks we are acting immorally. (Ewing, 1962:51-54.)

wishes to do what ought to be done" (p. 115). For ordinary people there is conflict for they have to "choose between rights and between goods as well as between right and good" (p. 115). What is needed is what Barnard (1976:272-278) called a capacity for the creative resolution of moral conflicts.

Out of his model, Hodgkinson (1978:116) postulates "Type I values are superior, more authentic, better justified, of more defensible grounding than Type II." Similarly with Type II over Type III: "There is a *hierarchy* or rank." His second postulate, "degeneration," is that "values tend to lower their level of grounding over time. For example: the issue of violence in hockey—at one time it was regarded by all as wrong whereas there are times now when it appears that, as Hodgkinson says, "one does one's own thing." His final postulate relates to *avoidance*. Here he points out there is "a natural tendency to resolve value conflicts at the lowest level possible in a given situation. We seek to avoid moral issues." An example of this would be anti-apartheid demonstrators (concerned with a moral issue) at a British-South African rugby match being arrested for obstructing traffic (a relatively minor offence). This is what Hodgkinson calls "a retreat to managerialism" (p. 122).

Right Sport Administrative Behavior

So we are now right back to the question of this learning design. Which decisions ought administrators to make? What I have written here makes it understandable why administrators hesitate to come to grips with value questions but such a stance is *not* forgivable. Sport administrators, through management, must seek "the best means for given ends and the best conduct for given means" (Hodgkinson, 1978:126). The supervisory function "has ethical imperative elements." Or, if moral relativity is not to eat away the foundation of sport, its administrators must bear the heavy responsibility for right action.

References

Barnard, Chester I.: *The Functions of the Executive*, 30th ann. ed. Cambridge, Massachusetts, Harvard University Press, 1976.
Ewing, A. C.: *Ethics*. New York, Collier, 1962.

Hodgkinson, Christopher: *Towards a Philosophy of Administration*. Oxford, Basil Blackwell, 1978.

Kissinger, Henry: *White House Years*. Boston, Little Brown, 1979.

McIntosh, Peter: *Fair Play: Ethics in Sport and Education*. London, Heinemann, 1979a.

McIntosh, Peter C.: Ethics, sport and education. In Jackson, John J. (Ed.): *Theory Into Practice*. Victoria, British Columbia, University of Victoria, 1979b.

Moore, G. E.: *Principia Ethica*. Cambridge, Cambridge University Press, 1903.

Russell, Bertrand: *The Problems of Philosophy*. Oxford, Oxford University Press, 1978 (Eighth impression). (First published in Home University Library 1912.)

Simon, Herbert A.: *Administrative Behavior*, 3rd ed. New York, Free Press, 1976.

Important Related Readings

Hodgkinson, *Towards a Philosophy*, 1978, ch. 6.

McIntosh, *Fair Play: Ethics in Sport and Education*, 1979a. ch. 6-8.

Supplementary Readings

Beauchamp, Tom L., and Bowie, Norman E. (Eds.): *Ethical Theory and Business*. Englewood Cliffs, New Jersey, Prentice-Hall, 1979.

Ewing: *Ethics*, 1962.

McIntosh, Ethics, sport and education. In Jackson, John J. (Ed.): *Theory Into Practice*, 1979b.

Shea, Edward J.: *Ethical Decisions in Physical Education and Sport*. Springfield, Thomas, 1978. (Deals with pornography, homosexuality, corporal punishment, human rights, racial discrimination, sport as a business, and drug abuse.)

Case 2.21

The End's In Sight

Young Rick Coulter finally got the position he wanted as physical education teacher and soccer coach at New High. The school had a poor athletic record but Jake Bland, head of physical education and athletic director, saw soccer developing and decided to make the school's athletic reputation better through soccer. In fact, he had been advised that if he did not produce a winning team within two years, he would lose his job.

Coulter was enthusiastic about all aspects of his duties and particularly made sure his players knew and respected the laws and insisted they properly interpret the spirit of fair play. At university he had been impressed by the broad ideals of "education through the physical" and was determined to put them into practice.

The soccer league competition was fierce. Appealing players, unnecessary fouls, swearing, and arguing with referees was common. After four games New's record was two wins and two losses. Coulter was quite pleased with his team's performances and behavior. Bland, however, was not pleased with the results. He told Coulter to "toughen up" and began advising soccer players "on the side"—particularly defender John Evans.

A crucial game came. Evans brutally brought down a break-away striker from behind and then stood near the ball to prevent the free kick being taken quickly. The referee was weak and the attackers lost their advantage. Soon afterwards, with the goalkeeper beaten by a fine shot at goal, Evans fisted the ball over the bar. The resulting penalty was missed, and the game was saved, but Coulter was livid and cut Evans from the lineup for the final two games from which the league title would be decided. Bland called Coulter to his office and said Evans must be allowed to play.

Case Analysis Method
CAM A or CAM B (see Chapter 1).

Case 2.22

Field House Blues

Finetown's field house was a versatile facility which served many city-wide sports and recreational groups. A major part of its initial capital cost was donated by a service club, which later formed two-thirds of a committee and advised Roy Bentham, city superintendent of recreation, on its use. The city council was tiring of capital gifts, which led to operating expense problems, so told Bentham that he must make the field house break even on operating costs. The service group's stance had always been that it should be used for "worthy" amateur sports and recreational pursuits and felt that the city should be prepared to absorb some costs; particularly considering the tremendous "good" provided by the field house.

Against the Advisory Committee's wishes, Bentham gave permission for a series of three rock concerts to be held. Financially they were a success and the operating expense problem was resolved for the year. However, after each concert, the hundreds of rock adherents left a trail of damage and mess: burn marks on the cushioned floor surface, four big barrel loads of broken glass and bottles, washroom doors broken off, washbasins smashed, mirrors broken, and a lingering stench of drug smoke. Many extra police had to be employed to attempt to keep the crowd's behavior within the law. When the third concert was over the head janitor resigned (after ten year's service) and the manager pleaded with Bentham to stop the concerts. The service club members were very angry. What should Bentham do?

Case Analysis Method
CAM A or CAM B (see Chapter 1).

Case 2.23

Where There's Smoke

Smithville had a population of 900,000 people and excellent recreational facilities. Recreational program delivery was controlled centrally through a director, but the city had six geographical districts and each district had a recreation manager who reported to the director. The recreation director reported to the city manager.

Personnel
City Manager: Tom Lewis, ex-recreation director.
Recreation Director: Peter Linski, 40, married, three children, new to Smithville.
District Recreation Manager: Bill Kane, 54, married, four children, salary $24,000.

Gathering Storm
Lewis told Linski that his new department had many signs of organizational pathology and that he wanted the "climate to be healthy" within eighteen months. Particularly, he wanted District Five "sorted out" and its Manager, Kane, removed. From his

own previous experience, Lewis warned Linski that supervising Kane was "like trying to catch smoke with your hands."

Kane had been employed in the department for twenty years. During Lewis' tenure he had been removed from central office to District Five in the hope that he would leave on demotion. However, he did not leave but instead built an "empire," which he controlled with considerable skill. The following list of words and phrases help to describe him: artistic, intelligent, political, wheeler-dealer, witty, tardy, wore several big rings and necklaces, off-duty wore kaftans, treated female staff roughly, loved music, practiced "group sensitivity," regarded himself charismatic—particularly with young males whom he gathered on his district staff, to bed at 3 A.M., rarely in his office in the mornings, where?

At first Linski was prepared to give him a chance to prove himself to be unlike the "smoke" reputation. However, Linski watched carefully and began to document the following isolated incidents.

1. Kane's budget submission was "padded" and Linski removed $20,000 without affecting programs.
2. In a new swimming pool budget submission Linski found "two snooker tables" and these were cut.
3. Kane attempted to have the city buy a private country club, which was in financial trouble, for use as District Five's offices and major facilities. Linski and Lewis blocked that maneuver, which had considerable aldermanic support thanks to Kane's "wheeler dealing."
4. Though working in District Five, he had kept some city-wide responsibilities and still attended meetings—one reason why his secretary rarely knew his whereabouts and why he was late for meetings with Linski and other district managers.
5. From the beginning, Linski had been warned that Kane used narcotic drugs; at this point (after six months), the staff began to tell him. Then a local professional organization officer reported the drug use to Linski on the grounds that it was being done on duty and was badly influencing other young men.
6. Linski began tighter control by telling Kane (verbally and in writing) that he was to confine his work activities to District Five.

7. Ann Preedy, city-wide cultural activities advisor, asked for a private appointment with Linski. She described Kane's rude treatment of her in District Five, that she could no longer advise his staff, and that she "smelled pot" all the time she was there; finally she cried.

8. At a meeting on December 4, 1978, Kane slipped a handwritten "speedy-memo" to Linski as he left early. It stated his intention to hire a night watchman to sleep in District Five's offices because of a recent break-in. Linski called Kane next day, refused permission, and told him to consult the city police department.

9. Kane's secretary asked for an appointment with Linski on December 7, 1978. She reported that a "hippie boy" was living in District Five's office basement and that "pot smoke" was sifting into her office.

10. December 8, 1978 at 8:30 A.M. Linski went to District Five offices, met the secretary, and went into the basement where he saw a "hippie pad" and a nude, long-haired male youth fast asleep. No recreation professionals were in the building. When he reached his own office, Kane had made an appointment for 11 A.M. to discuss "security."

11. Linski and Lewis had waited for such a time and such "hard evidence." Linski dictated a memorandum to be sent to Kane telling him to clear the youth out immediately and asked his secretary to hand it to Kane at 11 A.M. At that time, Linski and Lewis were with the city police chief and the head of the morality squad. Strategy was discussed. The police said a noon raid would lead to newspaper "headlines" regarding drugs in city buildings so advised a midnight raid when they were sure there would be evidence of drug use, if drugs had been used. The recreation department officials agreed with the night raid but pointed out that Kane had received so many warnings that he would have cleared every trace by that night.

12. At midnight Linski, Lewis, and two armed plainclothed morality squad officers drove into the District 5 office parking lot. There was one car there already: it was Kane's. Linski let them all in the building and led them to the basement. Kane, half dressed, met them on the stairs, said "Oh my

god!" and ran back into the basement room. The detectives burst in and barked out orders. The search revealed quantities of hashish, pipes, knives, large quantities of pornographic magazines, and a homosexual film that was being projected onto a screen. The eighteen-year-old youth was arrogant and taken into custody. After other offices were searched and more drugs found, Kane was released by the police and told to be at the police station by 8 A.M. next morning.

Case Analysis Method
CAM E or CAM D (see Chapter 1).

Summary

1. Administration can be traced back to 3,000 B.C. and there is evidence of its existence and development from then to the present time.
2. Sport administration is equally old and has developed in parallel with general administration.
3. Administration and management are often viewed as synonymous in sport and elsewhere.
4. In this book a clear distinction is made between administration and management.
5. Administration concerns the formulation of policy, the value-laden issues, and the human component of organizations. Administration is philosophy in action. It is more an art than a science.
6. Management refers to aspects of organizational behavior that are more routine, definite, programmatic, and susceptible to quantitative methods. It may be more scientific.
7. There is no approximation to purity at either end of the administration-management spectrum.
8. Administration has a general nature which is applicable in many fields, including sport.
9. Administrators'-managers' roles may be grouped under the following headings: interpersonal, informational, decisional.
10. Sport administrators ought to know better than "the man on the street" which decisions to make.
11. Nothing has value but it may be given value by us.

12. "Good" refers to what is enjoyable, likeable, and pleasurable while "right" refers to what is proper, moral, duty-bound, or simply what ought to be.
13. Type III values constitute the individual's preference structure. Type II values are grounded in the will of the majority and may be Type II*b* (consensus) or Type II*a* (consequences). Type I values are grounds of principle.
14. There is a hierarchy or rank in those values with Type I being superior to Type II and Type II superior to Type III.
15. Values tend to lower their levels of grounding over time (degeneration).
16. There is a tendency to resolve value conflicts at the lowest level possible (avoidance).
17. Sport administrators, through management, must seek the best means for given ends and the best conduct for given means. The supervisory function has ethical imperative elements.

Concepts For Review

Administration-management	Executive
Administration's general nature	Administrators' roles
Fact and value	Good and right
Values (Types I, II, III)	Values (hierarchy, degener-
Categorical imperative	ation, and avoidance)

Questions For Oral and Written Discussion

1. Why has the need for more sport administrators grown?
2. Why should students study administration?
3. What is the difference between a sport administrator and a hospital administrator?
4. "We are all either administered or administering" (Hodgkinson, 1978:206). Discuss.
5. "With everyone sold on the good how does all the evil get done?" (Saul Bellow). Discuss.
6. What is "fair play?" Should administrators enforce it?
7. "Value skills are best left to chance—the democratic answer. To education—the Platonic answer" (Hodgkinson, 1978: 207). Discuss.

8. "Means and ends are always intertwined. Their disentanglement is a problem in administrative philosophy" (Hodgkinson, 1978:216). Discuss in a sport context.
9. What will sport be like twenty years from now if administrators' values degenerate steadily?
10. CAM C applied to instructor-specified topics taken from this chapter.

Chapter 3

THE FORMAL STRUCTURE
OF ORGANIZATIONS

LEARNING DESIGN 3.1

BUREAUCRACIES

In this learning design, formal organizations are defined and aspects of the historical development and understanding of bureaucracies are traced. The cases relate some issues that arise to sport (cf. Notes of Learning Design 2.2) organizations.

Organizations

Sport has a multitude of organizations: many varied special interest clubs; elementary and high school physical education departments; college and university physical education divisions, departments, schools, and faculties; educational institutions' athletic and recreational units; sport governing bodies at local, regional, national, and international levels; local, regional, and national governmental sport ministries, departments, and branches; professional clubs and commercial sport organizations; non-profit private sport clubs; religious, ethnic, and political sport organizations. Of course, as Etzioni (1964:1) pointed out, we are born in organizations, educated in organizations, work in organizations, play in organizations, and put to final rest after the largest organization (the state) has granted official permission. We are in a society of organizations but this is not to say that organizations are new for they have existed in various forms as long as administration (cf. Chapter 1).

Parsons (1960:56) defined an organization as "a social system which is organized for the attainment of a particular type of goal." Included are corporations, armies, schools, hospitals, churches, and prisons; but tribes, classes, ethnic groups, friendship groups, and families are excluded (Etzioni, 1964:3). Etzioni further stated that organizations are characterized by:

> (1) divisions of labor, power, and communication responsibilities, divisions which are not random or traditionally patterned, but deliberately planned to enhance the realization of specific goals; (2) the presence of one or more power centers which control the concerted effort of the organization and direct them towards its goals; these power centers also must review continuously the organization's performance and re-pattern its structure, where necessary, to increase its efficiency; (3) substitution of personnel, i.e. unsatisfactory persons can be removed and others assigned their tasks. . . . Hence organizations are much more in control of their nature and destiny than any other social grouping.

It is generally agreed that organizations, including many sport organizations, have increased in scope and rationality above their ancient counterparts. Some of this development is good and right but some is bad and wrong. Thus, a major problem of modern organizations is how to structure human groupings which are as rational as possible whilst at the same time producing as few as possible undesirable side effects.

All organizations have to make provisions for their continuing activities that are directed towards the achievement of their aims. Through power, communication, and members' involvement, regularities such as task allocation, supervision, and coordination are developed. Such regularities constitute the organization's structure. A particularly important structural type, the bureaucracy, will now be discussed in more detail.

Bureaucracy

In this learning design the concern is to describe organizational structures and particularly, here, the bureaucratic structure. To do that it is desirable for students to be aware of the origin of the term and concept *bureaucracy*. This is so because it has different and contrasting meanings; further, it is only the organizational structural "Ideal Type" which is of interest in this book.

Albrow (1970:16) pointed out that the concept "bureaucracy" probably has origins that are too remote to trace but there is evidence of it as far back as 337 B.C. in Chinese written principles which can be likened to twentieth-century theories of administration. There are also examples in the writings of Machiavelli when he advised princes to pay officials so they would not need to receive money from elsewhere. The word "bureaucracy" is believed to have been invented by de Gournay who was reported in 1764 to have said that a French illness was "bureaumania" and he invented "a fourth or fifth form of government called a bureaucracy." Other forms were monarcy, aristocracy, democracy, and tyranny; thus he was identifying a new group of rulers and a method of governing. His complaint being that government had become an end in itself (Albrow, 1970:17). In the language of the eighteenth century, "bureau" meant a writing table and also a place where officials worked. Thus by adding a suffix from the Greek word for "rule" a term resulted which had power to penetrate other cultures. So the French *bureaucratie* led to the German *bureakratie*, and Italian *burocrazia*, and the English "bureaucracy" (plus its derivatives bureaucrat, bureaucratic, bureaucratism, bureaucratist, and bureaucratization).

Around 1800, French, German, and Italian dictionaries broadly defined "bureaucracy" as signifying the power of officials in public administration. However, the French academy also called it "a regime where bureaux multiply without need." This dual meaning was the beginning of the complex development through which the concept would pass (Albrow, 1970:18). Thus, "bureaucracy" is sometimes regarded as an efficient organization and sometimes an inefficient organization. Others have viewed it as a capitalist system of government which Marxists have deplored; however, Marxist regimes have developed their own big bureaucracies. Here, then, the purpose is to describe the "Ideal Type" organizational structural form as outlined by Weber.

Weber And Bureaucracy

Max Weber (1864-1920) was born in Thuringia, Germany in a well-to-do family. He originally studied law and became a full professor of economics at Freiburg University in 1894 before moving to a chair at Heidelberg in 1896. When he was thirty-three he suffered from exhaustion and anxiety to such an extent he was unable to carry out formal academic duties but an understanding university, and private means, enabled him to carry on with wide-ranging academic endeavours until he died in 1920 (Rogers,

1969:4-5). He wrote on many related topics and he wrote in German; the result is that there is "a dearth of detailed exposition of his work" (Albrow, 1970:37). What follows, then, is an attempt to describe his main contributions to the issues here.

Weber's principal endowment to the study of organizations was his theory of authority (*Herrschaft*) structures and he categorized organizations in terms of the authority relations within them. He was interested in answering the question, "Why do people obey commands?" In answering this he made an important conceptual distinction between power and authority. A person had power in a social relationship if his will could be enforced without resistance. Authority, on the other hand, was a special instance of power needed for structuring human groups; it existed when a command was voluntarily obeyed by receivers. The subordinate saw the issuing of a directive by a superordinate as legitimate (i.e. justified). Weber, then, distinguished between organizational forms according to the way authority was legitimized (Albrow, 1970:39-40; Pugh, Hickson, and Hinings, 1971: 19). He outlined three pure organizational types.

1. CHARISMATIC. In this type of organization the authority lies in the charismatic qualities (or personal qualities) of the leader. Weber took his meaning from the Greek word *charisma*, which means set apart from the ordinary, endowed with supernatural powers, or exceptional powers. Examples are a prophet, Messiah, and a political leader whose organization consists of himself and a set of disciples who mediate between the leader and the mass. Actual instances have been Henry Ford, Hitler, Trudeau, and perhaps certain coaches such as Vince Lombardi. This type of organization has a built-in instability for as soon as the leader dies there is no charismatic leader; disciples are often divided and so the charismatic organization must change to become one of the other two types.

2. TRADITIONAL. Commands are obeyed out of reverence for old established patterns of order. Precedence and usage are all important; the great arbiter is custom. When charisma is traditionalized by making the transmission hereditary, the leader's authority is part of his *role* and not his personality. Weber distinguished two organizational forms of traditional organization: *patrimonial* when officers are personal servants

(dependent on the leader for remuneration) and *feudal* when the officers have more autonomy but have to be loyal through customary rights and duties such as titles. Though historical, such organizations exist in modern life in family businesses and dynasties based on heredity. Actions are not based on rationality.

3. RATIONAL—LEGAL ("IDEAL TYPE" BUREAUCRATIC). Sometimes Weber wrote of a bureaucracy as a body of officials in a general and broad sense; however, it is his pure and rational type that is described here. In conformity with what was stated above about legitimacy, Weber first stated five related beliefs on which legal authority depended. Here they are in abbreviated form as taken from Albrow (1970:43):

    I. That a legal code can be established which can claim obedience from members of the organization.

    II. That the law is a system of abstract rules which are applied to particular cases and that administration looks after the interests of the organization within the limits of the law.

    III. That the man exercising authority also obeys this impersonal order.

    IV. That only *qua* member does the member obey the law.

    V. That obedience is due not to the person who holds authority but to the impersonal order which has granted him this position.

Based on the above conceptions of legitimacy, Weber formulated eight propositions about the structuring of legal authority systems. Taken from Albrow (1970:43-44), they are:

    (a) Official tasks are organized on a continuous, regulated basis.

    (b) These tasks are divided into functionally distinct spheres, each furnished with the requisite authority and sanctions.

    (c) Offices are arranged hierarchically, the rights of control and complaint between them being specified.

    (d) The rules according to which work is conducted may be either technical or legal. In both cases trained men are necessary.

    (e) The resources of the organization are quite distinct from those of the members as private individuals.

(f) The office holder cannot appropriate his office.

(g) Administration is based on written documents and this tends to make the office (bureau) the hub of the modern organization.

(h) Legal authority systems can take many forms but are seen at their purest in a bureaucratic administrative staff.

Albrow makes the important point that (*h*) above is vital for understanding Weber's thinking on bureaucracy; that is, other kinds of administration (e.g. collegial) could be based on these conceptions and principles. However, bureaucracy, in its most rational form, presupposed the preceding propositions on legitimacy and authority and had the following defining characteristics (Albrow, 1970:44-45):

1. The staff members are personally free, observing only the impersonal duties of their offices.
2. There is a clear hierarchy of offices.
3. The functions of the offices are clearly specified.
4. Officials are appointed on the basis of a contract.
5. They are selected on the basis of a professional qualification, ideally substantiated by a diploma gained through examination.
6. They have a money salary and usually pension rights. The salary is graded according to position in the hierarchy. The official can always leave the post and under certain circumstances it may also be terminated.
7. The official's post is his sole or major occupation.
8. There is a career structure, and promotion is possible either by seniority or merit; according to the judgement of superiors.
9. The official may appropriate neither the post nor the resources that go with it.
10. He is subject to a unified control and disciplinary system.

These ten features constituted Max Weber's renowned ideal, pure, most rational type of bureaucracy. It should be noted, contrary to what is often stated, that "Weber never defined bureaucracy"; what he did was "specify the features of what he considered the most rational form of bureaucracy" (Albrow, 1970:40-41). Albrow says this is without a doubt "the single most important statement on the subject in the social sciences, its influence has been immense." Weber, himself stated (trans. Gerth and Mills, 1946:214-216):

> The fully developed bureaucratic mechanism compares with other organizations exactly as does the machine with non-mechanical modes of production. Precision, speed, unambiguity, knowledge of the files, continuity, discretion, unity, strict subordination, reduction of friction and of material and personal costs—these are raised to the optimum point in a strictly bureaucratic administration.
>
> Its specific nature . . . develops the more perfectly the more bureaucracy is "dehumanized," the more completely it succeeds in eliminating from official business, love, hatred, and all purely personal, irrational, and emotional elements which escape calculation.

It should be understood that this is an "Ideal Type utopian construct which is primarily rational and abstract" (Rogers, 1969:91). As Rogers elaborated further: "It is normatively ideal, therefore, in its conceptual purity it cannot be found empirically anywhere in reality. While it does not describe a concrete course of action, it does describe an 'objectively possible' course of action." These last points are worth remembering when considering some of the criticisms of Weber's Ideal Type, which are presented in the next section. Weber knew it was an Ideal Type that could serve for comparison purposes with actual actions (cf. Parsons 1964:92).

Limiting Bureaucracy

De Gournay, Mill, and Michels saw bureaucracy and democracy as opposite systems of government but Weber sought to show that the nature of the administrative apparatus and government were distinct; that is, a democratic government could have a bureaucratic administration. However, Weber knew that bureaucracies accumulated power and he sought mechanisms which would prevent such power accumulation reaching a point where it could control the policy of the organization it was supposed to serve. Albrow (1970:47-48) pointed out that this was usually a neglected aspect of Weber's work but, nevertheless, Weber had described five major mechanisms designed to limit bureaucracy's powers.

1. COLLEGIALITY. In this structure Weber was influenced by the nineteenth century German administrative concept of the

collegium, which was a body of officials charged with the collective responsibility for advising the ruler and taking responsibility for a particular function of government. In a pure bureaucratic structure, one person only at each hierarchical stage has decision responsibility. As soon as others are involved as of right, then a collegial principle is being employed. Among the twelve forms of collegiality which Weber identified were the Roman consulate, the British cabinet, various senates, and various parliaments. Though important in limiting bureaucracy, its decisions are slow and it "receded in the face of the monocratic principle" (Albrow, 1970:27,27).

2. THE SEPARATION OF POWERS. In bureaucracy, tasks are divided into relatively distinct functional spheres. If two or more bodies are given responsibility for the same function, then a compromise solution must be reached. Weber‚ thought such arrangements unstable because one of the authorities would win preeminence (Albrow, 1970:47-48).

3. AMATEUR ADMINISTRATION. This occurs when governments select people with public esteem and private means to administer. Weber's position was that such systems could not measure up to the demands of modern society and, when assisted by professionals, it was the latter who made the real decisions (p. 48).

4. DIRECT DEMOCRACY. In these organizations officials are guided by, and answerable to, an assembly. It is only possible in small organizations and Weber thought "the need for expertise was a decisive counterweight" (p. 48).

5. REPRESENTATION. This occurs when leaders represent their followers (cf. also charismatic and traditional leaders). In the modern organization it happens when a collegial representative body's elected members make decisions and share authority over those who elected them. Through this mechanism, Weber saw the greatest possibility of a check on bureaucracy (p. 48).

Albrow (1970:49) summarized such arrangements, as advocated by Weber, as not being ideally democratic but, "it steered a middle course between the Scylla of mass irrationality and the Charybdis of bureaucratic tyranny."

Some Critical Observations Of Weber's Model

Here some critical observations of Weber are recorded because they were made by eminent scholars and they highlight important factors. Readers will recognize, from the first part of this design, that they are not always valid adverse criticisms of Weber's Ideal Type but some do lead to important understandings about managing organizations, which are dealt with later in this book.

Albrow (1970:50) pointed out that Weber's work paid very little attention to bureaucratic "inefficiency" and one form of attack has been on the rationality of his "rational bureaucracy" (p. 55). Merton (1952:361-371) argued that emphasis on precision and reliability in administration may have self-defeating consequences; that is, rules designed as means to ends may become ends in themselves. So "rational" structure of Weber's type can easily generate consequences that are detrimental to the achievement of the organization's objectives.

Albrow (1970:56) cited Parsons, one of the translators of Weber's *Wirtschaft und Gesellschaft*, on the internal consistency of the Ideal Type. The administrative staff was defined as having professional expertise and the right to give orders. But what happens in organizations when people in high authority positions do not have enough expertise? Parson's pointed out that this leads to conflict because people have the problem of deciding whom to obey: the person with greater expertise or the one with the right to command.

Parson's criticisms were a starting point for Gouldner (1955 a and b). Applying bureaucratic structure to a previously lax U.S. gypsum mine's organizational structure, Gouldner found a drop in worker morale, management-worker conflict, and a wildcat strike. This led Gouldner to identify three patterns of bureaucratic behavior.

Mock bureaucracy occurs when rules, which are not regarded as legitimate by anyone, are imposed by an outside agency. Examples of such rules may be an insurance company "no smoking rule" or "official statistical returns" (red tape); management and workers may ignore or give superficial attention to them. In such joint violation, morale may be high and they all "get on with the real job."

The second type was what Gouldner called *representative* bureaucracy. In such structures rules are promulgated by experts whose authority is acceptable to all members of the organization.

Members regard the rules necessary on technical (and/or safety) grounds and to be in their own interests. The final pattern was *punishment-centered* bureaucracy in which rules arise out of pressure from either management *or* workers. Examples may be management's strict production controls or workers' "no over-time regulation" or redundancy fund. With either of these stances only one side considers the rules legitimate; a gain for one is a loss for the other and, therefore, conflict and tension ensues.

Gouldner pointed out that this third pattern is most commonly found; impersonal rules specify what is not allowed and this leads to minimum acceptable behavior becoming standard behavior, which results in inefficiency and more conflict. Therefore bureaucracy is unstable; however, varying degrees of the three patterns may coexist in any one organization.

Finally, referring back to Gouldner's starting point with Parson's comments on "experts," and those with the right to command who may not be "experts," Gouldner called the former "cosmopolitans" and the latter "locals." Cosmopolitans' main loyalty is to their speciality and not to the organization; locals have great loyalty to the organization and have little commitment to special skills. Organizations want both types so this is another source of conflict (cf. Pugh, Hickson, and Hinings, 1971:25-29.)

Some other criticisms of Weber have been made but they are beyond the scope of this design. They refer to such concerns as cultural differences (Bendix, 1947:493-507), human attitudes to rules (Blau, 1955:201), disregard of efficiency (Blau and Scott, 1963:534; Albrow, 1970:89-91; Mouzelis, 1969), and the need for different structures in different situations, i.e. not "timeless" (March and Simon, 1958:36; Woodward, 1965; Pugh, Hickson, and Hinings, 1971:36-55). Albrow (1970) conceded that Weber did disregard the problem of efficiency but can adequately defend him on most other counts (as readers here should be able to do by careful reference to the early part of this design). Albrow's (p. 66) final defensive comment was "he (Weber) would never have needed to retract his view that modern bureaucracy involved formal rationality."

Etzioni's Compliance Structures

In critical examination of Weber's model, Etzioni (1964:56-57) points out that there are many "mixed" types of organizations that combine "charismatic" organization with "traditional" and "bureaucratic" organization. Also, that the degrees of each may shift over time; for example, peacetime armies are highly bureaucratic but are less so in combat.

It is with the element of "compliance" that Etzioni has made a particularly important contribution to organizational structure. Etzioni (1975:3-4) defines *compliance* as "both a relation in which an actor behaves in accordance with a directive supported by another actor's power, and to the orientation of the subordinated actor to the power applied." The power means may be physical, material, or symbolic rewards or deprivations. The orientation of the subordinated actor is called *involvement*, which may be positive (commitment) or negative (alienation). Etzioni's (1975:4-12) precise terms and abbreviations of their meanings are:

Power
   (1) *Coercive* power rests essentially on the (possible) application of physical force to make sure that members of an organization comply with orders (e.g. a concentration camp).
   (2) *Remunerative* power is based on control over material resources and rewards such as wages, commissions, and "fringe benefits" (e.g. a business organization).
   (3) *Normative* power rests on the allocation and manipulation of symbolic rewards and deprivations (e.g. as in voluntary associations, religious organizations, and universities).
Most organizations employ all three kinds of power to varying degrees, usually emphasizing one kind over the other two.

Involvement
   (1) *Alienative* involvement designates an intense negative orientation (e.g. convicts, prisoners of war).
   (2) *Calculative* involvement designates either a negative or positive orientation of low intensity (e.g. business relationships).
   (3) *Moral* involvement designates a positive orientation of

high intensity (e.g. committed church workers, loyal political party members).

Taken together, the varieties of power and involvement produce nine types of compliance relations (Figure 2):

KINDS OF POWER	KINDS OF INVOLVEMENT		
	Alienative	Calculative	Moral
Coercive	1	2	3
Remunerative	4	5	6
Normative	7	8	9

Figure 2. A typology of compliance relations (Etzioni, 1975:12). (Courtesy of Macmillan Publishing Co., Inc.)

Etzioni points out that the nine types are not equally likely to occur empirically: types 1 (coercive compliance), 5 (utilitarian compliance), and 9 (normative compliance) are found more frequently because these three constitute "congruent" relationships. Coercive power produces alienative involvement, and vice versa; remunerative power and calculative involvement are found together; and normative power and moral involvement are congruent with one another. Organizations are under pressure to be effective and to shift their compliance structure from incongruent to congruent types, which are more effective. The incongruent types are of interest to those studying organizational change, conflict, strain, and similar topics. Finally, Etzioni's conceptual framework lays a base for comparative analysis of a wide range of organizations for his typology applies to them all (cf. Pugh, Hickson, and Hinings, 1971:30-35).

Summary

This design has paid particular attention to the formal structure of organizations. In doing so it has described "Ideal Types" which are not found empirically in pure form. Some of the debate with Weber points to the fact that the human factor in organizations was not given sufficient attention. That does not matter here but it is given more attention in subsequent chapters (as it was in Chapter 2). By contrast, all Etzioni's types of compliance relationships are found empirically.

References

Albrow, Martin: *Bureaucracy*. London, Macmillan, 1970.

Bendix, R.: Bureaucracy: the problem and its setting. *American Sociological Review, 12:*493-507, 1947.

Blau, Peter M.: *The Dynamics of Bureaucracy*, rev. ed. Chicago, University of Chicago Press, 1963.

Blau, Peter M., and Scott, W. Richard: *Formal Organizations*. San Francisco, Chandler, 1962.

Etzioni, Amitai: *A Comparative Analysis of Complex Organizations* rev. ed. New York, The Free Press, 1975.

Etzioni, Amitai: *Modern Organizations*. Englewood Cliffs, New Jersey, Prentice-Hall, 1964.

Gouldner, Alvin W.: *Patterns of Industrial Bureaucracy*. London, Routledge and Kegan Paul, 1955a (and Glencoe, Illinois, The Free Press, 1955).

Gouldner, Alvin W.: *Wildcat Strike*. London, Routledge and Kegan Paul, 1955b.

March, J. G., and Simon, H. A.: *Organizations*. New York, Wiley, 1958.

Merton, R. K. et al. (Ed.): *Reader in Bureaucracy*. Glencoe, Illinois, The Free Press, 1952.

Mouzelis, Nicos P.: *Organization and Bureaucracy*. Chicago, Aldine, 1969.

Parsons, Talcott: *Structure and Process in Modern Societies*. Glencoe, Illinois, The Free Press, 1960.

Parsons, Talcott (Ed.): *Max Weber—The Theory of Social and Economic Organization*. New York, The Free Press, 1964.

Pugh, D. S., Hickson, D. J., and Hinings, C. R.: *Writers on Organizations*, 2nd ed. Harmondsworth, England, Penguin, 1971.

Rogers, Rolf E.: *Max Weber's Ideal Type Theory*. New York, Philosophical Library, 1969.

Weber, M.: *Essays in Sociology*. Translated by Gerth, H. H., and Mills, C. W. New York, Oxford University Press, 1946.

Woodward, Joan: *Industrial Organization: Theory and Practice*. London, Oxford University Press, 1965.

Important Related Readings

Albrow, *Bureaucracy*, 1970, ch. 1-3.

Etzioni, Amitai: *A Sociological Reader on Complex Organizations*, 2nd ed. New York, Holt, Rinehart and Winston, 1969.

Pugh, Hickson, and Hinings, *Writers on Organizations*, 1971. Section 1 is a useful overview.

Supplementary Readings

Albrow, *Bureaucracy*, 1970, ch. 5. Deals with bureaucracy as: rational organizational inefficiency, rule by officials, public administration, administration by officials, the organization, and modern society.

Bendix, *Bureaucracy*, 1947.

Blau, *Formal Organizations*, 1963.

Etzioni, *Modern Organizations*, 1964, ch. 1 and 5.

Gouldner, *Industrial Bureaucracy*, 1955a.

Mouzelis, *Organization*, 1969, ch. 1-2.

Rogers, *Ideal Type Theory*, 1969, ch. I, IV, and V.

Pugh, D. S. (Ed.): *Organization Theory*. Harmondsworth, England, Penguin, 1971, Part 1.

Hall, Richard H. (Ed.): *The Formal Organization*. New York, Basic Books, 1972.

Case 3.11

Use Or Ornament?

Dr. Ling, a Parksville M.D., was honored when the mayor's office called one day and invited him to join the Parks and Recreation Advisory Board. He was very concerned about people's general health which he thought could be enhanced through the services of city-provided recreational programs. Thus, he reasoned, he would be able to influence city policies towards programs which would encourage active lifestyles. It was pointed out to Dr. Ling that evening meetings would take place every two weeks and that the board's function was to "advise" the mayor's office—it had no executive power.

Dr. Ling began his work enthusiastically but after awhile began to be disillusioned with the board's role. Meetings began at 7:30 P.M. and often lasted until midnight or later—most time being consumed with considering grant applications from local recreational groups and then putting them in priority order. The board never seemed to debate any broad policy issues.

During Dr. Ling's second year on the board the city learned that it would receive $5 million of state funds for the development of a "Centenary Park." Ling saw this as a wonderful chance to build a racquet sports facility with provisions for racquetball, squash, badminton, and tennis—mainly sports which he knew would be popular and likely to encourage vigorous activity. He gained the support of fellow board members and they then wrote a detailed proposal for the mayor's office.

In the meantime, the Parksville Recreation Department Head was having a most difficult time with operating budgets. Recreationally worthy programs were steadily being "cut" by the city council's Economic Affairs Committee. So many capital facilities existed that they could barely afford to operate and certainly did not want any more. Consequently, the department advised council that a "natural" park should be built with the state funds so that operating expenses would be minimized.

Thus, through the advice of the department and the Economic Affairs Committee, the mayor and council agreed to build the "natural" state centenary park, which was ceremoniously opened by a state minister. Dr. Ling was not present at the opening and resigned from the Parks and Recreation Advisory Board soon afterwards.

Case Analysis Method
CAM B (see Chapter 1).

Case 3.12

The Piper Calls The Tune

When Dr. Gray was appointed president of the University of Chicago, she was reported to have said, "You don't tell people what to do in universities—you try to persuade them."

Such a state of affairs led three deans at Apex University to resign within six months of each other and their average time in office had been 2.1 years. Said one, "*Nothing* can be done without it being considered in detail by one or several committees—such a situation would not be tolerated in business." Another retiring dean complained, "I became nothing but a messenger boy between the faculty members and the university administration—it's an awful position to be in." The third reasoned, "Almost all the budget is earmarked for spending before a dean takes over so there is no latitude for innovation and no excitement under this structure. Even though there are associate and assistant deans, everyone wants to talk to 'the person in charge,' thus the dean bears the brunt of the attack but has no power."

Shortly after this, Frank Thom was appointed dean of physical education and recreation. Apex President Wilson promised him full support of the senior administration to "tighten control" on the physical education and recreation faculty. Wilson believed that the organization was not being democratically responsible to the wider population that was funding it. Indeed it was only "democratic" to its self-serving clique of faculty members—many of whom were incompetent, lazy, and used the job as a "cushion."

Thom knew he was in a tricky situation because it may be possible eventually for his faculty to vote him out of office. Nevertheless, because he had Wilson's support, he was determined to be responsible to the wider public who paid his salary. He decided to operate objectively; to ignore irrational, purely personal, and emotional elements. A faculty member not doing his job would be called to task and every effort would be made to make him accountable.

During early interviews with faculty members, Thom let them know his expectations for their teaching, research, and other duties. Several welcomed this approach but others said nothing and carried on in as lax a fashion as before. When the time came for salary assessments, Thom told four people that their performances were unsatisfactory and that they would not receive a pay raise. Also he refused to recommend two of them for promotion to associate professor. It was his ultimate intention to encourage them to leave; "firing" was extremely difficult because they had tenure.

After this episode the "atmosphere" in the faculty deteriorated. There was little trust between members and all decision-making ground more slowly than usual in the many committees. The situation "festered" in this manner for over two years until the time came to consider whether or not to reappoint Thom for a second term as dean. Thom, himself, made some attempts to gain support from his "good workers" and from the senior administration. However, he had caused too much overall dissention within his faculty and he was not successful in his bid for a second term.

Case Analysis Method
CAM A or CAM D or CAM E (see Chapter 1).

Case 3.13

The Annual Report

Brian Harms (regional director) had worked his way up to his leadership position with the National Sports Council. When young Elain Kopp had been employed in the region for just under one year, Harms told her that she must write a comprehensive annual report of all her activities and programs; it would then be sent to the national office.

Kopp viewed this as an important assignment and spent close to two weeks collecting data and writing a polished document. When she had just finished it, Jack Collins, with whom she shared an office, returned from a week of travel and was given the same task. Kopp noticed that Collins finished his complete report in just over one hour, so she asked how he did it. "Oh," replied Collins, "there's lies, damn lies, statistics, and the annual report!"

Case Analysis Method
CAM B (see Chapter 1).

LEARNING DESIGN 3.2

ORGANIZATIONAL STRUCTURE

Here, common *formal* organizational structural characteristics are described. By bearing in mind what was dealt with in Learning Design 3.1, selected concepts are given specific attention and the way that "formal structure" is depicted graphically is outlined. The cases focus on some of the types of problems that arise when sport organizations' structures are not adequately formulated; the point being that learners will know *better* what structures ought to be like.

Formal Relations

"Line"
"Line" relationships are the simplest ones to understand in organizational structures. They indicate the "chain" of command from the superordinate to the subordinate. Examples from sport administration are in Figure Three where the lines of authority run through the "scalar chains" from city council to program specialist, and from school board to student. Thus, these lines of authority enable superiors to direct subordinates to carry out actions that will enable the organization to reach its goals.

Sport Administration

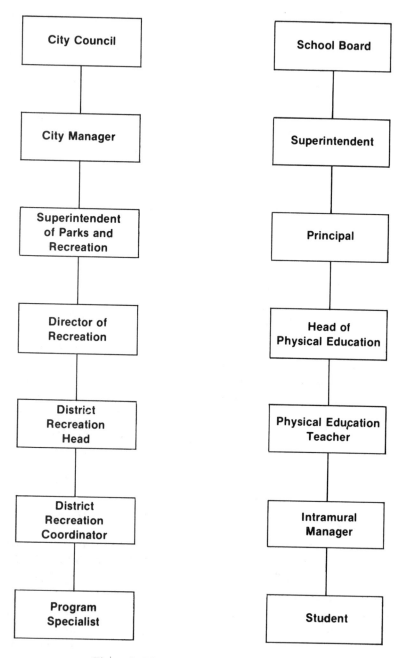

Figure 3. Hierarchies of "line authority"

Closely related to this concept are the principles of authority, definition, and correspondence, which are defined in Chapter 1 under "An Example of Case Analysis Method B." Students wishing to read more about this should consult Pugh, Hickson, and Hinings (1971:105-107) where they cite the writings of L. F. Urwick and E. F. L. Brech. Urwick and Brech took many of their ideas from Henri Fayol's work (which is described in Chapter 5). Whether or not the additional reading is done, students are urged to learn and apply these principles. Without them there is the certain outcome of organizational dysfunction.

"LINE" GROWTH. Line structures expand vertically through delegation of authority and horizontally through division of labor. Thus, a typical sport organization's line structure combines levels of authority with functional specialization at each level, as is illustrated in Figure Four.

"Staff"

When a sport organization grows, so do the responsibilities of its chief executive. Firstly, then, the chief executive appoints subordinate managers (e.g. cf. director of intramurals in Figure 4) and delegates some authority to them. In time, if growth continues, the chief executive may have too many people reporting directly to him to be able to give them adequate attention or to plan and coordinate properly. At that point he may create a "personal staff" to help him perform duties he cannot delegate. Later, the "personal staff" may not have the needed expertise in such areas as labor relations, law, and accounting. Thus, the "personal staff" is inadequate. Subordinate managers also need expert guidance to be able to carry out line duties. Ultimately, then, every line organization reaches a point where specialized staff contributions are required. Haimann and Scott (1974:177) define *staff* work as revolving "around the performance of specialized activities, the utilization of technical knowledge, and the creation and distribution of technical information concerning the functions which are important to line management."

Haimann and Scott (1974:177-178) point out further that a "staff" department (e.g. "personnel" in parks and recreation departments) may have its own lines of command. Such a line is

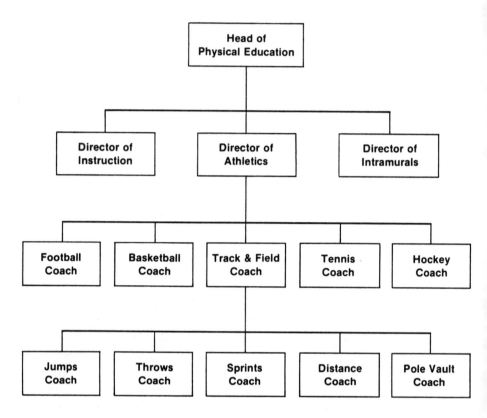

Figure 4. Vertical and horizontal growth of line structures

termed *secondary* to distinguish it from the "primary" chain, which links the organization's basic levels of authority. Mostly, "staff authority" provides its service to managers who have "line authority," but staff do not have the right to command the managers. The exception to this is when the staff has "functional authority" over the line in a restricted sphere of activity.

FUNCTIONAL AUTHORITY. Functional authority is that authority which a chief executive gives to a "staff" member to apply in his narrow area of expertise. Less commonly, it may be given to a line manager for some special purpose. So, for example (in Figure 5), the accounting revenue officer may command the district recreation head and pool manager to carry out particular

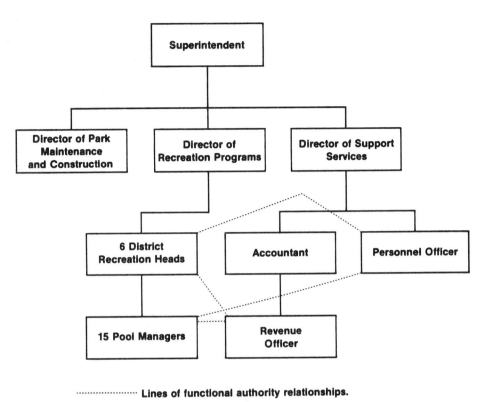

Figure 5. Functional authority

accounting procedures; and the personnel officer may command the district recreation head and pool manager to assign duties to subordinates in a fashion that is in accordance with the union agreement.

Students will see immediately that functional authority uses special knowledge well but it violates the unity of command concept of the principle of authority. Such violation often causes considerable friction and subsequent organizational dysfunction. However, it is usually necessary for chief executives to allow some restricted functional authority to specialist staff on the grounds that it increases overall efficiency more than it lessens overall efficiency.

Line-Staff Relations

The point immediately above brings into focus the possibility of line-staff conflict. The common line complaint is that staff usurp line authority. Also, that staff advice is often too academic, theoretical, and unrealistic; staff people are "cosmopolitans" and not "locals" (cf. Gouldner in Learning Design 3.1). Such complaints are often valid criticisms of staff and particularly so when line personnel are held responsible for failure to achieve organizational objectives.

On the other hand, staff complain that line managers will not listen to new ideas, will not take technical advice (particularly those who need it most!) and sometimes take advice but then do not use it. Often line managers feel they will undermine their own authority if they seem ignorant enough to seek advice from staff.

Executives must be constantly aware of the possibility of this line-staff conflict and ensure that there is intelligent two-way communication between the two authority types which are based on position (line) and expertise (staff).

"ASSISTANT—TO." Haimann and Scott (1974:184) describe such positions as belonging to a single executive's personal staff to do a variety of jobs without line authority. They say such people are an "extension of the arms and mind of the chief executive." Sometimes such positions are used for executive training.

In sport organizations they are seen in a number of guises: administrative assistant, associate dean, assistant dean, and others. A danger with such positions is that they sometimes assume line authority and become an unnecessary barrier between, say, a dean and a department chairman so that conflict ensues. For a harsher treatment of the "assistant-to" see Townsend (1971:4-6) who says, "anyone who has an assistant-to should be fined a hundred dollars a day until he eliminates the position."

PROJECT ORGANIZATION. This concept began in advanced military and space technology. Its purpose is to secure a higher degree of coordination than is possible in regular line structures. A project is of limited time duration and has a manager responsible for its completion. He in turn can *use* the line and staff resources of the organization to complete his task. This type of structure introduces a whole new set of organizational relationships which are too complex to discuss here (cf. Clelland, 1967:63-70). Usually, the project relationships are horizontal and diagonal within a usual vertical structure (Haimann and Scott, 1974:338-340).

A prime example in my sport experience was the building of the 1978 Commonwealth Games Facilities which cost $36 million and became the property of the city of Edmonton. A project manager, Ron Ferguson, worked in the parks and recreation department and skillfully completed his most difficult task on time within budget.

Communication

The regularities of organizations' structures are brought about by superiors' authority, member involvement, and communication. In this design communication has been indirectly referred to when discussing "relations" above, and here some additional formal communication concepts are identified. Generally, of course, the formal communication structure is the same as the authority structure.

Communication involves at least two people: a sender and a receiver. The sender has intention which must be encoded, pass through a communication medium, and be decoded for meaning to be understood by the receiver (cf. Kelly, 1969:473). Various possibilities exist, then, for a message not to be understood.

Downward communication occurs when superiors send messages down the scalar chain to subordinates, usually to initiate action. Upward communication is in the reverse direction and informs, discusses, and reports. Management should encourage upward communication for it helps determine whether or not messages have been understood. Lateral and diagonal communication is also needed as was demonstrated when discussing "staff" and "project organization."

COMMUNICATION MEDIA. Words, pictures, and actions are the media and all are important. Written word messages are indispensible at times as permanent records, as definitive statements, and for mass circulation. They are very time consuming however, for senders and repliers; also they may not transmit complete, true intentions.*

Oral word messages may be by telephone, tape, or face-to-face. The last mentioned are the most important for day-to-day organizational communication between superiors and subordinates. Feedback is instantaneous and a facial expression may be the only "reply" needed for understanding. Thus, a manager must try to develop effective face-to-face communication skills by cultivating a suitable voice and manner (cf. Haimann and Scott, 1974:316-328).

Pictures, in the form of blueprints, charts, models, posters, slides, and movies are often very effective media for transmitting messages in organizations.

Actions include such gestures as the facial expression mentioned above but also encompass the overall organizational behavior of a member. A superior who "practices what he preaches" (and more) has a tremendous positive effect on his subordinates; the reverse is also true. Subordinates, likewise, impress superiors by their actions.

Formal Organization Charts And Manuals

Charts

Partial organization charts are depicted in Figures 3—5. A complete chart graphically portrays the formal structure of an organization; the rectangular boxes indicate functions (and people sometimes) while the lines joining the boxes demonstrate the relationships between the functions (and people). Responsibility for preparing, reviewing, and approving charts rests with executives at various levels; with overall approval being the responsibility of the chief executive.

ADVANTAGES. The purpose of an organization is to achieve its goal and an organization chart helps to portray any structural faults, such as duplication of effort, which may exist. Thus, they help the chief executive and other managers to attain a conceptual view of the whole.

---

*Electronic "discussions" by computer are not considered here. Their proponents claim they are very good because objectivity is needed to win a point; as opposed to a domineering personality.

One important aspect of structure which charts make clear is the *span of control* that various individuals have. "Span" refers to the number of people a manager has reporting directly to him. Various opinions are held as to what is the ideal number; frequently this is said to be six for an executive who is controlling a diverse department such as a big city parks and recreation department or a large university faculty.

This ideal span number obviously varies by job complexity. If fifty clerks are doing routine filing, one supervisor can oversee them all. By contrast, a city director of recreation may have six district heads reporting to him who each in turn may have ultimate responsibility down the scalar chain for one hundred employees. It may be unwise for him to have any more diverse reportees. However, the point here is that shorter span leads to more levels and wider span leads to fewer levels. Charts help to clarify this and therefore encourage thoughts about ideal span in particular situations. The advantages of wide span are greater decision speed, more efficiency, and less frustration below. The reverse is true when spans are too narrow. Careful experienced judgement is required in each situation but the critical consideration should first be at span and *not* at levels (cf. Simon, 1976:26-28).

LIMITATIONS. Charts are a very current picture so must be kept up to date or they are useless. Also, charts only show the surface picture of formal relationships and do not depict the informal relationships, which may be many. Furthermore, charts cannot show precise functions, amounts of authority, or responsibility (Haimann and Scott, 1974:188).

TYPES. Usually charts are vertical but sometimes they are horizontal; particularly when it is wished to de-emphasize levels. In the latter the chief executive is on the left of the page and the other positions are depicted moving to the right across the page. For similar reasons, some charts are circular, with the chief executive in the middle and the subordinates branching out at right angles all the way round the circle.

OTHER CONSIDERATIONS. Those responsible for preparing sport organization charts should keep in mind that they may be by function (recreation programs, park maintenance, intramural, extramural), product, or geographical location (district, provincial governing body, regional sports council). It is useful (but not always necessary) to distinguish between line and staff functions; some do this by means of light and heavy lines or by the position of lines (cf. Haimann and Scott, 1974:192). Finally, always date the chart.

Organization Manuals

The manual should include the sport organization's objectives, its organization charts, and the scope of its personnel. The latter (i.e. job descriptions) should include the principal duties, functions, and authority channels relating to the positions (cf. principles of definition and correspondence). Note that "job description" specifies the elements of a position while "job specifications" list the qualities a person should have to perform it.

Townsend (1971:73) calls job descriptions "strait jackets" which are all right for key-punch operators but "insane for jobs that pay $150 a week or more." Certainly there is a danger that they discourage judgement and "freeze" the job. Also, they consume too much time in being kept up to date by personnel people who do not understand the jobs.

My view is that manuals have value for sport organizations but the possible limitations should be guarded against by executives (cf. Chapter 10).

References

Clelland, David I.: Understanding project authority. *Business Horizons,* *Spring*:63-70, 1967.

Haimann, T., and Scott, William G.: *Management in the Modern Organization,* 2nd ed. Boston, Houghton Mifflin, 1974.

Kelly, J.: *Organizational Behavior.* Homewood, Illinois, Dorsey, 1969.

Pugh, D. S., Hickson, D. J., and Hinings, C. R.: *Writers on Organizations,* 2nd ed. Harmondsworth, England, Penguin, 1971.

Simon, Herbert A.: *Administrative Behavior,* 3rd ed. New York, Free Press, 1976.

Townsend, Robert: *Up the Organization,* Greenwich, Connecticut, Fawcett Crest, 1971.

Important Related Reading
Haimann and Scott, *Modern Organization,* ch. 10, 12, 13, 23.

Supplementary Readings

Case, Robert L.: The communication structure of a physical education unit. In Zeigler, Earle F., and Spaeth, Marcia J. (Eds.): *Administrative Theory and Practice in Physical Education and Athletics.* Englewood Cliffs, New Jersey, Prentice-Hall, 1975.

Conrath, D. W., and Johnson, G. A.: *Analyzing an Organization Via its Internal Communication Patterns.* Paper read at Institute of Management Science International Meeting, Houston, Texas, April, 1972.

Parkinson, Northcote C.: *Parkinson's Law,* 5th pr. New York, Ballantine, 1973 (First published 1957).

Peter, L. J., and Hull, R.: *The Peter Principle.* New York, Bantam, 1970.

Porter, Lyman W., and Roberts, Karlene H. (Eds.): *Communication in Organizations.* Harmondsworth, England, Penguin, 1977.

Simon, H. A., Smithburg, D. W., and Thompson, V. A.: *Public Administration.* New York, Knopf, 1962, ch. 13.

Williams, Trevor: "Structure and Involvement in a Voluntary Sport Organization." Unpublished M.A. thesis, University of Victoria, British Columbia, Canada, 1979.

Yeager, Beatrice V.: Interpersonal communication patterns in physical education. In Zeigler, E. F., and Spaeth, M. J. (Eds.): *Administrative Theory and Practice in Physical Education and Athletics.* Englewood Cliffs, New Jersey, Prentice-Hall, 1975, ch. 15.

Zeigler, Earle F.: Advantages of a totally unified organizational structure for physical education and sport in a university setting. In Zeigler, Earle: *Issues in North American Sport and Physical Education.* Washington, D.C., AAHPER, 1979.

Case 3.21

Great Divide University

Great Divide University's community consisted of 9,000 people. The "sport"-related functions are depicted in Figure Six, which shows Rocky Mountain Center, the sport complex, as being the responsibility of a line manager under the director of buildings and grounds. Using the complex are participants in athletics and recreation (whose manager reports to the director of student services) and students preparing for teaching/academic careers in physical education (whose director reports to the dean of education).

The manager of Rocky Mountain Center was "management oriented" and keen to keep buildings, sports fields, and equipment looking clean and in perfect order. He was very building security conscious.

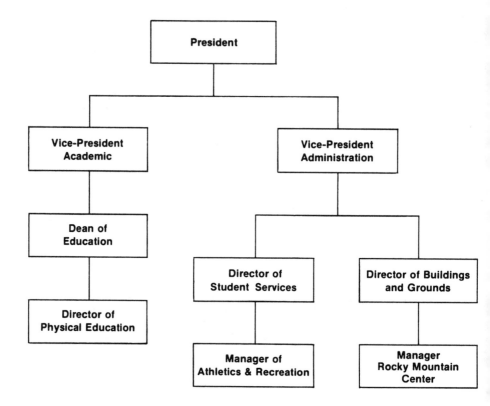

Figure 6. Great Divide University

Here are some statements from users of Rocky Mountain Center that should be of interest to someone in the higher reaches of line authority.

P.E. PROFESSOR. "Why can't I have a key for the gym? I have to prepare my lessons *before* 9:00 A.M."

SOCCER COACH. "How come the drains were put in the field just at the start of the season when the field was not needed in the previous four months?"

FIELD HOCKEY COACH. "Why was the newly constructed field, which was supposed to be smooth, sited where all other field users would have to walk across it to reach their fields? There were plenty of other sites."

BADMINTON INSTRUCTOR. "Is it true that the fans in the gym can't be turned off here and that they are controlled by a computer twenty-five miles away? And that it takes a week to change the program?"

FIELD HOCKEY INSTRUCTOR. "I'm pleased to hear of the computer-controlled field watering arrangement but why is it set to come on in the middle of my class?"

TENNIS INSTRUCTOR. "In the fall my students and I have to sweep leaves off the courts every day. It really cuts into instructional time so why can't I get someone from maintenance to do it?"

FOOTBALL COACH. "Who gave permission for that dog show to take place on the football field? There was mess all over the place."

DIRECTOR OF P.E. "I can't answer any of these questions."

MANAGER OF ATHLETICS AND RECREATION. "Nor can I."

What should be done and by whom?

Case Analysis Method
CAM A or CAM B (see Chapter 1).

Case 3.22

Ring-A-Ring Of Roses

Brogan Junior High School had 600 students. The principal, Dr. Letniak, believed in "freedom with responsibility" and was on first-name terms with all his staff. He did not regard the staff as being in "departments" but did have five people teaching physical education and rather more than that coaching teams.

Two physical education teachers were strictly 9:00 A.M. to 3:00 P.M. "types." Two were very keen on teaching and coaching but, after two years, were practically "worn-out." The fifth teacher taught conscientiously and coached wrestling, which was not popular with students.

One of the two "worn-out" teachers went to the principal and complained about gymnasium scheduling clashes, shoddy equipment, lack of equipment, poor student behavior, lazy colleagues, and other ills. The principal then directed the P.E.

teachers to form a "circular structure" with no one in the middle. Each would be in the perimeter and take it in turns (annually) at being responsible for coordination.

Was the principal right? If not what would you do in his position? What would you do as one of the worn-out teachers?

Case Analysis Method
CAM A or CAM B.

Case 3.23

"O Canada"

Burton and Kyllo (1974) pointed out that the government of Canada has been involved in the provision of leisure services for about one hundred years. Recently, the involvement had grown to a point where "almost all federal departments and agencies have responsibility for some form of leisure services."

Services provided included: dissemination of information (53 of 66 agencies), policy development (41), research (41), coordination (39), planning (34), licensing and regulation (14), safety and protection (17), provision of areas and facilities (20), provision of programs (22), training and education (27), and financial support (31).

The orientations of services were: sports and physical recreation (39), social activities (39), outdoor activities (40), tourism and travel (40), and arts and culture (45).

The departments and agencies listed above were only included if they reported directly to a minister or government department. They were:

Departments	*Agencies*
Agriculture	Economic Council of Canada
Communications	National Research Council
Consumer and	Treasury Board Secretariat
Corporate Affairs	Farm Credit Corporation
Energy, Mines, and	Canadian Radio-Television
Resources	Commission
Environment	National Energy Board
External Affairs	Fisheries Research Board
Finance	International Joint Commission

Indian and Northern Affairs
(3 sections)
Industry, Trade, and
Commerce
Justice
Labor
Manpower and Immigration
National Defence
National Health and
Welfare
Post Office
Public Works
Regional Economic
Expansion
Secretary of State
Solicitor General
Transport
Urban Affairs
Veterans Affairs

Industrial Development Bank
Canadian Government Office of
Tourism
National Design Council
Statistics Canada
Information Canada
Defence Research Board
Medical Research Council
National Advisory Council on
Fitness and Amateur Sports
Prairie Farm Rehabilitation
Administration
Canadian Council on Rural
Development
Ministry of State for Science and
Technology
Science Council of Canada
Canada Council
Canadian Broadcasting
Corporation
Canadian Film Development
Corporation
Company of Young Canadians
National Arts Centre
Corporation
National Film Board
National Library
National Museums of Canada
Public Archives
Minister for Multiculturalism
Canadian Penitentiary Service
Royal Canadian Mounted Police
Crown Assets Disposal
Corporation
Royal Canadian Mint
Air Canada
Canadian National Railway
Canadian Transport
Commission
National Harbours Board

> St. Lawrence Seaway Authority
> Central Mortgage and Housing
>   Corporation
> National Capital Commission
> Veterans' Land Administration

You have just been appointed as consultant to "help rationalize the provision of leisure services by the federal government of Canada." Bear in mind that there are provincial and municipal levels of government as well. What will you advise?

Reference

Burton, Thomas L., and Kyllo, Leo T.: *Federal-Provincial Responsibilities for Leisure Services in Alberta and Ontario: Volume 1, Analysis and Commentary*. Toronto, Ontario Research Council on Leisure for the Ministry of Culture and Recreation, 1974.

Case Analysis Method
CAM A or CAM B (see Chapter 1).

Case 3.24

Little Boxes

Figure Seven focuses on the recreation programs branch of a city parks and recreation department; the other two directors' branches are not considered. The numbers in the boxes two levels below the director of recreation represent the numbers of professionally qualified staff; non-professional and part-time employees are excluded.

Based on your experience, and knowledge of formal structure, advise the superintendent on the quality of his recreation branch's structure (which costs $8 million per year to operate). Explain the reasons for any changes you may suggest.

Case Analysis Method
CAM A or CAM B (see Chapter 1).

Summary

1. Sport has many varied organizations. An organization is a

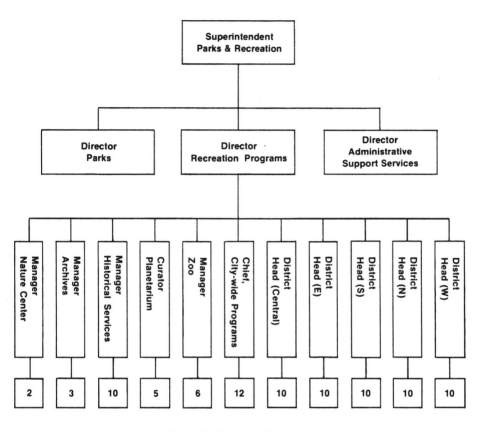

Figure 7. Spans and levels

social system that is organized for the attainment of a particular type of goal.

2. Organizations are characterized by planned divisions of labor, power, and communication responsibilities that are designed for specific goal achievement.

3. Through power, communication, and members' involvement, regularities such as task allocation, supervision, and coordination are developed. Such regularities constitute the organization's structure.

4. The concept "bureaucracy" is ancient. The word originated in about 1764 and has a variety of meanings (cf. Supplementary Readings of Learning Design 3.1).

5. Weber's "pure" organizational types were: charismatic, traditional, and rational-legal ("Ideal Type" Bureaucratic). A person had power if his will could be enforced without resistance; authority when his command was voluntarily obeyed and perceived as legitimate (i.e. justified). Based on legitimacy propositions and authority, Weber defined his most rational form of bureaucracy, which had: precision, speed, unambiguity, knowledge of files, continuity, discretion, unity, strict subordination, impersonality, and reduced friction.

6. Weber suggested limiting bureaucracy's power by collegiality, separation of powers, amateur administration, direct democracy, and representation.

7. The "Ideal Type" was criticized by a number of scholars, but, it is not empirical.

8. Etzioni identified three types of power and three types of member involvement; respectively they were: coercive, remunerative, normative, and alienative, calculative, moral. Nine compliance relationships evolve of which three are congruent and all are found empirically.

9. "Line" relationships are those in the scalar chain of command. They are associated with the principles of authority, definition, and correspondence.

10. "Staff" work revolves around the performance of specialized activities and using technical knowledge for the benefit of line managers.

11. "Functional" authority is held by staff in narrow areas of expertise.

12. "Communication" may be downward, upward, lateral, or diagonal and by words, pictures, or actions. Oral, face-to-face communication is most important in organizations; particularly when linked with appropriate actions.

13. Organization charts and manuals present conceptual views of organizations and help to develop appropriate structures.

14. Span of control refers to the number of people a manager has reporting to him.

Concepts For Review

Organizations   Bureaucracy

Formal Structure   Weber's "Ideal Type"
Power   Limiting bureaucracy
Authority   Mock bureacracy
Representative bureaucracy   Punishment-centered bureaucracy
Cosmopolitans   Locals
Compliance structures   Line
Staff   Principle of authority
Principle of definition   Principle of correspondence
Functional authority   Communication directions
Communication media   Organization charts and manuals

Questions For Oral Or Written Discussion

1. Identify, and discuss, sport organizations in each of the categories of meaning which "bureaucracy" has.
2. Select the sport organization you know which most closely resembles a Weberian "Ideal Type" structure. Describe it and discuss the deviations.
3. From your experience, describe a "collegial" sport organization then discuss its strengths and weaknesses. Do you advocate such structure? Give reasons.
4. Identify nine organizations (sport organizations if possible) that fit into each of Etzioni's compliance relationships. State what is likely to happen within each one.
5. Construct your ideal organizational structure for sport in your university, college, school, or agency.
6. CAM C (see Chapter 1) applied to instructor-specified topics taken from this chapter.
7. Sport committees are a mode of responsible irresponsibility. Discuss.
8. Managing a collegial sport organization is the art of the impossible. Discuss.

Chapter 4

LEADERSHIP

LEARNING DESIGN 4.0

LEADERSHIP THEORIES

The last chapter dealt with the concepts of power and authority which here are merged in a consideration of leadership. But what is leadership? Fiedler (1967:8) defined the leader, "as the individual in the group given the task of directing and coordinating task-relevant group activities or who, in the absence of a designated leader, carries the primary responsibility for performing these functions in the group." More concisely, and synthesizing several views, leadership is the process of influencing individuals or groups to direct their efforts towards the achievement of particular goals (cf. Hodgetts, 1975:342; Haimann and Scott, 1974:349; Sikula, 1973:143; Barrow, 1977:232). Chelladurai (1979:2) points out that this is interpersonal in nature and serves "to distinguish the leadership functions of an administrator or manager from his other functions."

Bearing in mind the wide variety of sport organizations that were identified in Chapter Three, it can readily be suspected that understanding the leadership of them must involve complex analyses. This design traces the way general thoughts on leadership have developed, pays particular attention to sport-related findings, and links important leadership concept variables with actual case problems.

General Theories

Trait Theory

For hundreds of years it was believed that certain people were born to be leaders having inherited a set of unique traits or characteristics. This belief arose from the fact that leaders frequently emerged in the same prominent families. Overlooked, of course, was the point that strong class barriers made it almost impossible for people outside the prominent families to acquire the skills, knowledge, and power to become leaders (Haimann and Scott, 1974:351).

Later, leaders did emerge from the so-called lower classes, and 1930s behavioral scientist researchers focused on leadership traits which they said could be acquired through experience, education, and training as well as by inheritance (Gordon, 1975:47). Thus, researchers said that leaders seemed to possess similar personalities, physical traits, and psychological characteristics. In the 1940s, however, Byrd (1940:378) examined twenty lists of purported leadership traits and found that none appeared on all lists. Similarly, Jenkins (1947:74-75), after reviewing leadership studies of diverse groups, said, "No single trait or group of characteristics has been isolated which sets off the leader from the members of his group."

These observations, and those of others (cf. Gibb, 1947:267-284; Stogdill, 1948:35-72), heralded the death knell for the trait theories. In sport situations, similar limitations have been identified by Chelladurai and Carron (1978:6). Summarizing, Hodgkinson (1978:92) says the trait theory "has been exploded" and "set aside if not entirely discounted."

It is not entirely discounted, for numerous later researchers certainly consider leaders' traits as one set of factors involved in analysing the whole concept of leadership (Fiedler, 1967; House, 1971; House and Mitchell, 1974; and Vroom, 1959). Citing Davis (1972:103:104) and Fiedler and Chemers (1974:22-28, 31-34), Hodgetts (1975:343) lists the following traits as appearing to be related to successful leadership: intelligence, social maturity and breadth, inner motivation and achievement drives, and human relations attitudes. All in all, though, traits alone cannot be used to predict successful leadership.

Behavioral Views

TECHNIQUES. Among others, Albers (1969:588-91) has differentiated leadership into three types: authoritarian, democratic, or laissez-faire. The first type makes all the decisions without subordinate participation. The laissez-faire leader, if he can be called a leader, gives the group complete freedom in determining activity. The democratic leader falls between the two extremes: seeking advice which he often acts on and generally giving group members a range of discretion in performing their activities.

Albers (1969:588-91) cited Lewin, Lippitt, and White's (1939) Iowa experiment, which sought to find a relationship between types of leadership and group behavior. Whilst engaged in mural painting, soap carving, and model airplane construction, four groups of ten-year-old boys were variously subjected to authoritarian, democratic, and laissez-faire leadership techniques. To control for leaders' personalities the four leaders used different techniques as they moved from group to group after six-week periods.

Autocratic leadership produced tension, frustration, and some aggression. Laissez-faire leadership gave rise to most aggression while democratic leadership fell between the aggressive authoritarian-led group and the four non-aggressive autocracies. Based entirely on the leadership techniques (not the people), nineteen boys liked their democratic leaders better than their autocratic ones. Seven out of ten preferred laissez-faire leaders over autocratic ones and more favorable comments were made about democratic leadership than the other two types. Albers pointed out that discretion should be used in generalizing from this small sample, uncontrolled experiment. Of interest in sport is the point that leadership techniques of coaches have often been described as being authoritarian (Meggyesy, 1970; Ogilvie and Tutko, 1971; Sage, 1973; Scott, 1971; Tutko and Richards, 1971).

Weber's charismatic, traditional, and rational leaders were dealt with in Chapter 3. Here, only the first receives further comment for, despite what has been written here about traits of leaders, there are "forceful or magnetic personalities who possess the elusive quality of charisma" (Hodgkinson, 1978:93). Hodgkinson thinks the concept is "unpleasantly vague" but the phenomenon is sometimes "disturbingly real." He suspects "the charismatic leader has a special gift of being able to verbalize the wishes (conscious or unconscious) of the followership . . . and thereby a sense of meaning or purpose." In his search for this,

". . . man will reach beyond life itself. And certainly beyond logic."

The Ohio State Studies

After the trait theories were discarded, leader behaviors were investigated in what are usually referred to as The Ohio State Studies and The Michigan Studies.

Early studies at Ohio State (Hempill and Coons, 1959; Halpin and Winer, 1957; Fleishman, 1957a and b; Fleishman and Harris, 1962) used factor analytic techniques to isolate two major dimensions of leadership behavior; they were *consideration* and *initiating* structure. Consideration connotes rapport between supervisor and supervised (which is not simply superficial back-patting or use of first names). Initiating structure, on the other hand, refers to definition of roles of members, forward planning, and pushing for production. Thus, these are the two major classes of behavior used by leaders—one is interpersonal in nature (consideration) and the other is production/task/goal oriented (initiating structure).

In carrying out this research a number of well-known measurement instruments were developed that contained items relating to consideration and initiating structure and were designed to describe how a leader carries out his activities. The first was the *Leadership Behavior Description Questionnaire* (LBDQ), which dealt with such areas as leader's rules, regulations, task assignments, friendliness, and willingness to change or listen (Hemphill and Coons, 1959). Halpin and Winer (1957) developed a short-form LBDQ and Fleishman (1957a) the *Supervisory Behavior Description Questionnaire* (SBDQ), which was primarily applicable in industrial settings. However, the resulting questionnaires again measured consideration and initiating structure. Finally, the *Leader Opinion Questionnaire* (LOQ) was developed by Fleishman (1957b) to assess leadership attitudes. It assessed attitudes to consideration and initiating structure in contrast to the other scales' measurement of behavior. (Note that LBDQ and SBDQ assess behavior as perceived by leader or follower.)

The findings of these studies are that employees desired more consideration but that supervisors' superiors emphasize initiating structure. Attempts to make supervisors more consideration oriented has little effect unless there is a real change in their superiors. Though initiating structure and consideration are separate dimensions, a person could rank high on one without being low on the other. So a leader may be: (1) high on structure, low on consideration; (2) high on consideration, low on structure; (3) low on structure, low on consideration; or (4) high on structure, high on consideration. These Ohio State leadership "quadrants" permit simultaneous consideration of two factors, which is certainly better than viewing leadership on a continuum.

MANAGERIAL GRID. Though not originating at Ohio State, the managerial grid of Blake and Mouton (1966:31) is another two-dimensional approach. They rejected the Ohio State four-quadrant paradigm and constructed their own grid. In it, there are two axes and each has nine divisions; one axis is "concern for people" (cf. consideration) and the other "concern for production" (cf. initiating structure). This grid reveals five basic leadership styles:

1. Little concern for people or production (1,1 or "impoverished").
2. Great concern for people but little for production (1,9 or "country club" leader).
3. Great concern for production but little concern for people (9,1 or "task manager").
4. Balanced concern for people and production (5,5 or "middle of the road manager").
5. Maximum interest in people and production (9,9 or "team manager").

Some claim that the managerial grid has been a very useful tool for developing effective managers. For example, in redirecting a 1,9 manager to be more interested in production, or a 9,1 manager to be more interested in people (Hodgetts, 1975:351-353).

The Michigan Studies

Starting in 1946, at the University of Michigan Survey Research Center, Rensis Likert (1961, 1967) developed research to determine what contributes to a group's productivity and to the satisfaction group members derive from participation. So, again, the attempt was to find behaviors that leaders universally exhibited. The initial research used non-directive interviews and

derived two leadership behavior dimensions: "employee orientation" (cf. consideration) and "production orientation" (cf. initiating structure) (see Likert, 1950; Katz, Maccoby, and Morse,
1950; Katz, et al., 1951).

Later Michigan researchers identified five major dimensions of
the supervisor's effectiveness:
1. *His definition of his role.* A leader cannot act merely as a group
   member; he must spell out his job so that his people can
   define their jobs and their relationships to him.
2. *His orientation toward the work group.* Usually "employee-
   centered" supervisors rather than "production-centered"
   supervisors are associated with high producing groups.
3. *The closeness of his supervision.* Refers to "looseness" of
   supervision, and "employee-centered" supervisors are "looser"
   but have the confidence and goodwill of the workers. "Production-centered" supervisors are sometimes called "snoop-
   ervisors" (see Cribbin, 1972:34).
4. *The quality of his group relations.* Refers to the leader's
   ability to promote group cohesiveness.
5. *The type of supervision he receives from superiors.* High-
   producing work groups' supervisors' managers feel high production is one of the most important factors but not the most
   important factor. Low-producing groups' supervisors' managers act as if high production was the most important work
   aspect.

From the above it is clear that there are some similarities and
some differences in the conclusions of the Michigan studies and
those of the Ohio State. In an attempt to build on both groups'
efforts, Bowers and Seashore (1971) proposed a model containing
four factors, namely: *support* (behavior that enhances others'
feelings of personal worth and importance); *interaction facilitation* (behavior that encourages members of the group to develop
close, mutually satisfying relationships); *goal emphasis* (behavior that stimulates an enthusiasm for meeting the groups'
goals or achieving excellent performance); and, *work facilitation*
(behavior that helps goal attainment by such activities as
scheduling, coordinating, planning, and by providing resources)
(cf. Chelladurai and Carron, 1978:14).

Chelladurai and Carron (1978:14-15) point out that the Ohio

State and Michigan studies have been important in defining and describing leaders' behaviors and roles. Also, that the LBDQ, SBDQ, and LOQ scales, which measure consideration and initiating structure, have been most used by other researchers. This is not, however, without some concerns; for example, the two dimensions have not been successfully correlated with either performance or satisfaction of subordinates. And, if one of the four Ohio State quadrants (high consideration, high initiating structure) is considered best, there is not sufficient empirical evidence to support the view. In fact, Chelladurai and Carron (1978:15) cite a number of studies which propose "that the specific effects of consideration and initiating structure are dependent upon the situation." This leads appropriately to the next section.

Situational Approaches

A useful differentiation of the types of leadership theory that includes "situation" as a considered variable was made by Chelladurai and Carron (1978:20); one category was Fiedler's trait approach while the other endeavors were behavioral.

FIEDLER'S CONTINGENCY MODEL. Fiedler (1967) has been a prolific writer on leadership for more than twenty-five years. Out of his research, he developed his contingency model, which attempts to account for the interrelationships between the leader's motivational characteristics (traits), the situation, and the productivity.

With his associates he identified three major factors that could be used to classify group situations: (1) position power of the leader, (2) task structure, and (3) leader-member personal relationships. For example, the leader who has high position power, a clear-cut task, and is liked by his group has everything in his favor. Alternatively, the leader with weak position power, an unstructured task, and poor relationships with his group will be unlikely to exert much influence.

If the various possible combinations of these factors are the situations, which "style" of leader will achieve most in each? Fiedler's instrument for measuring style is his *Least-Preferred Co-worker* (LPC) scale. The LPC score is obtained by summing the item scores on a scaled questionnaire that describes the leader's least-preferred coworker. The scale's sixteen items are bipolar adjectives such as: friendly-unfriendly, tense-relaxed, boring-interesting, gloomy-cheerful, and open-guarded. The continua between the bipolar adjectives each have eight divisions; thus, the score is eight at one extreme and one at the other extreme (Fiedler, 1967:267-269). A high-LPC leader (who perceives his least-preferred co-worker in a relatively favorable manner) is a person who derives his major satisfaction from successful inter-personal relations. By contrast, a low-LPC leader (who describes his least-preferred co-worker in very unfavorable terms) derives his major satisfaction from task performance (Fiedler, 1967:45). So, the LPC score indicates the degree to which a leader is task oriented or relationship oriented and this is purported to be a stable characteristic in all circumstances.

The next issue is to consider how the two leadership styles react in the various group situations to produce desired results. Fiedler looked back at the leadership studies he had been conducting for more than ten years in business management, schools, military units, boards of directors, creative groups, and scientists doing pure research. Then he correlated the effectiveness of the groups' performances with the leadership styles. By plotting the correlations of leadership style against group situations it was possible to see which style worked best in each situation. When the median points of each column were connected, a bell-shaped curve resulted—showing that a task-oriented leader performs best in situations at both extremes (i.e. those in which he has a great deal of influence and power and also when he has no influence and power over the group members). Relationship-oriented leaders tend to perform best in mixed situations where they have only moderate influence over the group.

These results demonstrate that it is not possible to talk simply about good leaders or poor leaders, for a leader who is effective in one situation may not be effective in another. Therefore, the "situation" in which a leader performs well or badly must be specified. Fiedler (1967) contended that anyone who wanted to become a leader could do so if he carefully chose the situations that were favourable to his leadership style. Further, that a leader's performance could be improved by fitting the job to the leader; it being easier to change a work environment than to change a personality. For example, the leader's position power can be changed in either direction or the task structure changed to suit the leader's style; that is, the leader can be given explicit instructions or a vague and nebulous goal. Finally, the leader-member relations can be changed by, for example, making the group homogeneous in culture, language, or educational background.

Some sport-related research, using the contingency model and LPC scale, is reviewed later in this chapter but here this subsection closes by drawing attention to some limitations. These were summarized by Chelladurai and Carron (1978:29-31):

1. Limitations arise when completed research is used to develop a theory and then the same results to support the theory; particularly when subsequent research has not appreciably supported the theory (citing Graen et al., 1970).
2. LPC has been shown not to measure a stable trait of leaders. This is a serious conceptual flaw, and Fiedler (1973) has amended his interpretation of the scale.
3. Leader-member relations are not independent of the leader's style over long association.
4. The subordinates' impact on leadership effectiveness is not considered (but is discussed later in this chapter).
5. Style and substance of leader behavior are confounded.

The contingency model has led to many studies but it has not received much substantial support. Chelladurai and Carron (1978:31) cite some as suggesting it should be abandoned but their view is that the theoretical framework may be alright if the constructs could be validly measured.

BEHAVIORAL VIEWS. The researchers referred to in this section tried to account for leadership differences by focusing on the behaviors of leaders across different situations. This is a brief summary of their findings, which is adapted from Chelladurai and Carron's (1978:31-50) monograph and from the primary sources.

1. *The Path-Goal Theory and Role-Making Model.*

In contrast to Fiedler's (1967) contingency model, the path-goal theory places its emphasis on the needs and goals of the subordinates and their situations. Thus, the leader's strategic functions "are to provide for subordinates the coaching, guidance, support and rewards necessary for effective and satisfying performance that would otherwise be lacking in the environment" (House and Dessler, 1974:31). Two important groups of situational variables influence the leader behavior: (a) the subordinates' characteristics, and (b) the environmental demands and pressures on the subordinates which affects their reaching satisfying achievements. So, a leader may have to be task oriented or relationship oriented (depending on the subordinates' needs) and vary his behavior according to whether or not the tasks are routine, satisfying, and/or independent.

Graen and Cashman's (1975) role-making model of leadership is an extension of the path-goal theory. Its proposition is that the leader's behavior must be heterogeneous to the extent that a dyadic role-set is developed between the leader and each subordinate. Cummings (1975:184) disapproved of this model on the grounds that leaders would be accused of preferentially treating some subordinates and would have neither the time nor the energy to be so heterogeneous.

2. *The Situational Theory of Leadership.*

This theory has not been empirically tested but has been proposed by Hersey and Blanchard (1977:163). In earlier editions of their book it was named the "Life Cycle Theory of Leadership" and here is why. As a person matures from childhood to adulthood he requires different behavior from his parents; similarly is the case in work situations. An immature child/ worker requires high-task and low-relationship behavior from his parent/leader; a more mature young person/worker needs high-task and high-relationship behavior from his parent/leader; one with a further maturity requires low-task behavior but high-relationship behavior from parents/leaders; and finally, a fully mature person/worker requires little of each type of parent/ leader behavior.

3. *An Adaptive-Reactive Theory of Leadership.*

This was developed by Osborn and Hunt (1975) who viewed the leader's behavior as consisting of adaptation to the conditions of the organizational system ("macro-variables" of unit size, level of technology, and formal structure; "micro-variables" of task demands and subordinates' personalities) and reactions to the wants, desires, and pressures of subordinates. The reactions consist of "discretionary influence" and are the "essence of leadership." So, the micro-variables alter the impact of the leader's behavior and the macro-variables influence the leader behavior itself (Chelladurai and Carron, 1978:45).

4. *The Normative Model of Decision Making.*

Vroom and Yetton's (1973) normative model is a device for choosing appropriate leadership styles for specific situations with particular outcomes in view. It focuses on one aspect of leadership behavior: that of participation in decision making. The decisions, broadly, may be made autocratically, by consultation, or by group consensus.

Initially, Vroom and Yetton outlined eight possible problem attributes in the form of questions and then developed a flow chart that was designed to lead to the correct decision style for a particular situation. Their empirical testing of the model revealed that the "influence of situational factors in determining choice of leadership methods is roughly four times the influence of individual differences" (Vroom and Yetton, 1973:104).

This model is too cumbersome for full exposure here but it is worth further study. Sashkin and Garland (1979:86) point out that, though not without its critics (including Argyris, 1976) the model is "one of the most hopeful indications that scientific knowledge about leadership can be developed. . . ." It has been adopted in the athletic context by Chelladurai and Haggerty (see Chelladurai and Carron, 1978:50-53).

Sport Research And Theory

Sport-Related Leadership Research

The research reviewed here is presented in approximately the same sequential order as were the general theories described. Just as the trait theory was "set aside" there, so it is in the athletic context where Chelladurai and Carron (1978:6) cited five sports psychologists as considering traits only to be too limiting in trying to understand leadership behavior.

When Olafson (1975:89) completed his doctoral study in 1969, no physical education or athletics research had used the LBDQ. Using that instrument, it was his primary objective "to measure the leader behavior of the physical education chairman at two levels of higher education—the university and the junior college." After surveying physical education department chairmen at all "Big Ten" universities and thirty-two selected junior colleges, he found general support for situational and behavioral approaches. Thus, future department leaders would be better if they "understood the theoretical complexities of modern management techniques" and have "an expanded knowledge of the situation. . . ."

Using an adapted LBDQ, Olafson and Boucher (1978:11) sought to describe and analyse the perceived leadership styles of minor hockey coaches in Ontario, Canada. Their major finding was that coaches "need to increase the congruence of their expectations with the players perceived expectations" (p. 15). That is, leadership style is not what leaders think it is but how followers perceive it; too much incongruence is dysfunctional.

Danielson, Zelhart, and Drake (1975:333) modified the LBDQ and administered it to 160 hockey players aged twelve to eighteen years. The main finding was that "commonly perceived behaviors in hockey coaching are mainly of a communicative nature with surprisingly little emphasis on domination." This, of course, contradicts the usually held view of authoritarian coaches. Applying a similarly modified instrument and testing the path-goal theory (see following), Chelladurai and Saleh (1978:85-92) examined the relationship between preferred leader behavior of eighty male and eighty female undergraduate physical education students and the type of sport preferred. The analysed results revealed five different dimensions of preferred leadership behavior: training behavior, autocratic behavior, democratic behavior, social support, and rewarding behavior. Further, that: (1) athletes in interdependent sports (e.g. synchronized swimming, basketball) preferred their coach to emphasize more training behavior than athletes in independent sports (e.g. golf, tennis); (2) athletes in closed sports (e.g. golf, synchronized swimming) preferred their coach to emphasize more training behavior than athletes in open sports (e.g. tennis, basketball); (3) males preferred more autocratic behavior and social support than females; and (4) males in closed sports expected more supportive behavior than males in open sports and females.

Chelladurai and Saleh's (1978) findings regarding the dimensions of "training behavior, social support, and rewarding behavior" exactly parallel Danielson, Zelhart, and Drake's (1975) "competitive training, social, and recognition." Autocratic and democratic behavior reflect decision style preferred (Chelladurai and Carron, 1978:19-20).

The LPC scale is a component of an earlier scale named *Assumed Similarity between Opposites* (ASO); that is, between the most- and least-preferred co-workers. Fiedler (1954) used ASO in what was probably the first sport-related study of leadership in basketball teams. Results revealed "that the successful teams tended to choose highly task-oriented persons as informal leaders while the less successful teams chose the more relationship-oriented group members as informal leaders" (Fiedler, 1967:72). Fiedler (1967:225), also, cited two other sport studies: (1) DeZonia's (1958) bowling league research used ASO and found the correlation between the elected team captain's ASO score and team performance was only .06; and (2) Myer's (1962) investigation of rifle teams which also showed the leader's influence over the group to be minimal when his position power was weak.

Chelladurai and Carron (1978:26-27) reviewed some athletic context studies that tested Fiedler's contingency model by using LPC. Inciong (1974) assessed leadership style and group atmosphere among some seventy high school basketball coaches and 535 players; hypothesizing that "the LPC score would be positively correlated with performance effectiveness in moderately favourable situations and negatively correlated in very favourable and unfavourable situations." However, though correlation directions were as expected, they were nonsignificant so leadership style was not related to team success in high school basketball. Similarly, after using the LPC scale, Danielson (1976) found that leadership in hockey situations was more effective when leaders were relationship oriented rather than task oriented. Thus the model was not supported even though the LPC scale was used (cf. Fiedler's model and LPC earlier in this chapter).

Yet another LPC basketball study was reported by Loy, McPherson and Kenyon (1978:84-85); it was Vander Velden's (1971) doctoral dissertation which, among other things, tested the hypothesis that task-oriented leaders (low LPC) would be more effective. His study found no empirical support, but he noted that few coaches were task oriented. By contrast, the same authors reviewed Kjeldsen's (1976) dissertation, which investigated the leadership of thirty gymnastic coaches who had fairly strong position power. His findings generally supported Fiedler's model.

Finally, regarding LPC, Bagley (1975:98-112) tested Fiedler's model in university graduate departments of physical education by particular reference to LPC, group atmosphere, task structure, position power of the leader, and effectiveness measures. Her findings did not support the model and she concluded that graduate departments of physical education require primarily relationship-oriented leaders who, of course, do not ignore the task.

For the second part of Chelladurai and Saleh's (1978) preferred leadership in sports study, which was referred to earlier in this section, the *path-goal theory* was tested. Its emphasis was on the needs and goals of the subordinate in contrast with Fiedler's leader orientation and situation favourableness. When the undergraduate physical education students had stated their preferred sports, the researchers grouped them as (1) independent-open; (2) independent-closed; (3) interdependent-open; and (4) interdependent-closed. (For example, badminton is open, and a track sprint is closed; dependence related to individual or team sports.) The path-goal theory was supported so far as the task attribute of dependence was concerned; it was not, however, regarding task variability. That is, those "who preferred closed sports showed greater preference for training behavior than individuals with a preference for open sports" (Chelladurai and Carron, 1978:38-39). Also, they noted sex differences in preferred leader behavior: males preferring more autocratic and socially supportive behavior while females preferred democratic coaches who did not provide as much social support.

Sport-Related Leadership Theory

Most of the theories referred to in this chapter have their origins with industrial psychologists; most (not all) empirical testing of the theories in sport settings has been on coaches. Sage (1975) and Chelladurai and Carron (1978) have reviewed and advanced the theoretical knowledge in the athletic context. However, it is Chelladurai's (1978) "Multidimensional Model of Leadership" that is described here. It is one that synthesizes a number of factors to present a more complete conceptualization of leadership. Figure 8 schematically depicts the 1978 model in the slightly modified form that Chelladurai used in his 1979 paper.

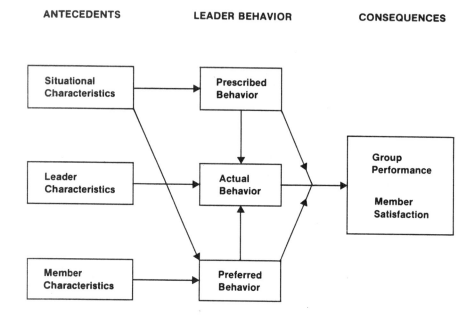

ANTECEDENTS　　　**LEADER BEHAVIOR**　　　**CONSEQUENCES**

Figure 8. Chelladurai's multidimensional model of leadership. (Courtesy of Dr. P. Chelladurai.)

The consequences of leadership (i.e. satisfaction and performance of subordinates) are the product of the interactive effects of three types of leader behavior: (1) prescribed leader behavior, (2) the leader behavior preferred by subordinates or group, and (3) the actual leader behavior. The antecedents of these types of leader behavior comprise the three separate categories of: (1) the characteristics of the situation; (2) the characteristics of the leader; and (3) the characteristics of the group member or subordinate.

PRESCRIBED LEADER BEHAVIOR. Drawing on, and adding to, the work of Osborn and Hunt (1975), Chelladurai (1978) pointed out that macro-variables such as unit size, level of technology, normative forces, organizational goals, group task, and formal organizational structure directly influence/control leader behavior. Thus, Chelladurai also calls this "required" leader behavior, which arises from situational variables and tends "to be task oriented and/or instrumental in the realization of the group's objectives" (Chelladurai, 1978; Osborn and Hunt, 1975).

PREFERRED LEADER BEHAVIOR. Chelladurai (1978) considers preferred leader behaviors to result from the combined variables of the situation and the members' characteristics (see Figure 8). This is because the leader and members are socialized into the behavioral prescriptions for an occupation (cf. Jackson and Lowe, 1978).

ACTUAL LEADER BEHAVIOR. From Figure Eight, it can be seen that actual leader behavior is centrally affected by the characteristics of the leader (personality and ability) and indirectly by the preferred behavior of subordinates plus the prescribed (required) behavior dictated by the situation. Osborn and Hunt (1975) view the leader's reaction to macro-variables as "adaptive" and his response to the needs and desires of his subordinates as "reactive." Chelladurai (1978) proposed that adaptive behaviors would be homogeneous across all group members while reactive behaviors would be heterogeneous; being in response to individual subordinate's needs and desires.

Further, Chelladurai (1978) pointed out that the environment for the leader varies from more favourable to less favourable according to the degree to which it is possible for the leader to engage in adaptive versus reactive behavior. That is, organizations impose different constraints; for example, in a bureaucracy with structured tasks the leader's behavior would be largely prescribed; therefore, the leadership process is easier. Alternatively, the leadership environment is less favourable when there is a greater proportion of discretionary behavior, since the leader and the subordinates may have different preferences.

Nevertheless, despite the influences of the organizational situation and the subordinates, the leader's actual behavior is mainly determined by his own personality and ability. Chelladurai and Carron (1978:68) hypothesized that "task-oriented leaders would emphasize adaptive behaviors while relations-oriented leaders would emphasize reactive behaviors."

PERFORMANCE AND SATISFACTION. Chelladurai's (1978) model stipulates that as the degree to which the three states of leader behavior (i.e. prescribed, actual, preferred) are congruent, so performance and satisfaction will be facilitated. For example, total congruence would lead to an "ideal" outcome; no congruence would lead to chaos (similar to laissez faire type leadership); and, actual leadership incongruence with prescribed and preferred leadership would lead to the removal of the leader.

Chelladurai (1978) viewed the interrelationship of performance and satisfaction from two perspectives: First, "insofar as subordinates (athletes) are oriented towards task accomplishment and, insofar as the leader (coach) meets these preferences, *both* satisfaction and performance should be enhanced" (as a direct result of leader behavior); and secondly, "the athlete (or subordinate) may obtain satisfaction as a result of the leader's reactive (i.e. interpersonal) behavior." That is, for example, if a coach meets an athlete's preference he is like a "benefactor" who bestows something. To achieve equity, the athlete must reciprocate and provide some benefit to the coach. So if, for example, "the athlete perceives the leader to be task oriented, this payoff could be given through enhanced performance." Consequently, Chelladurai (1978) reasons, "satisfaction with leadership would contribute to performance." (Chelladurai uses Adams' (1963) equity theory, which proposes "that every individual wishes to maintain a balance between interpersonal rewards bestowed to others versus those received.") Chelladurai is saying, then, that "performance leads to satisfaction" in the case of satisfaction with technical leadership, and "satisfaction leads to performance" in the case of satisfaction with interpersonal leadership.

Implications stemming from the model are recorded later in the "Conclusion" section of this chapter.

Innovation

An aspect of leadership is bringing new ideas to fruition— either those of the leader or those of another organizational member. Indeed, a leader is expected to *lead*, so must have good new ideas himself and encourage others to bring forward new notions. But what is the mechanism through which a new idea must pass before it is accepted? An area of study called the "Diffusion of Innovations" provides useful guidance. Here it is briefly reviewed from the work of Rogers and Shoemaker (1971).

Elements In The Diffusion of Innovations

An *innovation* does not have to be objectively new, the crucial point is that it is perceived as new by the would-be adopters. That is, previously, they *may* have heard of it but have never had to make a considered decision whether to adopt or reject it. For example, soccer was popular in much of the world before it was adopted in many North American organizations. *Diffusion* is the process by which innovations are communicated to the members of a social system. Rogers' and Shoemaker's (1971:20-40) elements in the diffusion of innovations, then, are:

1. Inventors, scientists, change agents, or opinion leaders.
2. The innovation, which will have important perceived attributes that will affect the rate of adoption. They are: relative advantage (the degree to which the innovation is perceived as better than the idea it supersedes); compatibility (the degree to which the innovation is perceived as consistent with existing values, past experiences, and need); complexity (the degree to which the innovation is perceived as difficult to understand and use); trialability (the degree to which an innovation may be experimented with on a limited basis); and, observability (the degree to which results of an innovation are visible to others).
3. Communication channels which may be mass media or interpersonal.
4. Members of the social system. Rogers and Shoemaker (1971) define a social system as "a collectivity of units which are functionally differentiated and engaged in joint problem solving with respect to some common goal." And, they point out the importance of this, "because the system's social structure can have an important influence on the spread of new ideas."
5. Consequences over time. These include: (a) knowledge, (b) attitude change (leader's persuasion), and (c) behavior change (adoption or rejection).

Rogers' And Shoemaker's Generalizations

Drawing from many fields of inquiry, Rogers and Shoemaker (1971:347-385) synthesized 1,500 diffusion studies and based generalizations on the overall findings. To qualify for inclusion, a study had the "elements" described here. Thus, they have been able to generalize about such things as the psychosocial characteristics of early adopters, laggardly adopters, and early knowers; ages of adopters; social status of leaders with reference to adopters'; and authority-imposed adoption, collective adoption, and optional adoption. Their list is too extensive for inclusion here but a few examples will illustrate their applicability in sport situations.

Some Sport Diffusion Studies

One of the earliest studies was Loy's (1967) doctoral dissertation from which he wrote a number of papers on the socio-psychological attributes associated with the early adoption of sport innovations and new technologies (Loy, 1968). He found a significant multiple correlation of 0.80 between the time of adoption by coaches of a new swimming training technique and ten social-psychological attributes of such coaches. Thus, sociological factors and psychological factors were shown to be important in leadership studies and behavior as well as traits (Loy, McPherson, and Kenyon, 1978:75-76).

Jackson (1979:66-69) reported two studies on promoting mass physical recreation in social systems, which supported some of Rogers' and Shoemaker's generalizations. The studies investigated "consequences" of Sport Participation Canada's (SPC) attempts to promote more physical activity (the innovation) among all Canadians (the particular social systems studied being Saskatoon and Victoria, British Columbia). Saskatoon people were subjected to an intense mass media communications campaign plus some interpersonal communication; Victorians only received the national mass media influences.

RESULTS OF JACKSON'S STUDIES. In Saskatoon, 94 percent of the population were aware of SPC, while in Victoria the figure was 72 percent. As a result of SPC's Saskatoon campaign, 27 percent initially adopted the innovation and, later, 10 percent discontinued. In Victoria, the initial adoption figure was 10 percent. There were some other more detailed findings but let's see how these results compare with the generalizations.

Appropriate Rogers' and Shoemaker (1971) generalizations were:

1. Mass media channels of communication are relatively more important at the knowledge function, and interpersonal channels are relatively more important at the persuasion function in the innovation-decision process (p. 382).
2. Cosmopolite channels (originating outside the social sys-

tem) are relatively more important at the knowledge function and localite channels are relatively more important at the persuasion function in the innovation-decision process (p. 383).

The third and fourth generalizations, which are appropriate for the example here, introduce two unusual words: "Homophily" is the degree to which individuals who interact are similar in certain attributes such as beliefs, values, education, and social status; and (2) "Heterophily" is the mirror opposite. Thus:

3. Interpersonal diffusion is mostly homophilous (p. 376).
4. When interpersonal diffusion is heterophilous, followers seek opinion leaders of higher social status (p. 377).

Jackson's (1979) findings from the two studies clearly substantiate the generalizations. Thus, the mass media cosmopolite channels made most people aware of SPC; more so in Saskatoon than in Victoria, but there was some interpersonal communication in the intense Saskatoon campaign. However, in both cities the behavior change was relatively slight. Again, this is not surprising since behavior change is most likely between homophilous dyads, and Jackson pointed out that much of the interpersonal communication was heterophilous. Indeed, it often is in sport situations.

The Leader's Role In The
Innovation-Decision Process

Although the example immediately above is "macro" relative to most leadership situations in sport organizations, nevertheless, important principles remain the same. Thus, the leader should use mass media to create awareness but "engineer" exchange between homophilous dyads to effect behavior change. The latter is possible by using opinion leaders at various levels in the organization to bring about the change among those organizational members with similar degrees of homophily. These ideas are useful supplements to Chelladurai's (1978) model in that a skilled leader can affect situational factors to assist his own leadership objectives.

Summary

It has been shown that none of the earlier theories of leadership were sufficiently comprehensive because they did not consider enough of the relevant variables. Chelladurai (1978) synthesized the various theories and his model presents a better understanding of the concept. Table I is my summarization of the implications for some sport organizations (adapted from Chelladurai, 1979).

TABLE I

LEADERSHIP STYLES APPROPRIATE FOR TYPES OF ORGANIZATIONS

Organizational Type[1]	Prime Beneficiary[1]	Sport Example[2]	Leadership Style[2]
Mutual-benefit associations	The membership	(a) Sport clubs	Democratic-considerate
		(b) Athletic team (Intramural)	Low structuring/ high consideration
Business concerns	Owner(s)	(a) Selling fitness, recreation, sport	Structuring (subordinates)[3]
		(b) Selling sport, entertainment	Structuring (subordinates)[3]
		(c) Athletic team	Low structuring, low consideration [of team members who are assumed to be "athletically mature" (cf. Chelladurai and Carron, 1978).]
Service	Client group	(a) Educational Institutions	Minimum interference (Because of bureaucratic controls and the subordinates' professional orientation to independently satisfying tasks.)
		(b) Athletic team (Varsity)	High structuring/ high consideration
		(c) Athletic team (Juvenile)	Low structuring/high consideration [Athletes assumed to be not athletically mature.]

[1]From Blau and Scott (1962) but omitting "commonweal organizations" whose prime beneficiary is the public-at-large. Prime examples are police forces and prisons.
[2]Adapted from Chelladurai (1979). [Also, cf. Miner, 1975.]
[3]But, see Chapter Five.

Thus, it can be seen from Table I that a person in a sport leadership position must be sensitive to all the factors outlined in Chelladurai's (1978) model, "and provide the appropriate level of guidance and coaching (structuring or task orientation), and/or social support (consideration or relationship orientation)" (Chelladurai, 1979).

Finally, here, leaders may appear in various levels of an organization. If the leader is an administrative leader (see Chapter 2), then he ought to lead in the right direction.

References

Adams, J. S.: Toward an understanding of inequity. *Journal of Abnormal and Social Psychology, 67:*422-436, 1963.

Albers, Henry H.: *Principles of Management: A Modern Approach*, 3rd ed. New York, Wiley, 1969.

Bagley, Martha: Leadership effectiveness contingency model: Implications. In Zeigler, Earle F., and Spaeth, Marcia J.: *Administrative Theory and Practice in Physical Education and Athletics.* Englewood Cliffs, New Jersey, Prentice-Hall, 1975.

Barrow, J.C.: The variables of leadership: A review and conceptual framework. *Academy of Management Review, 2:*231-251, 1977.

Blake, Robert R., and Mouton, Jane S.: Managerial facades. *Advanced Management Journal,* 31, July, 1966.

Blau, P. M., and Scott, R. W.: *Formal Organizations.* San Francisco, Chandler, 1962.

Bowers, D. G., and Seashore, S. E.: Predicting organizational effectiveness with a four factor theory of leadership. In Hinton, B. L. (Ed.): *Groups and Organizations.* Belmont, California, Wadsworth, 1971.

Byrd, Charles: *Social Psychology.* New York, Appleton-Century Crofts, 1940.

Chelladurai, P.: "A Multidimensional Model of Leadership." Unpublished manuscript, University of Western Ontario, London, Canada, 1978. (This paper is reviewed in Chelladurai and Carron [1978] and Chelladurai [1979].)

Chelladurai, P.: *Leadership: Implications for Various Types of Sports Organizations.* Read before the Canadian Association for Health, Physical Education, and Recreation, Administration Committee at the Annual Conference of CAHPER, Winnipeg, June 28-30, 1979.

Chelladurai, P., and Carron, A. V.: *Leadership.* CAHPER Sociology of Sport Monograph Series. Calgary, University of Calgary, 1978.

Chelladurai, P., and Saleh, S. D.: Preferred leadership in sports. *Canadian Journal of Applied Sport Sciences, 3:*85-92, 1978.

Cribbin, James J.: *Effective Managerial Leadership.* New York, AMACOM, 1972.

Cummings, L. L.: Assessing the Graen/Cashman model and comparing it with other approaches. In Hunt, J. G., and Larson, L. L. (Eds.) *Leadership Frontiers.* Kent, Ohio, Kent State University Press, 1975.

Danielson, R. R.: *Contingency Model of Leadership Effectiveness: For Empirical Investigation of its Application in Sport.* Read before The International Congress of Physical Activity Sciences, Quebec City, 1976.

Danielson, R. R., Zelhart, P. F., and Drake, C. J.: Multidimensional scaling and factor analysis of coaching behavior as perceived by high school hockey players. *Research Quarterly, 46:*323-334, 1975.

Davis, Keith: *Human Behavior at Work,* 4th ed. New York, McGraw-Hill, 1972.

DeZonia, R. H.: "The Relationship Between Psychological Distance and Effective Task Performance." Unpublished doctoral dissertation, University of Illinois, 1958.

Fiedler, F. E.: Assumed similarity measures as predictors of team effectiveness. *Journal of Abnormal and Social Psychology, 49:*381-388, 1954.

Fiedler, Fred E.: *A Theory of Leadership Effectiveness.* New York, McGraw-Hill, 1967.

Fiedler, Fred E.: Personality and situational determinants of leader behavior. In Fleishman, E. A., and Hunt, J. G. (Eds.): *Current Development in the Study of Leadership.* Carbondale, Illinois, Southern Illinois University Press, 1973.

Fiedler, Fred E., and Chemers, Martin M.: *Leadership and Effective Management.* Glenview, Illinois, Scott, Foresman and Co., 1974.

Fleishman, E.A.: A leader behavior description for industry. In Stogdill, R. M., and Coons, A. E. (Eds.): *Leadership Behavior: Its Description and Measurement.* Columbus, Ohio, The Ohio State University Press, 1957a.

Fleishman, E. A.: The leadership opinion questionnaire. In Stogdill, R. M., and Coons, A. E. (Eds.): *Leader Behavior: Its Description and Measurement.* Columbus, Ohio, The Ohio State University Press, 1957b.

Fleishman, E. A., and Harris, E. F.: Patterns of leadership behavior related to employee grievances and turnover. *Personnel Psychology, 15:*43-56, 1962.

Gibb, C. A.: The principles and traits of leadership. *Journal of Abnormal Psychology, 42:*267-284, 1947.

Gordon, Thomas: *Group-Centered Leadership.* Boston, Houghton Mifflin, 1955.

Graen, G., and Cashman, J. F.: A role-making model of leadership in formal organizations. In Hunt, J. G., and Larson, L. L. (Eds.): *Leadership Frontiers.* Kent, Ohio, Kent State University Press, 1975.

Graen, G. et al.: Contingency model of leadership effectiveness: Antecedent and evidencial results. *Psychological Bulletin, 74:*285-296, 1970.

Haimann, T., and Scott, William G.: *Management in the Modern Organization,* 2nd ed. Boston, Houghton Mifflin, 1974.

Halpin, A. W., and Winer, B. J.: A factorial study of the leader behavior description. In Stogdill, R. M., and Coons, A. E. (Eds.): *Leader Behavior: Its Description and Measurement.* Columbus, Ohio, The Ohio State University Press, 1957.

Hemphill, J. K., and Coons, A. E.: Development of the leader behavior description questionnaire. In Stogdill, R. M., and Coons, A. E. (Eds.): *Leader Behavior: Its Description and Measurement.* Columbus, Ohio, The Ohio State University Press, 1957.

Hersey, P., and Blanchard, K. H.: *Management of Organizational Behavior,* 3rd. ed. Englewood Cliffs, New Jersey, Prentice-Hall, 1977.

Hodgetts, Richard M.: *Management: Theory Process and Practice.* Philadelphia, W. B. Saunders, 1975.

Hodgkinson, Christopher: *Towards a Philosophy of Administration.* Oxford, Basil Blackwell, 1978.

House, R. J.: A path-goal theory of leader effectiveness. *Administrative Science Quarterly, 16:*321-338, 1971.

House, Robert J., and Dessler, Gary: The path-goal theory of leadership: Some *post hoc* and *a priori* tests. In Hunt, James G., and Larson, Lars L. (Eds.): *Contingency Approaches to Leadership.* Carbondale, Illinois, Southern Illinois University Press, 1974.

House, R. J., and Mitchell, T. R.: Path-goal theory of leadership. *Journal of Contempory Business, 5:*81-97, 1974.

Inciong, P. A.: "Leadership Styles and Team Success." Unpublished doctoral dissertation, University of Utah, 1974.

Jackson, John J.: Promoting physical recreation in social systems. *Recreation Research Review, 6:*66-69, 1979.

Jackson, John J., and Lowe, Benjamin: *Sport as a Career.* CAHPER Sociology of Sport Monograph Series. Calgary, University of Calgary, 1978.

Jenkins, William O.: A review of leadership studies with particular reference to military problems. *Psychological Bulletin, 44:*54-79, 1947.

Katz, D., Maccoby, N., and Morse, N.: *Productivity, Supervision, and Morale in an Office Situation.* Ann Arbor, University of Michigan Press, Survey Research Center, 1950.

Katz, D. et al.: *Productivity, Supervision and Morale Among Railroad Workers.* Ann Arbor, University of Michigan Press, Survey Research Center, 1951.

Kjeldsen, E. K.: "An Investigation of the Leadership Process in Organizationally Embedded Task Groups." Unpublished doctoral dissertation, University of Massachusetts, 1976.

Lewin, K., Lippitt, R., and White, R. K.: Patterns of aggressive behavior in experimentally created "social climates." *The Journal of Social Psychology, 10:*271-299, 1939.

Likert, R.: Foreword. In Katz, D., Maccoby, N., and Morse, N. C.: *Productivity, Supervision, and Morale in an Office Situation.* Ann Arbor, University of Michigan Press, Survey Research Center, 1950.

Likert, Rensis: *New Patterns of Management.* New York, McGraw-Hill, 1961.

Likert, Rensis: *The Human Organization.* New York, McGraw-Hill, 1967.

Loy, John W., Jr.: "Socio-Psychological Attributes of English Swimming Coaches Differentially Adopting a New Technology." Unpublished doctoral dissertation, University of Wisconsin, 1967.

Loy, John W., Jr.: Socio-psychological attributes associated with the early adoption of a sport innovation. *Journal of Psychology, 70:*141-147, 1968.

Loy, John W., McPherson, Barry D., and Kenyon, Gerald: *Sport and Social Systems.* Reading, Massachusetts, Addison-Wesley, 1978.

Meggyesy, D.: *Out of Their League.* Berkeley, California, Ramparts Press, 1970.

Miner, J. B.: The uncertain future of the leadership concept: An overview. In Hunt, J. G., and Larson, L. L. (Eds.): *Leadership Frontiers.* Kent, Ohio, Kent State University Press, 1975.

Myers, A. E.: Team competition, success, and the adjustment of group members. *Journal of Abnormal and Social Psychology, 65:*325-332, 1962.

Ogilvie, B. C., and Tutko, T. A.: Sport: If you want to build character, try something else. *Psychology Today, 5:*61-63, 1971.

Olafson, Gordon A.: Leader behavior of junior college and university physical education administrators. In Zeigler, Earle F., and Spaeth, Marcia J.: *Administrative Theory and Practice in Physical Education and Athletics.* Englewood Cliffs, New Jersey, Prentice-Hall, 1975.

Olafson, Gordon A., and Boucher, Robert L.: "Leadership in Coaching: An Investigation of Player/Coach Relationships in Minor Hockey." Read before the NCPEAM/NAPECW Conference, Denver, Colorado, June, 1978.

Osborn, R. N., and Hunt, J. G.: An adaptive-reactive theory of leadership: The role of macro-variables in leadership research. In Hunt, J. G., and Larson, L. L. (Eds.): *Leadership Frontiers.* Kent, Ohio, Kent State University Press, 1975.

Rogers, Everett M., and Shoemaker, F. Floyd: *Communication of Innovations: A Cross-Cultural Approach,* 2nd ed. New York, The Free Press, 1971.

Sage, G. H.: The coach as management: Organizational leadership in American sport. *Quest, 19:*35-40, 1973.

Sage, G. H.: An occupational analysis of the college coach. In Ball, D. W., and Loy, J. W.: *Sport and Social Order.* Reading, Massachusetts, Addison-Wesley, 1975.

Sashkin, M., and Garland, H.: Laboratory and field research on leadership: Integrating divergent streams. In Hunt, James G., and Larson, Lars L.: *Cross Currents in Leadership.* Carbondale, Illinois, Southern Illinois University Press, 1979.

Scott, J.: *The Athletic Revolution.* New York, The Free Press, 1971.

Sikula, Andrew F.: *Management and Administration.* Columbus, Ohio, Merrill, 1973.

Stogdill, R. M.: Personal factors associated with leadership: A survey of the literature. *The Journal of Psychology, 25:*35-72, 1948.

Tutko, T. A., and Richards, J. W.: *Psychology of Coaching.* Boston, Allyn and Bacon, 1971.

Vander Velden, L.: "Relationships Among Member, Team, and Situational Variables and Basketball Team Success: A Social-Psychological Inquiry." Unpublished doctoral dissertation, University of Wisconsin, 1971.

Vroom, V. H.: Some personality determinants of the effects of participation. *Journal of Abnormal and Social Psychology, 59:*322-327, 1959.

Vroom, V. H., and Yetton, P. W.: *Leadership and Decision-making.* Pittsburgh, University of Pittsburgh Press, 1973.

Important Related Reading
Hunt, James G., and Larson, Lars L.: *Cross-Currents in Leadership.* Carbondale and Edwardsville, Illinois, Southern Illinois University Press, 1979, chs. 2, 4, 7, 10, and 14.

Supplementary Readings
Chelladurai and Carron, *Leadership,* 1978.
Gibb, *Principles of Leadership,* 1969.

Case 4.01

Integrated Leaders

Dr. Richard Revons was appointed principal of newly integrated Mellow Street High School, which had 1,750 students from a racially mixed urban community. Dr. Revons believed that an important factor in developing school morale was a successful sports program. So, he decided to appoint the best possible leader he could find to be director of physical education and athletics. He advertised the position and told the four short-listed candidates that they would be given lessons to teach that were designed to assess their leadership capabilities.

Two female teachers and two male teachers were invited for interviews and tests; one of each sex was black and the other white. Dr. Revons explained that each of the contenders would have to teach two lessons and their performances would be judged by two experienced teachers and himself. The lessons were to be as noted below and the preparation time for each was forty-five minutes.

Lesson One (30 minutes)

OBJECTIVE. Using the limited amount of gymnastic equipment and class members, build a structure over which a small gymnastic horse could be transported by the students from one end of a basketball court to the other end without the horse, or the students, touching the gymnasium floor once the apparatus was in place. En route, the horse must pass over an eight feet high beam and be swung by ropes across a twenty-five feet wide gap between two benches.

STUDENTS. Fifteen of known "moderately good" behavior; five white, five black, five of other ethnic origins, and eight of the total were girls.

Lesson Two (35 minutes)

OBJECTIVE. Design, and have the class present, a five-minute modern dance routine to music.

STUDENTS. Five girls and five boys (all of the same ethnic origin as the teacher but having had no previous modern dance training).

Deputy Principal Hawkes was opposed to the tests and argued with Dr. Revons that they were not valid tests of leadership ability. The principal, however, insisted they were just what was needed to select the much needed sports leader for Mellow Street.

Case Analysis Method

CAM B (see Chapter 1).

Case 4.02

Horses For Courses

Annette Winter was recreation coordinator for the downtown core area of a Canadian city. Residents were from a varied cross section of society: native indians, senior citizen white Canadians; immigrants of long and short duration from China, Greece, Italy, Portugal, the United Kingdom, and the West Indies. Being keen to revitalize her area's programs, Annette took a number of new tacks; one was to develop a day camp program to operate in a variety of styles and locations throughout the summer.

With this in mind, Michael Moore, a recent recreation graduate, was hired as head playground leader. Michael was very enthusiastic and set about his task in earnest. He decided on suitable locations, developed varied challenging programs that had "something for everyone," and designed his publicity material with the expert assistance of the city public relations department. The advertising information was widely distributed through local newspapers, radio stations, television, and other recreational outlets. Finally, an eager group of recreation administration students was hired for the summer and trained for their playground leadership duties. Michael felt sure he had prepared everything well and he received a "pat on the back" from Annette.

However, all the camps were very poorly attended; a $70,000 budget seemed to have been wasted. Michael wrote his report to

Annette expressing dismay at what had happened and saying there was nothing else he could have done. He really had tried hard and done his best to lead a successful program. Annette read his comments with a furrowed brow.

Case Analysis Method
CAM A or CAM B (see Chapter 1).

Case 4.03

The Hired Gun

Kormoran Winter Club was a private multi-sports club, which was administered by a board of directors who were elected by the 1,200 member-shareholders. By 1975, family dues were $50 per month. The club took its name from the fact that curling and indoor racquets enthusiasts had founded it; however, in addition to curling, squash, and badminton, the club had gradually added indoor and outdoor tennis, figure skating, ice hockey, and racquetball.

For several years prior to 1975, Steve Mudd had been the general manager directly responsible to the board of directors for the club's operations. Steve was a pleasant, easy going, and friendly individual who was liked by the members and the employees. Unfortunately, the club was gradually getting into debt and the debt costs were further injuring the financial situation. Finally, the board decided to fire Mudd and hire Ken Kincaid, a business graduate whose job was to save the club.

Within six months of his appointment in 1975, Ken had fired nearly half of the paid employees and had given the volunteer chairmen of the various sports committees clear instructions that their programs must break even. Few liked Ken but it was difficult to argue with his style for he got the results the board wanted. By 1978, the club was out of debt but only just keeping ahead financially. Further, dues were up to $65 per month and total membership was down to 960. Ken argued that the membership decline was due to the fact that certain sports people, such as tennis players and curlers, do not mix; especially when tennis upkeep costs are low and curling ice is expensive. This confrontation was additionally complicated by the contrast between the big revenues from curlers' drinking compared with negligible income from tennis players' or figure skaters' drinking habits.

By mid-1978 some directors felt Ken's leadership style was too tough. They acknowledged he was so damaging the morale of members and employees that he would have to be dismissed. The board chairman, however, firmly argued that the board had a responsibility to the shareholding members to keep the club financially viable; without tough leadership it would go bankrupt. Thus, the board became divided and the chairman asked all directors to consider the issues very carefully and be prepared to vote at the next meeting. The question simply being, "Do we keep our task-oriented manager?"

Case Analysis Method
CAM A or CAM B or CAM D or CAM E (see Chapter 1).

Case 4.04

The Mutual Admiration Society

The Organization:	A university physical education and recreation department.
The Dean:	Supervised ten departments of which physical education and recreation was one.
The Department Head:	For whatever reason, leniency in supervision was his potent leadership strategy (cf. Blau, P. M.: *Bureaucracy in Modern Society*. New York, Random House, 1956, pp. 70-78).
The Faculty Members:	A few worked too hard.
	A few worked as was reasonably expected.
	A majority worked too little, committing minor and major infractions of organizational policy.

The department head "went along" with everyone. Thus, a sense of obligation was built up within individual faculty members for past "favors" done for them by the department head. Therefore, they tended to return the "favors" when the head needed "to look good." The dean, from experience and observation, knew that the organization was not fully satisfying its policy objectives and was determined to rectify the situation, but what could he do? The department head was virtually elected by the faculty members.

Case Analysis Method
CAM A or CAM B or CAM D or CAM E (see Chapter 1).

Summary

1. Leadership is the process of influencing individuals or groups to direct their efforts towards the achievement of particular goals.
2. Traits alone cannot be used to predict who will be a successful leader.
3. Two major dimensions of leadership behavior are:
   (a) Consideration which connotates rapport between supervisor and supervised (relationship orientation).
   (b) Initiating structure refers to definition of roles of members, forward planning, and pushing for production (task orientation). These factors are dependent upon the situation in finally determining leadership effectiveness.
4. Fiedler's contingency model classified group situations according to the leader's powers, the task structure, and the leader-member personal relationships. He concluded that task-oriented leaders performed best in unfavourable situations (no influence and power) and favourable situations (much influence and power). Relationship-oriented leaders tended to perform best in mixed situations where they had moderate influence over the group. The theory has not been widely empirically supported and several other limitations are evident.
5. The path-goal theory (cf. role-making model) suggests that a leader may have to be task oriented or relationship oriented (dependent on the subordinates' needs) and according to the nature of the task situations. Critics say such heterogeneous leader behavior is impossible in practice.
6. The situational theory of leadership (life cycle theory)

states that just as a person matures from childhood and requires different behavior from his parents, so does a maturing worker from his leader.

7. The adaptive-reactive theory views leader behavior as consisting of adaptation to the conditions of the ogranizational system and of reactions to the wants, desires, and pressures of subordinates.

8. The normative model of decision making is a device for choosing appropriate leadership styles for specific situations with particular outcomes in view. It focuses on autocratic, consultative, or group consensus decisions.

9. Chelladurai's multidimensional model synthesizes a number of factors to present a more complete conceptualization of leadership. The consequences of leadership are the product of the interactive effects of three types of leader behaviors whose antecedents comprise the separate characteristics of the situation, the leader, and the group member.

10. Diffusion is the process by which innovations are communicated to the members of a social system. Mass media informs but does not, by itself, change behavior. Behavior change occurs when communication is between homophilous dyads. This knowledge can be usefully applied in Chelladurai's model and additional implications for practice are summarized in Table I.

11. Leaders ought to lead in the right direction (see Chapter 2).

Concepts For Review

Leadership

Leader types
   —autocratic
   —democratic
   —laissez-faire
   —charismatic

Managerial grid

LPC

Role-making model

Adaptive-reactive theory

Multidimensional model

Innovation

Heterophily

Trait theory

Consideration (relationship orientation)

Initiating structure (task orientation)

LBDQ, SBDQ, LOQ

Fiedler's contingency model

Path-goal theory

Situational theory (life cycle)

Normative model

Diffusion

Homophily

Innovation-decision process

Questions For Oral Or Written Discussion

1. (Comte de Mirabeau.) "There go the mob and I must follow for I am their leader." Discuss.
2. (Barnard.) "Leadership has been the subject of an extraordinary amount of dogmatically stated nonsense." Discuss.
3. Anyone can be a leader. Discuss.
4. What qualities would the ideal leader of your sport organization possess and how would that person behave? State your reasons in detail.
5. CAM C (see Chapter 1) applied to instructor-specified topics taken from this chapter.

Chapter 5

SUPERVISION OF WORKERS

T HE CONTENT OF THIS chapter is closely related with that on leadership (Chapter 4) and with organizational compliance relationships, which were dealt with in Chapter 3. It delves further into what motivates people to work, with the intention of illustrating how supervisors ought to behave if they want their subordinates to cooperate in accomplishing organizational goals.

Work is, "the social role performed by adult members of society that directly and/or indirectly yields social and financial consequences and that constitutes a major focus in the life of an adult" (Hall, 1975:8). Occupations may be classified into groups that describe functionally what a worker produces; the groups are primary production of raw materials, processing raw materials, transporting products, trading, administering related enterprises, and serving in other functions. "Serving" refers to consumers' personal needs for such services as education, health, religion, and recreation (Caplow, 1964:302). Thus, Hall's (1975:8) definition tells us what a sports worker is doing and Caplow's (1974:302) functional groups elucidate what he produces; that is, primarily a service (cf. Jackson and Lowe, 1978:8-9; and, Table I in Chapter 4).

Steers' and Porter's (1975:553) definition of motivation is used here and is, "that which energizes, directs, and sustains behavior." Before discussing this definition towards the end of the chapter, earlier management and motivational theories are presented with a view to synthesizing them into a more complete understanding of the interrelated complex phenomena. To achieve this objective, the chapter has two learning designs: the first deals with "early theories" and the second with "contemporary theories." Each design is followed by cases that show what happens when these general theories are applied in sport situations.

LEARNING DESIGN 5.1

MOTIVATION TO WORK: EARLY THEORIES

This design traces important approaches to the supervision of workers from about 1900 up to, but not including, "contemporary approaches." Aspects of the included approaches are still extant.

Traditional Approaches

Scientific Management

The impact of the Industrial Revolution on management and workers was great, and some attempts to deal with the problems during the 1800s have been reviewed by Hodgetts (1975:12-20). The problems were: (a) *technological* (how to increase productivity by making the work easier to perform); and (b) *human* (how to motivate workers to use the new techniques). The technological problems were easier to solve than the human ones and by as late as 1886, "virtually nothing had been written about how to coordinate and motivate human effort in a business operation" (Haimann and Scott, 1974:21). When Henry R. Towne was elected president of the American Society of Mechanical Engineers (ASME) in 1886 he appealed to members to contribute management articles to the group's magazine *Transactions*. The response was not overwhelming but one who did write was Frederick W. Taylor (1856-1917); he became known as the "Father of Scientific Management" and his major writings, reviewed here, are illustrative of the "traditional approach."

F. W. TAYLOR'S PRINCIPLES OF SCIENTIFIC MANAGEMENT. Taylor presented "A Piece Rate System" to the ASME members in 1885 and followed it with "Shop Management" in 1903. However, it was in his *Principles of Scientific Management* (1911) where he set forth his major ideas. He believed the main object of management "should be to secure maximum prosperity for the employer, coupled with maximum prosperity for each employee" (p. 9). One could not exist, in the long run, without the other. So, why was there antagonism between the two?

Taylor (1911:15-16) listed three reasons which may be summarized as:

(1) Workers' fallacious belief that increased output for man or machine would lead to unemployment for many.
(2) Defective management systems made it necessary for each workman to "soldier" [work slowly] to protect his interests.
(3) Inefficient rule-of-thumb work methods wasted effort.

So, Taylor reasoned, scientific management principles would lead to gaining the "initiative of workmen" because of new types of work done by management and this would be "much more efficient than the old plan" (p. 37). He listed the new management duties under four heads:

> *First.* They develop a science for each element of a man's work, which replaces the old rule-of-thumb method.
> *Second.* They scientifically select and then train, teach, and develop the workman, whereas in the past he chose his own work and trained himself as best he could.
> *Third.* They heartily cooperate with the men so as to insure all of the work being done in accordance with the principles of the science which has been developed.
> *Fourth.* There is an almost equal division of the work and the responsibility between the management and the workmen. The management take over all work for which they are better fitted than the workmen, while in the past almost all of the work and the greater part of the responsibility were thrown upon the men (pp. 36-37).

The "science" in this scheme was, for example, in the "science of shoveling" and Taylor (1911:65) said: "For a first-class shoveler there is a given shovel load at which he will do his biggest day's work. What is this shovel load? Will a first-class man do more work per day with a shovel load of 5 pounds, 10 pounds, 15 pounds, 20, 25, 30, or 40 pounds? Now this is a question which can only be answered through carefully made experiments."

By conducting such experiments, Taylor sought to convince his readers "that every single act of every workman can be reduced to a science" (p. 64). He believed in job specialization and first-class men receiving much higher wages; all this would lead to efficiency and the financial rewards that both management and workers wanted.

Similar work has been done by Gantt, the Gilbreths, Halsey, Bedaux, and Emerson (Hodgetts, 1975:33-35, Pugh, Hickson, and Hinings, 1971:101). It has developed into "work study" or "industrial engineering." However, even in Taylor's lifetime, the principles led to bitter controversy because they were alleged to be inhuman and to treat men like machines.

Often, Taylor's tenets have been misunderstood; for example, he advocated no limit on wages for more work but management's incentive schemes often involve such limits (Pugh, Hickson, and Hinings, 1971:101).

HENRI FAYOL (1841-1925). Whilst Taylor was making his contributions to management in the United States, Fayol, a French mining engineer, was making his in Europe. Fayol's ideas were presented in *Administration Industrielle et Generale* (1916), which was translated into English and retitled *General and Industrial Management* in 1949. He was "the earliest known proponent of a theoretical analysis of managerial activities—an analysis which has withstood almost half a century of critical discussion" (Pugh, Hickson, and Hinings, 1971:65).

In defining "management" in *any* "undertaking" he said the following six groups of activities or essential functions were always present: technical, commercial, financial, security, accounting, and managerial. He is famous for his definitive breakdown of the last mentioned of these activities (Fayol, 1949:3).

First, he identified the five "elements" of management that are still useful concepts for sport managers (and administrators) to use when clarifying their thinking about what they are supposed to do. The elements are: (1) to forecast and plan, (2) to organize, (3) to command, (4) to coordinate, and, (5) to control (pp. 43-110).

Second, he listed fourteen principles of management that he had to apply most frequently. They were: division of work; authority; discipline; unity of command, unity of direction; subordination of individual interests to the general interest; remuneration; centralization; scalar chain (line of authority); order; equity; stability of tenure of personnel; initiative; and esprit de corps (pp. 19-42).

CONCLUSIONS. In his *Foreword* to Fayol's (1949:ix-x) book, Lyndall F. Urwick drew attention to the fact that some saw Fayol and Taylor "in competition or contrast." However, Urwick described how, in 1925, Fayol publicly spoke of his and Taylor's positions as being "essentially complementary." Both saw personnel management at all levels as the "key to industrial success." Both applied scientific method to this problem. Taylor concentrated at the operative level (from the bottom upwards), while Fayol "concentrated on the managing director and worked downwards. . . ." Urwick saw this as a reflection of the two men's very different careers. So, Taylor was noted for "scientific management" and Fayol for his conceptual framework for analyzing the management process. Taylor believed management had to be learned the hard way in the shop while Fayol thought a theory of administration could be developed and taught. This, according to Hodgetts (1975:49), "put him in the forefront of classical management theoreticians."

Human Relations Approaches

The Hawthorne Studies (1924-1932)

Scientific management's premise was that man was rational and economically motivated to work; the human relations movement added another dimension to the understanding of work motivation.

ELTON MAYO (1880-1949). An Australian by birth, Mayo originally trained as a psychologist and then spent most of his working life at Harvard's Graduate School of Business Administration. He is regarded as the founder of both the human relations movement and of industrial sociology.

MAYO'S MULE SPINNING INQUIRY. Whilst a faculty member at the University of Pennsylvania in 1923, Mayo was interested in fatigue, accidents, and labor turnover. At a Philadelphia textile mill, the department of mule spinning had a labor turnover of 250 percent compared with one of 5 or 6 percent per year in other departments. Financial incentives had not worked so Mayo and his colleagues were called in to experiment and offer advice.

When rest pauses were introduced, production and morale improved. Then the operatives were involved in fixing the frequency and duration of the rest periods; further production improvements occurred and morale in the whole factory rose. By the year end, turnover in the mule-spinning department was down to the level of the others.

At first it was thought the rest pauses made the job less monotonous and so improved the physical and mental conditions of the men. Subsequently, Mayo modified this explanation as a result of later studies (Hodgetts, 1975:71).

ILLUMINATION STUDIES. The Hawthorne studies were conducted at the Hawthorne Works of the Western Electric Company near Cicero, Illinois and were sponsored by the National Research Council. Their roots were in scientific management, and, prior to Mayo's joining the studies, experiments were carried out to discover the effects of illumination on the worker and his work. The control group's lighting was held constant and the experimental group's lighting was varied. There were no significant differences in output between the groups, and, whatever was done to the lighting, production rose in both groups (Roethlisberger and Dickson, 1939). At this point in the studies, Mayo became involved.

RELAY ASSEMBLY TEST ROOM. To control more factors affecting work performance, a group of five female assemblers and a layout operator were isolated in a room away from other workers. A researcher was with them to record what happened and to help maintain a friendly atmosphere. The girls were told to work at their regular pace, and the experiment was designed to study various types of working conditions. In five years there was a group payment scheme, varied rest pauses, fewer working hours, refreshments, and some others. There was always prior consultation with the girls and, almost always, output increased with each change.

Then original conditions were reverted to and output rose to its highest level. These findings were a mystery at the time. Later, Mayo pointed out that the six girls had become a social group whose intensified interaction and cooperation lead to informal practices, values, norms, and social relationships that produced high group cohesion. The communication with the researchers was very effective, and the workers felt important. Mayo generalized that, given such a situation, physical conditions have little importance (Hodgetts, 1975:73-74; Mayo, 1933).

BANK WIRING OBSERVATION ROOM. In the third stage of the

Hawthorne studies, workers were observed constantly in a natural setting. Output was restricted and the group standard was not exceeded by anyone. The group was indifferent to the company's financial incentive scheme and had a highly integrated social structure with a code of behavior that clashed with management's. Therefore, again confirming the importance of informal social groups in determining levels of output.

INFORMAL ORGANIZATIONS. The major importance of these studies is that they "discovered" the informal organization that is now known to exist in *all* organizations. Barnard (1968:114-115) described it as "the aggregate of the personal contacts and interactions and the associated groupings of people . . . when their relationships are not part of or governed by any formal organization" (p. 123). Further, that informal organization gives rise to formal organizations; that formal organizations are necessary to any large informal or societal organization; and that formal organizations, once established, in their turn create informal organizations. Also, that informal organizations result in greater organizational cohesion, protect the integrity of the individual, and serve as a means of communication.

The worst aspects of informal organizations are that they withhold or distort information that is of value to colleagues, promote personal aims, and foster cliques which may be organizationally dysfunctional (cf. Selznick, 1952). On the relationship between formal and informal structures, Simon (1976: 149) maintained that the formal structure performed no function unless it actually set limits on the informal relations that developed within it.

Returning to Mayo, he found that better output was not caused by scientific management (rest periods) but by socio-psychological phenomena (i.e. a restructuring of social networks). A major task of management was to organize spontaneous cooperation. Finally, that "management succeeds or fails in proportion as it is accepted without reservation by the group as authority and leader" (Mayo, 1933).

CONCLUSIONS. Resulting from the human relations approaches, managers began making workers feel important, they encouraged vertical communication, they allowed workers to make routine decisions, and they initiated group incentive schemes. So, motivation was seen as a social process but management's strategy remained as in the traditional model; that is, the work did not change and the aim was to secure employee compliance with managerial authority (Steers and Porter, 1975: 18-19).

Human Resources Approaches

Human relations theories have been challenged as too incomplete to be an explanation of human behavior at work. The approaches reviewed here are representative of those Steers and Porter (1975:19) include in their "Human Resources Model."

McGREGOR'S THEORIES

Douglas McGregor (1906-1964) was a social psychologist who ended his career as a professor of management at M.I.T. In his most noted work, *The Human Side of Enterprise* (1960), he examined management's assumptions about worker behavior and placed them in one of two categories: *Theory X* or *Theory Y*.

Theory X

Assumptions in this theory are implicit in much managerial literature and practice. They are that human beings naturally dislike work and must be coerced into putting forth adequate effort on the job; further, that most people want security above all and will avoid responsibility whenever they can (pp. 33-43). This approach, McGregor believed, was why managers failed when using traditional or human relations approaches. In contrast, he advocated Theory Y.

Theory Y Assumptions

1. The expenditure of physical and mental effort in work is as natural as play or rest. . . . Depending upon controllable conditions, work may be a source of satisfaction . . . or a source of punishment. . . .
2. . . . Man will exercise self-direction and self-control in the service of objectives to which he is committed.
3. Commitment to objectives is a function of the rewards associated with their achievement. The most significant of such rewards (e.g. the satisfaction of ego and self-actualization needs) can be the direct products of effort directed toward organizational objectives.

4. The average human being learns, under proper conditions, not only to accept but to seek responsibility. . . .
5. The capacity to exercise a relatively high degree of imagination, ingenuity, and creativity in the solution of organizational problems is widely, not narrowly, distributed in the population.
6. Under the conditions of modern industrial life, the intellectual potentialities of the average human being are only partially utilized (McGregor, 1960:47-48).

Theory Y has some obvious attractions over Theory X but Theory Y also has its critics. Hodgetts (1975:321-322) has summarized some of them, namely: not everyone is self-directed or self-controlled; many like security but shun responsibility (Fromm, 1955:318); unrestricted indulgence can lead to irresponsibility, psychopathic personality, and inability to bear stress (Maslow, 1962:153-154); many seek "satisfaction" in leisure time and not at work; finally, the individual and the organization are not always in conflict.

Which theory is better? Argyris (1957, 1962, 1964) has written extensively on related topics. Generally, he sees managements using more Theory X than Theory Y. He identified seven maturing stages a person passes through from infancy to adulthood—an immaturity to maturity continuum. Management tends to treat mature adults as parents would treat immature children and, hence, many formal organizations are incongruous with the mature person.

Argyris, then, advocates management showing real feeling for workers, encouraging upward and downward communication, and giving descriptive non-evaluative feedback. All this reduces organizational tension.

It should be noted, however, that McGregor (1960:246) did not want managements to "choose sides"; rather he wanted assumptions to be realistically tested with a view to improvements taking place later in the future.

Likert's Systems

Rensis Likert is an American psychologist who has been a professor at the University of Michigan for many years. His management systems fit this human resources section and are often referred to in the literature. Here they are briefly described.

"System 1" is the exploitative-authoritative type (e.g. fear, threats, downward communication); "System 2" is the benevolent authoritative type (e.g. rewards, subservience to superiors, restricted upward communication); "System 3" is the consultative type but with broad policy coming from the top; and, "System 4" is characterized by participative group management, which leads to high production and satisfied workers (Likert, 1961).

Summary

The human *relations* approach assumed that worker satisfaction will lead to good performance; by contrast, the human *resources* approach assumes that meaningful job performance leads to job satisfaction. The human resources approach has only recently begun to be adopted; often in a piecemeal fashion. In fact, all three approaches reviewed in this design still have their staunch advocates in current practice.

References

Argyris, C.: *Personality and Organization*. New York, Harper and Brothers, 1957.
_____: *Interpersonal Competence and Organizational Effectiveness*. Homewood, Illinois, The Dorsey Press, 1962.
_____: *Integrating the Individual and the Organization*. New York, John Wiley and Sons, 1964.
Barnard, Chester I.: *The Functions of the Executive*, 30th Ann. ed. Cambridge, Massachusetts, Harvard University Press, 1968.
Caplow, T.: *The Sociology of Work*. New York, McGraw-Hill, 1964.
Fayol, H.: *General and Industrial Management*. London, Pitman and Sons, 1949. (Translated by Constance Stoms from Fayol's (1916) *Administration Industrielle et Generale*.)
Fromm, E.: *The Sane Society*. New York, Holt, Rinehart & Winston, 1955.
Haimann, T., and Scott, W. G.: *Management in the Modern Organization*, 2nd ed. Boston, Houghton Mifflin, 1974.
Hall, R. H.: *Occupations and the Social Structure*, 2nd ed. Englewood Cliffs, New Jersey, Prentice-Hall, 1975.
Hodgetts, Richard M.: *Management: Theory, Process, and Practice*. Philadelphia, W. B. Saunders, 1975.
Jackson, J. J., and Lowe, B.: *Sport as a Career*. CAHPER Sociology of Sport Monograph Series. Calgary, University of Calgary, 1978.
Likert, R.: *New Patterns of Management*. New York, McGraw-Hill, 1961.
McGregor, D.: *The Human Side of Enterprise*. New York, McGraw-Hill, 1960.
Maslow, A. H.: *Toward a Psychology of Being*. Princeton, New Jersey, D. Van Nostrand, 1962.
Mayo, E.: *The Human Problems of an Industrial Civilization*. New York, Macmillan, 1933.

Pugh, D. S., Hickson, D. J., and Hinings, C. R.: *Writers on Organizations,* 2nd ed. Harmondsworth, England, Penguin, 1971.

Roethlisberger, F. J., and Dickson, W. J.: *Management and the Worker.* Cambridge, Harvard University Press, 1939.

Selznick, P.: *The Organizational Weapon.* New York, McGraw-Hill, 1952.

Simon, Herbert A.: *Administrative Behavior,* 3rd ed. New York, The Free Press, 1976.

Steers, Richard M., and Porter, Lyman W.: *Motivation and Work Behavior.* New York, McGraw-Hill, 1975.

Taylor, F. W.: *The Principles of Scientific Management.* New York, Harper and Brothers, 1911.

Important Related Readings

Fayol, *General Management,* 1949.

Hodgetts, *Management,* 1975, ch. 2.

Likert, *New Patterns,* 1961.

McGregor, *Human Side,* 1960.

Mayo, *Human Problems,* 1933.

Steers and Porter, *Motivation,* 1975, ch. 1.

Taylor, *Scientific Management,* 1911.

Supplementary Readings

Barnard, *Functions Executive,* 1968, Parts I and IV.

Emerson, H.: *Efficiency as a Basis for Operation and Wages.* New York, The Engineering Magazine Co., 1900.

––––––: *The Twelve Principles of Efficiency.* New York, The Engineering Magazine Co., 1924.

Gantt, H. L.: *Work, Wages, and Profits.* New York, The Engineering Magazine Co., 1910.

Gilbreth, F. B.: *Bricklaying System.* New York, Myron C. Clark, 1909.

––––––: *Motion Study.* New York, D. Van Nostrand, 1911.

Gilbreth, L. M.: *The Psychology of Management.* New York, Sturgis and Walton, 1914.

McGregor, D.: *The Professional Manager.* New York, McGraw-Hill, 1967.

Miles, R. E.: Human relations or human resources? *Harvard Business Review, 43:*148-163, 1965.

Munsterberg, H.: *Psychology and Industrial Efficiency.* Boston, Houghton Mifflin, 1913.

Myers, M. S.: *Every Employee a Manager.* New York, McGraw-Hill, 1970.

Pugh, Hickson, and Hinings, *Organizations,* 1971, chs. 2, 3, and 4.

Roethlisberger and Dickson, *Management,* 1939.

Schein, E.: *Organizational Psychology.* Englewood Cliffs, New Jersey, Prentice-Hall, 1972.

Taylor, F. W.: *Scientific Management.* New York, Harper and Brothers, 1947. (Comprising: *Shop management, The principles of scientific management,* and *Testimony before the special House Committee.*)

Case 5.11

Jack's A Dull Boy

The recreation department was in need of a coordinator for evening recreation programs who would also be responsible for instructing floor hockey, creative movement, and gymnastics. Jack Imwood, a University of the Ocean recreation student was hired because of his interests and past instructional experiences. His job also included the opening and closing of the facilities for the various programs and making sure that all classes were running smoothly. He worked a 30-hour week, Monday to Friday evenings at $4.60 an hour. Programs ran for twelve weeks and involved children aged four to seven years and eight to thirteen years.

Three weeks after the start of the first 12-week period, Imwood became tardy and often absent from his programs. He lacked enthusiasm for the classes he taught, was not prepared, and was inconsistent in his supervision. As a result of this behavior, his teaching methods were poor and this reflected on the entire recreation department. There were phone calls from parents complaining that their children were left unsupervised in the facility, safety rules were being ignored, and they were not receiving the instruction they had expected. Participants were losing interest and a few were demanding their fees be returned.

The supervisor became extremely concerned and arranged a meeting with Imwood to discuss his tardiness, inconsistency, unreliability, poor attitude, and absenteeism. Imwood agreed to be more efficient and was given a second chance. However, his behavior did not improve and he was fired at the end of the sixth week.

The supervisor was sure he acted wisely but knew there would be difficulties. The program was already at the halfway stage and it would be difficult to find another supervisor for the programs. Learning would be disrupted and the participants may lose interest. Imwood was replaced by a number of high school students who would share the work and begin immediately. The students had to write objectives for the remainder of the programs after reviewing the previous lesson plans. The student workers were not properly trained and were inconsistent in their teaching methods. Because of Imwood's behavior, enrollment had dropped, the remaining participants were not enthusiastic, and the parents were not keen to support the programs. The result was pressure on the untrained high school students who were easily discouraged. The additional long-term outcome was that next season there was little support for the proposed programs and they had to be cancelled before they were due to begin.

Case Analysis Method
CAM B (see Chapter 1), on the assumption that you are the F. W. Taylor—H. Fayol management consultants. Would Mayo, a Theory X proponent, or one who favors Theory Y agree with your optimum solution? Explain all reasons for your decisions.

Case 5.12

I Am A Music Man

The head office of Oiltown's recreation department filled two whole floors high in a multistory building. As well as recreation specialist personnel, there were such support workers as payroll clerks, booking clerks, mail handlers, and filers.

During the previous two years, ever since Hugh Speniski had been commissioner of the department, worker turnover had gradually increased to alarming proportions. Speniski reasoned that the employees must be unhappy, so decided to "stop the rot," as he put it. "Muzak" was installed, for Speniski was quite sure that it would relax the workers, make them more friendly to each other, and generally make the department head office a more efficient work place.

Case Analysis Method
CAM B (see Chapter 1).

Case 5.13

Summer Follies

Those involved in this case were mainly university and high school students who worked for the San Obeyo Leisure Center during the summer. The group of students had been hired on the premise of working as a unit with shared responsibility and authority, however, as it turned out the program coordinator "ran" the group. Job positions held were program coordinator, playground coordinator, two project aids, a community consultant, a secretary, and two playground aids. The program coordinator was a social work graduate, a very enthusiastic and rather dominant person. Her responsibility was to coordinate the various summer programs and to report on the group's progress to the full-time recreation director. The playground coordinator, who worked closely with the program coordinator, was an arts student at SOU and was a very talented, conscientious, and helpful worker. The two project aids worked together on two specific summer programs; both were education graduates and were very responsible and efficient workers. The remaining jobs were held by five other university and high school students.

The physical setting for the summer employees was rather bleak: a makeshift office, which was in a hockey locker room and with no windows. The room had one small filing cabinet, two large tables, six chairs, and a typewriter. The social setting was relatively good, as the summer employees were all of similar age and had been hired, among other qualifications, on the basis of their overall compatibility. In the beginning, the summer staff were told to use the general office more often instead of staying segregated, yet later they were told that they were in the office too often.

Initially the four major positions within the group, i.e. program coordinator, the two project aids, and the playground coordinator, had been hired with well-defined jobs and had worked easily together. The extra job positions had been opened as a result of extra funding and their job duties were far less-defined and at times there was very little for the people in those positions to do. Each person was supposed to write detailed activity reports and give them to the program coordinator, however, because of the constant turmoil of finding jobs and promoting programs, that essential duty was not stressed by the program coordinator and was neglected. In turn, the program coordinator did not regularly report on the progress of the group to the director. Near the end of the summer, when programs and projects needed to be finished and final reports written, the lack of initiative and work being done by some group members became evident. Those members who realized this situation were not in the position to discipline or direct those who were not working. While attempts were made to correct this problem by the program coordinator, they were too late.

The problem was finally noted by the director near the end of the summer and an informal meeting was held over a lunch for everyone to express feelings of the summer's events. Harbored ill feelings were vented and some general conclusions were made.

Case Analysis Method

CAM B (see Chapter 1), on the assumption that you are the F. W. Taylor—H. Fayol management consultants. Would Mayo, a Theory X proponent, or one who favors Theory Y agree with your optimum solution? Explain all reasons for your decisions.

Case 5.14

The Grape Vine

Commissioner Speniski (see Case 5.12) was under pressure from the city council to reduce his department's expenditures so he decided to find out what people were really doing with their time. Not only were people in the head office under scrutiny but also a variety of personnel in the district recreation offices. Speniski's suspicion was that several people were underemployed; if he could objectively determine how many were wasting time, he could probably eliminate a number of positions without affecting current programs.

The city "Systems" experts were called in to observe varieties of workers. They carried out the following sorts of tests and observations: the length of time it took to copy the daily mail for the filing system; the time to process outgoing mail; the number of phone inquiries dealt with by the main head office receptionist; the time it took for a recreation specialist to "set up" a 10-week course and the number of such courses prepared by each worker; the number of meetings recreation specialists attended and an assessment of how necessary they all were.

After the first three days, the work study people advised Speniski that it looked as though they would have some very interesting findings for him. They were "pretty sure" the work being carried out could be done much more efficiently. Thus, there was a good chance that money could be saved.

However, by the end of the second week the work study experts were not so sure. Everyone seemed to be very busy and many were involved in quite complicated interactions that could not be done quickly. When the month of investigations ended, the "systems" experts reported to Speniski that they could not recommend any staff cuts.

Case Analysis Method
CAM B or CAM E (see Chapter 1).

LEARNING DESIGN 5.2

MOTIVATION TO WORK: CONTEMPORARY THEORIES

Contemporary theories of motivation, as they relate to work situations, are described in this learning design. The theories are then synthesized into a more complete conceptualization of the total issue as it may be applied in sport administration.

Maslow's Need Hierarchy

Maslow's need hierarchy is a most popular theory of motivation and had its origin in the field of clinical psychology in the early 1940s. It was not until the 1960s that it became a model used to consider human behavior in work organizations. Then, McGregor (see Learning Design 5.1), for example, used the idea and Maslow (1965), himself, produced *Eupsychian Management*.

According to Maslow (1943:370-396), man always has some need he wants to satisfy. Once a need is satisfied it no longer motivates him so he turns to another need for satisfaction. A need, however, does not have to be 100 percent gratified before he will move to the next. So, Maslow put his needs in the following hierarchical order: physiological, safety, social, esteem, and self-actualization.

Physiological Needs
Physiological needs are those that are basic to sustain life and include food, water, clothing, and shelter. Lacking food, safety,

love, and esteem, a person would probably want food more than anything else (Maslow, 1954:37). Money, indirectly, can usually satisfy these needs but less easily than the others as progression is made up the hierarchy.

Safety Needs

When physiological needs are basically gratified, safety needs become important and take a variety of forms, namely economic security, an orderly environment, and protection from physical danger. So, for example, parents who have suffered often transfer overprotection to their children who seek non-competitive sports and sheltered environments (cf. Hodgetts, 1975:314).

Social Needs

After physiological and safety needs have been basically satisfied, social needs become important motivators. People need to feel needed. "Stroking" is important; not necessarily physical "stroking," perhaps psychological. A pat on the back or a kind word is reciprocated and affiliated groups form (cf. Schachter, 1959).

Esteem Needs

After physiological, safety, and social needs have been basically gratified, esteem needs become dominant. That is, the person needs self-esteem *and* the esteem of others. One, without the other, does not satisfy the esteem need. Given both, a person feels self-confident, prestigious, and powerful.

Self-Actualization Need

With all the other needs basically satisfied, the individual seeks self-actualization, which Maslow (1954:46) defined as the "desire to become more and more what one idiosyncratically is, to become everything that one is capable of becoming."

Conclusion

As Hodgetts (1975:318) noted, for the theory to be useful in work motivation, managers must know which of a worker's needs require satisfaction and this can only be an assumption. Also, it should be remembered that levels overlap and some people may only be interested in lower needs.

Of more serious concern is the validity of the whole theory. Lawler and Suttle (1972) reviewed research that has tested the theory and carried out some of their own empirical study—all of which is abridged in Steers and Porter (1975:39-46). Their conclusion was "... a close examination of Maslow's model ... points out the need for much more empirical work before it can be accepted as valid. ..."

Achievement Motivation

A second theory, using human needs as a base for analysis, is termed "need achievement theory" (abbreviated "n Ach") and "achievement motivation theory." It posits that "a major portion of an individual's will to perform can be explained or predicted by the intensity of his or her need for achievement" (Steers and Porter, 1975:47).

The idea had its origins in the 1930s when Murray (1938) developed the theory, which was based on clinical observations in the Harvard Psychological Clinic. Murray believed that individuals could be classified according to strengths of various personality need variables which included needs for achievement, affiliation, power, autonomy, nurturance, and deference. His clinical assessments were by means of thematic apperceptive tests wherein subjects make up imaginative stories that a series of ambiguous social or work situation pictures suggest to them. The stories are then analysed for evidence of the different kinds of imagery associated with various motives.

Since the early theory was developed, considerable work in the area has been carried out by McClelland (1971), Atkinson (1964), and their associates. Their findings were reviewed and critiqued in Steers and Porter (1975:47-86) and, here, McClelland's (1971:13) definition of a "need" is used to simplify understanding before describing the theories a little more fully. It is, "a recurrent concern for a goal state."

The Atkinson Model

The Atkinson (1964) model states that aroused motivation (striving for a particular goal) is a function of the strength of the basic need (M), the expectancy of goal-attainment (E), and the perceived incentive value of the goal (I). So:

$$\text{Aroused Motivation} = M \times E \times I$$

Note that a *motive* is a relatively stable personality characteristic (e.g. **n Ach, n Power, n Affiliation**) while *aroused motivation* is a "situationally" influenced action tendency.

NEED FOR ACHIEVEMENT. A person with high **n Ach** will seek out, enjoy, and do *entrepreneurial*-type jobs well. Also, (1) such people like situations in which they are personally responsible for solutions to problems; (2) they set moderately achievable goals and take calculated risks (high goals are too hard, low goals are too easy and, therefore, there is no achievement satisfaction at those levels); and, (3) they want concrete feedback on how well they are doing, (or how else can they get achievement satisfaction out of what they have done?). Thus, someone with high **n Ach** would probably be suitable for a sport business management position but perhaps not for a sport administrative position in a collegial university department (cf. McClelland, 1962).

Following the last point, a university administrator or school physical education department head should recognize this in subordinate teachers. Most likely, if this theory holds, individuals with high **n Ach** will not be teachers. But, teachers may well have high **n Power** (so they can directly influence others) or, perhaps, high **n Affiliation** (if they are very concerned about close relationships). It is thought that **n Power** is likely to be high in administrators, managers, and leaders; some **n Affiliation** is considered desirable in top quality executives (cf. McClelland, 1962).

Implications For Sport Administrators And Managers

Those in superordinate positions should learn to identify the motives, expectancies, and incentive values of their subordinates so that they can influence the E and I. In this way, the aroused motivation will clearly be greater for the benefit of all concerned. Further, knowing the jobs to be done, the superordinate should fit the job demands to the right person. In these ways, the subordinate will be aroused and satisfied so that the superordinate can build the persistent patterns of behavior he wants (cf. McClelland, 1962).

In another theoretical paper, beyond the scope of this learning design, McClelland (1965) outlined how motives may be acquired by various educational attempts.

Conclusions

Steers and Porter (1975:48-49) cite numerous field and laboratory studies that support this theory. They caution, however, when they cite Cofer and Appley (1964:374), who said, "the theory McClelland and his co-workers have developed is neither compelled by nor directly derived from their data, but is presumably consistent with the data."

Motivation-Hygiene Theory

Frederick Herzberg, Distinguished Professor of Management at The University of Utah, first published his famous motivation-hygiene theory in 1959 (Herzberg, Mausner, and Synderman) and, later, refined it in numerous other publications after further research had been done (e.g. Herzberg, 1966, 1968, 1976).

Theory Development

In the initial survey, 200 accountants and engineers, who represented a cross section of Pittsburgh industry, were asked to recall times when they had felt exceptionally good about their jobs. The interviewers then probed for the sequence of events that led to the good feelings before asking for the sequence of events that led back to "normal" feelings. Something objective had to be happening; Herzberg was not solely concerned with the workers' psychological feelings. Next, the workers were asked similar questions relating to when they had felt exceptionally negative about their jobs.

The important finding was that an entirely different series of events led to satisfaction (and motivation) than that which led to dissatisfaction. The major factors are summarized in Table II.

TABLE II

MOTIVATION-HYGIENE FACTORS

Motivators	"Hygiene" Factors
Achievement	Company policy and administration
Recognition	Supervision
Work itself	Interpersonal relations
Responsibility	Work conditions
Advancement	Salary

Lack of the major "motivators" did not lead to dissatisfaction; but a different range of environmental factors did (see "hygiene factors" in Table II). Thus, Herzberg (1968) concluded, "The opposite of job satisfaction is not job dissatisfaction but, rather, no job satisfaction; and, similarly, the opposite of job dissatisfaction is not job satisfaction, but no job dissatisfaction.

He explained further that two different needs of man were involved and both wanted satisfaction. The "animal nature" needs stemmed from man's overriding need to avoid physical and social deprivation from the environment. These, Herzberg called "hygiene" or "maintenance" factors; just as no hygiene leads to disease and the presence of hygiene does not, of itself, produce health, so lack of "job hygiene" will cause dissatisfaction, but its presence will not, of itself, lead to satisfaction. Such factors are listed under "hygiene" in Table II.

Man's need to realize his human potential for development, accomplishment, psychological growth, and self-realization is achieved through the work factors of achievement, recognition, the work's intrinsic nature, responsibility, and advancement. These are the "growth factors" or motivators and, when they are present, job satisfaction is experienced. Absence of the factors does not lead to job dissatisfaction (if "hygiene" is adequate) but to an absence of positive satisfaction.

Herzberg (1968) reports "at least sixteen other investigations, using a wide variety of populations . . . have been completed (since the 1959 study)," and all corroborate the original theory.

Implications For Sport Administrators

Sport administrators want their subordinates to be satisfied with their jobs, so what should they bear in mind if this theory holds?

(1) Do not try to produce satisfaction by increased "hygiene." Manage "hygiene" to reduce dissatisfaction but remember that workers expect management policies, working conditions, pay, and supervision to be good as a right. Thus, as Herzberg (1976:93) says, give "hygiene" for "hygiene" purposes for "what hurts" but keep it simple. Finally, "give it and shut up about it."

(2) To produce satisfied workers, superordinates must give

them interesting work, responsibility, opportunities for achievement, the chance for promotion, and recognition. Even dull jobs can be enriched by enlarging them within these guidelines (see Herzberg, 1976:94-164).

Criticisms

Herzberg's two-factor motivation-hygiene theory has attracted a great deal of attention (see Steers and Porter, 1975:87-134). Example critical comments are recorded here to illustrate some of the major reported concerns.

1. The theory is "methodologically bound." That is, the story telling critical-incident method of research in which the subject recounts extremely satisfying and extremely dissatisfying job events accounts for Herzberg's and others' findings. Subjects are more likely to attribute causes of satisfaction to themselves and dissatisfactions on the work environment (Vroom, 1964).
2. The research was faulty because the subject simply described the supervisor's behavior, which was then evaluated for coding by the rater (Vroom, 1964).
3. A given factor can cause job satisfaction for one person and job dissatisfaction for another, and vice versa. For example, wages and job security have been found to motivate blue-collar workers.
4. Citing other problems and many studies, House and Wigdor (1967:369-389) concluded, "the two-factor theory is an over-simplification of the relationships between motivation and satisfaction and the sources of job satisfaction and dissatisfaction."

Conclusions

Herzberg devoted a large part of his 1976 book to defend the theory in light of the numerous criticisms he has received. The criticisms, and his defense, certainly warrant further study by those readers who are particularly interested in this theory.

Prior to his theory, however, it should be remembered that managers and researchers concentrated on the individual (Maslow, McClelland, Atkinson) or the work environment (supervisory relations, pay, group influences) as potential sources of motivation. Herzberg drew attention to intrinsic aspects of the job itself (Steers and Porter, 1975:556).

Equity Theory

The basic theory under consideration here has been variously termed social comparison theory, cognitive dissonance theory, exchange theory, distributive justice theory, or inequity theory (Steers and Porter, 1975:135; Hodgetts, 1975:332). Adams' (1965) exposition of "Inequity in Social Exchange" is described.

Adams' Theory

Adams (1965:280) defined inequity as follows:

> Inequity exists for Person whenever he perceives that the ratio of his outcomes to inputs and the ratio of Other's outcomes to Other's inputs are unequal. This may happen either (a) when he and Other are in a direct exchange relationship or (b) when both are in an exchange relationship with a third party and Person compares himself to Other. The values of outcomes and inputs are, of course, as perceived by Person. Schematically, inequality is experienced when either:

$$\frac{O_p}{I_p} < \frac{O_a}{I_a} \qquad \text{or} \qquad \frac{O_p}{I_p} > \frac{O_a}{I_a}$$

> ... A condition of equity exists when:

$$\frac{O_p}{I_p} = \frac{O_a}{I_a}$$

(O = perceived sum of outcomes per exchange, I = perceived sum of inputs per exchange, p = Person, a = Other).

Thus, for example, a physical education teacher's inputs may be a master's degree, the right sex, substantial experience, a willingness to coach, and an enthusiasm for leading outdoor recreation trips. This teacher, then, is Person, and Other has a bachelor's degree, is the wrong sex for the assignment, is inexperienced, and will not put in time out of regular school hours. But Person knows that Other receives the same salary and, therefore, feels a state of inequity exists; Person feels dissatisfied.

In this example, the situation described is as perceived by Person. Other's perception may be quite different; perhaps Other teaches creative dance all day, regards the master's degree as unimportant for the task, age a handicap, and does not value athletics. Clearly, Other sees the inequity equation unbalanced the other way.

The third party in this exchange relationship is the school principal. The principal may say to Person (not literally), "I value your inputs and give you a pay increase of $500 per year." Person is pleased and thinks the equity has been restored. What Person does not know at first is that the principal has said to Other, "I value your inputs and give you a pay increase of $750 per year." Obviously, as soon as Person finds out, inequity will be perceived to exist again.

Alternatively, Other may perceive he/she is being overpaid relative to Person. Social inequity would be perceived to exist, and Other would quite likely work harder (at least at first) to justify receiving the higher salary.

GENERAL CONSEQUENCES OF INEQUITY. Adams (1965) proposes that "the presence of inequity will motivate Person to achieve equity or to reduce inequity, and the strength of motivation to do so will vary directly with the magnitude of inequity experienced." Thus, Person may, (1) alter his inputs; (2) alter his outcomes; (3) cognitively distort his inputs and outcomes; (4) leave the field; (5) act on Other; or (6) change the object of his comparison.

Implications For Sport Administrators

Sport organizations contain many people who are irritated by their feelings of dissatisfaction and low morale. Adams does not contend that all these dysfunctional feelings can be directly related to injustice in social exchanges but many are. Sport administrators should try to understand these processes and supervise workers in such a way that injustice will be eliminated or minimized.

Conclusions

A detailed analysis of research that tests Adams' theory has been carried out by Goodman and Friedman (1971:271-288). They conclude:

(1) "Some assumptions and hypotheses derived from the theory

have relatively clear empirical support" (e.g. inequity is a source of tension, the greater the inequity the greater the drive to reduce it).

(2) Some assumptions and hypotheses have "tentative empirical support" (e.g. Person will resist changing his comparison Other once Other has become a referent).

(3) Some hypotheses have been inadequately tested (e.g. Person will leave the field when inequity is high and other reduction strategies are unavailable).

So the theory has considerable empirical support but also numerous gaps (see Goodman and Friedman, 1971, or their reprinted article in Steers and Porter, 1975:155-179). Apart from the social equation aspect, it differs in other ways from the other contemporary work motivation theories reviewed so far. They identify specific factors in the individual or the environment as important determinants. Equity theory concentrates on the dynamic processes by which behavior is aroused/sustained and on perceived situations (which are not necessarily actual).

Expectancy/Valence Theory

A second "process" theory has been called "expectancy/valence" by Steers and Porter (1975:180) on the grounds that such a title is descriptive of the two major variables of the formulation. Others have been involved in the development of the concepts and have sometimes used other similar names. Here, the theory, as summarized by Steers and Porter (1975:180-218), is described then illustrated by a sport administration example.

The Theory
At least three factors significantly influence job performance:
(1) *Motivation*—A person must *want* to perform (or what happens?);
(2) *Abilities and traits*—The education, training, and personality traits required by the job; and
(3) *Clear role prescriptions*—Unclear role perception may lead to poor performance even if the person is motivated and has abilities.

EXPECTANCY. Most theoretical and empirical work on this

theory has focused on "motivation." The theory is that "motivational force to perform—or effort—is a multiplicative function of the expectancies, or beliefs, that individuals have concerning future outcomes times the value they place on those outcomes" (Steers and Porter, 1975:181).

An expectancy may theoretically range between 0 (absolutely no belief that an outcome will follow a particular action) and +1.0 (complete certainty that an outcome will follow a particular action).

Expectancy has two types, namely:.

(1) E——→P represents the belief that effort will lead to desired performance; e.g. a coach believes that more team practices will produce a winning team. That is, "the closer the perceived relationship between effort and the resulting job performance, the greater the E——→P expectancy."

(2) P——→O represents the belief that performance will lead to particular outcomes; e.g. a coach believes he will be paid more if his team wins (high P——→O), or that winning would make no salary difference (low P——→O). "The multiplicative combination of these two types of expectancies, then, determines the 'expectancy' part of the expectancy/valence equation" (Steers and Porter, 1975:182).

VALENCE. Is the "value, or preference, which an individual places on a particular outcome. Valencies may take on theoretical values from +1.0 to –1.0" (Steers and Porter, 1975:182).

The final motivational force in the expectancy/valence model is:

(E——→P expectancy) × (P——→O expectancy) × (outcome valences)

For example, the coach places high probability on producing a winning team (E——→P = 0.8); similarly, that such a performance has a very good chance of leading to a pay increase or promotion (P——→O = 0.8); and, finally, if the coach really places high value on the outcome (pay increase or promotion) the equation becomes:

Motivational force = 0.8 × 0.8 × 0.9 = 0.58

Such is a strong motivational force to perform so, if the coach's ability is high and his role prescription is clear, a successful job performance would be expected.

On the other hand, if the coach had no real desire for increased pay or promotion, his valence may have been 0.1. Then, the motivational force would have been (0.8 × 0.8 × 0.1), i.e. 0.06 or little desire to perform.

Conclusion

The work reviewed by Steers and Porter (1975:180-218) indicates that expectancy/valence is "a fairly well developed theory of work motivation . . . although it shows definite promise, (it) still requires a firmer empirical-analytical base . . ." (p. 183). The implications for sport administrators in a wide range of situations are clear.

The theories and associated research presented in this learning design demonstrate considerable progression in the understanding of the work motivational processes since the days of "scientific management." Thus, it is now known that work motivation is not solely a function of money and that a satisfied worker is not necessarily a productive one. Workers in sport organizations expect extrinsic and intrinsic rewards from their jobs, so sport administrators and managers must continuously work with motivational models which encompass the known complexities. A most useful conceptual model is that presented by Steers and Porter (1975:20-25), which is after Porter and Miles (1974).

Steers-Porter-Miles' Conceptual Model

In the model it is first assumed that work motivation "can best be understood within a multivariate framework" which takes into account several, often distinct, factors (Steers and Porter, 1975:20). Secondly, the factors "must be viewed within a systems framework" that considers interrelationships and interactive effects among the motivationally relevant factors (Steers and Porter, 1975:20).

If motivation is concerned with energizing, directing, and sustaining human behavior, at least three important variables must be accounted for. These are:

    I. Characteristics of the individual (e.g. interests, attitudes, needs);

    II. Characteristics of the job (e.g. intrinsic rewards, autonomy, direct performance feedback, task variety);

III. Characteristics of the work environment (e.g. immediate environment, peers, supervisors, reward practices, organizational climate) (Steers and Porter, 1975:20-24).

But considering these motivational factors in isolation is not sufficient. For example, a physical education professor may truly want to teach advanced exercise physiology but may lack the ability. Thus, the interactive effects of the motivational variables must be accounted for.

Reverting to the contemporary theories presented in this design, which is best? The need theories (Maslow, McClelland, Atkinson) concentrate on the characteristics of the individual, though situational links are clearly implied. Herzberg concentrates on the characteristics of the job in the belief that an enriched job will lead to a satisfied worker. Again other factors are implied.

Adams' inequity theory does take into account the interactive effects of the individual's characteristics and those of the environment. Finally, expectancy/valence theory encompasses the interactive effects of environmental factors, the job tasks, *and* how the individual workers view their jobs and work environments.

Generally, then, sport administrators and managers should be aware of this Steers-Porter-Miles conceptual model, perhaps experiment with various combinations of the contemporary theories, and choose whichever "works best" in a particular situation (cf. Steers and Porter, 1975:555).

Further Implications And Guidelines
For Sport Administrators

SPORT RESEARCH. In this work motivation area of sport administrative theory Zeigler's (1973:137) ". . . where we aren't" assessment is particularly applicable. My review, which may have deficiencies, indicates that none of the theories presented in this chapter have been empirically tested in sport situations. Some useful related work has been completed and is summarized in Table III. Here, then, is a challenge for researchers, but, for the present, the following general guidelines are useful for sport administrators and managers.

PRACTICAL GUIDELINES. For the purpose here, imagine you have just been appointed administrator or manager of your sport

TABLE III
STUDIES OF WORK MOTIVATION/JOB SATISFACTION
IN SPORT ADMINISTRATION

Doctoral	Master's	Journals/Papers
Daniel (1971)	McCaffery (1976)	Adams and Maloney (1978)
Gilbert (1977)		Petrak and Klein (1978)
Greenberg (1969)		Snizek *et al.* (1978)
Maloney (1974)		Zeisner (1976)
Perry (1976)		

Note: A study by Holdaway (1978) of teachers in nine subject areas revealed that physical
education teachers were least satisfied. He recommended further studies to
determine the causes.

organization. For ease of expression, it is assumed you are a sport
manager and here are the steps you should take and maintain:

(1) Identify your own strengths and weaknesses as objectively
as you possibly can. Try to assess the congruence of your
self-perception with that your subordinates are likely to have
of you. Develop congruence.

(2) You must deliberately "manage" the motivational processes
that you now know to exist; the theories really are practically useful. Do not simply leave it to chance. So, for
example, try Herzberg's theory; I am fairly confident (from
experience) that it will work if skillfully put to use. If it
does, try to develop your control of the total milieu by
applying one of the process approaches described in this
learning design.

(3) Be very sure that the roles of all your workers (e.g. janitors,
groundsmen, teachers, professors, secretaries) are clear and
try to enlarge their jobs as much as possible.

(4) Appropriately reward superior performances. A reward system not based on performance leads to mediocrity. This issue,
if my suggestion is adopted, leads to organizational dysfunction if not properly managed. So, involve your subordinates in goal setting and monitor performance regularly.
Further details on this point are in Chapter Ten.

(5) Try to identify barriers to cohesion anywhere in your
organization's environment and then develop a strategy to
eliminate them.

(6) Compare numbers one to five with, and blend them into, Chelladurai's leadership model (see Chapter 4) (cf. Steers and Porter, 1975:558-559).

References

Adams, J. S.: Injustice in social exchange. In Berkowitz, L. (Ed.): *Advances in Experimental Social Psychology*. New York, Academic Press, 1965, vol. 2.

Adams, P., and Maloney, T. L.: Role conflict, role ambiguity and job satisfaction in simple and multiple leadership situations. In *Proceedings*, (Vol. II), Sixth Commonwealth Conference on Sport, Physical Education, and Recreation, Edmonton, Alberta, 1978.

Atkinson, J. W.: *An Introduction to Motivation*. Princeton, D. Van Nostrand, 1964.

Cofer, C. N., and Appley, M. H.: *Motivation: Theory and Research*. New York, Wiley, 1964.

Daniel, Juri V: "Differentiated Roles and Faculty Job Satisfaction Within Departments of Physical Education and Athletics in Ontario Universities." Ph.D. dissertation, University of Illinois, 1971.

Gilbert, M.A.: "Organizational Approach to the Study of Productivity, Efficiency, and Satisfaction of AAA High School Basketball Teams Based on Fiedler's Contingency Model and Taylor and Bowers' Survey of Organizational Conditions." Ph.D. dissertation, University of Oregon, 1977.

Goodman, Paul S., and Friedman, Paul S.: An examination of Adams' theory of inequity. *Administrative Science Quarterly, 16*:271-288, 1971.

Greenberg, Jerrold S.: "The Relationship Between the Frequency and the Effectiveness of Selected Supervisory Behaviors as Perceived by Physical Education Teachers and their Supervisors in Selected Secondary Schools in New York State." Ed.D. dissertation, Syracuse University, 1969.

Herzberg, F.: *Work and the Nature of Man*. New York, Thomas Y. Crowell, 1966.

————: One more time: How do you motivate employees? *Harvard Business Review, 46*:53-62, 1968.

————: *The Managerial Choice: To be Efficient and to be Human*. Homewood, Illinois, Dow Jones-Irwin, 1976.

Herzberg, F., Mausner, B., and Snyderman, B.: *The Motivation to Work*. New York, John Wiley and Sons, 1959.

Hodgetts, Richard M.: *Management: Theory, Process, and Practice*. Philadelphia, W. B. Saunders, 1975.

Holdaway, E. A.: *Teacher Satisfaction: An Alberta Report*. Edmonton, Department of Educational Administration, University of Alberta, 1978.

House, Robert J., and Wigdor, Lawrence A.: Herzberg's dual-factor theory of job satisfaction and motivation: A review of the evidence and a criticism. *Personnel Psychology, 20*:363-389, 1967.

Lawler, Edward E., and Suttle, J. Lloyd: A causal correlational test of the need hierarchy concept. *Organizational Behavior and Human Performance,* 7:265-287, 1972.

McCaffery, D. T.: "Relationship of Teacher Satisfaction to Student Attitudes in Compulsory Physical Education Classes." M.A. thesis, University of Alberta, 1976.

McClelland, David C.: Business drive and national achievement. *Harvard Business Review,* 40:99-112, 1962.

————: Toward a theory of motive acquisition. *American Psychologist,* 20:321-333, 1965.

————: *Assessing Human Motivation.* New York, General Learning Press, 1971.

Maloney, T. L.: "Job Satisfaction of Canadian Physical Educators." Ph.D. dissertation, University of Alberta, 1974.

Maslow, Abraham H.: A theory of human motivation. *Psychological Review,* 50:370-396, 1943.

————: *Motivation and Personality.* New York, Harper and Row, 1954.

————: *Eupsychian Management: A Journal.* Homewood, Illinois, Richard D. Irwin and The Dorsey Press, 1965. (Maslow (p. xi) defined "Eupsychia" as "the culture that would be generated by 1,000 self-actualizing people on some sheltered island where they would not be interfered with . . . implying only real possibility and improvability rather than certainty, prophesy, inevitability, necessary progress, perfectibility, or confident predictions of the future . . . it can mean 'moving toward psychological health' or 'healthward' . . . the far goals of work.")

Murray, H. A.: *Explorations in Personality.* New York, Oxford University Press, 1938.

Perry, Jean L.: "Job Satisfaction as it Relates to Similarity in Philosophic View Between Physical Education Faculty Members and their Department Chairperson." Ph.D. dissertation, University of Illinois, 1976.

Petrak, B., and Klein, M.: Sociological factors concerning the motivation to work attitude of honorary coaches and assistants. *Leistungssport,* 8:173-179, 1978.

Porter, L. W., and Miles, R. E.: Motivation and management. In McGuire, J. W. (Ed.): *Contemporary Management: Issues and Viewpoints.* Englewood Cliffs, New Jersey, Prentice-Hall, 1974.

Schachter, S.: *The Psychology of Affiliation.* Stanford, California, Stanford University Press, 1959.

Snizek, W. E., Showmaker, D. J., and Bryant, C. D.: Job satisfaction and perceived bureaucratization in recreational delivery organizations: A comparison of federal and state park and forest rangers. *Leisure Sciences,* 1:147-161, 1978.

Steers, Richard M., and Porter, Lyman W.: *Motivation and Work Behavior.* New York, McGraw-Hill, 1975.

Vroom, V. H.: *Work and Motivation.* New York, John Wiley and Sons, 1964

Zeigler, Earle F.: Administrative theory and practice: A conference summary. In Hunsicker, P. (Ed.): *Administrative Theory and Practice in Athletics* and *Physical Education*. Chicago, The Athletic Institute, 1973.

Zeisner, R. E.: Job satisfaction and the volunteer coach. *Coaching Association of Canada Bulletin*. *15*, 5-23, 1976.

Important Related Reading

Steers and Porter, *Motivation*, 1975, ch. 2-5, 14-16.

Supplementary Readings

Adams, *Injustice*, 1965.

Atkinson, *Motivation*, 1964.

Goodman and Friedman, *Adams' Theory*, 1971

Herzberg, *Nature Man*, 1966.

———: *One More Time*, 1968.

———: *The Managerial Choice*, 1976.

Herzberg, Mausner, and Snyderman, *Motivation*, 1959.

House and Wigdor, *Dual-Factor Theory*, 1967.

Ibbetson, J. F. R., and Whitmore, D. A.: *The Management of Motivation and Remuneration*. London, Business Books, 1977.

Jaques, E.: *The Measurement of Responsibility*. London, Tavistock, 1956.

———: *Equitable Payment*. New York, Wiley, 1961.

Katz, Daniel: The motivational basis of organizational behavior. *Behavioral Science*, *9*:131-146, 1964.

Lawler and Suttle, *Need Hierarchy Concept*, 1972.

McClelland, *Business Drive*, 1962.

———: *Motive Acquisition*, 1965.

———: *Human Motivation*, 1971.

Maslow, *Human Motivation*, 1943.

———: *Personality*, 1954.

———: *Eupsychian Management*, 1965.

Murray, *Explorations*, 1938.

Porter and Miles, *Motivation*, 1974.

Schachter, *Affiliation*, 1959.

Schwartz, A. P., Ronan, W. W., and Day, G. J.: Individual differences and job satisfaction. *Studies in Personnel Psychology*, *6*:35-53, 1975.

Vroom, *Work*, 1964.

Case 5.21

Utopia?

Gerry Wilcocks was dean of the large faculty of physical education, recreation, and sport at Utopian University, which had one of the highest student enrollments in North America. The faculty had its own specialist library, which employed two librarians and eight library clerks.

In 1976, Mrs. Jan Wallace, an experienced physical education teacher, took a clerk's job in the library while her husband pursued his doctoral studies. Miss N. Picky, a Clerk III, outlined in detail the duties of Mrs. Wallace (Clerk I): she was to check out books, replace returned books on the shelves, and "read the stacks" to see that books were in the right place. Thus, Mrs. Wallace would always be occupied carrying out one of the three functions.

For awhile Mrs. Wallace enjoyed her work; she discussed useful books with students, occasionally advised them, and read some herself during quiet periods. The library operated as smoothly as always but students liked the new clerk who took an interest in their work instead of sullenly checking them out.

After three months, Miss Picky sent a memorandum to Mrs. Wallace saying she must visit her for review of her "three-month report." Miss Picky gave a "grade" out of ten on the following items: attendance; punctuality; efficiency (in each of three areas); appearance; and relations with peers, supervisors, students, and faculty. This enabled Miss Picky to assign a grade out of 100 and 70 was required for continuing employment. Mrs. Wallace received 75 percent; she was told she talked too much to users, had taken five minutes too long on two coffee breaks, and had been observed reading books! She received eight out of ten for attendance even though she had never been absent.

Mrs. Wallace thought it was a joke at first, but it was not. So she explained why she talked to students, that she only read books when all other work was done, and asked "How did I lose my two attendance points?" Miss Picky subsequently reported Mrs. Wallace to the head librarian as most likely unsuitable for the job. Mrs. Wallace was very upset, badly needed the money from the work, and asked her husband to explain the situation to Dean Wilcocks.

Case Analysis Method
CAM A or CAM B (see Chapter 1).

Case 5.22

A Hiding To Nothing

In April, 1980, Dr. Tim Ongena was appointed head of the

Department of Human Kinetics and Leisure Studies at Southern University* and was thrilled to achieve a long-term ambition. Southern produced "discipline" specialists, physical education teachers, recreation administrators, and had a very big graduate program. The department had forty-five faculty members.

That June, Ongena visited the campus for discussions with the retiring head, Dr. Alice Keen. Keen had just read Schoen's (1979:118) book *Pat* (New York, Harper and Row) which contained this quote:

> If you decide to join a University faculty, you must accept the fact that at any given hour for the rest of your professional life someone, somewhere, will be saying something unpleasant about you. You cannot avoid this. Your only option is to choose between having the successful or the unsuccessful professors take you apart. If you are successful your less fortunate colleagues will consider the disreputable means by which you have attained your position. If you are not successful, those who are will remark at length on the shortcomings which made this outcome inevitable. If you are in between or otherwise difficult to define, everyone will be nasty about you.
>
> —Pat Moynihan, 1960

Keen showed the quote to Ongena and said, "It may be my fault, but that's exactly the situation you're about to take over at Southern. You must try to change it."

Case Analysis Method

CAM B (see Chapter 1) assuming that you are Dr. Ongena and that you believe in, (1) Adams' Theory of Inequity; (2) Expectency/Valence Theory; and, (3) Machiavelli's organizational methods.†

Case 5.23

O' Brother!‡

My brother Jim's physical education teacher, Mr. Peach, is in his third year of teaching after being appointed by the School Board. I emphasize "board" because Frank Swift, head of

---

*A high school may well be substituted as the institutional setting.

†To complete this part of the analysis it is necessary to read: Machiavelli, N.: *The Prince*. Harmondsworth, Penguin, 1961 (Translated by George Bull).

‡As told by Jim's brother.

physical education, was not involved in the appointment process; in fact, Mr. Swift was a fine sportsman who had built a sound physical education and sport tradition at Oakridge School.

In physical education classes Peach uses dictatorial methods and shows no sensitivity to less able students: he ridicules fat boys and goads Andrew Euridge, who has a slightly deformed foot. Jim is a skillful games player (racquet sports) but has no interest in basketball, which is Peach's speciality. When Peach coaches the team his sole concern is winning. Sometimes only five boys play while the rest "warm the bench." More likely Peach will scream at someone for a mistake and literally yank him off the court; the sub then enters the arena in trepidation. Peach receives technical fouls nearly every game and the local officials are fed up with him.

One day, without pre-training, Peach instructed Jim's class to run five miles in the lesson and anyone who didn't beat him (Peach) would have to run it again the next day. About ten students didn't finish ahead of Peach and Jim was one. In truth, Jim didn't try because he had an important squash game that night. During the evening contest Jim strained his groin and the club trainer advised him to rest for a week so he would be likely to recover for the Nationals.

Dad wrote a note to Peach explaining that Jim was unable to run the penalty five miles. Jim handed the note to Peach who glanced at it and said, "Crap! Get changed and run." Jim struggled round the course, aggravated his injury and Dad was livid. Immediately, he called Mr. Swift and urged appropriate action. Mr. Swift was sympathetic for he had taught Dad when he was at school.

Case Analysis Method
CAM A, CAM B, or CAM E (see Chapter 1).

Summary

1. Work is "the social role performed by adult members of society that directly and/or indirectly yields social and financial consequences and that constitutes a major focus in the life of an adult" (Hall, 1975:8). Sport workers primarily produce services.

2. Motivation is "that which energizes, directs, and sustains behavior" (Steers and Porter, 1975:553).
3. Frederick W. Taylor was the "Father of Scientific Management." He believed that every single act of every workman could be reduced to a science, that managers should fit men to jobs and pay first-class men more money. Such would bring the efficiency and rewards which *both* management and workers wanted.
4. Henri Fayol said technical, commercial, financial, security, accounting, and managerial functions were present in any undertaking. Management had five elements, namely: (1) to forecast and plan; (2) to organize; (3) to command; (4) to coordinate; and, (5) to control. He also listed fourteen "principles of management."
5. Elton Mayo's studies identified the importance of the informal organization that is now known to exist in all organizations.
6. The human relations approach (Mayo) assumes that worker satisfaction will lead to good performance while the human resources approach (Theory Y) assumes that meaningful job performance leads to job satisfaction.
7. Maslow's needs were in the following hierarchical order: physiological, safety, social, esteem, and self-actualization.
8. Aroused Motivation = $M \times E \times I$.
9. According to Herzberg, "hygiene" should only be given for what hurts to reduce dissatisfaction. Workers are motivated by interesting work, responsibility, opportunities for achievement, the chance for promotion, and recognition.
10. Social inequality is experienced when either:

$$\frac{O_p}{I_p} < \frac{O_a}{I_a} \quad \text{or} \quad \frac{O_p}{I_p} > \frac{O_a}{I_a}$$

Equity exists when $\quad \dfrac{O_p}{I_p} = \dfrac{O_a}{I_a}$

11. In expectancy/valence theory three factors significantly

influence job performance: motivation, abilities and traits, and clear role prescriptions. Motivational force is:

$$(E \longrightarrow P \text{ expectancy}) \times (P \longrightarrow O \text{ expectancy})$$
$$\times \text{ (outcome valences)}$$

12. Work motivation is not solely a function of money, and a satisfied worker is not necessarily a productive one. Sport organization workers expect extrinsic and intrinsic rewards from their jobs. Steers and Porter (1975) see three important variables interacting, namely: the individual's characteristics, the job's characteristics, and the work environment's characteristics.

Concepts For Review

Work	Motivation
Scientific management	Fayol's management functions
The Hawthorne studies	Fayol's five elements
Informal organizations	Fayol's fourteen principles
Human relations approaches	Human resources approaches
Theory X and Theory Y	Argyris' maturing stages
Likert's Systems 1 to 4	Maslow's need hierarchy
n Ach, n Power, n Affiliation	Motive
Aroused motivation	Motivation-hygiene theory
Equity theory	Expectancy/Valence theory
Steers-Porter-Miles' conceptual model	

Questions For Oral Or Written Discussion

1. Describe a "scientific management" style of management as it could be applied in a school physical education department. Discuss the consequences you would expect.
2. Describe and compare Herzberg's and Maslow's theories as they apply in work motivation. Use sport examples to illustrate your points of view.
3. Evaluate Adams' theory of inequity with reference to the Steers-Porter-Miles conceptual model.
4. Evaluate Expectancy/Valence theory with reference to the Steers-Porter-Miles conceptual model.
5. Assume you are head of a sport department and are unable to give additional money to motivate your workers. Specify

the department setting and describe other methods you would use to improve performance *and* keep your workers satisfied.

6. Describe an individual you know in a sport organization who fits Theory X. What would you do about him if you were his boss and you had no real grounds for firing him?

7. CAM C (see Chapter 1) applied to instructor-specified topics taken from this chapter.

Chapter 6

SUPERVISION OF CLIENTS

T WO LEARNING DESIGNS constitute this chapter on the supervision of clients. "Clients" are those people who receive services directly in the wide variety of sport organizations under consideration in this book. Thus, clients are school students, adult recreational class members, casual visitors to parks, athletes, spectators, and others. Sometimes clients are compelled to be sport organization members, as in curriculum physical education classes, while in other situations the clients' involvement may be entirely voluntary. In either of the latter situations, the clients may desire the organizations' goals be met or they may only intend to behave deviantly (cf. Figure 2, Chapter 3).

"Supervision" is used here on the assumption that it has two particular purposes; firstly, to ensure the maintenance of organizational effectiveness and, secondly, to contribute to clients' development. So, administrators or managers (e.g. department heads, teachers, coaches, recreation directors) have the responsibility to preserve their organizations so that particular goals may be met but, also, they must be particularly concerned about the overall welfare of their clients.

Some aspects of organizational maintenance and client development are dealt with elsewhere (e.g. right behavior [Chapter 2], leadership [Chapter 4], supervision of workers [Chapter 5], legal considerations [Chapter 7], policies [Chapter 8], and evaluation [Chapter 10]). Such areas as "planning for instruction" and "effective teaching" do contribute to this chapter's two major concerns but they are not dealt with in detail. The overriding approach is a general one that is designed to help sport administrators and managers to maintain their organizations and develop their clients.

LEARNING DESIGN 6.1

MAINTAINING ORGANIZATIONAL EFFECTIVENESS

In this design a "framework" is outlined that identifies the client-related phenomena of which sport administrators must be aware if they are to maintain organizational effectiveness. It does not suggest answers to all likely problems, for that would be too glib. However, having identified the phenomena, the process of understanding them is discussed in a general, pastoral care fashion and cases further illuminate the issues. Client development concerns cannot be entirely divorced from consideration but they are not of primary interest.

Involved Client-Related Phenomena

The client-related phenomena are listed in Table IV along with example problems, example solutions, and related readings. Generally, if the persistent problems are not appropriately dealt with, organizational dysfunction or demise will ensue.

Pastoral Care

Oscar Wilde is reputed to have held the view that, "to give advice is always foolish but to give good advice is absolutely fatal." Nevertheless, looking at Case 6.11, a student died; was it an accident or did he commit suicide? No one knew. Indeed, the university administration knew very little about the student and certainly no university employee had given him advice. Obviously an extreme case but, without committing suicide, many university students go through months of mental agony without consulting anyone; thus leading to wasted years. Considerable expansion in higher education has led to increased mechanization of administration with the consequent virtual elimination of significant contact between students and professional adults on school and university campuses. To begin to put this type of student personnel administrative problem into focus, a brief look

TABLE IV

FRAMEWORK OF CLIENT-RELATED PHENOMENA INVOLVED IN
ORGANIZATIONAL MAINTENANCE

Phenomena	Example Persistent Problems	Example Solutions	Related Readings
A. The admisintration-client relations.	1. Client participation in decision making. (Which decisions?; How?)	1. Student councils, athletic councils, booster clubs, recreation commissions.	1. Godbey (1978: ch. 16-17) and Case 6.12.
	2. Legal.	2. Risk planning.	2. Chapter Seven.
	3. Discipline.	3. (a) Positive, organized democratically-based leadership; *not* a "buddy" approach.	3. (a) Insley (1973: 92-112) and Case 6.12.
		3. (b) Policies.	3. (b) Chapter Nine and Case 6.14.
	4. Learning "climate."		4. Learning Design 6.2.
B. Organization for formal instruction.	1. Large class size and impersonality.	1. Houses, colleges, homerooms.	1. This design (below).
	2. Teaching assistants doing most activity work.	2. Ensure regular professors do most of the teaching.	
	3. Underqualified recreation leaders.	3. Minimize dangers.	3. Chapter Seven.
	4. Little student learning.	4. Hire teachers who understand what constitutes effective teaching.	4. Locke (1979).
C. Co-curricular activities (Intra- and extra-mural).	1. Staffing.	1. Non-specialists must be used well.	1. Chapter Five.
	2. Scope and status.	2. Preferably keep all under the control of a "right" director.	2. Chapter Two, Case 3.21, and Case 6.12.
D. Integrative services which assist clients (usually students) in relating to the organization's formal structure.	1. Impersonality (cf. B1 above).	1. Counselling services.	1. This design (below).
	2. Disabled clients.	2. Specialized and/or therapeutic services and appropriate facilities.	2. Godbey (1978: ch.6), Gunn (1975), Kraus (1973), Peterson (1976), Ibrahim & Crandall (1979: ch. 10).
	3. Disadvantaged clients.	3. Homophilous dyad network.	3. Nesbitt, Brown, & Murphy (1970).

		4. Develop good working arrangements with allied community organizations.	
	4. Functioning in a "vacuum."		
E. Special programs which assist vocational preparation or personal development.	1. Anti-team sport students.	1. Outward Bound, Duke of Edinburgh Award programs, or other youth-serving agencies.	1. Godbey (1978: ch, 9).

at the situation on a Canadian university campus follows.

Until recently, the Faculty of Agriculture and Forestry was relatively small and fraternity between (and among) faculty and students was considerable. Recently, the faculty has suffered from rapid growth with a resultant considerably less personal interaction between faculty and students. To help alleviate possible problems for students, a compulsory non-credit course was given to first-year students in which academic requirements and expectations were fully explained and student queries were sought. Additionally, all students were encouraged to consult faculty if they had any kind of problem. The "Ag" club, one of the most active on campus, organized a "Big Brother-Little Brother" arrangement so that a newcomer always had a homophilous person to turn to for advice about the "system." Despite this, however, one department chairman believed students should be treated as adults and left alone while another felt they should be treated more as his own children with, consequently, considerably more faculty input.

In the Faculty of Physical Education, Recreation, and Athletics, every student had a "faculty adviser" who was supposed to deal with any of the student's academic or personal problems. If the adviser could not adequately solve the problem he referred the student to the professional officer, department chairperson, or dean, in that ascending order. The ratio of advisers to students was about one to fifteen and it was thought the arrangement worked reasonably well. As with Agriculture, however, the pastoral care of students was better when the faculty had fewer students. In recent years the dean had witnessed male students, ranging from first year undergraduates to final year Ph.D. students, crying, with big tears rolling down their cheeks.

A former head of the student health service did a study on university suicides and found, for example, that there were twelve per year at the University of Texas and that the University of Alberta had never had more than three per year.

Generally, it was faculty disinterest in students that led to the formation of the student counselling services. Since the service started a few years ago, almost 8,000 students had taken advantage of the confidential help offered and 55 percent of their problems had been "personal." Psychiatric consultation was available to all students registered at the university through the university health service and, through referral arrangements, the service claimed to have been able to help with almost any student problem. Indeed, it was through referrals that the student counselling service received most of its clients; not just from the health service but also from faculties. However, the counselling service would have liked more referrals to be made to it from academic staff who often had not the time nor training to deal adequately with student problems. Several thousand students per year used the service but details of cases were not reported to anyone.

Other services were available to individual students. For instance, the foreign student adviser, the dean of women, the dean of men, and residence personnel were all willing to try to meet the requirements of their sectional interests. The Students' Union offered very varied assistance through handbooks and even had a confidential 24-hour "hot line" telephone service through which a student with any problem could receive confidential help.

Universally (not just at the Canadian university) there seems gradually to be a change in emphasis in the counsellor's role—moving away from an exclusively one-to-one interview service to one that includes an involvement in the campus community; an involvement which aims at modification of institutional procedures and which tries to humanize the impact of the institution on students and to give the kind of professional support that will increase the effectiveness of those students and faculty who are in a position to offer direct services to students (Dawes, 1973:270). Drum and Figler (1973) readings outline the evolving position more fully; all in a fashion which will contribute positively to an understanding of how sport administrators may contribute, in this pastoral area, to maintaining their organizations and helping their students to develop.

Interim Design Summary

The phenomena of which sport administrators need to be aware so far as their clients are concerned, if they wish to maintain organizational effectiveness, were outlined in Table IV. Example persistent problems were identified as were brief suggested solutions. Some of the phenomena are dealt with elsewhere in the book. An approach to pastoral care of student clients was discussed as illustrative of what is needed in increasingly impersonal sport organizations. It is intended that readers study the cases that follow and carry out the case-related activities—all with the particular intention of maintaining the organizations in an appropriately functional fashion.

References*

Dawes, Richard V.: The role of the counsellor in mass higher education. *Higher Education, 2*:267-270, 1973.

Drum, David J., and Figler, Howard E.: *Outreach in Counseling.* New York, Intext Educational Publishers, 1973.

Godbey, G.: *Recreation, Park and Leisure Services: Foundations, Organization, Administration.* Philadelphia, W. B. Saunders, 1978.

Gunn, Scout L.: *Basic Terminology for Therapeutic Recreation and other Action Therapies.* Champaign, Illinois, Stipes, 1975.

Ibrahim, H., and Crandall, R.: *Leisure: A Psychological Approach.* Los Alamitos, California, Hwong, 1979.

Insley, Gerald S.: *Practical Guidelines for the Teaching of Physical Education.* Reading, Massachusetts, Addison-Wesley, 1973.

Kraus, Richard: *Therapeutic Recreation Service Principles and Practices.* Philadelphia, W. B. Saunders, 1973.

Locke, Lawrence F.: Learning from teaching. In Jackson, John J. (Ed.): *Theory into Practice.* Victoria, British Columbia, University of Victoria, 1979.

Nesbitt, John A., Brown, Paul D., and Murphy, James F.: *Recreation and Leisure Service for the Disadvantaged.* Philadelphia, Lea and Febiger, 1970.

Peterson, Carol A.: *A Systems Approach to Therapeutic Recreation Program Planning.* Champaign, Illinois, Stipes, 1976.

*Note that some of these references are from Table IV as "related readings" which are not specifically referred to in the design.

Case 6.11

Tragic Trio: Part One

North University was founded in 1836 and had a philosophy based on excellent scholarship. Many of the 7,000 students lived in fine halls of residence, a few in lodgings, and the remainder at home in a city of 200,000 people situated on the coast and yet close to mountains.

The value of physical recreation for assisting the physiological, psychological, and social needs of the students had long been recognized by the university administration and the first director of physical recreation was appointed in 1925. During the next thirty years he developed a useful, though limited by present standards, program of physical recreational activities and then, when he retired, he was replaced by Peter Plymouth.

Peter Plymouth, age forty-two, had been a major in the army during World War II and a school teacher for seventeen years—all at the same high school. His good reputation at the greatly respected school led to his appointment at the university. Peter was happily married and lived in a well-ordered household with his wife and two children. His daughter was in high school and his son was a geography student at North University.

When Mr. Plymouth was appointed to the university in 1955, the physical recreational facilities consisted of a small multi-purpose gymnasium and ample outdoor playing fields. He had only one professional colleague, who carried the title of director of physical recreation for women, and she was technically under Mr. Plymouth's jurisdiction. By 1966 (the year of the incidents to be described) the physical recreational staff numbered seven professionals and several auxiliary workers such as the swimming pool superintendent. Facilities included a new physical recreational complex that consisted of a two-court basketball hall, eight squash courts and a twenty-five meter swimming pool. Playing fields had been extended, tennis courts had been added, and an outdoor activities center had been built in the mountains about fifty miles away. The department owned two vehicles for towing canoe and dinghy trailers to the mountain center, which was at Nab Mountain.

This progress had been achieved largely because of Mr.

Plymouth's powerful committee work and by close liaison with the Student's Union; particularly with the Students' Athletic Union, which was the body responsible for controlling all the athletic and recreational clubs. For instance, the ski club had 400 very active members and several sport clubs competed nationally. The Athletic Union was very old and well controlled by its constitution. Any new sports club was given a "model constitution" that enabled it to become established quickly along sound lines, and all clubs received recreation department assistance whenever they asked for it.

Mr. Plymouth's long experience in physical education had taught him a great deal about the safety precautions necessary when physical activities are being performed. In his own family, Mr. Plymouth was more than reasonably prudent and he carried this philosophy over to his department where he tried to do the same for the recreational clubs.

Incident Number One
(Incidents Two and Three are in Chapter 7, Case 7.02.)

Paul Chambers was a first-year student who hoped eventually to specialize in English literature. From a "normal" background he had just scraped into university and was taking seven courses throughout his first year. At the Christmas examinations he did moderately well; certainly not badly enough for anyone to notice. But, during the first year, classes were very large (100+) and there was no very effective personal tutor system and no university-wide counselling service. From his school report, the Arts Faculty knew that his father was a schoolteacher and that he had one sister. He was reported to be "fairly quiet" and he had no known physical defects. Indeed, all students were medically examined by the university health service doctors and could not get green "athletic passes" if they were "unfit." Some were given red passes that indicated defects; thus, for example, a diabetic could be observed carefully on entering the swimming pool.

The pool superintendent had one assistant and both of them were in the pool area at busy times. At quiet times one was on duty and his sole responsibility was to watch the pool users. Additionally, a big notice warned, "Do not swim alone." At 10:00 A.M. one day in January 1966, Paul Chambers entered the pool area and showed his green pass to the superintendent who was on duty by himself. There was no else in the pool so Paul was asked not to swim until someone else came. Soon, Gary North, a second-year student, arrived and they began to swim. Just then, the superintendent heard a strange noise coming from the filtration room and so he rushed out and was away about ten minutes rectifying the fault. Gary North swam twenty lengths and then sat on the side to regain his breath. Just then, the superintendent returned and said, "Where's the other student?" Gary had not been taking notice and did not know. The superintendent looked round and saw a dark shape on the bottom at the deep end. He dived in immediately and pulled the boy out. Artificial respiration was unsuccessful; Paul Chambers was dead.

Case Analysis Method

CAM B (see Chapter 1) without considering any legal liability implications.

Case 6.12

A Few Too Many

Tilton High School had just over 1,000 students in grades nine through twelve and a good physical education and athletics program. As soon as football ended, basketball was the given major emphasis in the athletic department. Mr. Dillon, the well-qualified and respected boys' coach, asked all the players to stay behind for a meeting after practice one day in November, 1972. His procedure was to make team policy decisions by democratic vote among members.

At the meeting, he reported having seen a player drinking beer after the last practice: a violation of school and training rules. He chose not to name the player but asked the offender to see him privately; otherwise, the player would never be allowed to represent the school again.

The disgruntled players left with a problem because five of them had been drinking. Who had Dillon seen? They decided it must have been Jim Rudge, a starting guard. Jim's father was a principal at another school in the district and Jim had high hopes of a basketball scholarship and a career in medicine. However, he didn't really think the odd beer would hurt him and yet the possible consequences of the incident troubled him. He made an appointment to see Mr. Dillon.

Meanwhile, Dillon discussed the problem with Principal Hallett. Hallett said he would leave it to Dillon but reminded him of Rudge's key position on the team and the school's good chance of winning the conference.

Finally, all five drinkers decided to go with Jim to see Mr. Dillon. A shocked Dillon discussed the issue with the players for two hours before asking them what he should do. Their suggestion was that none of them should be allowed to play in the next game as punishment but, after then, the incident should be forgotten. Visualizing a heavy defeat, Dillon warned them about the dangers of drinking and the need to obey rules. But, he decided to let them all play.

The five drinkers and the other squad members all thought Mr. Dillon had used bad judgment. Two weeks later, Dillon saw Rudge and another player drinking beer in the student parking lot soon after a practice ended.

Case Analysis Method
CAM A or CAM E (see Chapter 1; also, cf. "decision making" in Chapter 9).

Case 6.13

The Bounty Hunters

The following occurred during the summer of 1978 at Cypress Lake Park, which includes three lakes and is operated by the city of Nordest. The park is located fifteen miles from downtown Nordest and is intensively used in the months of July and August. It presents a wide variety of problems for the administration including vandalism, unsupervised pets, whether to lifeguard the beaches, the proper response to nude bathers, understaffing, periodic fire closures, indecent exposures, and a host of others.

The lifeguards at Cypress Lake Park, during the fire hazard season, made hourly trips around Lower Cypress Lake because it received most of the public usage. The purposes of this circuit were to give the guards a break from sitting in the sun, to caution smokers, douse campfires, and enforce park regulations. On returning from one of these patrols on a weekday afternoon, the lifeguard reported to the park foreman, Mike Orton, that he had encountered three massively proportioned males who were causing trouble. They were sitting on a picnic table near the main beach area, were obviously intoxicated, and were drinking straight from a bottle of rye. When the lifeguard approached them and informed them that they were not permitted to consume alcohol in the park he was reportedly met with a stream of abuse and a threat to break both of his kneecaps should they ever see him again. The lifeguard also reported that the men in question were harrassing members of the public as they passed.

Of the two park staff members (as distinguished from lifeguards) who were on duty with Mike, one was a slight girl and the other was John Lemm. Mike thought John was the more appropriate to assist him with the situation so the two set off at a brisk pace in the direction of the malefactors with Mike in the lead. Mike was not the type of foreman to shy away from a confrontation, nor was it usually necessary, because he was tall and weighed over 200 pounds. Normally his physical presence was enough to diffuse any situation with belligerent park users. Directly behind Mike was John Lemm, who, although tall, was relatively scrawny and didn't look much of a threat to anybody. Following, were two fairly short lifeguards who were not keen on going first. Mike and John were dressed in casual work clothes while the lifeguards were in their distinctive uniform.

When the crew arrived at the picnic site where the three were drinking, the lifeguards were met with a chorus of insults. One of the drinkers was at least as large as Mike but considerably heavier and another was significantly larger still. Both were generously tatooed, had long hair and beards, were wearing leather jackets with the sleeves cut off, and blue jeans. The third was rather short and stocky, but he didn't pose much of a threat because he was intoxicated to the point that he had trouble standing. Attempting to be as diplomatic as possible while trying to appear firm, Mike suggested that the group might like to continue their party somewhere else. This approach had little effect on the three and the biggest launched into a monologue on the subject of individual liberty and the role of government in regulating the drinking habits of its citizens. He concluded his barely coherent speech with a surprisingly distinct invitation to physically attempt to remove them if the park's staff thought they could survive the attempt. At that point, Mike, with his public relations talent rapidly deserting him, informed the three that not only were they violating a section of the criminal code but also a Nordest municipal bylaw that specifically prohibited the consumption of alcohol in Cypress Lake Park. At the mention of police intervention the two larger culprits offered "to settle this like men." Mike was shoved backwards by the largest of the group who continued to advance upon him. John was literally thrown into the surrounding shrubs by the other one. The park staff hastily retreated.

A decision on how to handle three large belligerent drunks had to be made. With their pride severely wounded, the park workers lost no time in deciding to "fix their wagon" and promptly called the nearest detachment of the RCMP. The RCMP had never appeared keen to enforce regulations in Cypress Lake Park, because the park was city property and the city had its own police force (about fifteen miles away). However, under stress the RCMP detachment never failed to show up, so in due course two constables in separate cars arrived. The same crew as before, augmented by two RCMP officers, set off in the direction of the culprits at a more subdued pace than previously.

Long before the arrival of the police, the three had disposed of all evidence of their drinking. Presumably the contents were dispatched and the bottles went into the lake. It was their turn to be humbled but instead they explained to the police how they had been accosted and unjustly accused of drinking in a public place by the alleged park staff who wore no uniform and did not carry identification. They explained that they didn't know that they had been dealing with the park staff; instead, they thought the lifeguards were merely playing a joke on them. Further, they explained that they were members in good standing of the Bounty Hunters, the local motorcycle gang, and should the park deal with them unfairly they thought their friends wouldn't be kindly disposed to the park or its staff.

The police seemed to be affected by this last revelation and promptly concluded that there was no evidence that the three had been drinking and, because the staff had no identification, the actions of the accused had been perfectly justified. Meanwhile the shortest and most intoxicated of the three had attempted to walk and had fallen backwards into a ditch where he promptly passed out.

Mike, concluding the police were about to leave the three right where they were, demanded that the police evict the three from the park. He declared that the owner of the park had vested in him the authority to prohibit anyone from the property and the three had thus become trespassers. To add to this, he continued, they were obviously drunk in a public place and were in clear violation of the criminal code. Faced with this outburst the two constables felt compelled to take some action so they requested that the three leave the park. After much discussion, the largest of the bikers threatened to come back and kill Mike Orton. The bikers eventually left the park, carrying the unconscious member of their party, but not before shoving Mike to the ground in the presence of the police.

Case Analysis Method
CAM A or CAM B (see Chapter 1).

Case 6.14

The Lesson

Tom Gaunt was a student teacher of physical education at Springbank High School. As his class members came into the gymnasium, they dropped their valuables, such as watches and wallets, into an open cardboard box for safekeeping. Gaunt then handed the box to Greg, a boy who was injured and not participating, to look after during the lesson. After showering, the boys collected their valuables from the box and, when it was empty, Greg gave the box back to Tom Gaunt. At the same time, however, Michael Gretsky claimed that he had not got his watch back. It was new and worth $150.

Gaunt went to the principal to explain. The principal advised Gaunt to try to resolve the issue himself. So, with the help of the deputy principal, Gaunt recalled the class into a room and quietly explained what had happened. He asked for the watch to be put in his mailbox within two days and no further questions would be asked.

When Gaunt was back in the staff changing room a student came in and said he knew who had taken the watch and named the boy. Gaunt, still trying to settle everything himself, told the deputy principal what had transpired. The deputy said, "We can't accuse the boy but I believe he may be guilty—we must get the police in." A police officer came and the suspect was brought out of his class for questioning. Present in the room were Gaunt, the deputy principal, the policeman, and Gretsky. The policeman's questions were skillful and lengthy but the suspect denied taking the watch.

Case Analysis Method
CAM A (see Chapter 1).

Addendum
This is intended to help with parts five and six of CAM A *after* parts one to four have been attempted

WHAT ACTUALLY HAPPENED. The watch was not found and Gretsky's father complained to the School Board that his son had been improperly treated. The principal then found that he ought to have adhered to the following policy:

Ministry Position
1. It should be a matter of policy that, except as indicated in the next sections of this circular, children are not interviewed by police officers at school premises.
2. If they are, it should be considered essential that either a parent or a guardian be present at the interview.
3. Teachers should not take part in these interviews.
4. The policy should provide for appropriate modification in the case of an emergent situation where there is no question of compromising the legal rights of the child and where immediate information is necessary for quick action.
5. The policy should also provide that, where a police officer insists on interviewing a child immediately and on school premises, any member of the board's staff should: (a) request the police officer to delay the interview until

such time as the school can obtain the presence of a parent or a guardian, (b) if such a request is refused, then the staff member should attend the interview and:

    (i) ensure that the child is instructed and that the child understands that he has a right to remain silent:

    (ii) ensure that the child's parents are contacted immediately:

    (iii) request the district superintendent of schools or the secretary-treasurer to consult the School Board's solicitor immediately for advice.

Mr. Gretsky left the school with a satisfied smirk on his face and several school staff members, including Gaunt, were considerably wiser.

Case 6.15

The Silly Season

In November 1976, Tom Dooley decided there should be nude swimming in Great Divide University's pool so he organized a petition, collected many signatures (including William Shakespeare's and Mae West's), and sent it to the Pool Users' Committee. It was not accepted so Tom, ten other males, and two females "skinny dipped" whilst an audience of 200 sniggered, jeered, and/or applauded. The student newspaper gave front page attention to the story and began to write editorials on the issue; mainly attacking various administrative actions which, in time, were called "sleazy shuffles."

First the Users' Committee approved nude bathing "in principle" and sent the issue to the President's Committee on Athletics from where it was immediately returned. So the Users' Committee sought legal advice and were told that nude swimming constituted an offence if it took place in a public place (which the university pool was). Appropriate notices were posted on the pool walls and lifeguards were told to ask nude bathers to leave.

The student paper, meanwhile, suggested that the legal advice could just as easily have said it was a "private" place and a little notice to that effect could have legally permitted the nude bathers to have their freedom.

Undeterred, "hang-down-your-head Tom Dooley," as the paper called him, organized a second "skinny dipping session." In front of a large crowd, ten people began to swim and four of them refused to leave when asked to do so by the lifeguards. The lifeguards also snatched two reporters' cameras and took out the films. An "official" asked the local police for assistance but the police refused to answer the call.

Case Analysis Method
CAM A or CAM B (see Chapter 1).

LEARNING DESIGN 6.2

CONTRIBUTING TO CLIENT DEVELOPMENT

Recognizing that sport administrators, in their supervision of clients, are concerned with organizational maintenance *and* client development, this learning design is particularly concerned with client development. Usually, here, the client is a student.

It is easy for a sport administrator to think his/her task is only to provide conditions for sport skill learning to take place or for sport contests to be played. Learning, in such circumstances, is mediated in the teacher-student relationship. But, as McIntosh (1974) and Gallagher (1973) pointed out, students learn from other aspects of their organizational experiences. For example, ". . . a student learns about social status and prestige when he or she notes that some members of a school staff have offices and others do not . . . and so on" (McIntosh, 1974).

At Dawson Community College in Montreal, Gallagher (1973) created an organizational environment for learning in which students could experience personal effectiveness and responsibility; conditions often lacking in students' institutional experiences. This, he regarded as part of his administrative responsibility and, thus, he rejected an often popular stance typified by Bereiter (1972:391), who, when writing about early childhood education, stated: ". . . Schools should drop their educational function in order to do a better job of child care and training. . . . Schools cannot cease to be places where intellectual growth and personality development go on, but they can cease to be places where an effort is made to direct or shape these processes. . . . [this] is to say that schools should narrow their teaching efforts to a simple concern with getting children to perform adequately in reading, writing, and arithmetic."

Having rejected the above approach, Gallagher (1973) committed himself to a fundamental stance in his approach to education. Briefly he subscribed to the following view which was presented by Kohlberg and Mayer (1972:493):

1. . . . the aims of education may be identified with development, both intellectual and moral.
2. . . . education so conceived supplies the conditions for passing through an order of connected stages.
3. . . . the understanding of logical and ethical principles is a central aim of education.

In this design the latter view is held; the overall development of the student is the concern of the sport administrator, and the student's general life in the sport organization is recognized to be influential in this development. Learning Design 2.2 is closely related with what follows and its concepts should be reviewed before reading further.

Developmental Theories

Kohlberg's Stages Of Moral Development
A re-reading of Learning Design 2.2 will have clarified the point that moral development is closely allied with intellectual development and both are suggested aims for sport administrators so far as their clients are concerned.

Kohlberg (1972) claimed that schools were not successful in teaching moral education because they went about it in the wrong way: teachers preached or used a system of rewards or punishments. Usually, the moralizing was about relatively trivial behaviors that were disruptive to others in the classroom. Kohlberg believed that moral education could be taught not by pre-determined teacher values being indoctrinated into the students but by stimulation of the child's moral judgment and character.

Based on research among many subjects in several different cultures, Kohlberg (1972:460), found that a person's development of moral judgment passed through three levels with each level having two stages. Everyone begins at "Stage 1," and the stages occur in order, but not everyone reaches "Stage 6."

Level 1 (Premoral)

Stage 1: Moral judgments are based on considerations of obedience and punishment. Physical consequences determine "good" or "bad" and people obey rules to avoid punishment.

Stage 2: "Naively egoistic orientation." "Right" action is that which satisfies the self's needs and occasionally others'. People conform to obtain rewards or have favors returned—typified by, "You scratch my back and I'll scratch yours."

Some sport is conducted at this "Level 1."

Level 2 (Conventional role conformity)

Stage 3: "Good-boy" (nice-girl) orientation." People behave in a way that will lead to others' approval by pleasing or helping them. At this stage people conform to stereotypical images the majority holds for them, and they maintain the expectations of the family, the group, or the nation regardless of the consequences. Consider the impact on a team member when the coach says, "Winning is not the main thing, it's the only thing"; and, "Nothing stokes the fires like a good dose of hatred."

Stage 4: "Authority and social-order-maintaining orientation." The person's orientation is towards authority, doing duty, fixed rules, and the maintenance of social order. The law is frozen.

Much sport is conducted at this "Level 2." For instance, the young hockey player being influenced by a frenzied crowd of whom few have passed beyond "Stage 4" and some are still at "Stage 1." Also, many "rules" and "laws" in sport can only go to this stage.

Level 3 (Self-accepted moral principles)

Stage 5: "Contractual legalistic orientation." People accept a starting point in rules or expectations for the sake of agreement. "Duty defined in terms of contract, general avoidance of violation of the will or rights of others, and the majority will and welfare." Thus, there is an effort to define moral values and principles that have validity apart from the authority group. People at this stage are willing to change laws after rational consideration.

This is the highest stage to which a sport governing body can go in attempting to regulate participants' conduct.

Stage 6: "Conscience or principle orientation. Orientation . . . to principles of choice involving appeal to logical universality and consistency . . . to conscience as a directing agent and to mutual respect and trust" (cf. Hodgkinson's Type I values in Learning Design 2.2). People are motivated to act in this fashion to conform and to avoid self-condemnation.

IMPLICATIONS FOR SPORT ADMINISTRATORS. McIntosh (1979) described what might happen by way of analogy with learning sport skills for precise, particular situations. For example, on meeting an unexpected obstacle, the skilled downhill ski racer takes immediate evasive action; the racer has made a "decision of principle" that was only possible because of prior training. Similarly, moral decisions of principle can be taught by skilled individuals. The skilled individuals must recognize at which of Kohlberg's stages their clients are; then, clients' moral development (and intellectual development) can be progressively trained. Just as the skier was trained. If the training is successful and the client reaches "Stage 6," right actions will follow.

The point, here, is that sport administrators do have a role to play in striving for right action (as previously explained in Learning Design 2.2). When trying to develop clients, they can do so by example and by trying to hire competent staff to conduct programs.

Intellectual Development

Reaching Kohlberg "Stage 6" ensures a good deal of intellectual development has taken place. There are, however, some other general aspects of client development of which sport administrators should be aware.

MASLOW'S THEORY. Consider, for example, Maslow's theory, which was outlined in Learning Design 5.2. Its validity was questioned but it has some merit which is applicable here. When considering clients, try to determine where they may be in Maslow's hierarchy. According to Maslow (1954), self-actualized people have a more than usually efficient perception of reality; they accept self and others; they are spontaneous; they lack ego-centeredness; they are autonomous; they derive inspiration and strength from ordinary experiences of life; they have frequent peak experiences; they feel for mankind by way of sympathy and identification; they form deep personal relationships; they are democratic and form relationships irrespective of class, education, race, and religion; they can differentiate between ends and means; they have a sense of humor; they are creative; and they are relatively detached from their culture so that they more readily discover their "growth needs" or "being values."

Thus, sport administrators must aim to provide a range of activities that are likely to bring about actualized states of being (cf. Arnold, 1979). This does not mean they must accept all Maslow's theory but, at least, strive to develop some of the qualities of self-actualized people in their clients.

ROGERS' VIEWS. Carl R. Rogers (1969) has recorded his opinions on student development that are relevant for consideration here. He begins with the question, "What sort of human being do we wish to grow?" Then he draws analogy with a psychotherapist (A) and his client (B).

1. (A) is extensively client centered.
2. (A) and (B) have an immensely personal relationship, and (A) has no barriers in sensing what it feels like to be the client.
3. (B) would have explored increasingly strange, unknown, and dangerous feelings within himself, possibly because of gradually realizing unconditional acceptance. Finally (B) discovers he/she has experienced himself/herself.

Then Rogers (1969) posed the question, "What personality characteristics would develop in a client as a result?" He concluded:

1. The client would be open to experience. Every stimulus would be freely relayed through the nervous system without distortion; he/she would be able to empathize; be able to communicate (hear and be heard); and, prize or accept or trust another's feelings, opinions, and person.
2. The client would live in an existential fashion, be adaptable, and creative.
3. The client finds his organism to be a trustworthy means of arriving at the most satisfying behavior in each existential situation. Thus, the client is independent, aware of his/her own values, and feels competent to cope with situations.

Implications For Sport Administrators

It has been demonstrated that sport administrators ought not to be solely concerned with teaching sport skills to their clients and with maintaining their organizations—they must also try to educate their clients. That is, develop their clients' intellects and moral values.

Much of what may be done by sport administrators with reference to moral issues was dealt with in Learning Design 2.2 and under the Kohlberg heading above. A further suggestion is that heed of Peter McIntosh (1979) ought to be taken. He points out that research has shown that uncontrolled competitive sport, without higher values, leads to antagonism, hostility, and violence between competing groups. It also leads to withdrawal from sport at young ages (cf. Orlick and Botterill, 1975).

McIntosh's (1979) wise contention is that the problem of controlling competition within a framework of moral education is easier if attention is paid to challenge rather than competition. With competitive success of secondary importance, the challenge for clients is in mastering skills within the sport's rules and spirit. By themselves, children play fairly; in adult-structured sport, they often play unfairly and/or eliminate themselves from competition. Thus, administrators ought to recognize these points and acknowledge that some clients want totally non-competitive recreation while a few clients desire highly competitive sport. Whichever it is, the administrator's policy should be for managers (coaches, officials, captains, players) to develop and enforce high moral standards.

Such standards contribute to client's intellectual development. Careful monitoring assists clients to "actualize" as Maslow advocated and to be as open to experience as Rogers recommended. This is not to say administrators should be "soft" or "wishy-washy" in supervising clients for, as Gordon McIntosh (1973) demonstrated, "It isn't easy being green" (cf. Reich, 1970).

References

Arnold, Peter J: Intellectualism, physical education, and self-actualization. *Quest, 31*:87-96, 1979.

Bereiter, C.: Schools without education. *Harvard Educational Review, XLII:* 391, 1972.

Gallagher, P.: Administration without hierarchy: The Dawson Approach. In McIntosh, R. Gordon and Bryce, Robert C. (Eds.): *School Administration for a Humanistic Era.* Edmonton, Alberta, Council on School Administration, The Alberta Teachers' Association, 1973.

Kohlberg, L.: Moral education in schools: A developmental view. In Purpel, D. E., and Belanger, M.: *Curriculum and the Cultural Revolution.* Berkeley, California, McCutchan, 1972.

Kohlberg, L., and Mayer, R.: Development as the aim of education. *Harvard Educational Review, XLII:*493, 1972.

McIntosh, P. *Fair Play: Ethics in Sport and Education.* London, Heinemann, 1979.

McIntosh, R. Gordon: "It Isn't Easy Being Green." Paper read before the South Peace Teachers' Convention, Grande Prairie, Alberta, March 1, 1973.

———: "Administrative Behavior and Student Development." Unpublished paper, Department of Educational Administration, University of Alberta, 1974.

Maslow, A. H.: *Motivation and Personality.* New York, Harper, 1954.

Orlick, T., and Botterill, C.: *Every Kid Can Win*, Chicago, Nelson, 1975.

Reich, Charles A.: *The Greening of America.* New York, Bantam, 1970.

Rogers, Carl R.: *Freedom to Learn.* Columbus, Ohio, Merrill, 1969.

Important Related Readings

Kohlberg, *Development*, 1972.

McIntosh, *Fair Play*, 1979, ch. 12-13.

Supplementary Readings

Allport, Gordon W.: *Becoming.* New Haven, Connecticut, Yale University Press, 1955.

Arnold, *Intellectualism*, 1979.

Fromm, E.: *Escape from Freedom.* New York, Farrar and Rinehart, 1941.

Gerber, Ellen W., and Morgan, William J. (Eds.): *Sport and the Body: A Philosophical Symposium*, 2nd ed. Philadelphia, Lea and Febiger, 1979.

Girdano, Dorothy D., and Girdano, Daniel A.: *Drugs: A Factual Account*, 2nd ed. Reading, Massachusetts, Addison-Wesley, 1976.

Kesey, K.: *One Flew Over the Cuckoo's Nest.* New York, Signet, 1962.

Pooley, John C.: *The Sport Fan: A Social-Psychology of Misbehavior.* CAHPER Sociology of Sport Monograph Series. Calgary, University of Calgary, 1979.

Reich, *America*, 1970.

Rogers, *Freedom*, 1969.

Schein, Edgar H.: *Organizational Psychology*, 2nd ed. Englewood Cliffs, New Jersey, Prentice-Hall, 1970.

Sergiovani, Thomas J., and Starratt, Robert J.: *Emerging Patterns of Supervision: Human Perspectives.* New York, McGraw-Hill, 1971.

Case 6.21

Advantage Ass

A very talented tennis player was noted for his court antics, which were particularly nasty at times. A few years ago he reached the semi-final of a major tournament and a capacity crowd turned out to watch. He lived up to his reputation to such an extent that the umpire finally disqualified him and awarded the match to his opponent. The crowd then began to jeer the umpire, and the tournament referee came onto the court; he spoke briefly to the umpire, who angrily left the arena. Shortly afterwards, another umpire took the chair and the match continued.

Case Analysis Method

CAM A or CAM B (see Chapter 1).

Case 6.22

Rule Britannia

At the 1978 Commonwealth Games in Edmonton, Alberta, the badminton team matches were very keenly contested. The officials and linespersons were well qualified for their responsibilities but they were unpaid volunteers. Many courts were used simultaneously and each match required eight linespeople, a service judge, and an umpire; thus, there were a very large number of such volunteers. The service judges were always well-qualified umpires, and there was always a capacity crowd.

One of England's best female players appeared to foul-serve in the eyes of several experienced observers. She was thought to be hitting the shuttle above her waist. The service judge, who happened to be a top female umpire in that match, called her for foul-serving three times. At that point, the English team official stormed to the tournament referee's table and demanded that the service judge be replaced with another; the referee carried out his request.

At the next interval, a meeting of all umpires and service judges was called; the discussion concerned withdrawing their services from the games, which still had one week to go.

Case Analysis Method

CAM B (see Chapter 1) on the assumption that you are the chief administrator of the entire games.

Case 6.23

Let The Punishment Fit The Crime*

John interacted and cooperated with his thirteen-year-old peers but Gordon was not so well adjusted and stood out as deviant and over-emotional. John was from a "stable middle class" family whereas Gordon was from an "unstable lower class" family. The two boys were enrolled in the summer sports adventure program at Pine Recreation Center and the group of sixty students were roller skating in the rink one wet afternoon. It was very easy to slip away unnoticed from the designated activity and the two lads left the instructional area and went on the balcony overlooking the center's main foyer. From there they began to spit over the balcony at passersby on the main level. One of the unfortunate recipients of this rather disgusting behavior was Bill Smith, the assistant manager of the recreation center, who gave chase after yelling at them. Bill caught them at the bottom of the back stairs.

It was then that I appeared on the scene to hear Bill giving my guilty students a severe reprimand. The two were sent back to the roller rink with another staff member and Bill Smith and myself moved into an office where a decision had to be made about disciplinary action. Several options were available to us:

1. Contact their parents and let them handle the punishment.
2. Not permit the boys back in the sports program.
3. Ban them from free "choice" activities.
4. Give them unpleasant chores to do in their own time.

Fortunately, I was aware of Gordon's home life and knew it would be very dangerous for us to contact his parents for his father would beat him. As for John, the problem could have been handled well by his parents, however, since the penalty had to be the same for both boys, it was concluded that the punishment

---

*The recreation instructor's tale.

would have to originate within the recreation center. We decided that both John and Gordon could reflect on their deed as they washed all the staff's cars over several lunch breaks.

Case Analysis Method
CAM A or CAM B (see Chapter 1).

Case 6.24

Pot Hunting*

It was a Friday night and the first day of the British Columbia Schools' Track and Field Championships was over. Both Chris and Mick failed to qualify for Saturday's finals and thus were finished for the weekend. Keith and I were still contenders for the 400 meters and 800 meters respectively, which were slated for Saturday afternoon.

We arrived back from the track to our motel rooms, and Keith decided to call up two guys he knew from Vancouver. About a half-hour later they came over and had brought some marijuana. They offered us some and we accepted despite the fact that we knew we were breaking the rules set down before the trip. Anyone caught offending in such a way was to be sent home on the first ferry in the morning. Ten minutes had gone by since Kevin's friend had come into our room when there was a knock on the door and in came Mr. Stu Gaunt, our Vancouver Island "zone representative" for the championships. I could now see myself going home on the ferry and kissing good-bye to any hope for a medal. Instead he just asked the two guys to leave and take their marijuana with them. He said he would leave all disciplinary matters up to our coach. Our coach was sleeping and never knew about the incident until the morning. She allowed us to compete but told us some action would be discussed later. As it turned out, Keith placed seventh and I was third.

On our way back on the ferry we discussed the incident with our coach. She felt she had to tell the principal about it or she would be neglecting her duties as a sponsor. She suggested we write three letters of apology. One was to be sent to Mr. Stu Gaunt

*As told by Dwayne.

because he was the Island Zone Representative; another to the principal of Elm Grove for letting down the school; and the third to our coach for putting her in an embarrassing position.

The awards day was coming up and all four of us were contenders for awards of excellence: Keith for track, myself for track and basketball, Mick and Chris for rugby. Chris was also slated to win the prestigious rugby trophy for the most outstanding player. As it turned out, because of our escapade in Vancouver, we did not receive any awards.

Case Analysis Method
    CAM A or CAM B (see Chapter 1).

Case 6.25

Priorities

Munsey Park is a junior secondary school, with a student population of approximately 600, located in the interior of British Columbia. It draws from a middle to high-class population and has a very active athletic department which works effectively with an extensive intramurals program. The head of the physical education department was Terry Wilson who had taught at Munsey Park for five years. He was leaving to assume a vice-principal's position in the Fraser Valley. He had been head of the P. E. department for three years and, because of the relative inexperience of the rest of the department, it was felt that an experienced teacher should be hired. Munsey Park, being located in the Okanagan Valley, received many applications for the position from well-qualified personnel. After extensive interviews and much deliberation, Bill Johnson was hired.

Bill Johnson had taught for seven years, the last two as head of a P. E. department in a large school in the lower mainland. As well as having excellent qualifications, he was a well-known basketball coach, a position he would fill when he replaced Terry Wilson.

In the physical education department there were four other teachers, two males and two females, and each was actively involved in both the extramural and intramural programs. Munsey Park had a small gymnasium that contained one basketball court and two volleyball courts running across the basketball court. The intramural program ran four days a week: two for females and two for males. Intramural sports included soccer, field hockey, volleyball, and basketball. In the spring, an afternoon was devoted to an intramural track meet. All indoor intramural competition was run at noon hour with exclusive use of the gymnasium.

Practices for the athletic teams were held after school, and the school was locked when practices ended at 7:00 P.M. During the basketball season there were six basketball teams and a large badminton club who used the gymnasium. As a result, the basketball team practiced twice a week for an hour-and-a-half each session. Because of a lack of funds to pay overtime, the custodians would not allow practices to be held in the morning.

The year before Bill Johnson arrived the senior basketball team had done fairly poorly, having the nucleus of the team consisting mainly of grade nines. However, the following year saw these students in grade ten, and, as well, there was the addition of two new players who had moved to town. Johnson knew of these players (who were brothers) from the lower mainland and knew he had the basis for a very strong team. He looked forward to coaching them with much enthusiasm.

The intramural and extramural programs ran much like the preceding years until the start of the basketball season. At that time Johnson was unhappy with the fact that he could only practice twice a week. He approached the principal with his complaint and asked if the gymnasium could be opened in the mornings before school for practices. After a day's thought and a few phone calls, the principal informed him that he would have to abide by the restriction and outlined why. Johnson then took it upon himself to approach the custodians and was flatly refused by the head custodian, with whom he got into a heated argument. As a result, a complaint was filed by the custodians with the principal.

The same day the issue was brought up in a staff meeting by a very forceful Johnson. It had also come to the principal's attention, by way of one of Johnson's fellow P. E. teachers, that Johnson had reduced intramural programs to get more practice time for the basketball team.

Case Analysis Method
CAM D (see Chapter 1).

Case 6.26

Flunk Flunks*

Somehow, Dave Knome had reached fifth-year status at State University's School of Physical Education and Recreation. It was his intention to become a teacher of physical education. Now he was in my final (I was to retire in June) professional year class and I would have to decide whether or not to pass him.

From previous brief contacts with him and from colleague's reports, I knew he was lazy, sloppy, unreliable, inattentive (often absent), and incompetent. So I wondered: how had he got into fifth year? I thought about illiterate scholarship athletes who obtained passing grades so long as they had eligibility, but he was not one of them. I reflected on my own training nearly forty years earlier: then our instructors gave it to us straight and "C" was the most common grade; "A's" were very rare.

What had happened? Well, socio-psychological ideas and pluralistic educationists who had spent very little time in classrooms had hoodwinked the rest of us into believing all their hogwash. Thus we had opened doors to everyone, passed ignorance, accepted plain stupidity, been influenced by teary-eyed low grade getters, and accepted all kinds of sentimental excuses from shaky students. All this had led us to mediocrity and worse. We had to do it to fill the oversupply of universities. The many good students thought faculty members were weak for much of what these flunks were allowed to get away with and they then competed with good students for scarce jobs, sometimes successfully.

Yes, I was partly guilty but not so much as some of my colleagues. So, I decided to watch Knome carefully during his fifth year. By March he had failed to hand in two assignments, had missed four peer teaching sessions, and always had Billy Liar-type excuses. Finally, he was absent for three weeks, without a word, before showing up again on crutches (but no plaster). He

---

*The elder's tale.

said he was keen to complete his final teaching practicum in April and May.

I'd had enough and decided that, at least, I would end my own career with a semblance of professional self-respect. I called Knome into my office and told him he was finished, I would not allow him out on the practicum and that would prevent him from receiving certification to teach.

Case Analysis Method
CAM A (see Chapter 1).

Summary

1. Clients are those people who receive services in sport organizations (e.g. students, athletes, park visitors, and spectators).
2. Supervision of clients should contribute to their development and aim to maintain organizational effectiveness.
3. Some aspects of client supervision are dealt with elsewhere in the book.
4. The client-related phenomena of which sport administrators must be aware, if they are to maintain organizational effectiveness, are listed in Table IV.
5. An organized system for pastoral care of students, in otherwise impersonal sport organizations, helps to alleviate problems.
6. An aim in supervision of clients is to contribute to their intellectual and moral development. Learning Design 2.2 should be reviewed and linked with Kohlberg's six stages of moral development which are:
   (i) Obedience and punishment orientation.
   (ii) Naively egoistic orientation.
   (iii) Good-boy, nice-girl orientation.
   (iv) Authority and social-order-maintaining orientation.
   (v) Contractual legalistic orientation.
   (vi) Conscience or principle orientation.
7. Everyone begins at the first stage, and the stages occur in order, but not everyone reaches the sixth stage. Administrators, through managers, should train clients to develop towards "Stage 6."

8. To develop Maslow-like actualization qualities in clients is desirable.
9. A Rogers-like supervisor-client relationship can be of benefit to clients and organizations but it should not be too "soft" on clients, otherwise they will not be objectively developed.
10. Remember that it is not only elite clients who are to be developed, though they are to be developed as well.

Concepts For Review

Clients	Purposes of supervision
Organizational maintenance phenomena	Pastoral care
	Self-actualization
Client development	Learning Design 2.2
Kohlberg's stages of moral development	McIntosh's "challenge"
Carl R. Rogers' views	

Questions For Oral Or Written Discussion

1. CAM C (see Chapter 1) applied to instructor-specified topics taken from this chapter.
2. List other example persistent problems that would be appropriate for inclusion in Table IV and, briefly, suggest solutions to them.
3. Discuss Kohlberg's stages of moral development in light of your own experience.
4. Discuss McIntosh's "challenge" with reference to a large high school physical education and athletics department of which you are the head.
5. Assume you are dean of an all-inclusive sport faculty in a large university and describe in detail the procedures you would adopt for the pastoral care of your students.
6. With reference to Case 6.11 (Tragic Trio: Part I), what information would you want (and how would you record it) on any student who was going to use the physical recreational facilities.
7. Discuss the views of Carl R. Rogers that are presented in this chapter in light of your experience in sport situations.
8. Would it be possible for a "self-actualized" person to compete in the 1980 Olympics and, if so, describe what you think such a person would be like?

Chapter 7

DYNAMIC LAW

T HE CONCEPTS OF this chapter are initially described with particular reference to school gymnastics. Gymnastics is the example sport because of its often perceived high risks and the need for stringent standards of supervision. The supervision principles are the same in other sport situation; thus, these are useful general guidelines for sport administrators to follow. The cases presented for analysis enable students to test their knowledge of principles in real situations and the suggested supplementary readings provide substantial additional information on this complex field of study.

Part of Learning Design 7.0 is adapted from my chapter in Gerry Carr's *Safety In Gymnastics* (Vancouver and Seattle, Hancock House, 1980) and is used here with the permission of the publishers. The referencing style is not the same as that generally used in this book but conforms to that found in legal publications.

LEARNING DESIGN 7.0

LEGAL STANDARDS OF CARE[1]

The assurance that is given in this design is consistent with the theme that gymnastics, from a teacher's legal responsibility viewpoint, is very worthy of inclusion in school physical educational programs so long as certain basic precautions are taken. Here, then, the legal terminology that has applicability to gymnastics teaching is described, and a course of action for teachers to follow is suggested. If these procedures are followed, there is *no* need to fear any hostile legal actions being successful.

One of the problems in trying to generalize about how the law will be applied is that the law is dynamic. As Betty van der Smissen has said, with respect to the interpretation of laws in the different United States of America, ". . . it is impossible to give a statement of status that will remain correct even one year."[2] Thus, when trying to present guidelines that also apply in Canada, and in other countries whose laws have older common law English origin, the task is even more complex. With this in mind, the attempt is to describe principles that are presently applicable that will, if followed, permit teachers to present the fine sport of gymnastics to their students without fear of successful lawsuits.

Legal Terminology And Processes

Torts

A tort is a civil injury or wrong. As Heuston stated: "A civil wrong is one which gives rise to civil proceedings—proceedings, that is to say, which have as their purpose the enforcement of some right claimed by the plaintiff as against the defendant."[3] The wrongdoer may be compelled, in a civil action, to make compensation or restitution to the injured person.[4] But, as Heuston explained further: "Although a tort is a civil injury, not all civil injuries are torts, for no civil injury is to be classed as a tort unless the appropriate remedy for it is an action for damages."[5]

Negligence

For what, then, may a teacher of gymnastics be held liable in the courts? Heuston guides us further: "The wilful wrongdoer is he who desires to do harm; the negligent wrongdoer is he who does not sufficiently desire to avoid doing it."[6] So, negligence is that part of tort law that attempts to define for which careless acts, whether in omission (not doing something that should be done) or commission (doing something that should not be done), a person will be held responsible.[7] What must be shown is that the defendant had a duty to make sure that the act complained of did not happen and that he should have forseen that the undesirable consequences would follow as a result.[8] In legal terms the plaintiff must show:

(a) that the defendant had towards him a duty of care;

(b) that the defendant's act or omission to act constituted a breach of that duty;

(c) that the defendant should have foreseen that his act or omission would damage the plaintiff.[9]

The plaintiff must plead and prove on a balance of probabilities, all of these three elements in a cause of action in negligence in order to obtain a judgment against the defendant.[10]

DUTY OF CARE. In countries having the common law, liability in negligence requires a finding that the defendant owed a duty of care to the plaintiff. (Originally, this concept stemmed from the principle that "we owe a duty of care to our neighbour."[11]) This duty will almost invariably be based upon some relationship between the plaintiff and the defendant (e.g. the relationship of driver and pedestrian will raise a duty of care). While in some areas of human activity, the common law has been slow to find a relationship between the plaintiff and the defendant (e.g. the relationship of driver and pedestrian will raise a duty of care). While in some areas of human activity, the common law has been slow to find a relationship that gives rise to a duty owing to the plaintiff. In most factual situations that involve a teacher of gymnastics it is reasonably clear that the teacher will owe to the student a duty of care. Therefore, for the purpose of the present discussion, it will be assumed that the student would have little difficulty establishing that the teacher owed a duty of care to the student.

BREACH OF THE STANDARD OF CARE. The plaintiff must also show that the defendant breached the relevant standard of care before liability will be found. In other words, the defendant is held liable, or legally at fault, only in those situations where he failed to do what the hypothetical "reasonable person" would have done in the same situation. The primary issue in many negligence cases is whether the defendant's conduct met the standard of the "reasonable person." If the defendant failed to do something that the "reasonable person" would have done, or if he did something that the "reasonable person" would not have done, then the defendant has breached the standard of care and the plaintiff has established this element.

While the "reasonable person" guideline is the primary test in most areas of human activity, if the defendant either has special knowledge or special skills, or ought to have, or holds himself out as having special knowledge or skills, he will be judged by the hypothetical expert having such knowledge or skills. For example, a medical doctor will be judged by whether his act or omission was what the hypothetical medical practitioner would have done in similar circumstances.

From the above discussion it is relatively clear that the standard of care required by the law varies both according to the circumstances and according to the type of the defendant. In regard to teachers, the courts have frequently stated that the standard is to act as the "careful parent of a large family."[12] However, in the same case, the judge also suggested that a teacher may be required to meet a higher standard to that of a professional physical education teacher: ". . . the practice of a profession, art or calling, which, from its nature, demands some special skill, ability, or experience carries with it a duty to exercise, to a reasonable extent, the amount of skill, ability and experience which it demands."[13] Furthermore: "A person who provides anything for the use of another is bound to provide a thing reasonably safe for the purpose for which it is intended, even though the person using it uses it only by the permission or consent of the person providing it and has no legal claim to the use of it."[14]

It is with reference to the experience of a professional that guides us on what to interpret is meant by foresight. The law refers to "reasonable foresight . . . to keep in touch with the needs of ordinary men."[15] However, the disadvantage of this stance is that it makes an appropriate standard of forseeability difficult to set.[16] Heuston explains this point by citing the case of the steamship *Wagon Mound*, which carelessly discharged oil into Sydney harbour. The oil later caught fire and damaged the wharf and other ships. The defendants claimed they could not have expected the wind and tide to take the oil under a wharf from which some molten metal would fall and start the fire. On appeal, the judgment was that "the defendants ought reasonably to have foreseen damage by fire against which precautions should have been taken;" so they were liable in negligence.[17]

In many of the school cases, the courts have noticed these two possibly different standards of care, and, without clearly deciding which one applies, have concluded that on either of the two standards the teacher was, or was not, acting in accordance with the relevant standard. Perhaps the trend is toward using the "hypothetical trained teacher" standard rather than the "hypothetical careful parent."

For the purposes of this discussion it will be assumed that the relevant standard of care in regard to a teacher of gymnastics will be that of a trained professional teacher. Although the courts may not impose this test, it is better to calculate the reasonability of actions against this standard because, if the act or omission is in accord with the act or omission of a trained professional gymnastic teacher, there will be no liability on either standard. Put shortly, if the teacher's act is something that the hypothetical professionally trained teacher would not have done, then the plaintiff has satisfied this element. If the teacher's omission is something that the objective professional teacher would not have omitted, again this element is established. The touchstone then is: what would this hypothetical and objective professional teacher do under the circumstances? So long as the teacher's conduct matches this standard, there is no liability in negligence.

DAMAGES AND PROXIMATE CAUSE. Even though the defendant may owe a duty to the plaintiff, and even though the defendant may have breached the relevant standard of care, there is no liability in negligence unless that breach caused damage or injury to the plaintiff. Frequently it is said that the breach must have been the proximate cause of the plaintiff's injury or loss. The term *promixity* is often used in this context and, if not understood, it may be misleading. For example, geographical proximity is not itself enough to establish liability. On the other hand, lack of proximity in time or space will not prevent the establishment of liability; for example: ". . . the manufacturer of poisonous tinned food is liable although his product has been shipped to the other side of the world and consumed months later."[18] Thus, what is meant by the term is: ". . . a convenient description of the state of affairs which exists when the relationship between the parties is such that there is a real likelihood of harm to some legally protected interest against which precaution should be taken."[19]

Some events that occurred in gymnastics settings and led to negligence suits will now be described; the legal outcomes will be stated and the reasons for them linked with what has been written above. Thus, what has been written above is a set of general legal principles against which teachers of gymnastics can set standards for themselves. What immediately follows are descriptions of how the law has dealt with some major gymnastics cases.

Resolved Cases

One case will be given a more comprehensive discussion than the remainder; the reason being that it highlights all of the elements that need to be the particular concerns of gymnastics teachers.

Thornton et al. v. Board of School Trustes et al.[20]

THE GYMNASIUM INCIDENT. On April 6, 1971, Gary Thornton (aged 15) and his Prince George, British Columbia classmates were offered three choices of activity in the physical education class by the instructor, Mr. Edamura: floor hockey, gymnastics, or weightlifting. The physical education teaching space consisted of a multipurpose large floor area and a stage at one end. Floor hockey was played in the larger space; weightlifting took place in a corner of the stage; and Gary Thornton, with six other boys, chose to do gymnastics on the major part of the stage. Mr. Edamura sat at his desk on the front left-hand side of the stage and occupied himself filling out student report cards. By looking ahead, he could see the floor hockey players but his back was towards the other students and he had to look over his right shoulder to see the gymnasts and weightlifters. The gymnasts:

> . . . positioned the springboard so that its "high" or spring end was facing toward the end of the stage where Edamura was seated. The leading edge of the spring, or "high" end, was at or near the middle of the stage in its length and breadth. Starting a short distance in front of the spring, or "high" end of the board, and extending forward from it they placed the wrestling mat. On top of the wrestling mat they placed the two bundles of foam chunks end to end. In the result, the end of the foam chunks furthest from the board was almost behind Edamura as he sat at his desk. Upon arranging this "configuration," as it was referred to, the young gymnasts commenced to run from the far end of the stage

onto the springboard and onto the foam chunks. They were trying to somersault into the foam chunks.[21]

Not being particularly good at gymnastics, or successful, the boys:

> . . . concluded that they did not have an adequate distance to run in order to obtain a spring that would elevate them high enough to complete the somersault. They then hit upon an idea to remedy the problem. They placed a box horse at the low end of the board so that they could jump from it down onto the high end, catapult upwards, do the somersault and come down onto the foam chunks. Edamura agreed to their request to use the box horse for that purpose and returned to his report cards.

Shortly afterwards, Larry Karlson attempted a double somersault and landed off balance: "He went over to Edamura complaining of pain in his arm, that he was winded, and that he had hurt his wrist on the floor. Edamura did not ask him what kind of stunt he had attempted to perform—he merely examined the wrist carefully, did not observe any gross swelling and suggested to the boy that he put it under cold water.

The boys and he then placed what are called "Add-a-Mats®" around the perimeter of the foam chunks."[23]

Despite the mishap, Mr. Edamura gave no warning to the boys and nor was the "configuration" tested for safety. Mr. Edamura returned to his desk.[24] Shortly afterwards, Gary Thornton attempted a somersault and landed head-first on the "Add-a-Mats." As a result, he suffered a severe spinal injury that will leave him a quadriplegic for the remainder of his life. His family sued the teacher, his principal, and the school board.

MR. JUSTICE ANDREWS' REASONS FOR JUDGMENT. The judge first carefully described Gary's previous gymnastics experience in Calgary and stated: ". . . as a gymnast . . . he had not progressed beyond the most elementary basic training, and there is no evidence from the defendant Edamura that he was aware of the extent of Gary's training, the degree of proficiency he had reached, nor the quality of the training he had received."[26]

The evidence at the trial indicated that Gary had not received any systematic gymnastic training whilst a member of Edamura's physical education class in the earlier part of the school year. The judge then discussed the "configuration" of the equipment and pointed out that expert witnesses of the plaintiff, and the defendant, agreed that it was an "unusual configuration." Further, that "All the witnesses, including Edamura ... had never used that configuration before." After describing that use of the springboard as "unpredictable," the judge turned his attention to the landing area and said, "I agree with those witnesses who say that the foam chunks as described are quite inadequate to that object. . . . This form of crash pad is intended to be landed on horizontally either on one's back or front."[27]

The judge's next concern was with "spotters"; his comments are important:

> . . . the evidence I accept convinced me that any gymnastic exercise should not be attempted by amateurs without the assistance of what are called "spotters." The placing of spotters is problematic given this configuration. As I understand the evidence, the object of spotting is not to catch the gymnast, but rather to assist him in completing his manoeuvre. . . . With this configuration the only conclusion I can draw is that considering the unpredictable trajectory of the gymnast a spotter would have been little or no use to him.[28]

With reference to the original apparatus of springboard and chunks the judge said he was satisfied that was not dangerous. However: ". . . when the "box horse" was added a whole new dimension was involved. I think it is important to remember that those boys had never before used this equipment in this fashion. They were not highly trained and had not done any gymnastics for approximately three months. . . . In my opinion, the "configuration" should have been recognized by any reasonable physical education instructor as one fraught with danger."[29]

Turning his attention to Karlson's injured wrist which had, in fact, been broken, the judge expressed puzzlement at Mr. Edamura's admission that he did not ask the boy what stunt he had attempted. Previous training did not qualify boys to attempt double somersaults, and Mr. Edamura must have recognized some risks when he added the "Add-a-Mats." In the event the judge said, "I accept that the reasonable practice is to stop the exercises when someone is injured until it is determined how and why."[30]

Considering the circumstances and Edamura's duty as a physical education instructor, the judge stated: "He must be taken to have knowledge that the equipment provided or allowed to be used is supposed to be reasonably safe for the purpose which it is intended"[31] (cf. Note 14 above when the judge was citing *Shrimpton* v. *Hertfordshire C.C.* [1911] 104 L.T. 145). He went on to describe what is expected of a physical education teacher with regard to his training, skills, and knowledge (cf. Note 13 above when the judge was citing 28 *Halsbury* 3rd ed. p. 19). What standard of care, then, was required in these particular circumstances? The judge continued: "The whole of the evidence leads me to find that these boys, possessing such limited expertise in gymnastics, had undoubtedly not progressed to the point where they could be trusted to somersault from this unpredictable, dangerous, configuration. I do not suggest that each piece of equipment was per se dangerous; I am concerned with the configuration. I think that Edamura should have taken care to instruct these boys on the use of the configuration. They had never used it before. He should have given them some advice, some instruction, a word of caution, and, at least imposed some limits on what they could or could not do in the circumstances. His attention to them was, in my opinion, casual."[32]

Quite apart from the breach just described, the judge then commented on Mr. Edamura's least duty to act as the "careful parent of a large family" (cf. Note 12 above when the judge was citing *Williams* v. *Eady* (1893) 10 T. 6 R. 41). Why, when Karlson hurt his wrist did Edamura not stop the action to find out why, and so possibly prevent another boy being injured? The judge thought a prudent parent would have done so. After commenting on precedents of "forseeability" the judge concluded:

> Edamura's duty as a physical education instructor was to recognize the "configuration" in this circumstance as an inherently dangerous one. He was in breach of that duty when he permitted these youngsters to use it to perform manoeuvers when he knew, or ought to have known, there was considerable danger for novices somersaulting on that configuration. In any event it seems to me Edamura failed in what might be described as a lesser duty of a careful parent not to forsee the risks of further injury once he learned of the injury to Karlson. He accordingly is liable.[33]

MR. JUSTICE ANDREWS' HOLDINGS CONCERNING THE LIABILITY OF THE SCHOOL AND THE PRINCIPAL. Since Mr. Edamura was at all relevant times a "servant or agent of the Board of School Trustees," the relationship of "master and servant existed between the board and the teacher."[34] The activity in question was part of "the physical training of the pupil and therefore within the scope of employment of the teacher." Thus, the judge ruled: "There can be no doubt that if the defendant Edamura is liable then the co-defendant Board of School Trustees is also liable."[35]

WAS THE PLAINTIFF, GARY THORNTON, CONTRIBUTORILY NEGLIGENT? Citing *Phipson on Evidence* (11th ed., para. 103), the judge explained that when a defendant pleads the provisions of the Contributory Negligence Act, the onus of proof "is upon him to establish a prima facie case that the plaintiff was also at fault to some degree." The defendants claimed that Thornton attempted an exercise he knew, or ought to have known, he could not do; he failed to get advice or assistance, and he failed to appreciate the "configuration." In judgment, Mr. Andrews said the defendants had failed to establish a prima facie case and that Thornton was only attempting a single somersault, which "should have been well within his competence." The student should not be taken "to possess the same familiarity and knowledge of the equipment as his instructors." So, the judge concluded that the defendants had failed to establish contributory negligence.[37]

ASSESSMENT OF DAMAGES. This is a complex process and will not be detailed here; instead the judge's interpretation of the situation and his reasons for the award will be given. Generally, the judge regarded Gary Thornton, as a result of his gymnastics injury, to be "in essence, just a living head attached to a metabolic machine that provides nutrition for his head."[38] He felt that, so long as Gary received optimal care, he had "a good chance of living a normal life expectancy." The judge's underlying principle in assessing the amount of damages, was "that the plaintiff should be put back into the position both in terms of finances and health that he would have been had he not been injured (as a result of a wrongdoer's negligence.) Whilst not wishing to "soak the wrongdoer," the judge stated: "I have endeavoured to use the wrongdoer's money to provide Gary with the dignity, comfort and length of life to which we all in this society feel so rightly entitled. The principles have not changed and that is fortunate for they make good sense. It is the medical evidence that has changed and warrants the large award assessed in this case in the amount of $1,534,058.93" (Vancouver, British Columbia, January 23, 1975).[39]

In making this final conclusion, it is worthy of note here that the judge said, "I have read and re-read all the Canadian, English, and American authorities referred to me by counsel in argument."[40] Earlier, with reference to assessment, he had been "most notably" influenced by *Bisson* v. *Powell River* (1968) (62 W.W.R. 707) and "the method used by the plaintiff therein."

The Thornton case was appealed to the British Columbia Court of Appeal (July 22, 1976) where the court ruled: "Appeal (of the defendants) as to liability and contributory negligence dismissed; appeal as to damages allowed in part; cross appeal as to damages allowed in part."[41]

Importantly, this means that Mr. Justice Andrews' opinions regarding negligence and liability were upheld but his assessed amount of damages were reduced to $649,628.87.[42]

Later still the case was taken to the Supreme Court of Canada, where the appellants (Thornton et al.) had leave to appeal "on the broad issue as to whether or not the court of appeal erred in law as to the assessment of damages." It was held: "The appeal should be allowed. The assessment of damages was set aside and an award to the appellant of $859,628 was substituted."[43]

FURTHER DISCUSSION. As Robbins pointed out: *"Barring statutory or contractual limits* there is nothing to prevent (1) the injured party from ignoring his claim against the board and seeking relief solely from the teacher, (2) the board from suing the teacher for the damages paid by the board to the injured party, or (3) the board's insurance company from suing the teacher for the damages paid."[44] Fortunately for teachers there usually are statutory or contractual limits that prevent this happening, but Robbins' advice as to how teachers can reduce their potential liability is worth noting: ". . . (1) by negotiating a contract with their board which holds them harmless in the event they are negligent in the course of their employment, (2) by obtaining statutory protection, (3) by convincing their board to carry adequate insurance which holds the teacher harmless in the event of a claim, and (4) by carrying professional liability insurance."[45]

Robbins discussed a number of related issues including the possibility of contributory negligence on the part of students and, also, the legal status of trustees. However, what he said about the principal in the Thornton case is worthy of further attention here. First he pointed out that "if you're going to sue, sue everybody remotely connected with the accident." Thus, the principal was a defendant and principals are responsible, according to most school acts, for "organization, administration, and supervision." So if a principal could be shown that he did not exercise his duties under law to a reasonable extent then he "might also be held negligent and consequently also liable for damages."[46] In the Thornton case, the judge ruled that no evidence causally linked the principal with the accident and so the action against him was dismissed.

An insurance coverage comment is also of interest. When the first damages of $1.5 million were assessed, the School Board only had insurance to cover $1 million; that being the amount required of School Boards by the British Columbia School Act. Subsequently, that minimum statutorily required was increased to $2 million and at least one board took out coverage for $5 million.

The dynamic nature of the law has been referred to earlier as making it very difficult to set absolutely definite guidelines. The teachers in the United States should investigate carefully how the doctrine of "governmental immunity" is being applied in their state. Basically, governmental immunity was designed to absolve the public purse of extra financial burden that it would have if it had to pay for governments' negligent acts on the grounds that it was only trying to do what was in the public interest (e.g. teaching gymnastics). Van der Smissen pointed out: "It appears that the trend is toward the effect of governmental immunity being tempered by permission to carry insurance and allowing the injured party to recover up to the amount of the insurance coverage. This is a definite inroad on the doctrine of governmental immunity."[47] Van der Smissen outlined the current (but changing) interpretation for each state in her 1975 Supplement.[48]

Some Other Gymnastics Cases

In her 1968 book, van der Smissen listed six cases involving horizontal bar, high bar, or chinning bar; five concerned with the horse springboard, and a ramp; three tumbling; three ladders and two jungle gym monkey bars; and one each head stand, trapeze, and beam.[49] A selection of these are very briefly reviewed.

BARS. "All cases alleged inadequate supervision and in all instances no recovery was held as the supervision was found adequate."[50]

HORSE. A fourteen-year-old boy broke his arm when vaulting but he had been instructed, a demonstration had been given, and the performance was supervised. In such situations the student then assumes the risk and so the instructor was found to be competent.[51]

SPRINGBOARD. The Superior Court of New Jersey awarded $1,180,000 to a boy injured after catching his foot in a defective springboard while the instructor was out of the room.[52]

TUMBLING. In an after-school tumbling class a ten-year-old boy broke his leg when the instructor tossed him in the air as he improperly executed a "flip." The instructor was found not negligent and there was no recovery.[53]

TRAMPOLINE. By the time of van der Smissen's 1968 book, no case had reached a state supreme court.[54] Later, a "skilled" eighteen-year-old boy attempted a double somersault, with one spotter and the instructor thirty to forty feet away. He fell to the floor, landing on his head and shoulders, and sustained serious permanent injury. The court held that a proficient performer "must exercise the same judgment in care for his own safety as a person of more advanced years when on a trampoline." The instructor was found not negligent.[55] Teachers now, however, should read carefully the AAHPER "Position Statement on Trampolines" (*JOPER*, October, 1978, 14.), the reason being that it may well become a recognized "professional" standard.

Professional Standard Of Care

Risk

In most human activity there is a risk; a person who spends most of his time sitting at home runs the risk of death from a heart attack because of his lack of exercise. The point is that the law knows this about risk and recognizes that no activity can be 100 percent free from danger. It is acknowledged, then, that there is a risk in gymnastics. What the law looks for was summarized by the British Columbia's Court of Appeal judge when considering the Thornton case:

> ... it is not negligence or breach of the duty of care ... to permit a pupil to undertake to perform an aerial front somersault off a springboard: (a) if it is suitable to his age and condition (mental and physical); (b) if he is progressively trained and coached to do it properly and avoid the danger; (c) if the equipment is adequate and suitably arranged; and (d) if the performance, having regard to its inherently dangerous nature, is properly supervised. These are the component criteria constituting the appropriate duty or standard of care . . .[56]

Supervision

From what is immediately above, it is clear what is required of gymnastics instructors as far as the law is concerned. Here, then, a little more specific guidance is presented. Van der Smissen has very usefully distinguished between "general" and "specific" supervision.[57]

GENERAL SUPERVISION. The instructor must be "immediately accessible to anyone who needs him" and should have a "plan of supervision."[58] He must also be "alert to conditions" that may be dangerous to gymnasts.[59] The law accepts that a teacher cannot be in all places but his lesson plan should include appropriate positioning of himself so that he can see all his students most of the time. Thus, if he is giving individual attention to a student doing head stands in one corner of the gymnasium, he should not face the corner. He should have his back to the corner, give individual aid to the head stander, but also be able to see everyone else. In that way, he can congratulate a performer in a distant corner or yell "stop" if danger is seen anywhere. Thus, his plan of general supervision becomes known to his students by his actions and appearance of seeing everything. His movements should be mainly around the perimeter of his class and he should never be "lost" in the middle of a group because there would be a number of students he could not see to supervise.

The final aspect of general supervision concerns first aid and emergency care.[60] The gymnastics teacher should be knowledgeable in first aid, particularly with regard to the types of accidents likely to happen in the gymnasium. Thus, it is a professional responsibility to be so prepared. Similarly, there must be an emergency procedure in the school that will always be operational when needed. Such policies should be established and enforced by sport administrators.

SPECIFIC SUPERVISION. Van der Smissen identified this type of supervision by stating: ". . . when introducing an activity you must stay with the participant until he is familiar enough with the activity to evaluate his own capacity to do the activity and to understand and adhere to safety practices and procedures which have been established, and . . . when an activity is going on under your general supervision and you note any failure to adhere to rules and regulations . . . then you must change . . . to specific supervision."[61] Here, then, van der Smissen is also saying that a teacher must make his students appreciate the risks they are taking (cf. the trampoline example above). This is best done by ensuring that all stunts are preceded by appropriate progressive training; also, that this is appropriate for the age and condition (mental and physical) of the student.

ADMINISTRATIVE SUPERVISION. Administrators should enforce all types of supervision outlined above and apply, also, the following:

1. Only hire qualified instructors.
2. Arrange in-service training, on a regular basis, to be sure staff know first aid[62] procedures and the most safe teaching methods (which would include spotting techniques).
3. Ensure that complete accident report forms are completed and regularly analyse them. Such may identify weaknesses and enable possible future accidents to be prevented.
4. Regularly inspect equipment and facilities so as to identify possible hazards. Arrange ongoing, regular preventive maintenance.
5. Check the particular local insurance situation and consult a good lawyer when in doubt.

As van der Smissen pointed out, such an "aura of caring" makes students and parents feel that the school "cares" and so creates a good public relations image. She felt it was "irritated" people who were likely to sue.[63]

Conclusion

It has been demonstrated that gymnastics teachers and administrators can only be sued for damages and held liable if they are negligent. Also, that such teachers have a duty of care that is of a specific standard. So long as: the gymnastic activity is suitable for the age and condition of the student; the student has been progressively trained; the equipment is safe and suitably arranged; and the activity is properly supervised; then, the teacher will not breach his duty and cannot be found negligent in law. The same is true in other similar sport situations.

This is clear and it is not frightening to a professional teacher or administrator. It does mean that teachers and administrators will probably have to become very alert to these factors. Good teachers and administrators are alert and will want to continue teaching fine sports. As Betty van der Smissen has said, "Be a positive professional person."

Notes and References

1. Professor Terence J. Wuester, B.A. (Bethany Nazarene Coll.), M.A. (Missouri), J.D. (Kansas), LL.M. (Yale), of the Bars of Saskatchewan and Kansas, advised on the content of this design for accuracy and legal interpretations. His assistance is gratefully acknowledged as a University of Victoria Faculty of Law colleague who is always very willing to share his experience with others. Any inaccuracies which remain are my responsibility. Subsequent notes and references are included to substantiate the material in the text but are not essential reading for those readers who simply want basic guidance.

2. Van der Smissen, Betty: *Legal Liability of Cities and Schools for Injuries in Recreation and Parks: Including those in Operation of Physical Education and Athletic Programs.* Cincinnati, Anderson Publishing Co., 1968 with 1975 Supplement, p. 259. This is an authoritative book which is constantly updated by "Supplements" as new cases are resolved. It is possible to be notified of new supplements as soon as they are published by asking for this service from The W. H. Anderson Company, 646 Main Street, Cincinnati, Ohio, 45201. Dr. Van der Smissen is Professor of Recreation at the Pennsylvania State University and of the Kansas Bar.

3. Heuston, R.F.V. (ed.): *Salmond on the Law of Torts.* 15th ed. London, Sweet and Maxwell, 1969, p. 10.

4. *Ibid.*

5. *Ibid.*

6. *Ibid.*, p. 249.

7. Lennon, C. B.: *Torts.* Vancouver, International Self-Council Press, 1974, p. 29.

8. *Ibid.*

9. *Ibid.*

10. *Ibid.*, pp. xiii-xiv.
11. Heuston, *op. cit.*, pp. 254-255.
12. British Columbia Supreme Court, *Thornton, Tanner, et al. v. Board of School Trustees of School District No. 57 (Prince George)*, Edamura and Harrower, [1975] 3 Western Weekly Reports 623, at p. 633.
13. *Ibid.*, p. 632.
14. *Ibid.*
15. Heuston, *op. cit.*, p. 285.
16. *Ibid.*
17. *Ibid.*, p. 286.
18. *Ibid.*, p. 260.
19. *Ibid.*
20. British Columbia Supreme Court, *op. cit.*
21. *Ibid.*, p. 625.
22. *Ibid.*
23. *Ibid.*, p. 627.
24. *Ibid.*, p. 629.
25. *Ibid.*, pp. 622 *et seqq.*
26. *Ibid.*, p. 623.
27. *Ibid.*, p. 626.
28. *Ibid.*, p. 626-627.
29. *Ibid.*, p. 628-629.
30. *Ibid.*, p. 633.
31. *Ibid.*, p. 632.
32. *Ibid.*, p. 633.
33. *Ibid.*, p. 634. It is worthy of note that one of the judges at the British Columbia Court of Appeal thought the standard should be that of a trained teacher; see [1976] 5 WWR 240, at 265 (B.C.C.A. per Carrothers, J.). However, the trial judge used the lower standard but could have used the higher standard *a fortiori*.
34. *Ibid.*
35. *Ibid.* The judge cited *Smith v. Martin* (1911) 2 K.B. 775; *Gary et al. v. McGonegal et al.* (1949) 4 D.L.R. 344, O.R. 749; and *Hall v. Thompson et al.* (1962) 4 D.L.R. 139.
36. *Ibid.*, p. 635.
37. *Ibid.*
38. *Ibid.*, p. 649.
39. *Ibid.*p. 650.
40. *Ibid.*, p. 649.
41. British Columbia Court of Appeal, *Thornton et al. v. Board of School Trustees of School District No. 57 (Prince George) et al.* 73 D.L.R. (3d) 62. In the case referred to above in the text, Bisson (plaintiff) became almost a complete quadriplegic when his head struck the sea bed after a dive from a five-meter diving platform mounted on a raft owned by the Corporation of Powell River. There were no warning

signs so a jury found Powell River to be 80 percent responsible and Bisson 20 percent responsible. Bisson was awarded $286,000 in general damages, although the amount was reduced by $90,000 on appeal.

42. *Thornton v. School District No. 57 (Prince George)* [1978] 2 S.C.R. 267.
43. *Ibid.*, pp. 267-268.
44. Robbins, Mel: Duty of care. *Education Canada, 16,* 8, 1976.
45. *Ibid.*
46. *Ibid.*, p. 9.
47. van der Smissen (1968), *op. cit.*, p. 256.
48. van der Smissen (1975), *op. cit.*, p. 8.
49. van der Smissen (1968), *op. cit.*, p. 154.
50. *Ibid.*, p. 155.
51. *Ibid.*, p. 156, citing *Sayers v. Ranger,* 16 NJ Super 22, 83 A (2d) 775 (1951).
52. *Ibid.*, citing *Kelley v. Board of Educ.* 191 AppDiv 251, 180 NJSupp 796 (1920).
53. *Ibid.*, p. 157, citing *Walter v. Everett School Dist.,* 195 Wash 45, 79 P (2d) 689 (1938).
54. *Ibid.*, p. 159.
55. van der Smissen (1975) *op. cit.*, p. 76.
56. British Columbia Court of Appeal, *op. cit.*, pp. 57-58 citing: *Murray et al. v. Board of Education of City of Belleville,* [1943] 1 D.L.R. 494, [1943] O.W.N. 44; *Gard v. Board of School Trustees of Duncan,* [1946] 1 W.W.R. 305, 62 B.C.R. 323; and *McKay et al. v. Board of Goven School Unit No. 29 of Saskatchewan et al.* (1968), 68 D.L.R. (2d) 519, [1968] S.C.R. 589, 64 W.W.R. 301.
57. van der Smissen, Betty: Legal responsibility in the gymnasium. In Wettstone, E. (Ed.): *Gymnastics Safety Manual.* University Park, Pennsylvania, The Pennsylvania State University Press, 1977, p. 107.
58. *Ibid.*
59. *Ibid.*
60. *Ibid.*, p. 108.
61. *Ibid.*, p. 109.
62. van der Smissen (1968) *op. cit.*, Section 4.13 and 4.14 regarding correct application of first aid to avoid successful lawsuits.
63. van der Smissen (1977), *op. cit.*, p. 116. It is also worthy of note here that one part of being a professional person is belonging to, and being active in, professional organizations. Professional journals, for example, frequently contain information which helps to make people "more professional."

Supplementary Readings

Appenzeller, H. *From the Gym to the Jury* (1970); *Athletics and the Law* (1975); *Physical Education and the Law* (1978); *Sports and the Courts* (1980). All published by Michie Bobbs-Merrill Law Publishing, Post Office

Box 7587, Charlottesville, Va., 22906 and available on approval.

———:Sports in the courts. *USSA News, 1:*4-5, 1977.

Blaufarb, M.: *Complying with Title IX of the Education Amendments of 1972 in Physical Education and High School Sports Programs.* Washington, D.C., AAHPERD, n.d. [ca. 1979.]

Drowatzky, John N.: On the firing line: Negligence in physical education. *Journal of Law and Education, 6:*481-490, 1977.

Hjelte, G., and Shivers, Jay S.: *Public Administration of Recreational Services.* Philadelphia, Lea and Febiger, 1972. (Ch. 2, Legal foundations for public recreational service; Ch. 5, Legislative authority and executive relationships in public recreational service.)

Ross, C. Thomas: Anatomy of a law suit. *USSA News, 2:*2-3, 1978.

van der Smissen (1968 and 1975), *loc. cit.*

Case 7.01

Peel County[1]

Case Incident

Myers transferred to Erindale Secondary School in grade ten where he was estimated to be in the bottom half of his physical education class. During that year he received his first instruction on the rings (Level 1) and was taught the functions and importance of "spotters." At the end of October, 1972, when in grade eleven, a four-and-one-half week gymnastic block began for Myers. Overlooking the gymnasium was an "exercise room," which contained several pieces of gymnastic equipment, including the rings. The exercise room interior was not visible from the gymnasium.

The physical education teacher was in his late twenties and described as "qualified, proficient, and dedicated." On the incident day, Myers and his spotter asked if they may go into the exercise room along with several other boys. The teacher allowed them to go while he tested some other grade eleven boys *and* supervised an extra grade twelve class in the gymnasium (from which he could not see the gymnasts). Myers had never done a straddle dismount from the rings before; it was a Level 2 stunt and should not be done until Level 1 stunts had been mastered. Having done some dismounts, he appeared to have ended his routine and his spotter moved away. Myers did not tell his spotter he was mounting the rings again and had a disastrous fall that resulted in serious injuries. Myers and his father sued Peel

County Board of Education and the physical education teacher for damages for negligence.

Case Analysis Method

CAM A (see Chapter 1) before reading further.

Trial Judgement

Judge O'Driscoll found the manoeuver was suitable to the plaintiff's age and condition and that he had been progressively trained to do the manoeuver properly to avoid danger. As to equipment, he found the mats used to be inadequate because Myer had broken his neck on them. Furthermore, he found that the supervision was inadequate in that the teacher was downstairs in the gymnasium. He said: ". . . the mere presence of a teacher in that upstairs exercise room probably would have deterred the plaintiff, Gregory Myers, from the foolish move that led to his injuries."

Thus the liability of the defendants was on two grounds: inadequate mats under the rings, and inadequate supervision of they gymnastics class. The plaintiff was found to have been 20 percent contributorily negligent but general damages were assessed at $80,000. The defendants appealed both the finding of negligence and the assessment of damages.

Court of Appeal Judgment

The appeal was allowed and the action dismissed in a two-to-one judgment in the Ontario Court of Appeals. Justices Arnup and Zuber thought the injuries could have been received even with thicker matting and that the supervision was adequate. They argued that the plaintiff had been warned of the dangers and that a careful father, having instructed his son not to perform without a spotter, and having knowledge that there was a spotter nearby, would not have hesitated to allow his son to use the rings unsupervised. The standard of supervision imposed on the School Board was no higher than that of a parent.

Dissenting Judge Blair's opinion was that the defendants failed to provide safe matting and failed to provide effective supervision. The injuries were reasonably foreseeable and the defendants were negligent.

Discussion

In the annotation section of the case report, John Barnes of the Department of Law at Carleton University points out that the majority view is: "consistent with a pedagogy stressing the internalization of safety norms by students, the growth of personal responsibility, and the perception of one's own limits of performance." Barnes regards such an attitude as, "the safest in the long term." Further, that the decision may help "allay the (unjustified) anxiety prevalent among Canadian physical education instructors. . . ."

Certainly this judgment would do that if it could be relied on. On consideration of what has happened, I do not think it can be totally relied on for the following reasons:

1. In the Peel County case, judges' opinions are now (April, 1980) equally divided at two v. two. Of the four judges who have held the teacher not liable; however, one of the justices at the court of appeal and the trial judge have found the teacher negligent.

2. The case is going to the Supreme Court of Canada where the decision *may* be reversed.

3. The Prince George case was finally decided by the Supreme Court of Canada. There the standard of care imposed on the teacher seems to be that of the "hypothetical expert" whose profession's nature demands some special skill, ability, and experience.

This is a higher standard than that imposed by the concurring judges in the Ontario Court of Appeal.

For the time being, at least, it is my view that teachers and administrators will be far safer to set themselves the standard of the "hypothetical expert," which is certainly not an unreasonable standard.

Reference and Note

1. Ontario Supreme Court (Court of Appeal), *Myers et al. v. Peel County Board of Education et al.*, (1978) 5 C.C.L.T. 271. Further references to the Peel County Case, and the Case's Annotation, are related to this reference.

2. I gratefully acknowledge the advice of Professor Terence J. Weuster, B.A, M.A., J.D. (Kansas), LL.M. (Yale), of the Bars of British Columbia, Saskatchewan, and Kansas. A member of the Faculty of Law at the University of Victoria.

Case 7.02

Tragic Trio

Part One is in Chapter Six as Case 6.11 and should now be dealt with from a legal consideration point of view, along with Incidents two and three which follow here.

Incident Number Two

The university sailing club sailed on a large lake at Nab Mountain. The officer-of-the-day decided whether or not sailing would take place if the weather was doubtful, and there had always to be a motor launch on the water when a dinghy was out. Further, it was required that all sailors wear life jackets.

Donald Chadwick was a pleasant, popular, and good student in his first year of medicine. His father was a bank manager in the south of the country and the family had two other teenage daughters. On February 16, 1966, the sailing club's officer-of-the-day decided "no sailing" because of high winds and hoisted the red flag before going home. Shortly afterwards, Donald Chadwick and two friends arrived at the lake with the intention of sailing. They saw the red flag, knew the launch was not out but, nevertheless, chose to sail. The friends wore life jackets but Donald did not. Suddenly, after sailing for a short while, the dinghy capsized and they could not turn her over again because of the choppy water and high wind. Rashly, Donald said he would swim to shore for the launch and was on his way before the others could stop him. He had 300 yards to go but went under about 100 yards from the shore. His body was not recovered for a week.

Incident Number Three

With winter over and the snow melted, mountaineering club members looked forward to some rock climbing. A favorite and suitable spot was on the granite sea cliffs ten miles to the north of the university.

Fourth-year civil engineering student, Ike McKay, was a prominent club member who had held several offices within the club and was about to leave the university to join a bridge building firm. He had been climbing for as long as he could remember and was considered to be, technically, one of the best climbers in the region. On a drizzly Saturday morning in late

April 1966, Ike was leading a climb up a very difficult route on the sea cliffs. Three climbers were tied on to the cliff as Ike began the fourth stage; he skillfully negotiated about fifteen feet when suddenly he slipped on the wet rock and fell. It was with such force that his number two man was also pulled off the rock face; fortunately, the number three man's belay held and number two survived with a severe bruising. Sadly, Ike crashed onto the rocky beach and was killed as a result of internal bodily and head injuries—he was not wearing a helmet.

All the autopsies indicated that the victims were not suffering from any physical illnesses and no traces of drugs were found. Peter Plymouth was a very worried man. What was he to do?

Case Analysis Method
CAM B (see Chapter 1).

Case 7.03

The Final Practicum

Janet Webster was in her professional year of physical education teacher preparation with only a final six-week period of practice teaching to complete before graduation. The practicum was in the interior of British Columbia and a long way from the university. Consequently, Janet was not able to visit the school before her assignment and she did not receive any comprehensive instructions from her sponsoring teacher; only that she would teach units of track, soccer, and tennis.

The Monday that Janet began teaching, Maude Tomb, her sponsor teacher, was busy preparing for a PTA gym display so she told Janet to begin her track unit and that she would be out to observe and help later. Janet Webster gave high-jumping instruction to all the students then split them into various activity groups for practice to improve personal performances. Brenda Smith, attempting a "Fosbury Flop," landed awkwardly and could not get up. She was carried into the school nurse's office on a stretcher and Principal Peel called Janet and Maude to his room.

Peel (upon hearing Janet's description of what happened):   What do you know about Janet's training?

Tombs: She's in her final year.

Peel: Did you tell her what had been taught previously in high jumping?

Tombs: No.

Peel: Did you review her unit and lesson plan?

Tombs: Well, no.

Peel: What was Janet's class control like?

Tombs: I don't know.

Peel: Was the landing area safe?

Tombs: I haven't seen it this morning.

Peel: There are a number of things to be dealt with immediately. I'll talk to you again later.

Case Analysis Method

CAM A (see Chapter 1) before reading further.

The Outcome

Brenda Smith was not seriously hurt, but the case demonstrates clearly the principles that should have been applied. If the guidelines of the early part of this design had been followed, Miss Tombs would not have been in the position of having to answer Mr. Peel's questions. She should have communicated earlier with Janet, she should not have allowed Janet to teach by herself until she knew Janet's control was satisfactory, she should have checked the unit and lesson plan for appropriate progressions, and she should have checked the safety of the landing area. Generally, a supervising teacher should observe constantly for awhile and then, if safe to do so, gradually allow the student teacher to be alone with classes except for periodic, unannounced observations. As Drowatsky (1980) summarized: ". . . the duty for supervision cannot be delegated. The public school teacher, not the student teacher, has responsibility for the care of pupils and their well-being."

Reference

1. Drowatsky, John N.: The cooperating teacher and liability during student teacher supervision. *Journal of Physical Education and Recreation,* *51*:79-80, 1980.

Case 7.04

Wills' Warning

At the end of Mr. Rickett's gym class, Michael Wills reported that one of the climbing ropes had some loose strands near the top. Mr. Ricketts glanced at it and made a mental note to have it repaired. Next day, Sam Sakowitz, a heavy youth, was in Mr. Rickett's class and near the top of the faulty rope. Suddenly, everyone heard a loud, dull thud and saw Sam motionless on the floor.

Case Analysis Method
CAM B (see Chapter 1).

Case 7.05

Backward Behavior

West Vancouver's ice skating rink measured 200 feet by 80 feet and had 100 skaters on it one night in 1971. Fifty-eight-year-old experienced skater Lawrence McLean was skating counterclockwise in conformity with the rink rules when, suddenly, he was knocked down by David Conroy. Conroy was moving in the same direction but was skating faster, and backwards. McLean's right elbow was fractured and he sued Conroy and the municipality for damages.

Case Analysis Method
CAM A (see Chapter 1) before reading further.

The Judgment
The British Columbia Supreme Court awarded general damages of $7,500 against Conroy and the District of West Vancouver. The judge ruled that Conroy deliberately decided to skate backwards, a mistake in judgment under the circumstances. Further, he held the municipality in breach of its duty in failing to declare a general prohibition of backward skating (under the conditions) before the accident happened and in failing to have anyone on the ice at the time Conroy was backward skating who might have stopped him doing so.

Reference

1. *McLean v. The Corporation of the District of West Vancouver and David Conroy.* 18699, March 12, 1976 (Supreme Court of British Columbia).

Summary

1. There are many legal aspects of which sport administrators need to be aware. Important supervision principles are given particular attention in this chapter and supplementary readings cover other concerns.
2. Sport administrators need not fear successful lawsuits so long as they take basic precautions.
3. The law is dynamic.
4. A tort is a civil injury or wrong, but not all civil injuries are torts. If the appropriate remedy is an action for damages, then the civil injury is classed as a tort.
5. The negligent wrongdoer is one who does not sufficiently desire to avoid doing harm.
6. To prove negligence, the plaintiff must show:
   (a) that the defendant had towards him a duty of care;
   (b) that the defendant's act or omission to act constituted a breach of that duty;
   (c) that the defendant should have foreseen that his act or omission would damage the plaintiff.
7. Sport administrators usually have a "duty of care" relationship with their clients.
8. The stardard of care varies but often is the "hypothetical expert" standard in sport situations. It is safest for sport administrators to set themselves the highest standards, in a professional fashion, without putting unnecessary fears into their instructors or clients.
9. In most human activity there is a risk, but correct supervision alleviates the risk.
10. Equipment and facilities that sport administrators allow clients to use must be reasonably safe for the intended purpose.

Concepts for Review

Dynamic Law   Tort

Negligence	Duty of care
Breach of duty	Plaintiff
Defendant	Standard of care
Foresight	Hypothetical expert
Careful parent	Damages
Proximate cause	Progressive training
Safe equipment	Contributory negligence
Liability insurance	Governmental immunity
Risk	General supervision
Specific supervision	Administrative supervision

Questions For Oral Or Written Discussion

1. CAM C (see Chapter 1) applied to instructor-specified topics taken from this chapter.
2. Find out if any of your local legal interpretations are at odds with any of this chapter's principles.
3. A trial court in Florida awarded $5.3 million in damages to a boy injured at football; the award was against the helmet manufacturers. Discuss this case and estimate what the long-term consequences may be.
4. Assume you are head of physical education and athletics in a large high school. List all the steps you would take to ensure that no successful lawsuit could be brought against the department staff or school.
5. In number four's school (immediately above), you have to organize a championship football game between your school and a keen rival school. Eight thousand spectators are expected to attend so list all you will do to ensure good crowd control procedures (cf. Appenzeller [1970], *op. cit.*, Appendix B; and van der Smissen [1968], *op. cit.*, Section 4.15).
6. Describe the risk management plan of your city recreation department, or your university, and then discuss its adequacy.
7. Draw up a "Facilities and Equipment Safety Inspection Form" that would be suitable for the sport department in the high school you attended.
8. By library research, find out what happened in Case 7.01 (Peel County) when it reached the Supreme Court of Canada. (It will probably be possible to do this by 1981.)

Chapter 8

BUDGETING AND FINANCIAL CONTROL

A MAJOR COMPLAINT against sport administrators is that they are often not competent enough to manage money. So, for example, individuals from other disciplines are often hired to head big recreational organizations; sometimes to the detriment of the programs. It is realized that large sport organizations usually hire specialists to control money but, nevertheless, sport administrators and managers do require stringent competence if they are to be really effective and reach their full potential. This chapter is designed to prepare sport administrators and managers to defy the common complaint referred to in the first sentence: to prepare them to utilize all revenues correctly and prudently whilst guarding against misuse.

LEARNING DESIGN 8.1

BUDGETING

Budgets: General Definitions

Stedry (1960:3-12) regarded the following definition of a budget as "the most comprehensive": (1) A financial plan serving as a pattern for a control over future operations; (2) hence, any estimate of future costs; (3) a systematic plan for the utilization of manpower, material or other resources (Kohler, 1956:67). Similarly, Horngren (1972:121) wrote: "A budget is a quantitative expression of a plan of action and an aid to coordination and implementation. Budgets may be formulated for the organization as a whole or for any subunit. The master budget summarizes the objectives of all subunits of an organization. . . . It quantifies the

211

expectations regarding future income, cash flow, financial status, and supporting plans."

Stedry (1960:3-12) saw budgets' two major functions as forcing planning and serving as a control; the latter being, for example, when anticipated performance and cost criteria can be compared later with actual performances and costs. Horngren's (1972:122) variety of budget functions were, "planning, evaluating performance, coordinating activities, implementing plans, communicating, motivating, and authorizing actions." Clearly, Horngren's list is more complete, with the "authorization" function being particularly important in most sport situations. Indeed Horngren's list epitomizes the need for, and value of, sound budgets in sport organizations.

The reference to budgets being for subunits of organizations is important to note here because that is usually the case with sport budgets. For example, a school physical education department is a subunit of a school and a city parks and recreation department is a subunit of a city government. These two examples also serve to illustrate the vast range of budget sizes in sport organizations: the former may be for a few hundred dollars while the latter is frequently for millions of dollars. Nevertheless, many principles remain for same for either, even though the complexity is different.

Budget Types

Time Coverage

It is usual for sport budgets to cover a time span of one year; thus a "fiscal year" is a twelve-month accounting period. However, some budgets may be for longer periods if, for example, large capital spending is proposed. Alternatively, the period may be for less than one year, as is often the situation with special projects.

"Continuous budgeting" occurs when one month, or one quarter, is added to a twelve-month budget as soon as a month, or quarter, is completed. This forces administrators always to think twelve months ahead whatever the month and it is becoming more common, particularly in business enterprises (cf. Horngren, 1972:126).

Current (or Operating) Budgets

Current or operating budgets in sport organizations are usually for a twelve-month period and are concerned with the operation of the organization for that time period only. Thus, a current budget includes such items as salaries, services, materials, and travel.

Capital Budgets

Capital budgets in sport organizations involve long-term planning for land, buildings, sports fields, equipment, and other long-lived assets that affect operations over a number of years. So, in organizations with good planning, a five-year capital budget program is reviewed/revised annually and then executed through the current operations budget.

Revenue Budgets

Revenue budgets are those that project all revenues that the sport organization expects to receive in the coming year. Thus, revenue may be from tax sources, grants, gate receipts, fees, charges, or other sources. It is important that these be as accurate as possible; otherwise, with the common under-budgeting, the overall budget picture is misleading.

Line-Item Budgets

A line-item budget is one that lists objects to be purchased and salaries to be paid. The validity of a request "is judged largely on the basis of comparison with previous expenditure experience" (Sherwood and Best, 1968). In a sport organization, part of a summary sheet may look something like Table V.

Many sport organizations prepare budgets in this fashion. In times of inflation, a department may be told it can have a 5 percent increase and such an amount may not buy the objects it could buy in the previous year. Then, some goods or services must be reduced or cut.

Performance Budgets and Program Budgets

In contrast with line-item budgets, the performance approach "calls for a budget in which the appropriation figures bear a clear relation to service standards, volumes of work to be performed,

TABLE V
EXAMPLE LINE-ITEM BUDGET

Account Number	Account Title	1978 Actual	1979 Actual	1980 Appropriations
14-100[1]	*Recreation Department*			
01[2]	Salaries	200,000	225,000	250,000
02	Heat and light	8,000	8,500	8,750
03	Telephone	2,800	2,870	2,900
04	Mail	1,800	1,900	1,950
05	Travel and training	5,000	5,000	5,600
06	Printing	500	481	560
07	Supplies (expendable)	2,500	2,600	2,700
08	Equipment	3,000	3,000	3,000
09	Towels and laundry	1,000	1,200	1,400
10	Dues	400	400	450
11	Medical supplies	300	400	500
12	Advertising	1,000	1,100	1,200
14	Books and periodicals	150	160	175

NOTES

[1]This number identifies for accounting purposes, the faculty and the department or the city department.

[2]This minor code number identifies the object. Often, further minor code subdivisions are used and the supporting folios would explain and try to justify the proposed expense.

methods of performing such work, and the cost element required by such standards and volume" (Sherwood and Best, 1968).

Budgets in this category are called variously performance budgets, program budgets, PPBS, and others. PPBS, or Planning-Programming—Budgeting System, perhaps best typifies these types. It was introduced into the United States federal government in the early 1960s as part of the continuing struggle to bring rationality into the budgetary process. Some of the system's advantages and disadvantages were outlined by Turnbull (1976: 602-607) and are adapted for use here:

ADVANTAGES.

1. Traditional approaches (line-item) accept past decisions without examination and apply primarily political criteria to requests for new programs; PPBS does not.
2. PPBS does not separate planning from budgeting.
3. A formal cost-benefit analysis is carried out.

DISADVANTAGES.

1. Democratic political systems make it impractical and unnecessary.

2. It is impractical because:
    (a) It is very difficult (often impossible) to isolate explicit measurable goals and then evaluate alternatives.
    (b) Politicians do not separate programs from goals.
    (c) It is often difficult to charge resources (inputs) to results (outputs). For example, how much of the cost of providing a gymnasium should be charged to instructional classes, intramurals, and athletics?
    (d) Some "staff" units have no public outputs.
    (e) Long-established traditional functions in departments are really hard to change in practice.
    (f) It is bound to have a too centralizing bias.
    (g) Even when PPBS is adopted, decision makers often do not act on the objective information.
    (h) There is "data overload." And, sometimes, managers do not want administrators to know everything, for knowledge is power!

So rationality "as defined by PPBS was abandoned by the United States government when it quietly directed the federal agencies to stop producing PPBS documentation as part of their annual budget requests" (Turnbull, 1976:607). It should be noted, however, that PPBS has survived in many states and local governments. With that in mind, the section below on "The Budget Process" uses the PPBS system as an example in a parks and recreation department. So, the system is given further explanation in the attempt to demonstrate the difficulties of rationality in the process (sequence of stages or "hurdles")—a process, incidentally, that must be followed whatever the type of budget.

Zero-Base Budgets

Zero-base budgets (ZBB) originally developed as an element of PPBS. The originator of the concept, Peter Pyhrr of Texas Instruments, defined it as follows in a speech: "An operating planning and budgeting process which requires each manager to justify his entire budget request in detail from scratch (hence zero-base) and shifts the burden of proof to each manager to justify why he should spend any money at all. This approach requires that all activities be identified in "decision packages" which will be evaluated by systematic analysis and ranked in order of importance."

Thus, managers develop a series of priority-ranked decision packages with details of projected expenditures and benefits. Decision makers are then offered a range of decisions, each of which has a cost and benefit summary attached. Proponents of ZBB claim it uncovers "what is really going on in an organization, why it's being done, what better ways might be available, and which activities are really important—as well as what they cost" (Cheek, 1977:18). Cheek calls it, "A goal, objective, strategy, policy, decision, scheme of control . . . an effective means to translate high-minded goals into reality. . . ."

Some disadvantages are similar to those described for PPBS. Long-established programs present real difficulties, information is hard to collect, it is time consuming, and priority ranking is often very difficult. Nevertheless, it is another attempt at a rational approach and it has produced some dramatic results when adopted. Though it is not widely used in public sport organizations, it is very close to what a rational individual would do in private business.

Special Project Budgets

Special project budgets often have to be made in sport organizations for such activities as conferences and athletic training camps. The funding for them is not in ongoing budgets and so they must be treated separately. Even so, the usual budget functions must be completed and an example of a line-item type is in Table VI.

Conclusions

This section identifies the types of budgets sport administrators are likely to encounter. Usually, they will have to operate within an existing system of a larger organization. When possible, however, they should strive to make rationality and budget processes coexist, by some of these means or by others that may be developed.

The Budget Process

In this section an example of a city parks and recreation department PPBS process cycle is described with the intention of illustrating the stages that must be passed before public funds can

TABLE VI
EXAMPLE SPECIAL PROJECT BUDGET

Proposed Budget for the Sixth Annual Conference		
Receipts		
Registration (400 at $40.00*)	$16,000.00	
Displays	400.00	
		$16,400.00
Disbursements		
Secretary	500.00	
Clinicians	3,530.00	
Printing	625.00	
Audio Visual	200.00	
Truck rental	125.00	
School rentals	265.00	
Equipment honorarium	200.00	
Entertainment	1,375.00	
Wine	450.00	
Food services	8,000.00	
Phone	100.00	
Returned cheques	50.00	
Miscellaneous	50.00	
		$15,470.00
Excess Receipts over Disbursements		930.00

*If last year's $35.00 fee was maintained the projected deficit would be $1,070.00.

be spent on such services. It is done in this fashion because the process stages are similar in the approval of many organization's budgets. Here, imagine you are the superintendent of the city parks and recreation department who is receiving the process instructions. Try to decide what sort of specific information you would provide for the commissioners (your public servant superiors) and council. Also, what information you would seek from your program managers (assuming it is a big, diverse, and complex department).

The major elements of this cycle are:
1. The determination of objectives, with measurement criteria;
2. The design of programs and the consideration of alternatives;
3. Budgeting and resource allocation;
4. Execution of programs; and,
5. Evaluation of results.

1. Determining Objectives

An objective should describe the desired end situation, not the means used to get there. Similarly, the measurement criteria should answer the question, "How do we know when we have accomplished our goal?" A good program objective is specific. Rather than "The objective is to provide citizens with clean drinking water," it would be better to have an objective of "drinking water will contain a bacterial count of less than 3 per 1000 cc in 1979." Rather than "To clear the streets after every major snowstorm, and sand when ice occurs," it would be better to have "Main streets will always be passable to a conventional car with snow tires on the driving wheels." The test can easily be made; the objective, classified by the criteria, clearly defines the level of service to be provided.

The method of measurement is not always quantitative; sometimes the judgement of an individual (possibly an accredited expert of some sort) is relied upon to determine whether the objective has been met. In other cases, a poll of citizen opinion would determine whether the level of service provided was satisfactory.

The objectives of various programs will relate to, and complement, each other. If the objectives of two distinct programs are the same, however, it should be considered whether the programs could be combined; possibly with some saving in resources or people.

To sum up, the reasons for identifying objectives for programs are:

(a) To make clear to ourselves, the commissioners, and council just what it is we expect to accomplish;

(b) To outline at the beginning the means by which we expect our performance to be measured, the target level of service, and the means by which the completion of a program can be identified;

(c) To detect programs that have identical, similar, or related objectives; and,

(d) To enable consideration of relative priorities by commissioners and council.

2. The Design of Programs and the Consideration of Alternatives

Theoretically, program design should not start until objectives and criteria have been specifically determined. In practice, programs and their objectives frequently develop side by side; often, programs exist before their objectives have been clearly identified. The annual budget submission is the time when a serious effort should be made to determine the most cost-effective way of accomplishing the objective; this implies that present programs and methods should be closely examined both for their cost and their effectiveness.

The choices, expressed briefly, can often be summarized as:

1. Prevention or cure?
2. Do it ourselves or persuade other people to do it?
3. Use people or equipment or some appropriate combination?
4. Do it now or later?
5. One type of activity or a mixture of various types of activity?
6. Can we hedge against unpredictable events, such as the weather?

There are many other questions that can be asked; the objective of program design is to plan a workable strategy while assuming that all possible alternatives, including "way out" suggestions and the "traditional" ways, are thoroughly compared. In some cases it may be necessary to carry out some study, possibly involving a "model" of the situation, to estimate the probable effectiveness of untried approaches.

3. Budgeting and Resource Allocation

When a program has been designed, it is possible to determine quite specifically what people, equipment, office space, funds, etc., will be required, how soon and for how long, and at what cost. The process of budgeting by program asks first what resources are needed and second from where these resources will come. Obviously, they may be drawn from many departments or from outside for any one program. Thus a budget for a program will probably specify participation by one or a number of departments, some on a direct cost basis, some (profit centers) on a charge-out basis. Also, since programs are typically longer than one year, the budget will estimate expenditures for three to five years in the future.

The department superintendent must naturally ensure that the limited resources—particularly staff—at his command do not become overcommitted. Thus, initial planning discussions between the program planner and the department head become the first process of resource allocation.

As in all budgeting systems, it is invariably found that the total resources required exceeds the resources available. Thus, further allocation (and, in effect, priority setting) will take place at commissioner and council levels.

4. Execution of Programs

The program manager is responsible for carrying out the program no matter what department is doing the work. He must plan and schedule all the elements in the program, arrange where necessary for work to be carried out in service and other departments, and originate changes and revisions to the budget if needed. He is, of course, primarily concerned with the achievement of the laid down objectives; should it appear that these are not being achieved by the program, he must initiate corrective action or possibly even abandonment of the program. At all times, however, he would work within the existing organization and use the present lines of authority. Where he does not have the direct authority he must ask for cooperation, especially from those in senior positions and in other departments.

The program manager needs up-to-date information on resources used (compared with budget) and progress towards objectives. Some of this information will be supplied by the central management information system; some must be gathered as part of the program.

5. Evaluation

Evaluation must be continuous—not just at the end of the budget year—and it is primarily the program manager's responsibility. Commissioners and council will be concerned, from time to time, with the success of ongoing programs and will initiate systematic reviews of vital programs at times during the year. However, the most searching evaluation will occur next budget time, when resources are requested to carry on the program. At that time, all programs will be reviewed and those that have not achieved their objectives will be in for close scrutiny to determine the reason. There may be extenuating circumstances, there may be poor planning, or just plain bad management. Evaluation is, at least in part, a learning process. It is also a people-to-people process and should not be reduced to a mere numerical exercise. More than anything else, it lays the groundwork for next year's planning.

The importance of human aspects in the whole process cannot be overemphasized. Without thoroughly educated and cooperative people, at all levels, the budget-making process is a waste of funds and a hindrance to efficient operation. As Horngren (1972:125) said, "Attitudes ideally are sympathetic, cooperative, and cost-conscious" (cf. also Horngren, 1972:Ch. 5; and Argyris, 1968).

The Detailed Schedule

A detailed schedule of events keyed to the proposed timing of major phases is presented below. Brief explanations of the activities to be carried out are also included; start and end dates and elapsed weeks are shown.

ORIENTATION SEMINARS FOR DEPARTMENTS. Weeks 1-3, June 5-23. In order to familiarize a maximum number of members of management with PPBS, program budgeting, and the objectives of the immediate task in the shortest possible time, a series of half-day seminars will be held. All department heads and program managers should attend, and seminars will be repeated until the demand is satisfied.

IDENTIFICATION OF PROGRAMS. Weeks 2-6, June 12-July 14. During this period the implementations team will work with departments to identify the programs on which the program budget will be based. This step will require close coordination and support within the team itself and will also serve the function of a "learning phase" for departmental staff.

ACCOUNTING POLICIES DECISIONS. Week 4, June 30 deadline. A number of accounting policies will be clarified prior to the detailed budgeting phases. Among these are:

(a) treatment of cost centers, pricing on internal services;
(b) charging of overhead to programs;
(c) treatment of depreciation, the cost of money, and debenture repayments;
(d) allocation of land holdings;
(e) integration of program accounting with utility accounting; and,

(f) integration of existing management reports with program cost reports.

Policy decisions, fundamental to both program budgeting and future accounting systems, must be made early in the budgeting process; research will be necessary to obtain a basis for these decisions.

HOLIDAYS. Week 7, July 17-21.

COMMISSIONERS REVIEW PROGRAM STRUCTURE. Week 8, July 24-28. In order to manage the preparation of program submissions, and ensure an even flow of programs for commissioners' review, a detailed schedule will be prepared indicating when each program write-up should be completed and thus guiding departmental and implementation team priorities for the remainder of the implementation project. Commissioners will have the opportunity to review the program structure at this point.

BUDGET GUIDELINES. Week 8, July 24-28. In order to guide superintendents and program managers in the planning and preparation of programs, commissioners will indicate guidelines for 1979 levels of activity and expenditure early in the process.

OBJECTIVES AND PERFORMANCE CRITERIA. Weeks 8-11, July 24-August 11. During this period the implementation team will work closely with program managers and superintendents to develop objectives and appropriate measures for results for each program. This phase will involve considerable analysis, discussion, and coordination on the part of team members.

COMMISSIONERS REVIEW OBJECTIVES. Week 12, August 21-25. Commissioners will review programs in their areas with superintendents and program managers where appropriate. This review will serve as a check on the 1979 planned operations and give commissioners an overview of the 1979 program budget contents.

PROGRAM COSTING AND WRITE-UP. Weeks 12-19, August 21-October 13. Detailed resource allocations and costs will be developed for each program. Costs will include:

(a) estimated actual for 1978;
(b) budget for 1979, and forecasts for 1980-83;
(c) both capital and operating costs;

(d) revenues from program (if any); and,

(e) costs from all departments directly participating in a program.

As each program is completed it will be keypunched for input of data into the city budget assembly system on the computer, which will produce running totals to assist in budget analysis. Each write-up will then be ready for review by the relevant commissioner.

COMMISSIONERS REVIEW PROGRAM AND COSTS. Weeks 15-19, September 11-October 13. Commissioners review all program submissions with superintendents and program managers. This review marks the completion of the program planning process and provides the opportunity for comprehensive discussion of objectives and costs.

COMMISSION BOARD CLEAR BUDGET FOR PRINTING. Week 22, October 30-November 3.

PRESENTATION OF BUDGET TO COUNCIL. Week 24, November 13. The completed budget, with the commissioners' summary report, will be presented to council. It is expected that it will be referred to the Economic Affairs Committee for review.

REVIEW BY ECONOMIC AFFAIRS COMMITTEE. Weeks 24-28, November 13-December 15. During the review by this committee, superintendents and program managers will be available to present details and answer questions about proposed programs as required by the committee.

RECOMMENDATION TO COUNCIL. Week 29, December 18. Economic Affairs Committee will present its recommendation to Council for review and approval.

The Program Budget Format

In the city, the immediate objective is to develop a program budget to cover 1979. For each program, the following information will be shown (see Figures 9 and 10):

1. Name of program.
2. Name of program manager (who is responsible for the results of the program).
3. Program number (for identification and accounting purposes).
4. Objectives of program (written out clearly).

5. Measurement criteria (how results are to be measured).
6. Council policy (if this program stems from a formal policy, resolution, or bylaw, this is indicated).
7. Other supporting information (maps and diagrams can be most helpful).
8. Costs of program (total costs, projected for five years and including an estimate of prior year's [1979] costs) by departments participating in this program, and including:
   (a) capital expenditures;
   (b) operating costs;
   (c) applicable revenues;
   (d) internal services;
   (e) external services; and,
   (f) other.
9. Man-years of work required (especially to establish a degree of control over the number of people employed) divided into:
   (a) existing permanent staff;
   (b) additional permanent staff; and,
   (c) temporary staff.
10. Effect on other programs (most programs affect, or are affected by, other programs so this should be indicated, in both narrative and dollar terms).

This format summarizes the essential information required for decision making at budget time. The programs outlined in the budget provide a framework in which to conduct the total PPB management process and improve both the management of the city and its accountability to citizens and taxpayers. (Note that "Management by Objectives" is given attention in Chapter 10.)

Economic Influences

The financial responsibility expected of managers of government-operated recreational facilities is inconsistent; for example, a library has virtually no non-tax revenue but continues to operate while a riding stable shuts down under the same conditions. Without discussing all the possibilities in between these two examples, it is evident that some recreational facilities' managers do have to demonstrate that the users of the facilities will pay a substantial part of the total operating costs. The degree

Program Name (1)				Program Number		(3)
Program Manager (2)						
Objectives						
(4)						
Performance Criteria						
(5)						
Relationship to Other Programs						
(10)						
Source of Funds	1979	1980	1981	1982	1983	

Identified Council Objective, Policy, or Approval
(6)
Illustrative Material
(7)

Figure 9. Program budget form—(left hand page)

1978 Costs $	Man Years 1979			Description		Program Name (1)		Department		1979 $	1980 $	1981 $	1982 $	Program Number (3)	
	Perm. Staff	Added Staff	Temp. Staff					Name	Code					1983 $	
(8)	(9)	(9)	(9)							(8)	(8)	(8)	(8)	(8)	
				Effect on Other Programs (10)						(10)	(10)	(10)	(10)	(10)	

Figure 10. Program budget form—(right hand page)

of subsidy is determined by politicians in processes similar to the one described above.

This section examines two British Columbia tennis bubbles (air-supported indoor tennis facilities) to demonstrate how fee setting (and hence budget making) may be done for the benefit of most potential users. Tennis bubbles are chosen as the focus here because a number have been forced to shut down and several exist or are planned in many parts of the world. The specific example is also intended to illustrate the economic concepts, which are particularly appropriate here.

Research Findings

TENNIS BUBBLE A. At the time of the inquiry (Summer, 1979), Tennis Bubble A had been open for two-and-one-half years. Figure 11 shows its court hours' percentage usage for that period.

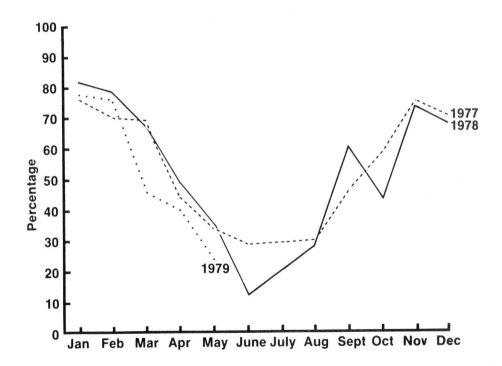

Figure 11. Bubble A: Usage (1977 to mid-1979)

Tennis Bubble B. At the same inquiry time, Bubble B had been open seven months and Figure 12 demonstrates that its percentage usage followed a very similar monthly pattern to that in Bubble A. This may be the density of usage others should expect.

The revenue from users and the operating costs (variable costs—see below) are depicted in Figure 13 (monthly) and Figure 14 (total).

Peak Load Pricing. Both of the bubbles used a system of peak load pricing; that is, more was charged for use of the courts when demand was highest. Both bubbles' peak times and prices were similar; in particular, Bubble B's peak times were 9:00 A.M. to 11:00 P.M. when the price was $6.00 per court hour as against $4.00 in off-peak times. Such a system was designed to spread the

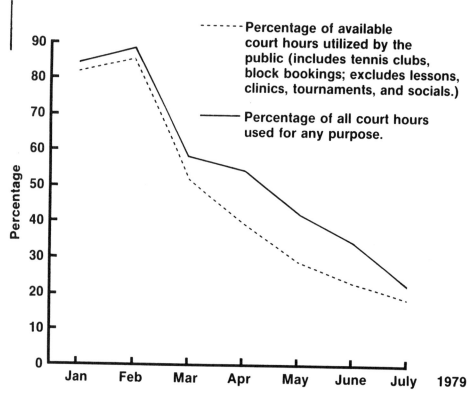

Figure 12. Bubble B: Usage (January-July 1979)

demand over a longer period and encourage more people to play; that is, endeavor not to exclude potential users because of high prices.

Economic Concepts

Economic concepts provide a framework within which to describe and discuss what is observed in the financial operation of

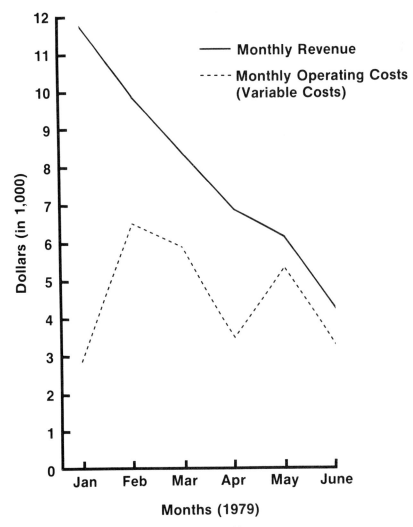

Figure 13. Bubble B: Revenue and expenditure

the bubbles. Here, the definitions are adapted for this context from the work of Lipsey, Sparks, and Steiner (1976:209-212).

1. *Total cost* (TC) is the total cost of producing any given level of output; in this case, the total cost of providing the service of tennis courts in a bubble. Total cost has two parts, total fixed costs (TFC) and total variable costs (TVC). *Fixed costs* are those that do not vary with output; they will be the same if one court

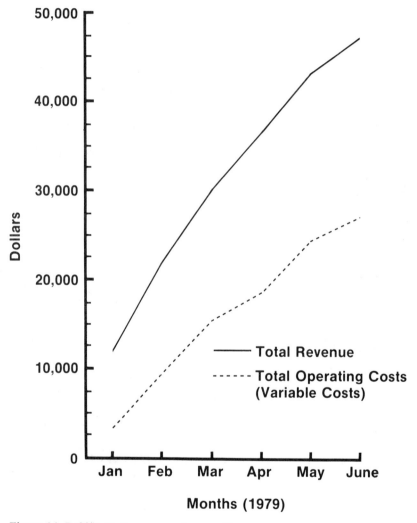

Figure 14. Bubble B: Revenue and expenditure

hour per day is used or if 150 court hours are sold. *Variable costs* are those that vary directly with output; they are likely to include labor costs, lighting costs, and material costs. Sometimes there is some overlap between these two types of costs.

2. *Average total cost* (ATC) is the total cost of producing any given output divided by the number of units produced, or the cost per unit (i.e. the cost of one court hour). ATC may be divided into average fixed costs (AFC) and average variable costs (AVC) just as total costs were divided above.

3. *Marginal cost* (MC) is the increase in total cost resulting from raising the rate of production by one unit. Because fixed costs do not vary with output, marginal fixed costs are always zero. Therefore, marginal costs are necessarily marginal variable costs.

Figures 15 and 16 show smooth curves to emphasize the interrelationships among the various cost curves. Figure 15 illustrates that fixed cost does not vary with output while TVC and TC rise with output (first at a decreasing then at an increasing rate). In Figure 15, AFC declines as output increases; AVC and ATC fall and then rise as output increases; MC does the same and intersects ATC and AVC at their minimum points. The output that corresponds to the minimum short-run ATC is called the *capacity* of the firm; it is not an upper limit so long as the firm recognizes that producing above capacity incurs higher per unit costs. In Figure 16, capacity output is q_c.

ACTION RULES FOR MANAGERS. Municipally operated bubbles are not "firms," but "rules" for firms offer good guidance. Common sense says only produce if that is better than not producing; or, only provide a service if it is better than not providing one. If nothing is produced (*no* service provided), the operating loss will equal the fixed costs. Unless the actual production (renting court time) adds as much to revenue as it adds to the cost, it will increase the loss of the firm (municipality); thus, Rule 1: "A firm should not produce at all if the average revenue from its product does not at least equal or exceed its average variable cost" (Lipsey, Sparks, and Steiner, 1976:211).

Remembering *marginal cost* (MC), a parallel concept is *marginal revenue* (MR), which is the change in total revenue resulting from the sale of one additional unit (one tennis court hour). Hence, the same authors' second rule: "Rule 2: Assuming that it pays the firm to produce at all, it will be profitable for the firm to expand output whenever marginal revenue is greater than marginal cost; expansion must thus continue until marginal revenue equals marginal cost."

Conclusions

Bubble B was the only one for which revenue figures were available. That municipality clearly had more revenue than variable costs and, therefore, could operate so long as the

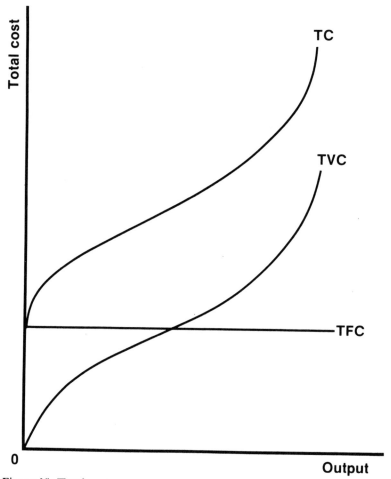

Figure 15. Total-cost curves

taxpayers were prepared to subsidize the TFC. Indeed, the revenue from court rentals was contributing towards the TFC and could, conceivably, cover them in the long run.

Sport managers who are familiar with these bubbles' experiences and economic concepts can readily see the flexibility they have. Some managers of private bubbles must recover TC while others usually must, at least, recover TVC. Without discussing motivational and promotional strategies designed to increase demand, the flexibility for managers lies in the setting of prices so as to contend with whatever other constraints are imposed on them.

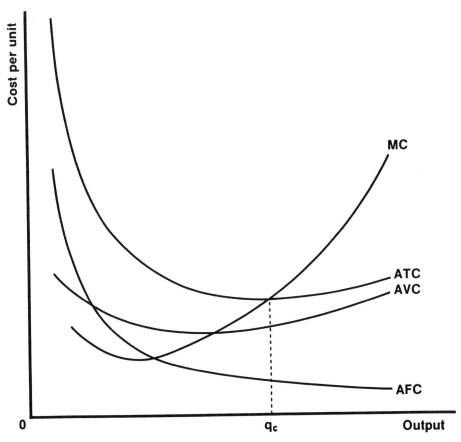

Figure 16. Marginal- and average-cost curves

References

Argyris, C.: What budgeting means to people. In Golembiewski, Robert T. (Ed.): *Public Budgeting and Finance*. Itasca, Illinois, F. E. Peacock, 1968.

Cheek, Logan M.: *Zero-Base Budgeting Comes of Age*. New York, AMACOM, 1977.

Horngren, Charles T.: *Cost Accounting: A Managerial Emphasis*, 3rd ed. Englewood Cliffs, New Jersey, Prentice-Hall, 1972.

Kohler, E. L.: *A Dictionary for Accountants*. Englewood Cliffs, New Jersey, Prentice-Hall, 1956.

Lipsey, R. G., Sparks, G. R., and Steiner, P. O.: *Economics*, 2nd ed. New York, Harper and Row, 1976.

Pyhrr, Peter A.: "Zero-Base Budgeting." Unpublished speech, International Conference of the Planning Executives' Institute, New York, May 15, 1972.

Sherwood, Frank P., and Best, Wallace H.: The local administrator as budgeter. In Golembiewski, Robert T. (Ed.): *Public Budgeting and Finance*. Itasca, Illinois, F. E. Peacock, 1968.

Stedry, Andrew C.: *Budget Control and Cost Behavior*. Englewood Cliffs, New Jersey, Prentice-Hall, 1960.

Turnbull, Augustus, B.: Rationality and budgeting: Is coexistence possible? In Golembiewski, Robert T., Gibson, F., and Cornog, Geoffrey Y. (Eds.): *Public Administration: Readings in Institutions, Processes, Behavior, Policy*, 3rd ed. Chicago, Rand McNally, 1976.

Supplementary Readings

Avedisian, Charles T.: PPBS—its implications for physical education. In Hunsicker, P. (Ed.): *Administrative Theory and Practice in Athletics and Physical Education*. Chicago, Athletic Institute, 1973.

Bole, Ronald: Economic factors influencing athletics. In Zeigler, Earle F., and Spaeth, Marcia J.: *Administrative Theory and Practice in Physical Education and Athletics*. Englewood Cliffs, New Jersey, Prentice-Hall, 1975.

Cheek, *Zero-base budgeting*, 1977. (Contains many ZBB budgets.)

Cumrine, J. P., and Frazier, D. H.: The application of program budgeting in collegiate athletics and recreation: Alternative program structures. In Hunsicker, P. (Ed.): *Administrative Theory and Practice in Athletics and Physical Education*. Chicago, Athletic Institute, 1973, pp. 17-42.

Doh, J. C.: *The Planning-Programming-Budgeting System in Three Federal Agencies*. New York, Praeger, 1971.

Golembiewski, Robert T. (Ed.): *Public Budgeting and Finance: Readings in Theory and Practice*. Itasca, Illinois, F. E. Peacock, 1968.

Haggerty, Terry R.: Physical education budgeting processes in an Ontario school system. In Zeigler and Spaeth, *Administrative Theory and Practice in Physical Education and Athletics*. Englewood Cliffs, New Jersey, Prentice-Hall, 1975, ch. 15, pp. 355-372.

Horngren, *Cost Accounting*, 1972.

International City Management Association: *Planning and Budgeting in*

Municipal Management. Chicago, International City Management Association, 1965.

Lyden, Fremont J., and Miller, Ernest G. (Eds.): *Planning-Programming-Budgeting: A Systems Approach to Management,* 2nd ed. Chicago, Markham, 1972.

Pyhrr, Peter A.: *Zero-Base Budgeting.* New York, John Wiley, 1973.

Case 8.11

Economic Affairs

Parks and recreation department Superintendent Brown and city museums Director Jones were appearing before the City Council Economic Affairs Committee to answer questions on the budget submissions. Committee chairperson Green was not in a pleasant mood.

Green: What's this $50,000 for "historical interpretation" going to be used for?

Brown: Students, holding temporary summer positions, will wear period costumes and explain to visitors what life was like for the pioneers. They'll bake bread, shoe horses, keep shop, and so on so that visitors use all their senses in experiencing the past. It's part of the "living museum" concept.

Green: What's your admission charge?

Brown: There is no charge.

Green: No charge! Do you mean to tell me that you're proposing to spend $50,000 so that a few people can use their senses to experience the past?

Brown: But we've already spent $2 million of capital funds and we're expecting 30,000 visitors this summer.

Green: Put fences round the buildings and let them look from outside. Cut $45,000; we'll resume at noon tomorrow.

Deflated Brown and Jones left the committee room. Brown told Jones that he required a detailed report by 9:00 A.M. the next day recommending how the program could operate under the new circumstances; it would require council approval at some time in the near future.

Case Analysis Method

CAM B (see Chapter 1).

Case 8.12

The Albatross

Economic Affairs Committee Chairperson Green (see Case 8.11) spent very little time looking at the budget submission for the service club fieldhouse before saying: "If these service clubs think all they have to do is provide a facility and then expect the taxpayers to operate it indefinitely, they are mistaken. I want to know how much it costs to operate and I'm not prepared to recommend *any* subsidy at present. Show me full details of all costs and hours of usage by types of participants; then, recommend appropriate charges to cover the costs. I'd like this by 4:00 P.M. tomorrow."

Superintendent Brown set his staff to work that night and had the following before him next morning:

Expense Figures (1975)

General Administration		$ 18,799
Operating Maintenance		92,895
Delivery of Programs		1,855
Total Direct Operating Costs		**$113,549**
Plus: Building Maintenance & Construction		
Preventive Maintenance	$ 9,728	
Master Key System	96	
Special Projects	4,560	
Recoverables	(31)	14,353
Total Current Expenses		**$127,902**
Plus: Direct Overhead		
Program Resources	$12,172	
Building Maint. & Construction	3,653	
Mechanical & Transportation	1,606	17,431
Total Current and Direct Overhead Expenses		**$145,333**
Plus: Indirect Overhead (service sections of department)		24,532
Total Current and Overhead Expenses		**$169,865**

Usage Statistics (1975)

Program	Actual Hours	Participants
Minor Sports	301	25,406
Adult Sports		
(e.g. soccer, hockey)	617	15,750
Tennis	1,785.5	4,331
Joggers' Club	887	53,690
Meeting Rooms		
Public	532	5,713
City	134	453
Special Events		
Commercial	368	110,405
Community Service	106	14,868
Weight Room	32.5	1,001
Locker Room	15	465
Board Room	140	458
Schools	102	4,080
Totals:	5,020	236,620

NOTE: Total hours available for use, assuming it is open for sixteen hours a day for 360 days a year, would be 5,760.

"Well," said Brown, "that's a start. Now give me what Adlerman Green asked for by noon today."

Case Analysis Method
CAM B (see Chapter 1).

Case 8.13

Your Money?

Dean Amhurst decided she would look very carefully at her physical education and recreation faculty's budget to find out if money was being wasted. This, because there was great pressure on her overall allocation; she was to receive a 10 percent cut next year. So, the dean told her chairpersons to assume they had no funds for next year; every expenditure must be justified and listed in priority order.

When the lists came in, Amhurst noted that several expensive items had low priority; particularly, the services of four faculty members. Detailed analysis revealed that the faculty was only 61 percent efficient. Amhurst said to herself, "I know what I'd do if it was my money."

Case Analysis Method
CAM B (see Chapter 1).

LEARNING DESIGN 8.2

FINANCIAL CONTROL

Accounting

Accounting crosses all aspects of sport organizations and "the management accountant's duties are intertwined with executive planning and control" (Horngren, 1972:3). Large sport organizations employ accountants to do the specialized financial work, but sport administrators and managers need some knowledge of accounting if they are to be effective.

According to Horngren (1972:3), the accounting system is "the major quantitative information system in almost every organization" and should provide information for three broad purposes, namely:

1. Internal reporting to managers, for use in planning and controlling routine operations.
2. Internal reporting to managers, for use in making non-routine decisions and in formulating major plans and policies.
3. External reporting to stockholders, government, and other outside parties.

Sport managers and external parties (e.g. elected representatives in governments) share interest in numbers one to three above. However, the emphases of "financial accounting" and "management accounting" (internal) differ; the former is concerned with the "historical, custodial, and stewardship aspects of external reporting" (Horngren, 1972:4) while the latter's emphasis is on numbers one and two above.

"Cost accounting's" purposes parallel numbers one to three above; in fact, one and two are identical. The third purpose, originally, was "accumulating and assigning historical costs to units of product (e.g. tennis court hours) and departments, primarily for purposes of inventory valuation and income determination" (Horngren, 1972:4). So, "cost accounting" is "management accounting" plus part of "financial accounting." Horngren (1972:4) believes that, today, "cost accounting is generally indistinguishable from so-called *management accounting* or *internal accounting*, because it serves multiple purposes."

Three Particular Types Of Information
Simon et al. (1954) identified three types of data, each serving a different purpose, often at various levels of management, which cost (management) accountants need. Horngren (1972:8) believes that Simon et al.'s (1954) data types are timeless in that they help answer three basic questions (which certainly require answering in sport organizations). They are:

1. *Scorecard questions*: Am I doing well or badly?
2. *Attention-directing questions*: What problems should I look into?
3. *Problem-solving questions*: Of the several ways of doing the job, which is the best?

Thus, in sport organizations, the accountant's task is threefold: (1) *Scorekeeping*, which means accumulating data that will enable internal and external parties to evaluate organizational performance; (2) *Attention directing* by reporting information to managers that will enable them to focus attention on operating problems, imperfections, inefficiencies, and opportunities; and, (3) *Problem solving* by quantifying relative merits of possible courses of action and sometimes recommending best procedures (see Horngren, 1972:8). The three facets of the accountant's task sometimes overlap or merge.

Accounting's Division of Labor
A problem faced by accountants is that they fulfill conflicting duties at the same time and this often causes friction within big sport organizations if not properly understood (and carried out). The conflict can arise because accountants are supposed to help

managers and "police" them. Because of this, the controller's department "should divorce attention directing from score-keeping wherever possible" (Horngren, 1972:12).

Figure 17 illustrates the organizational structure of the controller's section in a large city parks and recreation department. As Horngren (1972:13) points out, effectiveness is enhanced by having an accountant personally explain performance reports to line managers. Saying, for example, "This is your program budgeted amount for the year, here's what you've spent this month, and this signifies how much you've spent in the first seven months. Do you think you have enough left for the final five months? What economies can you make elsewhere?" Such interaction builds teamwork, mutual confidence, and saves overspending (which is a very real danger in large sport organizations).

Similarly, the person responsible for "accounts receivable" can have a "quiet word" with whoever should be collecting money, and the auditor can perform his functions in a fashion that makes those being checked feel secure (if that is how they deserve to feel!). Auditing is the official examination and verification of accounts to determine whether or not the organization is spending funds in accordance with the budget. It relates to the collection and disbursement of money, the certification of its deposit, contract payments, and receipt of the goods and services for which the money was used. An audit may also be carried out by a person external to the department.

Internal Control

The American Institute of Certified Public Accountants (1963: 27) defines as follows: "Internal control comprises the plan of organization and all of the coordinate methods and measures adopted within a business to safeguard its assets, check the accuracy and reliability of its accounting data, promote operational efficiency, and encourage adherence to prescribed managerial policies." Horngren (1972:667) regards "promote operational efficiency" as the key phrase and, therefore, *internal control* is more inclusive than *internal check*, which is confined to checking "the accuracy and reliability of its accounting data." In practice, however, the two are often used interchangeably. The

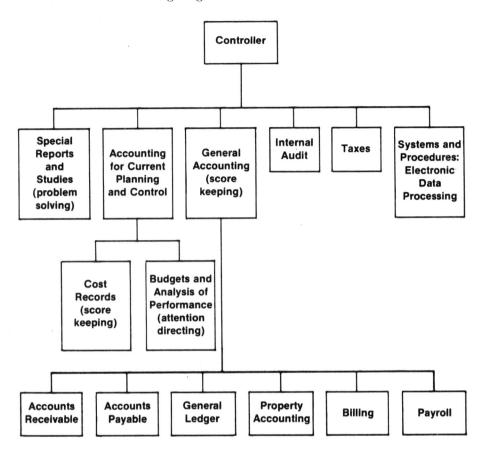

Figure 17. Accounting's division of labor

checklist that follows highlights the common features of good internal control systems that minimize errors, fraud, and waste. It is adapted from Horngren's (1972:667-670) *"principles* or *rules."*

1. RELIABLE PERSONNEL. Only hire, or continue employing, competent and reliable personnel. Low-cost workers may be expensive in the long-run and an accounting system, no matter how refined, can only be as good as the individuals who implement it.

2. SEPARATION OF POWERS. "Record keeping and physical handling of assets should not be in the hands of one person" (Horngren, 1972: 668). For instance, the cashier should not have

access to ledger accounts, the bookkeeper should not handle cash, the general-ledger bookkeeper should not have access to subsidiary records. Also, to ensure that objective, independent records are kept by operating personnel and accounting clerks, the entire accounting function should be separated from the operating function. So, for example, an accounting clerk should check swimming pool revenues against numbered tickets sold; and, a stores record clerk, not the storekeeper, should keep perpetual inventory counts.

3. SUPERVISION. Correctly structured organizations include everyone having a superior, who should oversee and appraise performance.

4. RESPONSIBILITY. By this is meant tracking actions as far down the "lines" in organizations as is feasible so that results may be related to specific individuals. Thus, for example, have part-time ski instructors sign time cards and requisitions. The psychological impact is that responsibility is fixed, and people tend to perform better if they must answer for inefficiency. Also, records of total department cost incurrences can only be made when there is a way of documenting each incurred cost.

5. ROUTINE AND AUTOMATIC CHECKS. Horngren (1972:668) likens this to doing things "by the numbers," which means that all financial transactions should be routinized with built-in checks and safeguards. So, for example, a disbursement will not be made for a gymnastic program specialist if the district recreation coordinator has not signed the voucher. Forms should be designed so that such omissions are readily seen and the transaction can be stopped before money is paid.

6. DOCUMENT CONTROL. Immediate, complete, and tamper-proof recording must be ensured by such measures as "having all source documents prenumbered and accounted for, by using . . . cash registers and locked compartments in invoice-writing machines, and by designing forms for ease of recording" (Horngren, 1972:669). This is particularly important when cash is handled and a useful device, say in a swimming pool, is to offer a reward to clients not offered a receipt when paying to enter.

7. BONDING, VACATIONS, AND ROTATION OF DUTIES. Key people such as executives, managers, and cash or inventory handlers may be subject to temptation to fraud so they "should be

bonded, have understudies, and be forced to take vacations" (Horngren, 1972:669). Another aspect of this principle is that clerks' duties should be rotated, say, every three months.

8. INDEPENDENT CHECK. All phases of a system should be periodically reviewed by outsiders: internal auditors, who normally do not have contact with the operation under review, or by independent public accountants.

This concept goes further, however: bank statements must reconcile with book balances and this check must be carried out by some clerk other than the cash receivables or payables clerk. Similarly, independent checks are made when monthly statements are sent to credit clients, and inventories are physically counted for check against perpetual records.

9. PHYSICAL SAFEGUARDS. ". . . losses of cash, inventories, and records are minimized by safes, locks, watchmen, and limited access" (Horngren, 1972:670).

10. COST FEASIBILITY. Highly complex internal control systems may "strangle people in red tape" or cost more than they are worth. It is not easy to answer this cost-effectiveness question but an attempt must be made. In sport organizations the needs vary greatly: a one-person physical education department in a school is already in a bigger system but can adopt some of the ideas in this checklist; a city parks and recreation department with a budget of $20 million needs to use all of the suggested items in the checklist.

Some Accounting Terms

What has been written so far in this learning design covers many of the non-specialist accounting principles of which sport managers and administrators ought to be aware. This section briefly explains some other common terms.

ASSETS. Anything a sport organization owns is an asset and should be listed in an inventory.

LIABILITIES. Anything owed by a sport organization is a liability; for example, accounts payable to suppliers and wages.

CAPITAL OR EQUITY. Is the difference between assets and liabilities.

THE JOURNAL. Every time a transaction takes place a written record should be made (e.g. receipts, check stubs, cash register tapes). In a journal the data from these pieces of paper are collected as records of daily transactions showing the date, brief descriptions, amounts of money involved, and the types of income or expense affected by the transactions. In big organizations there may be several journals while there may be only a modified one in a school physical education department.

THE LEDGER. Journal information becomes more usable when each item is later transferred (posted) in a ledger account. An account is a record of the increases and decreases in one type of asset, liability, capital, income, or expense. A book or file in which a number of accounts are kept together is called a ledger.

DOUBLE—ENTRY BOOKKEEPING. This refers to every transaction being recorded twice: as a debit in one account and as a credit in another. The sum of debit balances should equal the sum of credit balances.

THE BALANCE SHEET. At particular times, the balance sheet (or financial statement) summarizes assets, liabilities, and capital to show how the "accounting equation" (assets = liabilities + capital) "balances" in the organization. Thus, the *profit-and-loss statement* shows the resulting profit or loss (cf. Ragan, 1977:4-8).

Concluding Summary

Whatever size the sport organization, it will have assets and the administrator must have written documentation of what they are. Detailed financial records must be kept to show how the assets change over time; the records may be "scorekeeping, attention directing, or problem solving." All the data must be kept so as to minimize errors, fraud, and waste.

References

American Institute of C.P.A., Committee on Auditing Procedure: *Auditing Standards and Procedures*. New York, American Institute of Certified Public Accountants, 1963.

Horngren, Charles T.: *Cost Accounting: A Managerial Emphasis*, 3rd ed. Englewood Cliffs, New Jersey, Prentice-Hall, 1972.

Ragan, Robert C.: *Accounting for the Small Business*. Toronto, Coles, 1977.

Simon, H. A., Guetskow, H., Kozmetsky, G., and Tyndall, G.: *Centralization vs. Decentralization in Organizing the Controller's Department*. New York, Controllership Foundation, 1954.

Supplementary Readings

Hjelte, G., and Shivers, Jay S.: *Public Administration of Recreational Services.* Philadelphia, Lea and Febiger, 1972, ch. 13 and 14.

Horngren, *Cost Accounting,* 1972.

Simon, Herbert A.: *Administrative Behavior: A Study of Decision-Making Processes in Administrative Organization,* 3rd ed. New York, The Free Press, 1976, ch. IX.

Weston, J. Fred, and Brigham, Eugene F.: *Essentials of Managerial Finance.* New York, Holt, Rinehart and Winston, 1968.

Case 8.21

The Tennis Caper

Dramatis personae

Recreation department personnel in descending line order:

        Superintendent

        Director of Recreation

        District Recreation Head

        District Recreation Coordinator

        Tennis Program Supervisor (Af Said)

        Tennis Instructor (George Brinkley)

Also:

        The Police Chief

        Detective Gray

At the height of the tennis "boom" the *City Times* developed a sponsorship arrangement with the parks and recreation department: the *City Times* agreed to provide full-page advertising for "Learn-to-play tennis" classes on city courts and pay half the instructional costs. The scheme was designed to promote the paper (*City Times* Tennis Month) and tennis. Thus, the department had to manage the classes and only collect five dollars per participant for a five-day (one hour per evening) course of instruction. The city would pay other costs (if any) out of budgeted "Learn-to" funds. Several hundred people registered for the classes so many part-time instructors were required. Each instructor received five dollars per hour and had eight people in each class.

In the east district, the tennis program supervisor was Af Said who had to coordinate the activities of twenty-five instructors.

One was George Brinkley, and here is the story George told the superintendent later.

GEORGE'S STORY. Af told me that no one really knew exactly how many classes there were because many who registered did not show up; so he wanted to make a deal. Af said he would complete all the papers to say I was teaching ten classes when, in fact, I would only do five. In that way I would be paid 125 dollars I didn't deserve and we would then split the takings.

I thought his offer was disgusting so I decided to catch him out. I told the police chief what was going on and said it may be happening elsewhere. Anyway, he assigned Detective Gray to the case and Gray said he would need evidence of the final transaction. So, on payday I received my cheque and took Af along to the bank where I cashed it. I then handed Af sixty dollars at which time Gray arrested him.

AF'S STORY. (told to the superintendent with Detective Gray present). George Brinkley's a liar. He owed me that money from a previous loan and I was just going to collect it. I'd been pressing him to pay it back for some time.

The superintendent then called his other "line" people in and said (for starters): "Who signed George's worksheets and does anybody know if the classes took place?"

Case Analysis Method
  CAM B (see Chapter 1).

Case 8.22

The Racing Game

By the mid-1960s, skiing in Europe was a popular activity for British school students who went for about ten-day periods in school groups. Travel agents usually organized the trips and gave "free places" to sponsor teachers for each twenty paying students.

Physical education teacher Mike Efram had led two groups and planned to take a third around Easter 1965. Mike's wife went with him to provide general help and Margaret Bross, another physical education teacher, agreed to join the 1965 trip. Thirty students signed up to go to Austria so that meant one-and-one-half free places were available for the staff. Mike and Margaret agreed to share the one-half cost, which was twenty-two pounds. Margaret agreed to organize the pre-ski fitness training and the related social studies preparation, and Mike would deal with the travel agents and collect the money from the students. Each student had to pay ten pounds in October 1964 and the balance of thirty-four pounds by January 30, 1965.

Mike was regarded as a thoroughly trustworthy citizen and a happily married man with two teenaged boys. His second teaching subject was mathematics and he was very quick at mental arithmetic and strong on probability. With these qualities known at the local soccer club, a betting shop owner asked if he would like to earn extra money on weekends and during vacations. Mike agreed and thought it would help him to take the whole family to Austria. This work began in September 1964 and by Christmas Mike was "hooked" on gambling; mainly betting on horse races. He was modestly successful at first but by early January 1965 he had betting debts of 200 pounds.

The famous Grand National steeplechase was coming up in March. Mike worked out various complicated "odds" and estimated that he could make a small fortune with very little risk if he wisely placed bets with the total skiing fund. When the race ended, Mike had lost all the students' money; his wife told Margaret who explained to the students that the trip was cancelled.

Case Analysis Method
CAM B (see Chapter 1).

Case 8.23

A Stitch In Time

Barnoven, a large Canadian city, had an annual parks and recreation budget in 1976 of $20 million when Commissioner Mark Meehan was hired. Within a month of starting in his new job in August, Meehan had severe worries about the financial information his management team of four directors was receiving. Rough calculations led him to suspect that he could be $500,000 overspent by December. Meehan demanded immediate stringent savings measures be taken and he hired Corporate

Systems Analysts Ltd., (CSA) to provide him with a report on his controller's section by the end of November, 1976. There follows CSA's abbreviated report:

(a) *Transaction Listings and General Ledger Accounting*

The high number of coding and keypunching errors would make it desirable for more frequent edit listings to be issued throughout the month so that errors can be detected and corrections made before the month end.

(b) *Workorder Reports*

The effectiveness of the workorder system concept under which workorder numbers are used is limited as there is often no estimated cost against which the cost actually incurred can be controlled.

Cost summaries prepared monthly by computer for each workorder are bulky and difficult to effectively use when a large number of work orders are in use and costs need to be controlled on the workorder over a period of several months. The responsible manager finds it difficult to relate the cost summaries to the budget performance report for his area of responsibility.

The monthly workorder summary by account and the workorder summary by month are not generally distributed by the accounting department to the line operating manager.

(c) *Commitment Accounting*

The general ledger and budget performance reports are made less meaningful due to the delay in getting certain costs which have been incurred into the system. In particular:

The cash basis of accounting adopted within Barnoven means that invoices for materials and supplies received are not processed and included in the financial records until payment is actually made.

The bi-weekly payroll cutoff does not result in a full month's labor cost being charged during each month.

A commitment accounting system for purchase orders has recently been introduced which should be integrated into the budget performance reporting system. Parks and recreation is establishing its own system that will cover types of purchase orders not included in the automated system. This system too should be integrated into the budget performance reporting system.

(d) *Inventory Management Reports*

Two weekly stock status reports are received by parks and recreation relative to the management of the department's stores operation. The first report, covering all stock in parks and recreation stores and used to assist in the placing of orders, has the following deficiencies:

(1) It does not highlight stock items at or near order levels and no indication of usage is provided to assist in determining quantities to be ordered.

(2) Minimum and maximum stock levels have not been determined on economic ordering principles.

(3) There is no mechanism for the regular adjustment to reflect current demand patterns.

The second report, identifying stock by location and used by local storekeepers as a guide to the stock available in the local warehouse, is deficient as follows:

(1) The report is always out of date.

(2) There is no price data which could be useful to the local storekeeper.

(e) *Corporate Accounting Reports*

A lack of confidence in corporate accounting reports due to the high incidence of errors in coding and/or keypunching, lateness of reports, and unsuitability of data has led to the maintenance of manual accounting systems by many parks and recreation supervisors.

(f) *PPBS*

(1) *Definition of Programs and Activities is inconsistent*

Certain programs and activities coincide with an organizational unit; others do not.

Recreation has designated decentralized delivery into a district program whereas maintenance and construction has not.

Programs range in costs from approximately $30,000 to over $1 million.

(2) *Program Cost Elements are missing*

(3) *Program Revenue is not related to program costs*

(4) *There are no quantitative measures*

The **PPB** report covers cost only and does not, at present, attempt to measure the service provided either in terms of level of service or in terms of cost per unit of service. As a result, variances shown on the budget performance report reflect only rate of expenditure; they do not consider effectiveness, efficiency and service levels.

(5) *Variance analysis is not systematically undertaken*

The discipline of analyzing and reporting on variances, their causes, and the corrective action being taken is not in place.

Variances are shown for the program activity in total only and variances by type of expenditure are not shown.

(6) *Budgeting has largely remained traditional*

The budgeting process is still largely an incremental budgeting approach where the historical cost of each organizational element is increased to compensate for inflationary trends in planned organizational changes. Program orientation is lacking.

(7) *Timeliness*

PPBS reports are not timely.

Commissioner Meehan kept his fingers crossed until near the end of January 1977 when the final figures became available for 1976; his department was $200,000 underspent.

Case Analysis Method
   CAM A (see Chapter 1).

Summary

1. A budget is a quantitative expression of a plan of action and an aid to coordination and implementation.
2. Budgets usually cover one fiscal year though some span long periods.
3. Current budgets are concerned with the operation of the organization for a designated time period.
4. Capital budgets involve long-term planning for land, buildings, sports fields, equipment, and other long-lived assets. They are executed through current operations budgets.
5. Revenue budgets are those that project all revenues that the sport organization expects to receive in a designated time period.
6. Line-item budgets list objects to be purchased and salaries to be paid without attempting to justify the items.
7. Performance budgets show a clear relation of costs to service standards, volumes of work, and methods of working.
8. Zero-base budgeting forces each manager to begin the process from "scratch"; assuming nothing and so justifying every expenditure in decision-packaged priority order.
9. Special project budgets are used in sport organizations for special events of limited time duration.
10. The major elements of the PPBS cycle are:
    (a) the determination of objectives, with measurement criteria;
    (b) the design of programs and the consideration of alternatives;
    (c) budgeting and resource allocation;
    (d) execution of programs; and,
    (e) evaluation of results.
11. Total cost (TC) is the total cost of producing any given level of output. They consist of total fixed costs (TFC) and total variable costs (TVC).
12. Fixed costs are those that do not vary with output.
13. Variable costs vary directly with output.
14. Average total cost (ATC) is the total cost of producing

any given output divided by the number of units produced, or the cost per unit.

15. Marginal cost (MC) is the increase in total cost resulting from raising the rate of production by one unit.

16. Accounting systems have three broad purposes:
    (a) internal reporting to managers for use in planning and controlling;
    (b) internal reporting to managers for use in planning, policy-making, and in making non-routine decisions; and,
    (c) external reporting to stockholders, governments, and other outside parties.

17. The sport organization accountant's task is threefold:
    (a) Scorekeeping;
    (b) Attention directing; and,
    (c) Problem solving.

18. Accountants help managers and "police" them so they should divorce attention directing from scorekeeping.

19. Internal control (IC) systems should minimize errors, fraud, and waste. The IC checklist contains ten items.

Concepts For Review

Budget	Time coverage
Current budget	Capital budget
Revenue budget	Line-item budget
PPBS	Advantages of PPBS
Disadvantages of PPBS	ZBB
Advantages of ZBB	Disadvantages of ZBB
Special project budget	The budget cycle
The budget schedule	Peak load pricing
Total cost (TC) =TFC + TVC	ATC = AFC + AVC
Marginal cost	Capacity
Economic action rules for managers	Accounting
	Management accounting
Financial accounting	Internal accounting
Cost accounting	Attention directing
Scorekeeping	Helping *and* policing
Problem solving	Internal check
Internal control	Reliable personnel

Internal control checklist

Separation of powers

Responsibility

Document control

Independent check

Assets

Capital or equity

The ledger

The balance sheet

Supervision

Routine/automatic checks

Bonding

Physical safeguards

Liabilities

The journal

Double-entry bookkeeping

Profit and loss statement

Questions for Oral or Written Discussion

1. CAM C (see Chapter 1) applied to instructor-specified topics taken from this chapter.

2. Assume you are head of physical education at the high school you attended. Using any current equipment supply catalogue for guidance, prepare a line-item budget for what you think would be needed to operate the instructional classes for the coming year. Initially, estimate the total cost of what you need, then prepare a budget that will allow you to have 80 percent of what you need.

3. Obtain a copy of your sport organization's most recent budget. Next year you will have 15 percent less money; prepare a ZBB.

4. Visit a large sport organization (such as a city parks and recreation department), study all its internal control procedures, and then write a critique that identifies its strengths and weaknesses.

5. Frankton City Recreation Department seeks your advice; it has three competent clerical employees who must perform the following functions (each of which requires the same amount of time, except for *f* and *g*):

(a) Maintain general ledger;

(b) Maintain accounts-payable ledger;

(c) Maintain accounts-receivable ledger;

(d) Prepare checks for signature;

(e) Maintain disbursements journal;

(f) Issue credits on client registration cancellations;

(g) Reconcile the bank account; and,

(h) Handle and deposit cash receipts.

What would you recommend each of them should do to ensure the best internal control? Why? List four pairs of possible unsatisfactory combinations of the listed functions (Adapted from a CPA examination; cf. Horngren, 1972:672).

Chapter 9

POLICIES AND PLANS

A LL PREVIOUS CHAPTERS could be linked with the material of this chapter and so could the one that follows. However, here, the concepts of policies and plans are dealt with in a fashion which isolates facets of them from previous, and future, book content. The intended logical sequence of the chapter is as follows: decision making leads to policy formulation and, out of policies, plans can be developed.

LEARNING DESIGN 9.1

DECISION MAKING AND POLICIES

Decision Making

Immediately above, decision making was stated to precede policy formulation and planning. So it does, but it also occurs during policy formulation and during planning. Indeed during all aspects of administrative behavior. It is what readers of this book have been doing every time they analyzed a case. So, most decision making occurs after policy formulation; in fact, policy-making is to decision making as strategy is to tactics (cf. Chapter 2). The issue of values in decision making has already been emphasized (cf. Chapter 2); thus, administrators ought to make right decisions, but, their values will impinge anyway. First, the decision-making process will be examined as it has been identified by noted experts.

The Process of Decision Making
According to Simon (1960:1) decision making is synonymous with "managing" and comprises three principal phases:

1. Finding occasions for making decisions (i.e. surveying the economic, technical, political, and social conditions which call for new actions). This Simon (1960:2) calls the *intelligence* activity (using the military meaning of intelligence).
2. Finding possible courses of action (i.e. inventing, designing, and developing possible courses of action for handling situations in which decisions are needed). Simon (1960:2) calls this *design* activity.
3. Choosing among courses of action, which Simon calls *choice* activity.

Generally, "intelligence" precedes "design" which precedes "choice." However, the stages may be more complex, for "design" can call for new "intelligence" and sub-problems may develop at any stage that may require all three phases themselves. Ultimately, though, the three phases can be discerned (Simon, 1960:3).

To counter the possible objection that he ignores carrying out decisions, Simon (1960:3) observes that executing decisions is again decision-making activity for it falls to others to design new courses of action and make appropriate choices of action to carry them out. Hence, his decision-making paradigm, containing three phases, applies in most executive (and managerial) activity. It is worthy of note, however, that in the literature writers often add other phases to the three; for example, implementation, evaluation, and redefinition of alternate problems.

Addressing the issue of the basis for decisions, Simon (1976: xxix) distinguishes between "economic man" and "administrative man." The former deals with the "real world" in all its complexity and selects the rationally determined best course of action in order to maximize his returns. Alternatively, "administrative" man looks for courses of action that are satisfactory or "good enough." He is content with gross simplifications and does not search for the sharpest needle in the haystack but for one that will sew. So, as economic man "maximizes," administrative man "satisfices." He uses a simple picture of the situation "that takes into account just a few of the factors that he regards as most relevant and crucial" (Simon, 1976:xxx).

HODGKINSON'S PARADIGM. Hodgkinson (1978:62) does not regard the satisficing decision maker as irrational; rather such a person has modified "levels of aspiration in coming to terms with complexity" and settles upon practical solutions. Such action "is pragmatic but not unreasonable."

As a starting point in the decision-making process, Hodgkinson (1978:48) accepts Lichfield's (1956) cycle of events, which is: (1) definition of issue, (2) analysis of existing situation, (3) calculation and delineation of alternatives, (4) deliberation, and (5) choice. Clearly, this list can easily be collapsed into Simon's three phases. However, Hodgkinson (1978:48) is particularly interested in "the specifically administrative act," which is decision making. Like Lichfield (1956), he recognizes that it may be "rational, deliberate, discretionary, purposive," or "irrational, habitual, obligatory, random," or "any combination thereof."

Logically, Hodgkinson (1978:50-51) argues that a point, or time interval, is reached in the decision-making process when a choice has to be made. Though there may be several possible alternatives initially, finally it is always a choice between not more than two alternatives. Other options are eliminated along the way and indecisiveness or "dithering" occurs when rejected choices are reintroduced.

Rational administrators then, according to Hodgkinson (1978: 52), follow the following pattern or paradigm:

(1) *Delineation of the ultimate binary alternative.* "In the end it comes down to this or this."
(2) *Assessment of the consequences of each alternative.* This step can be subdivided as to fact and as to value....
(3) *Calculation of expected values* . . . The rational choice is the highest expected value.

In number two above, the decision maker is constrained by the extent of the facts and his/her capability to interpret them. Value was discussed extensively in Chapter Two. So Hodgkinson's (1978:52) paradigm (Stage Two) has the decision maker assigning probabilities (p) of selected outcomes and values (v) to the alternative outcomes. In the third, and final, stage, $p \times v =$ "expected value." The following example illustrates how the numbers are used.

Assume a new dean of physical education and recreation is to be appointed in a university, or a superintendent to a city parks and recreation department. Having used the process with all the candidates, it is down to one. Thus, there are four logically possible outcomes (o): (o_1) appointed and adequate, (o_2) appointed and inadequate, (o_3) not appointed and would have been adequate, and (o_4) not appointed and would have been inadequate. Assume the administration is indifferent between o_1 and o_4 (valuationally neutral) so that the point is to avoid hiring a failure (o_2) and failing to hire a success (o_3). Now, for *example*, the following v's are ascribed from a range of –1 (totally negative) through 0 (indifference) to +1 (totally positive): –0.6 to o_2 and –0.2 to o_3.

Finally, to conclude the illustrative example, it is assumed that likelihood of adequacy is uncertain so all the p's are 0.5. (However, note the p's could have been otherwise; e.g. 0.75, indicating a 75 percent chance of being adequate and a 25 percent chance of being inadequate.) The decisional calculation is then completed as follows:

Outcome	p	v	$p \times v$
o_1	0.5	0	0
o_2	0.5	–0.6	–0.3
o_3	0.5	–0.2	–0.1
o_4	0.5	0	0

Therefore, ($o_1 + o_2$) = –0.3 (possibilities for *hiring*) and, ($o_3 + o_4$) = –0.1 (possibilities for not hiring)

Since ($o_3 + o_5$) is a higher expected value, the decision is "do *not* hire" (cf. Hodgkinson, 1978:53-54).

Hodgkinson's (1978:54) point is that decision making, ultimately, is in the realms of probability and value. The decision maker must analyze (delineate the alternatives) and impute (ascribe p's and v's). However, he leaves the question open as to whether his paradigm is rational, logical, and amenable to science; probably not. Specifying p's may be scientific, specifying v's is philosophical and administrative (Hodgkinson, 1978:59-60).

In presenting his paradigm as simply as possible, Hodgkinson (1978:60-61) realized that he had omitted from consideration a number of key factors: personality variables; political considerations ("who really decides?"); plus complexities of setting, contingency, and decision type. Additionally, he drew attention to the fact that other aberrations are found in practice. For example, when democratic values "settle" but "do not prove"; when deciding is given over to so-called "experts"; and, when there is overconcentration on factual quantification. With reference to the last-mentioned aberration, Hodgkinson (1978:64) cites the indiscriminate use of computer hardware with reference to Kaplan's (1964:28) Law as a form of psychological retreat. The law states that when a small boy discovers the use of the hammer he tends to find that all objects need hammering!

Another form of insidious irrationality occurs when there is a pretence of open decision making when that is not really the case. For example, in Edmonton, Alberta, many people who lived near the 1978 Commonwealth Games stadium did not want it near their homes. Numerous public meetings were held and an expensive (about $20,000) "social impact" study carried out to assist in deciding the final site. However, the site decision had already been made by key parties and thus the "open" procedure was nullified.

Finally, illustrative but not exhaustive, is the practice of bureaucrats' "not ours to question why" attitude (Hodgkinson, 1978:64), which is a form of retreat to managerialism (cf. Chater 2).

Policies

A Link With Decision Making

Simon (1960:8) distinguished between two polar types of decisions: programmed and non-programmed. They are not mutually exclusive but make up a continuum of highly programmed decisions at one end to highly non-programmed decisions at the other end.

PROGRAMMED DECISIONS. Decisions are said to be programmed when they are routine and repetitive or when the organization has developed specific processes for dealing with them so that they do not have to be worked out afresh each time. Traditional techniques of programmed decision making are habit, clerical routines, standard operating procedures, and the organization's structural and cultural controls. Modern techniques are developing such as operations research, mathematical analysis, computer simulation, and electronic data processing (Simon, 1960:8-13). Simon, a Nobel Economics Prize winner, has done a great deal of work in cognitive psychology particularly linked with computer simulations. Those interested in such aspects should consult Simon (1979). The main point here is that some programmed decisions are often referred to as policies in many sport situations and are discussed under "internal policies" and "sport policies" below.

NON-PROGRAMMED DECISIONS. Decisions are said to be non-programmed when they are "one-shot, ill-structured novel . . . (and) handled by general problem-solving processes" (Simon, 1960:8). Or, they are the type discussed above in Hodgkinson's paradigm.

Policy Making

It has been shown that a decision must be made to make policy; that, in the terminology of this book, decision making is usually managerial more than administrative; and, that many programmed decisions in sport organizations are called policies. Now, the more precise definitions of policies are presented together with an analysis of the types of administrators who make them.

DEFINITIONS. These are some of the more reputable definitions which capture the essence of what policies are:

> . . . the decision aspect of that level of leadership which involves the alteration, origination, or elimination of organizational structure . . . the formulation of substantive goals and objectives for the organization as well as procedures and devices for the achieving of goals and the evaluating of performance (Katz and Kahn, 1966:259-260).
> . . . a body of principle to guide action . . . a design to shape the future by exerting influence upon trends that flow from the past into the present (Lerner and Lasswell, 1951:ix).
> . . . the setting of governing relations or norms, rather than in the more usual terms as the setting of goals, objectives or ends . . . (Vickers, 1965:31).

Hodgkinson (1978:66-67) regards policy making as "the epitome of administrative action" for "policy and philosophy coalesce." Thus, policymaking is "high level" in that it occurs high in organizational hierarchies and because it is concerned with ". . . values relating to the overall purpose, mission, or 'life' of the organization."

It should be noted that "levels" lead to organizational problems and even pathology for, once established at a high level, the policy may have to pass through a long chain of "sordid managerial detail" before it is effected. So, there is psychological distancing and the danger of ends and means being separated (Hodgkinson, 1978:76-77). For example, a university administration may establish a "right" sport policy which is ultimately carried out by a low level coach who wants to win at nearly any cost.

Reverting to the definitional effort, *internal* policy "establishes decision rules or parameters which determine and define whole realms of subordinate and contingent decisions," (cf. programmed decisions) and *external* policy is concerned with planning for the organization, as a whole, "in a context of competing and conflicting environmental factors" (Hodgkinson, 1978:68-69).

METAVALUES. Very likely to influence sport organization policies are metavalues. Hodgkinson (1978:180) describes organizations' value environments as "morally primitive" and corresponding with individuals' value levels when in Maslow's lower reaches. So, what are these values? Hodgkinson (1978:180) defines: "A metavalue is a concept of the desirable so vested and entrenched that it seems to be beyond dispute or contention . . . Examples . . . wealth, life . . . democracy (in a democratic society) . . . education, rationality, and consistency (amongst academics) . . . they go for the most part unquestioned, *beyond* value, and so intrude unconsciously to affect value behaviour."

The principal organizational metavalues are maintenance ("the organization must maintain itself"), growth ("the status quo is not enough"), effectiveness and efficiency (what is desirable but not necessarily right). Note that these four metavalues apply to organizations, not individuals. To illustrate, Hodgkinson (1978:185) says, "Thou shalt not destroy thine organization," and, "What's good for General Motors is good for the country," and, "My country, right or wrong." It should be noted that such metavalues may produce the opposite. Periodically, then, they should be examined (see the questions at the end of this chapter).

POLICYMAKERS. Administrators who make policies fall into one of three broad categories (Hodgkinson, 1978:67-68):

(1) Those who come to office by some form of political process (appointment, patronage, election; often with no formal administrative training).

(2) Career or professional administrators.

(3) Collegial administrators (organizational members who are professionals in some field appointed, or elected, from within the field for a specified term; with or without administrative training). A prime example is a university physical education department chairman.

Clearly then, personality and motivational factors affect policy-making; the term used to describe this additional complexity is the interest factor. There are three kinds: (1) self-interest; (2) organization interest (i.e. the collectivity which is the organization or the policymaker qua organization member); and, (3) extra-oganization (Hodgkinson, 1978:73). The three types are not mutually exclusive. Paralleling the kinds of interest are the modes, which are opportunistic, rationalistic, and doctrinaire. Alternatively, there may be anti-strategies of laissez faire and negativism. The former here means not having policies while the latter means just knowing what is not wanted. For example, the Economic Affairs Committee member whose aim is not to spend anymore money on recreation; he "doesn't care what they do with what they've got."

Sport Policies

The best way to keep sport organization policies current is to place them in loose-leaf ring binders so that they can be readily added to, deleted from, and amended. The extent of policies used in sport organizations varies considerably from those that require very thick manuals to others of much more modest proportions. City parks and recreation policies are very extensive, university departments are less so, and school physical education departments' manuals are often thin. Sometimes, the latter take the form of notices or are included in other documents. While this practice is useful, it is advisable also to have a complete and separate manual. A copy should either be given to all subordinates or, at least, one should be kept in a centrally known location. When clients need to know policies, means must be found to communicate the information to them. Newsletters and ringed clipboards placed on bulletin boards serve this purpose well. It is useful to type the policies on distinctively colored paper so that they are readily identifiable as policies.

External sport organization policies should serve the functions described above and also detail formal relationships with outside agencies. For example, a school and a parks and recreation department must have a written policy governing any joint facility use agreement they may have.

Internal sport organization policies cover such items as those listed in Table VII. This list is not intended for any one sport organization, nor is it complete.

For illustrative purposes, an example policy taken from a Canadian junior high school is in Table VIII. It is not a good idea to number policies (adding and deleting difficulties) but they should be dated and amendment dates should be included. The latter aspects are needed in case anyone is using out-of-date policies.

TABLE VII
TYPICAL TOPICS REQUIRING SPORT ORGANIZATION POLICIES

Topic	Notes
Gymnasium use	Priorities for classes, intramurals, athletics, band, drama, cleaning, repairs, or other.
	Dress, particularly shoes.
Security	Keys, alarm system.
Facility bookings	Particularly racquet courts.
Fitness/Medical	To participate—who decides (Dr., nurse, teacher).
Risk Management	Includes first aid procedure (see Chapter 7).
Travel	To contests, conferences, who pays, substitute teacher (?).
Outdoor Recreation	Field trip sponsors, qualifications, safety standards.
Class management	Attendance, grading, tardiness, dress, showers, towels, lockers.
Equipment control	Borrowing procedures, repair, replacement, storage.
Appeals	Teachers, coaches, managers, clients.
Budget making	Different organizational members' roles.
Expenditures	Who authorizes and to what extent.
Crowd control	
Fair play	
Visiting teams	
Public Relations	Who is responsible for press reports, for example.

TABLE VIII
GRADING POLICY

(1) *ATTENDANCE*

Students must attend physical education classes in proper P.E. strip to pass the course. If a student has missed more than 25 percent of his/her classes he/she will not receive credit for the P.E. course. In other words a student will be marked absent for missing and for not attending with P.E. strip (this will be marked as NO STRIP and will be noted on the student's report). Proper P.E. strip is considered to be athletic shoes, socks, shorts and/or sweat pants, t-shirts and/or sweat shirts. Cut-offs are not acceptable. P.E. strip is available through the school but it is not necessary to purchase it at school.

Twenty-five percent is the equivalent of approximately six classes per term.

A student who is excused for a period, either for illness or other class commitments, *MUST* see his/her P.E. teacher and ask to be excused. In such cases the student, if given permission, will be marked excused and these classes will not be considered as absences. They will also be marked on the report.

Students who miss more than a week of school (3 or more consecutive classes) because of illness or family business are asked to bring a note from their doctor in the case of illness and a note from home regarding extended vacations or the like. These absences may influence the grade for a term but will not carry over to the student's cumulative grades as the year progresses if documentation is produced. It is the student's responsibility to bring the appropriate written explanation to his/her P.E. teacher.

(2) *EXTENDED MEDICAL EXCUSES*

Any student who is going to miss P.E. due to injury or a medical problem for an extended period will be asked to take a curriculum outline to his/her family doctor and find out in which activities he/she is able to participate. If there are none, then the student and the class teacher will make arrangements for another non-vigorous activity to take place.

Students who are not allowed to take P.E. for the full year should see their teacher immediately as they will be reprogrammed into another course.

(3) *GRADING*

Criteria for grading in P.E. are as follows:
1. Attendance (in strip, ready to participate)
2. Attitude toward and during class
3. Effort—does the student work to his/her potential?

P.E. students will receive one of A, B, C+, C, P, I, F.

A - perfect or near perfect attendance
  - contributions in and to class are positive (outstanding, exceptional, excellent)
  - setting a good example to follow
  - effort is CONSISTENTLY his/her best in all class activities

B - good attendance
  - generally positive attitude
  - performance near potential consistently

C+/C
  - adequate, regular attendance

- generally positive attitude
- efforts not near potential consistently

P - irregular attendance (not exceeding more than 6 missed periods per term)
  - inconsistent attitudes and efforts
  - seldom puts forth more than minimal standards

I - incomplete attendance
  - excused periods are not counted as absences
  - this does not mean failure, rather that the student's poor attendance prohibits evaluation

F - fail

The attempt is to grade students against themselves. Talent and ability do not qualify the student for a high grade. Each and every student must work to his/her potential in all classes to earn his/her grade.

HEAD, P.E. DEPARTMENT

(Amended September 1976 and September 1978.)

References

Hodgkinson, C.: *Towards a Philosophy of Administration*. Oxford, Basil Blackwell, 1978.

Kaplan, A.: *The Conduct of Inquiry*. San Francisco, Chandler, 1964.

Katz, D., and Kahn, Robert L.: *The Social Psychology of Organizations*. New York, Wiley, 1966.

Lerner, D., and Lasswell, H. D. (Eds.): *The Policy Sciences: Recent Developments in Scope and Method*. Palo Alto, Stanford University Press, 1951.

Lichfield, G. H.: Notes on a general theory of administration. *Administrative Science Quarterly*, January, 1956.

Simon, Herbert A.: *The New Science of Management Decision*. New York, Harper and Brothers, 1960.

Simon, Herbert A.: *Administrative Behavior: A Study of Decision-Making Processes in Administrative Organization*, 3rd ed. New York, The Free Press, 1976.

Simon, Herbert A.: *Models of Thought*. New Haven, Yale University Press, 1979.

Vickers, G.: *The Art of Judgment: A Study of Policymaking*. London, Chapman and Hall, 1965.

Important Related Readings
Hodgkinson, *Towards a Philosophy*, 1978, ch. 3, 4, and 11.
Simon, *Thought*, 1976.

Supplementary Readings
Barnard, Chester I.: *The Functions of the Executive*, 30th anniv. ed. Cambridge, Massachusetts, Harvard University Press, 1976.

Braybrooke, D., and Lindblom, C. E.: *A Strategy of Decision: Policy Evaluation as a Social Process.* Glencoe, Illinois, The Free Press, 1963.

Gore, W. J., and Silander, F. S.: A bibliographical essay on decision making. *Administrative Science Quarterly,* 4:112, 1959.

Hodgkinson, C.: Philosophy, politics, and planning: An extended rationale for synthesis. *Educational Administration Quarterly,* XI:11, 1975.

Katz and Kahn, *Social Psychology,* 1966.

Kaufman, G. M., and Thomas, H. (Eds.): *Modern Decision Analysis.* Harmondsworth, Penguin, 1977.

Lindblom, Charles E.: The science of muddling through. *Public Administration Review,* Spring:155-169, 1959.

Lichfield, *General Theory,* 1956.

Scott, W. A.: *Values and Organizations.* Chicago, Rand McNally, 1965.

Self, P.: *Administrative Theories and Politics.* London, Allen and Unwin, 1972.

Simon, *New Science,* 1960.

Stufflebeam, D.L., et al.: *Educational Evaluation and Decision Making.* Itasca, Illinois, Peacock, 1971.

Vickers, *Judgment,* 1965.

Vickers, G.: *Value System and Social Process.* Harmondsworth, Penguin, 1970.

Waldo, D.: Organization theory: An elephantine problem. *Public Administration Review,* XXI:210, 1961.

Case 9.11

Be Prepared

Nova High School was located in a small city of 30,000 people, had an enrollment of approximately 700 students and was situated in a middle class residential district. The P.E. Department consisted of two full-time teachers: Mr. Cranston, the new department head, taught the boys' classes and Miss White taught the girls'. The classes were large but well organized, uniforms were mandatory, and a towel system was provided for student use after their required showers.

In the school's main building there was a nurse's room, which had a few cots and some basic first-aid equipment. The school nurse was only at the school one or two days a week because she serviced other schools in addition to Nova. In one corner of the basketball gym there was a small office in which Mr. Cranston had a desk and a chair, some bookshelves, and a filing cabinet. The walls and shelves were full of pictures and trophies, and the office was generally cluttered. The phone on the desk was connected to the main office.

Bob was enrolled in one of Mr. Cranston's P.E. 11 classes. An average student, he was a slightly better than average athlete. Although he was on the school's basketball team, Bob was only a "benchwarmer" but was a popular and friendly person. In March, the classes did a unit on basketball. Each class was divided into four teams and played a round robin schedule over the space of two weeks. On the next to last day of the basketball unit, Bob's team was playing and Mr. Cranston was refereeing while the Grade 12 teaching assistant refereed the game on the other court. About two-thirds of the way through the class period, Bob caught a long pass and dribbled down the court all the way to the basket before shooting a "lay-up." As he turned to go back up the court, he kept his eye on the ball, which hung on the rim before finally dropping through the basket. Just as he turned his head to see where he was going, he collided with another player who was still running quickly towards the basket. Both players fell to the floor, but while the other player was able to get up right away, Bob remained motionless on the gym floor.

Within thirty seconds Bob appeared semi-conscious and sat up; his nose was obviously broken. Many thoughts and questions flashed through Mr. Cranston's mind: Was it safe to move the boy? What if he had other head injuries? Was the nurse at school? Should he phone the main office to get an ambulance? Should he drive Bob to the hospital? Who would look after the class if he did? Several boys offered conflicting advice for they could see that Mr. Cranston was confused.

Case Analysis Method
CAM A (see Chapter 1).

Case 9.12

To Be Or Not To Be

V.P. Comprehensive School in England had 1800 students and the staff complement for boys' physical education was three specialists. Department head, Jack Jones, was a rugby enthusiast who coached the first fifteen and supervised other rugby coaches. Brian Walsh, the number two, was a keen cricketer who took overall responsibility for that major sport. The third position was vacant; another rugby player had just left and Jones thought it might be time to place more emphasis on other activities.

The advertisement asked for a physical education specialist who would take charge of a major sport. Finally, after a series of interviews, Jones, Walsh, and the headmaster narrowed the field down to a choice between Michael Field and Chris Shropshire.

Field had represented his county at cricket and rugby. He was a very fine all-round games player, an excellent teacher with five years of experience, and was liked by all three of the Selection Committee. Shropshire was slightly older, had served as a P.T.I. in the army before training as a teacher, and had been a member of the British Olympic Gymnastic team. Also, he was a very proficient basketball player and coach. The committee members liked him, personally, almost as much as Field, but he was not quite their "type."

The Selection Committee deadlocked and finally the head-master said, "Jones, you decide."

Case Analysis Method

Use Hodgkinson's paradigm (this design) and calculate the expected values to solve the problem.

Case 9.13

That Is The Question

With all her school sports teams, physical education teacher Mrs. Pat Foss stressed the importance of trying hard in a sporting fashion; winning was important, but not at all costs. The 1970 season was a particularly successful one for the senior netball team and a group of nine girls formed the squad from which seven played at any one time (substitutions were not allowed). Usually, one or two players were unavailable for some good reason or other so selection had not been a problem.

One girl, Susan Hitchen, had been unreliable and a poor sport on several occasions and missed the bus for two away games. She was also a general nuisance, but a very good player. By contrast, Pip Minly was not a good player, was very reliable, worked hard at team organizational chores, and was very enthusiastic.

The most important tournament of the year was the Devon County Championship. It was a straight knock-out and the finalists would play five matches in the day. Early games were easy for Mrs. Foss' team and Pip was one of the two shooters (only two are permitted) in three of them. The other shooter was a good player and a fine all-round student. With only eight available players to choose from for the fourth match, it was between Susan and Pip for the second shooter position. Having sat out for three matches, Susan played in the semi-final and was top scorer. The final promised to be very tough. To win, Mrs. Foss thought she would need her two best shooters yet, with the philosophy she preached, how could she leave Pip out?

Case Analysis Method

Use Hodgkinson's paradigm (this design) and calculate the expected values to solve Mrs. Foss' problem.

Case 9.14

The Baby Boom Busts

During the 1960s there was a rapid growth of universities in Ontario, Canada as a result of the post-war baby boom. Many of them offered physical education degree programs and several new schools of physical education expanded at a rapid rate.

Extrone University was one of these whose school of human kinetics had 40 faculty members and 400 students by 1970. The dean was proud of his extensive facilities and varied programs: B.P.E., B.Sc., B.A. (Rec.), M.A., M.Sc., and the beginnings of a Ph.D. program. In the early 1970s provincial funding was cut and the faculty was reduced to 35 members. Qualified students were finding it hard to get jobs and many did not find suitable ones. Nevertheless, the dean kept up his fight for funds, students, faculty, and the Ph.D. program.

Case Analysis Method

Give this organization a metavalue scrutiny with a view to reducing their primitive unconscious influence (cf. Hodgkinson, 1978:186). Do this by answering the following questions:
1. Is the organization justified in its basic purpose?
2. Is the organization justified in its complex of ancillary purposes?

3. Should the organization: (a) grow?, (b) consolidate?, (c) reduce?
4. What, so far as reasonable analysis can reveal, is the shape of the non-quantitative cost benefit account?
5. What consistency exists between the answers to these value questions and (a) Type II morality (see Chapter 2), (b) Type I commitments of the administrator? (Hodgkinson, 1978:186).

LEARNING DESIGN 9.2

PLANNING

A young preacher moved to a rural community and only one oldish farmer attended his first service. Nevertheless, he had a hymn, the first lesson, another hymn, a lengthy sermon, a second lesson, and a final hymn. Standing at the church door to bid goodbye to his "congregation," the preacher asked the farmer how he had liked the service. "Well," replied the farmer, "if I take a truckload of hay to a snow covered field and there's only one sheep there, I don't leave the whole load."

Similar problems have presented themselves in other designs but it is particularly salient here. Planning may be administrative, highly specialized, or sport organizationally ubiquitous. It has a literature too vast to attempt to summarize here. The approach, then, is to describe the general processes that sport administrators and managers need to know and to draw attention to some of the more pertinent reference sources. Of course, other aspects of detailed planning are dealt with elsewhere; for example, in the design on budgets and in that on M.B.O. (10.1).

The Planning Process

Definitions

Simon, Smithburg, and Thompson (1950:423) define planning as: ". . . that activity that concerns itself with proposals for the future, with the evaluation of alternative proposals, and with the methods by which these proposals may be achieved. Planning is rational, adaptive thought applied to the future and to matters over which the planners, or the administrative organizations with which they are associated, have some degree of control."

Steiner (1969:34) defines *strategic* planning as, "the process of determining the major objectives of an organization and the policies and strategies that will govern the organization, use, and disposition of resources to achieve those objectives." Thus, the two definitions serve to generalize administrative planning and Burton (1976:53) rounds out its *raison d'etre* when he says, "... it prevents the undesirable effects of change while promoting the desirable ones."

Sport Planning's Nature

Sport planning takes diverse forms of which the following is a partial list:

1. Planning for the conservation and use of natural resources (e.g. national, state, and provincial parks).
2. Planning for elite national sport (e.g. human, financial, and facility aspects).
3. Planning for national "mass" sport (e.g. human, promotional, and facility aspects).
4. Planning city sport facilities (e.g. arenas, pools, schools, parks, and golf courses).
5. Planning for disabled people's sport.
6. Planning for major sport festivals (e.g. Olympic, Commonwealth, Asian, Maccabean, World Student, Pan American, and African Games; also, Canada Games, provincial games, and U.S. Festivals of Sport).
7. Planning major and minor sport conferences.
8. Planning school track and field days.
9. Planning fixture schedules.
10. Planning curricula.

Thus, all sport programs require extensive planning efforts that are designed to influence human beings' future behavior. Figure Eighteen illustrates that sport opportunities (the planner's concern) are the product of a dynamic system of interrelationships among a set of both demand and supply variables (Burton, 1976:54).

So, following Burton's (1976:54) *raison d'etre* for planning (see above), it becomes "the process whereby man deliberately sets out to influence and control his environment so as to *improve* the quality of his life" (emphasis added).

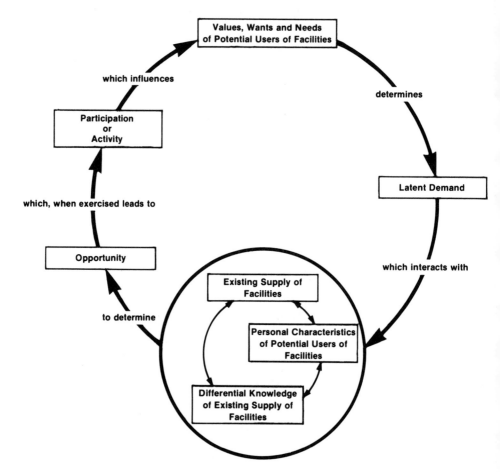

Figure 18. Planning's dynamic demand and supply variables. (Courtesy of Van Nostrand Reinhold, Ltd., Toronto.)

The Traditional Process

The traditional planning process sees the following steps occurring separately in distinct stages and leading to a "master plan" (cf. Sikula, 1973:59; and Burton, 1976:56):

1. Define goals.
2. Identify specific objectives and elaborate criteria for choice among alternatives.
3. Collect and analyse data.
4. Plan formulation (including development of a strategy,

identification of alternatives, and choice of preferred alternatives).

5. Plan implementation.

In the traditional process, each stage is carried out by appropriate "experts." Sometimes, this may be alright but usually it is not in sport situations for such a master plan is often out-of-date by the time it is completed and user needs/desires have not been taken sufficiently into account. To illustrate how a master plan can quickly be almost useless, consider the case of Edmonton, Alberta, which had a fine master plan in 1973. Then two unexpected major capital projects came to the city: the 1978 Commonwealth Games facilities ($33 million) and the Province of Alberta's capital city park system ($36 million). Each brought new major facilities and left Edmonton with large future operating costs. Thus, the new facilities plus the new costs dramatically affected the original master plan.

A Newer Process

A newer approach, which alleviates the problems mentioned above, is what Sikula (1973:65) calls the "creative method" with "feedback loops" occurring after each distinct stage. A representation of a further developed planning process is in Figure Nineteen as presented by Burton (1976:59).

With reference to the outer circles in Figure Nineteen, Burton (1976:60-63) explains them approximately as follows:

STATEMENT OF GOALS AND PHILOSOPHY: determined by: (a) lifestyles, needs, desires, and values of the population for which the plan is being developed; (b) current development patterns in the area or organization; (c) accepted goals and principles of the total society; (d) potential of the area/organization for various kinds of development in terms of resources and technology.

PRECISE DEFINITIONS OF OBJECTIVES: (a) emanate from the philosophy and goals of the organization/community and specify the precise purposes of the planning exercise; (b) identification of criteria for choice among alternatives.

DATA COLLECTION AND ANALYSIS: (a) compilation of an inventory of the organization's/area's capabilities and related existing resources; (b) analysis of population/client characteristics, needs, motivations, desires, and behaviors to determine

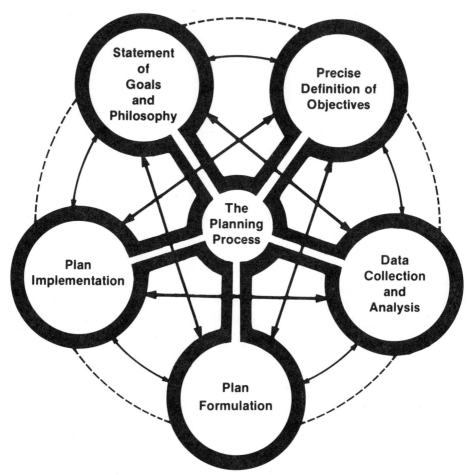

Figure 19. The planning process. (Courtesy of Van Nostrand Reinhold, Ltd., Toronto.)

how best to use resources to achieve the objectives of the plan (which may, of course, be modified after this stage).

PLAN FORMULATION AND IMPLEMENTATION: are dealt with together because they are intimately linked. The plan is formulated in spatial terms aimed at achieving the objectives. It should take into account: (a) objectives; (b) resources available; and (c) population characteristics. It includes development of an overall strategy, identification of alternatives, and the optimum choice based on the criteria developed earlier. After this phase, it may be advisable to modify the goals, objectives, and data analysis.

HISTORICAL PERSPECTIVE: Initially there was planning *of* people, then planning by experts *for* people. The newer, recommended approach is to plan *with* people, whether it be for a gymnasium, a swimming pool, or a comprehensive city plan. The attention should be on the actors and not the process; it is recognized that consultation of non-specialists leads to come conflict and frustration but, in the end, the administrator has a stronger mandate for the plan.

A Process Example

In this section, the planning steps actually used by a North American parks and recreation department are listed in note form. They bear close similarity with those suggested in the Burton process (above).

STEP ONE—INITIATION OF PROJECTS

Requests for projects may stem from a number of sources as follows:

(i) Recreation and Maintenance Districts—a number of projects may be initiated at this level, ranging from playground upgrading to the establishment of major district recreation facilities.

(ii) Community Leagues—building extensions through to major upgrading of neighborhood facilities.

(iii) Public Concerns—private clubs and others may wish to undertake a particular project.

(iv) Capital Budget Items.

(v) Approval of Subdivision Plans—projects as a result of dedicated reserve land.

(vi) School Boards—projects range from upgrading of playing fields to the establishment of major campus areas.

(vii) Other Civic Departments—projects range from roadside landscaping through to industrial landscaping.

(viii) Council and Commissioners—a number of projects are frequently requested from these offices.

(ix) Additional—projects may be initiated by parks planning and design personnel, the executive, the program resources section, the historical services section, and the cemeteries section.

STEP TWO—ASSEMBLY OF PROGRAM REQUIREMENTS

Once a project is initiated by one or any combination of the above parties, a program of requirements is assembled. The extent of the project determines the extent of involvement required to assemble the program of requirements. Any number of the following list of agencies may be involved in the preparation of a particular program.

   (i) Community Leagues—through district recreation co-ordinators and other parks personnel as required.

  (ii) District Recreation and Maintenance Personnel— problems of recreational program priorities, construction maintenance, and costs are discussed with appropriate personnel.

 (iii) Parks Planning and Design, Program Resources— the expertise of these personnel is solicited as required.

 (iv) School Boards—input solicited as to the effect any proposals may have on their programs.

  (v) Other Civic Departments—expertise of these departments is solicited as required.

 (vi) Private Consultants—expertise as may be required.

(vii) Public—meetings may be organized as necessary.

(viii) Fire Department.

 (ix) Police Department.

The initiators of any particular project are required to assemble programs. Parks planning has established a position with the assigned duties of aiding in the preparation of programs as requested. Parks planning, in some cases, is responsible for the assembly of programs and thus responsible for including the necessary agencies.

STEP THREE—REVIEW OF PROGRAM

Once the program is assembled, it is forwarded to the parks planning section. Parks planning reviews the program and is responsible for solving any problems that may arise. Problems may include elements ranging from utilities through safety and necessary land allocation. The necessary agencies must be contacted. (Refer to the list included in Step 2.)

STEP FOUR—APPROVAL OF THE PROGRAM

Once Step Three is complete, parks planning is responsible for obtaining approval from the director of maintenance and construction, and the director of recreation programs.

STEP FIVE—PRELIMINARY DESIGN SKETCHES

Upon completion of Step Four, parks planning forwards the final program to the design section. At this point, a number of alternative design sketches are prepared. These alternatives are forwarded for comments to those agencies involved in the preparation of the program and to any other agencies on which the project may have an effect. (Refer to list in Step 2.)

STEP SIX—FINAL DESIGN PLANS

The comments received on the preliminary sketches of Step Five are scrutinized. The design section incorporates those elements that can be practically accommodated into the final plan. The final design plan is recirculated to the same agencies as referred to in Step Five.

STEP SEVEN—FINAL WORKING DRAWINGS

Should the comments of Step Six require further changes, these are accommodated where possible, followed by the preparation of final working drawings.

STEP EIGHT—APPROVAL OF FINAL WORKING DRAWINGS

These final working drawings are forwarded through appropriate administrative channels for final signatures and approval. Signatures are required from the director of maintenance and construction, the director of recreation programs, and the superintendent of parks and recreation.

STEP NINE—IMPLEMENTATION

Actual construction of the project is to be completed. (Note: The directors and superintendent are responsible for financial implications; i.e. no money, no signatures.)

Complexities

The planning process is not so clear-cut and simple as it may appear from the above. For example, the diversity of sport and recreation needs and desires could easily lead to fragmentation; thus, standards of provision have been established for many purposes. In Canada, for instance, 75 percent of towns/cities have urban open space standards expressed as acres per 1,000 population. Similar standards exist in the United States and other urban-industrial countries (Burton, 1976:67).

In England and Wales, the Sports Council established standards for the scales of provision of golf courses, swimming pools, and indoor sports centers to meet the needs of international, national, regional, and local requirements. To supplement these broad planning standards, the Sports Council's "technical unit for sport" published numerous "design notes" on detailed aspects of the overall provisions. Some of these publications are listed at the end of this section in Supplementary Readings. The main point here is that sport administrators do not have to keep "re-inventing the wheel"; but they ought to be aware of where to find detailed information which they can use directly, or bring to the attention of architects when called upon to do so.

In the United States, the American Alliance for Health, Physical Education, Recreation, and Dance, together with the Athletic Institute, regularly produces an up-to-date manual called *Planning Facilites for Athletics, Physical Education and Recreation*. It is a very important reference source for most aspects of sport facility planning.

A further complexity is that facility planning stages vary and, therefore, it is quite difficult to prescribe from previous experiences. Thus, a broad city process was described above, but the planning and construction of a university sport facility is somewhat different and varies between universities as to administrative approval, design process, method of financing, and planning input during the construction phase (Peterson, 1975: 294-315).

Finally, though the future cannot be accurately predicted, it is very important to try to do so on many issues because of the *sunk costs* involved. Sunk costs are expenditures that produce services over a considerable period of time and an incorrect planning decision may serve in the short-run but prove to be very costly in the long-run (cf. Simon, Smithburg, and Thompson, 1950:427;

and Galloway's 1973 cost/benefit analysis paper).

Network Analysis (PERT)

A useful, short-term (usually), project planning technique is that carried out with a PERT-type system. PERT (Program Evaluation and Review Technique) was first used in 1958 by the United States Navy Special Projects Office to plan, schedule, control, and coordinate the Polaris missile program. About the same time, the Dupont Company developed another planning technique called CPM (Critical Path Method) to schedule and control its construction program. Since then, there have been other similar techniques but PERT and CPM are the best known and all similar means are often referred to as PERT-type systems (cf. Haimann and Scott, 1974:103-104; Campbell, Bridges, and Nystrand, 1977:226).

The salient feature of such techniques is that they force executives to pay particular attention to the allocation and management of *time*. It was estimated, for example, that the Polaris program was completed two years earlier than it would have been by conventional methods; clearly, then, PERT can lead to vast amounts of money being saved in big projects. The term *network* is used because the events and activities which constitute the total project are represented graphically by means of interconnected circles and lines (see Figure 20).

Developing A PERT-Type Network

The technique was first used in educational projects in the mid-1960s and, to my knowledge, in sport situations very slightly later. To illustrate the concept, and its use in a sport situation, a simple "Young Athletes' Camp" plan is described below.

For what follows, an event (depicted by a circle) is an instant of time marking either the start or accomplishment of a total plan phase. An activity, a time-consuming element, is the work required to accomplish an event and is depicted by an arrow. Several activities may be necessary to accomplish an event. All networks start and finish with a single event.

STEP 1. Prepare a list of all the activities necessary to complete the project. The example list is in Table IX (see the table "note" on the planning sequential order).

STEP 2. Determine the sequence in which the activities must be completed, make an event list, and draw the network showing that sequence of events (see Table X and Figure 20). The activities list, the event list, and the network need to be all visible at the same time to the manager; for example, on a desk, drawing board, or bulletin board.

STEP 3. Estimate the time required to complete each activity. In this example, a simplified time estimate is used which is quite adequate for these types of sport projects; for a more precise method, see Note One at the end of this design. In Figure 20, the

TABLE IX
1968 YOUNG ATHLETES' CAMP ACTIVITIES

Event Numbers	Earliest	Latest	Activity
1-2	Oct. 1, 67	Mar. 3, 68	Apply to County Education Dept. for grant.
2-3	Dec. 1, 67	Mar. 15, 68	Write to Senior Staff: availability, travel and accommodation requirements. Get timetable from Chief Coach.
2-4	Dec. 1, 67	Mar. 15, 68	Reserve university facilities.
3-6	Dec. 6, 67	Apr. 8, 68	Invite, confirm local staff.
3-7	Dec. 6, 67	Apr. 8, 68	Book Senior Staff travel and hotel.
3, 4-5	Dec. 6, 67	Mar. 15, 68	Complete budget.
4-19	Dec. 6, 67	Apr. 4, 68	Confirm equipment.
5-8	Dec. 7, 67	Mar. 17, 68	Design and print leaflet.
6, 8-9	Dec. 12, 67	Apr. 9, 68	Send information to local staff.
7, 8-9	Dec. 7, 67	Apr. 9, 68	Send information and tickets to Senior Staff.
8-10	Feb. 28, 68	Mar. 18, 68	Mail leaflets to schools, clubs, etc.
9-11	Dec. 13, 67	Apr. 16, 68	Arrange local transport for Senior Staff.
10-12	Mar. 1, 68	Apr. 1, 68	Arrange athlete selection meeting.
11-14	Apr. 16, 68	Apr. 17, 68	Entertain and brief Senior Staff.
12-15	Apr. 1, 68	Apr. 3, 68	Select athletes at meeting.
12-13	Apr. 1, 68	Apr. 2, 68	Provisionally book meals.
15-17	Apr. 3, 68	Apr. 4, 68	Inform selected athletes.
15-16	Apr. 3, 68	Apr. 4, 68	Book buses.
13-18	Apr. 3, 68	Apr. 4, 68	Confirm meals.

Notes:
1. Event numbers and dates are added *after* the network has been drawn.
2. It is often a good idea to have "action by" and "date completed" columns so the overall manager can clearly allocate tasks to others and monitor timing.

numbers on the activity arrows represent time estimates; the first number is an "optimistic time" (t_o in days) and the second bracketed number is a "pessimistic time" (t_p in days). Note that the same time unit (e.g. hours, days, weeks) must be used throughout a network and that when $t_p = 0$ it means there is little or no time flexibility.

STEP 4. Compute the total time required to complete the project. Sometimes it is necessary to estimate "expected times" (t_e) from the optimistic and pessimistic times of Step 3 but, in the example, it is known that the Young Athletes' Camp must begin on April 17, 1968. (Note that T_E is the time an event is expected to take to complete; it is computed from the t_e's of the activities needed for the event.)

TABLE X
1968 YOUNG ATHLETES' CAMP EVENTS

Event Number	Earliest	Latest	Event
1	Oct. 1, 67	Jan. 10, 68	Decisions on venue, staff, finance, type.
2	Dec. 1, 67	Mar. 10, 68	Grant approved.
3	Dec. 6, 67	Mar. 15, 68	Senior Staff accept.
4	Dec. 6, 67	Mar. 15, 68	Facilities confirmed.
5	Dec. 7, 67	Mar. 15, 68	Budget completed.
6	Dec. 12, 67	Apr. 8, 68	Local staff accept.
7	Dec. 7, 67	Apr. 8, 68	Travel and hotel reservations made.
8	Dec. 8, 67	Mar. 17, 68	Leaflet prepared.
9	Dec. 13, 67	Apr. 9, 68	Information sent to local staff.
10	Mar. 1, 68	Mar. 18, 68	Leaflets mailed.
11	Apr. 16, 68	Apr. 16, 68	Senior Staff arrive.
12	Apr. 1, 68	Apr. 1, 68	Applications received.
13	Apr. 2, 68	Apr. 2, 68	Meals booked.
14	Apr. 17, 68	Apr. 17, 68	Staff briefed.
15	Apr. 3, 68	Apr. 3, 68	Athletes selected.
16	Apr. 4, 68	Apr. 4, 68	Transport booked.
17	Apr. 4, 68	Apr. 4, 68	Athletes informed.
18	Apr. 3, 68	Apr. 3, 68	Meals confirmed.
19	Dec. 8, 67	Apr. 4, 68	Equipment confirmed.
20	Apr. 17, 68	Apr. 17, 68	Camp begins.

Notes:
1. The dates and event numbers are added *after* the network has been drawn.
2. The dates chosen here show considerable overlap, particularly with early events. That "crudeness" does not matter in practice but it is advisable for the manager to encourage subordinates to complete tasks early.

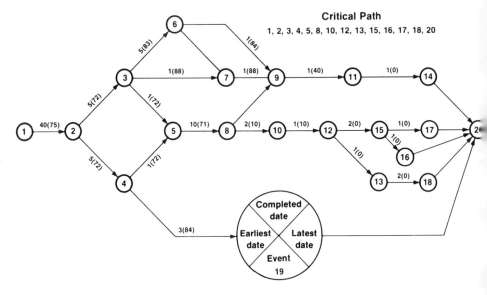

Figure 20. 1968 young athletes' camp pert-type network

STEP 5. Determine the times (dates) at which each activity must be completed for the entire project to finish on time. This is done by working backwards through the network; the "latest allowable time" (T_L) for an event is arrived by deducting the "expected times" (t_e). The "latest allowable time" (T_L) is the latest time an event can occur without affecting the completion of the objective event (Event 20 in the example). When T_L is greater than T_E, the event can be delayed for that time without affecting the outcome of the objective event; this difference is called the *slack* and is a most outstanding characteristic of PERT (see "Advantages" below). T_E cannot be greater than T_L.

In the Young Athletes' Camp example the latest and earliest event dates are recorded in Tables IX and X. It is useful, in practice, also to record them in, or close to, the event circles in the network (see Event 19 in Figure 20). The *critical path* is "that sequence of activities linking the starting event with the objective event which requires the greatest expenditure of time to accomplish" (Haimann and Scott, 1974:109). It is the longest path and has zero slack (see the following for further details or examples:

Dean, 1962; Evarts, 1964; Handy and Hussain, 1969; Cook, 1966; Campbell, Bridges and Nystrand, 1977).

Advantages

PERT-type techniques are not suitable for all types of planning but often are useful when the project is complex or non-routine. It is not only a planning technique but also one that enables executives to receive up-to-the-minute information on all aspects of a project's status. Thus, they can apply instant and effective control measures. For example, if one event has slack and another is behind schedule, resources can often be shifted from the slack activity. By contrast, in some non-PERT projects, executives cannot get precise information, they lose control of the project, and may put all workers on overtime (cf. Haimann and Scott, 1974:108-111).

Networks can be used in a wide variety of situations from constructing swimming pools through organizing young athletes' camps to planning badminton tournaments. Once made, some networks can be used many times; for example, a school "sports day" often requires complex planning each year and the network approach can save time and effort. Indeed, once made, it is quite easy to implement a plan indefinitely simply by working from a dated event list.

References and Note

Note 1: Those familiar with activity details make three time estimates (Haimann and Scott, 1974:109):

t_o = optimistic time

t_p = pessimistic time

t_m = most likely time

Then, t_e = statistically weighted expected time

$$= (t_o + 4t_m + t_p)/6$$

Burton, Thomas L.: *Making Man's Environment: Leisure.* Toronto, Van Nostrand Reinhold, 1976.

Campbell, Roald F., Bridges, Edwin M., and Nystrand, Raphael O.: *Introduction to Educational Administration*, 5th ed. Boston, Allyn and Bacon, 1977.

Cook, Desmond A.: *PERT: Applications to Education.* Washington, D.C., Office of Education Monograph no. 17, U.S. Government Printing Office, 1966.

Dean, K.L.: *Fundamentals of Network Planning and Analysis.* St. Paul,

Minnesota, Univac Division of Sperry Rand, 1962.

Evarts, Harry F.: *Introduction to PERT.* Boston, Allyn and Bacon, 1964.

Galloway, George M.: The use of cost benefit analysis in analyzing recreational facility expenditures. In Hunsicker, P. (Ed.): *Administrative Theory and Practice in Athletics and Physical Education.* Chicago, The Athletic Institute, 1973.

Haimann, T., and Scott, W. G.: *Management in the Modern Organization,* 2nd ed. Boston, Houghton Mifflin, 1974.

Handy, H. W., and Hussain, K. M.: *Network Analysis for Educational Management.* Englewood Cliffs, New Jersey, Prentice-Hall, 1969.

Peterson, James A.: The planning and construction of physical recreation facilities. In Zeigler, Earle F., and Spaeth, Marcia J. (Eds.): *Administrative Theory and Practice in Physical Education and Athletics.* Englewood Cliffs, New Jersey, Prentice-Hall, 1975.

Sikula, Andrew F.: *Management and Administration.* Columbus, Ohio, Merrill, 1973.

Simon, Herbert A., Smithburg, Donald W., and Thompson, Victor A.: *Public Administration.* New York, Alfred A. Knopf, 1950.

Steiner, G.: *Top Management Planning.* New York, Macmillan, 1969.

Supplementary Readings

American Association for Health, Physical Education, Recreation and Dance with The Athletic Institute. *Planning Facilities for Athletics, Physical Education, and Recreation.* Washington, D.C., AAHPERD and The Athletic Institute (Chicago), 1979.

Burton, T. L. (Ed.): *Recreation Research and Planning.* London, Allen and Unwin, 1970.

_____: *Experiments in Recreation Research.* London, Allen and Unwin, 1971.

Burton, *Man's Environment,* 1976.

Churchman, C. West: *The Systems Approach.* New York, Dell, 1968.

Dean, *Network Planning,* 1962.

Friedmann, John, and Alonso, William (Eds.): *Regional Development and Planning.* Cambridge, Mass., M.I.T. Press, 1967.

Hjelte, George, and Shivers, Jay S.: *Public Administration of Recreational Services.* Philadelphia, Lea and Febiger, 1962, ch. 16.

Murray, R. D.: *Planning Community-Wide Recreation,* Extension Bulletin E-684. East Lansing, Cooperative Extension Service, Michigan State University, 1970.

Peterson, *Recreation Facilities,* 1975.

Shivers, Jay S., and Hjelte, George: *Planning Recreational Places.* Cranbury, N.J., Associated University Presses, 1971.

Simon, Smithburg, and Thompson, *Public Administration,* 1950, ch. 20.

Sports Council (The), 70 Brompton Road, London, SW3 1EX, U.K. The following is a selected list of The Sports Council's planning publications: *Provision for Sport: Indoor Swimming Pools, Indoor Sports Centers, Golf Courses.* (HMSO, 1972).

Provision for Sport: Volume II, specialist facilities. (1973).

Hard Porous Playing Areas. [London and SE Sports Council, *c.* 1973].

Sports Halls: A New Approach to their Dimensions and Use. (1975).

Facilities for Squash Rackets. (1975) [TUS Bulletin 2.]

Sport for All in Converted Buildings: Making the Most of what Exists. (1975).

Recreation Facilities: Some Ideas on Reducing their Deficits. (1977).

The Changing Indoor Sports Centre. (Study 13, 1979).

Specification for Artificial Sports Surfaces. (1978).

Designing Public Swimming Pools. (1978).

Sport in a Jointly Provided Centre. (Study 14, 1978).

A Review of Studies of Sport and Recreation in the Inner City. (Study 17, 1978).

TUS Design Notes [The Technical Unit for Sport (TUS) is a professional group of architects and surveyors within The Sports Council which specializes in sport facility planning; it periodically publishes "Notes" and more extensive "Bulletins"].

TUS Design Note 1: *Plan for a Local Swimming Pool.* [*c.* 1970.]

TUS Design Note 2: *Plan for a Swimming Pool at Ashton-under-Lyne.* [*c.* 1971.]

TUS Design Note 3: *Film and Broadcasting Requirements in Sports Facilities.* [*c.* 1974.]

TUS Design Note 4: *An Approach to Low Cost Sports Halls.* [*c.* 1975.]

TUS Design Note 5: *Swimming Pool Hall Roofs in Timber.* [*c.* 1975.]

TUS Design Note 6: *Air Supported Structures as Sports Buildings.* [*c.* 1976.]

TUS Design Note 7: *Recreational Use of Church Buildings.* (1977).

Vancil, Richard F., and Lorange, Peter: Strategic planning in diversified companies. *Harvard Business Review,* (January-February):81-90, 1975.

Case 9.21

Palais de Basketball

For years Zenton University's community had to be satisfied with makeshift sports facilities until, finally, the state agreed to pay for an $8 million facility in 1975. Roger Rigar, dean of physical education and sport, headed the Building Committee and he was responsible for giving the program requirements to the architect.

Numerous subcommittees were set up among the future building users; the users included athletic teams through casual recreational participants from the entire university faculty, staff, and student communities. When the final program requirements ("desires") were assembled they filled a very thick black ring-binder and the cost estimate came to $12 million.

Rigar's committee then required all user groups to "prune"

their requests and this led to a second cost estimate of $10 million. Still not low enough. The Building Committee then decided to concentrate on two major items and work from there; the ones chosen were the main gymnasium and the swimming pool. A major requirement of the gymnasium was that it must accommodate basketball games and seat 4,000 spectators. The pool had to be at least twenty-five meters in one straight and had to have a five-meter diving board.

Thus, a gymnasium big enough for three basketball courts was decided on; pullout bleachers would cover two courts during the games. Such a floor space could easily accommodate a multitude of other activities; especially by using canvas dividing curtains. There was plenty of height for basketball so it would be fine for "volleyball and so on."

It was decided to build an L-shaped pool with a twenty-five meter length and a diving tank in the other part. The Program Committee was told that even a five-meter diving board required deep water, which had to be heated, and a high building ceiling, which also led to high space heating costs. Nevertheless, the committee said there must be at least that diving capability. After all, the pool length was a compromise on the requested fifty meters and the five-meter board was only half of what the divers wanted.

The building finally opened and two particular sport aspects only are commented on here: badminton and diving. There were fifteen badminton courts, but the players had great difficulty seeing the shuttles; the bright lights were immediately above the courts, the walls were light fawn and yellow with a shiny finish, and the floor was a shiny yellowish polished wood. The curtains did not help for they were cream-colored canvas. To further complicate matters, the ventilation system needed for the basketball games caused wind currents to blow the badminton shuttles off course, and the badminton nets were slightly too low because of the metal post and floor socket system that had been installed. Consequently, *no* good players would use the facility, and badminton, which was ripe for development, was retarded.

After one year of pool operation a survey was taken on the diving use. The figures were startling: there were only two serious divers and the five-meter board was mainly used by rather wild jumpers.

Case Analysis Method
CAM A or CAM B (see Chapter 1).

Case 9.22

Net-Work

Kokanee Winter Club was a private organization whose owners were trying to operate it as a profit-making enterprise. Manager Dick Orm's policy with the varied volunteer sports committees was to give them as much organizational help as possible; such arrangements served the members and the club's profit motive. On October 1, 1980 Jean Smith was appointed program co-ordinator soon after completing her degree in Recreation Administration.

The week after she began work, Dick Orm gave her the task of organizing the Pacific Northwest Junior Badminton Championships that were to be held at Kokanee from March 6-8, 1981. He advised her that the Badminton Committee would assist her but she must coordinate the planning. After a short discussion with Dick, Jean made the following list of jobs she would have to take care of:

Confirm availability of the club's facilities.
Gain the committee's support.
Arrange billets for an anticipated fifty young players.
Banquet for 100 players and officials (where?).
Buy shuttles (how many?).
Singles and doubles (boys' and girls') under 14, under 16, under 19.
Mixed doubles (all age groups).
Sponsor (preferably an equipment manufacturer).
Prizes (local dealers' gifts?).
Advertising.
Entry forms (out and in).
Budget (no profit required; refreshment sales would suffice).
Catering for refreshments and "Welcome Reception."
Draws and seeding (plus "B" and "C" consolation rounds).
Timing every scheduled match.
Tournament officials (referee, eight court coordinators, umpires and linespeople for semi-finals onwards).
News releases.

P.A. system.
Prizegiving (who?).
Banquet speaker.

Case Analysis Method

Assume you are Jean Smith and use a PERT-type plan to solve the problem. Work through the network planning process described in this design on the assumption that the above is a complete list of activities. Finally, you must have activity and event lists (*similar* to those in Tables IX and X) plus a fully completed network (similar to that in Figure 20).

Case 9.23

Weird

The state of Buritania's news releases about the capital city of Zok's new park system were given wide exposure by the news media and several government ministers saw to it that their pictures appeared close to the "artistic impressions" depicting some of the imaginative park concepts. Part of a news release sets the scene:

> The government of the state of Buritania, in keeping with its policy of bringing the state park system to the people, announces a major undertaking in Zok. The $40 million park is being planned, designed, and implemented as a joint effort between the state and the city of Zok. . .
> It will provide a wide range of sporting and recreational opportunities for all citizens . . . including the chances to wade, swim, water ski, skin dive, scuba dive, row, skull, canoe, kayak, sail, raft, and fish. . . . The water recreational opportunities are mostly made possible by the placement of an $8 million water control structure across the Zedar river to the east of Zok. The weir will increase upstream water depths and decrease water velocity, thereby creating favorable conditions for a wide range of water sports. The structure will also create an aesthetic waterfall and a pedestrian and bicycle crossing to link the park areas on both sides of the Zedar.

To implement the conceptual ideas, a vast committee structure was established including committees for *Policy*, Land and Agreement, *Planning and Development Management*, Implementation Management, Water Conservation, Technical Support, Trails and Recreation, Parks, and Ravines; each committee had *equal* representation of public servants from Zok and

Buritania. The italicised committees above were the most important strategic committees; the Policy Committee included elected politicians and took most of its technical advice from the Planning and Development Committee (which also included top elected representatives).

In gathering data, the Trails and Recreation Committee had a water quality study done by specialists whose summary reported: "Water quality is unsuitable for primary contact recreation within the entire study area. Therefore there can be *no* swimming, wading, water skiing, skin diving, scuba diving, skating, ice sailing, cross country skiing (ice surface), or snowshoeing (ice surface). The weir would improve resources for rowing, sculling, tour boating, and novice canoeing. It would depreciate resources for skilled canoeing and kayaking, and shorezone peripheral activity. Fishing would not be affected."

The Trails and Recreation Committee discussed the report's details and most professionals agreed it would be almost a total waste of money to construct an $8 million weir. State representatives warned, however, that their minister was "dead set on it."

Zok's representatives warned their representatives on the Planning and Development Management Committee of what may transpire. They urged efforts to convince advisors to the state minister and that was successfully done. Then came the key Planning and Development Management Committee meeting which the state minister attended.

He opened his remarks with a glowing description of the whole park concept and extolled the virtues of the weir. His officials looked uncomfortable but knew how they would have to vote. The Trails and Recreation Committee co-chairperson then spoke up and explained the findings of the "Water Quality Report." "Surely, Mr. Minister," he concluded, "you cannot possibly construct a weir."

"Why not?" said an irritated minister.

"It is not justifiable, for recreational reasons, and so my committee thinks it is an irresponsible waste of public funds that could be spent on more worthy needs."

"But the weir would have aesthetic value; it would be like a statue," retorted the cajoling minister.

"Yes, an $8 million statue!"

Case Analysis Method
CAM B or CAM E (see Chapter 1).

Summary

1. Decision making involves intelligence, design, and choice activities.
2. Decision making may be rational, deliberate, discretionary, purposive, irrational, habitual, obligatory, random, or any combination. Many administrative decisions are satisfice decisions, according to Simon.
3. Finally, a decision is made between not more than two alternatives.
4. "Rational" administrators delineate the ultimate binary alternative, assess the consequences of each (p's and v's) and calculate the expected values ($p \times v$). However, decision making is probably not amenable to science for it is philosophical and administrative.
5. Decisions are programmed when they are routine or repetitive. Non-programmed decisions are one-shot, ill-structured, and novel.
6. Policy making is the epitome of administrative action. It is the decision aspect of that level of leadership which involves the alteration, origination, or elimination of organization structure . . . the formulation of substantive goals and objectives for the organization as well as procedures and devices for the achieving of goals and the evaluating of performance.
7. A metavalue is a concept of the desirable so vested and entrenched that it seems beyond dispute or contention.
8. Planning is that activity which concerns itself with administratively controllable proposals for the future, with the evaluation of alternative proposals, and with implementation methods. It is rational, adaptive thought applied to the future which prevents the undesirable effects of change while promoting the desirable ones (and, hopefully, the right ones).
9. Planning involves the interrelationship of the following phases: statement of philosophy and goals, precise definitions of objectives, data collection and analysis, plan formulation

and implementation. It ought to be with people.

10. PERT-type network planning links activities and events and forces executives to pay particular attention to the allocation and management of time.

Concepts For Review

Decision making	Intelligence activity
Design activity	Choice activity
Economic man	Administrative man
Maximizing	Satisficing
Hodgkinson's paradigm	Kaplan's law
Policy definitions	Programmed decisions
Non-programmed decisions	Levels and policy
Internal policies	External policies
Metavalues	Policy makers
Interest factor	Negativism
Planning definitions	Sport planning's nature
Traditional planning process	A newer planning process
Notable references sources	Sunk costs
PERT	CPM
Events	Activities
PERT-type planning steps	Critical path
Slack	

Questions for Oral or Written Discussion

1. Make an appointment at as large a parks and recreation department as is convenient and ask a planner to describe the processes followed and to show you a range of plan types. Later, discuss what you have seen with colleagues.
2. As in number one but ask to see the policy manual.
3. To what extent do "politics" affect decision making and planning processes in sport organizations? Discuss and cite actual examples.
4. Which type of administrator is most likely to best serve the "extra organization" interest? Discuss.
5. Whether a sport administrator is political, professional, or collegial he/she abdicates his/her philosophical administrative responsibility if he/she allows his/her moral sense to atrophy or retreats to managerialism. Discuss and cite examples.

6. CAM C (see Chapter 1) applied to instructor-specified topics taken from this chapter.
7. Select the sport organization with which you are most familiar and give it the "metavalue scrutiny" described in the "analysis method" of Case 9.14 ("The Baby Boom Busts").
8. Assume you are head of physical education in a school that offers a very limited range of activities, on the grounds that "quality" is better than "quantity." The principal is pressuring you to broaden the program's scope so that you will offer many sports, at a low level, for two-week periods; the principal's reasoning is that you will interest more students overall. The principal says he "doesn't want to force it," but asks you and your staff to consider it carefully and decide before he finalizes next year's timetable in eighty day's time. You identify that the following activities must be carried out.

1. Select the teachers and coaches who will consider the issue.
2. Gather printed material dealing with the issues.
3. Identify schools which have a similar broad program.
4. Arrange for site visits.
5. Identify experienced curriculum specialists to offer advice.
6. Arrange for the specialists to meet your staff.
7. Meet teachers and coaches to explain the project, the resources, and the time deadline.
8. Have teachers and coaches make a report and conduct a vote on future policies.

Now, *complete* the network planning steps.

Chapter 10

CONTROLS:
GOAL-SETTING AND PERFORMANCE

C ONTROL IS ADMINISTRATIVE: Drucker (1973:494) says it is concerned with "what ought to be," with direction, ends, and future expectations. By contrast, controls are managerial; Drucker (1973:494) describes them as dealing with facts, measurement, information, and means. Mainly events of the past and present. Thus, controls are managerial means to administrative control.

In this chapter administrative control is linked to managerial controls by particular reference to "Management By Objectives" (MBO) and "Management Information Systems" (MIS). Though isolated for consideration here, the concepts and processes have clear connections with some other managerial topics that were dealt with in other chapters. For example, budgeting, financial control, policies, plans, and supervision of workers are all allied with goal-setting and performance.

LEARNING DESIGN 10.1

MANAGEMENT BY OBJECTIVES

The MBO Process

Terminology

In some sport organizations the words aim, objective, target, and goal are used synonymously or inconsistently. Here, the Steers and Porter (1975:437) interpretation of the concept of goals is accepted as "a dynamic process by which individuals and organizations determine their future aspirations within certain limitations." Thus, goal-setting is a "continual decision and reevaluation process" in which resources, such as manpower, money, and time, are allocated.

FUNCTIONS OF GOALS. Steers and Porter (1975:438) identify five functions which formulated goals serve:

(1) to guide and direct behavior by focussing attention and effort in a specific direction;

(2) as standards against which judgments can be made as to the relative effectiveness with which individuals or organizations achieve (or fail to achieve) their purposes (evaluation);

(3) they are a source of legitimacy since they justify various activities and the use of resources to pursue them;

(4) they significantly affect the structure of the organization itself; and,

(5) they illuminate what the goal-setter thinks is important and worthy of pursuit; that is, insight into the motives, character, and behavior of the actors.

GOAL TYPES. There are three types of goals (Steers and Porter, 1975:438-439):

(1) *Organizational goals* (i.e. organization-wide or department-wide goals which are statements concerning large segments of the organization's population);

(2) *Task-goals* are specific objectives assigned to an individual or small group. Organizational goals are not significant to individuals unless translated into task-goals; and,

(3) *Personal goals* are internally generated by the individual organization member and represent the personal aspirations (or the organizational task-goals) for which the individual is really trying (see the finer differentiation below).

Taken together, at the individual employee level, goal-setting behavior is a bargaining process and usually takes place between the individual and his immediate organizational superior. Thus, administration/management tries to set task-goals that are congruent with organizational goals and the closer they are to the individual's personal goals the greater the likelihood that the task-goals and the organizational goals will be realised (cf. Steers and Porter, 1975:439).

MBO ORIGIN. It is often stated in the literature that MBO was introduced in Drucker's (1954) *The Practice of Management.*

Indeed, he says that he "first coined the term" (Drucker, 1973:441) but Tarrant (1976:108) cites Drucker as saying it was used by Alfred Sloan (chief executive of General Motors for many years) in the 1950s as "a side effect." Drucker put it in "a central position" from which it has had a wide impact and generated a large literature. The wide use and literature has resulted in some of the terminology confusion mentioned above; here, I adhere to the goal types defined above and sometimes use "objective" interchangeably with "task-goal."

MBO Process Steps

The following steps illustrate how MBO is a continual decision and reevaluation process.

STEP 1: SET ORGANIZATIONAL GOAL(S). Organizational goal-setting is highly administrative. Thus, organizational goals may have a statutory basis, originate in a broad organizational policy statement, or stem from a strategic plan. Those setting such goals should examine two broad areas, namely:

    (a) What is the purpose of our organization?
         What is our unique contribution to society?
         What, exactly, are we trying to do? Why?
    (b) Who are our clients? Who uses our services, advice, or products?

The agreed upon answers to these questions, expressed in broad terms, become the organizational goal(s).

STEP 2: IDENTIFY MAJOR RESPONSIBILITY AREAS. Administrators' second step is to identify the major areas in which results must be achieved to fulfill the organizational goal(s). Each major area will have its own organizational goal(s), and clients, which relate to the organizational goal(s) of Step 1 (above). To illustrate what is meant by major areas, Drucker's (1954) "key areas" include: profitability, innovation, market standing, productivity, financial and physical resources, manager performance and development, worker performance and attitude, and public responsibility. The list is not intended to be complete but it is a good basis from which to begin.

STEP 3: DETERMINE PERFORMANCE INDICATORS. The third administrative step is to pose, and then answer, the question: "How can we tell if we are achieving good results in each major responsibility area?" The answers to the question are the performance indicators; each must be significant (not trivial) and measurable. That is, the performance indicators must consider quality, quantity, cost, time, and morale. They are made more managerial and specific in Step 5 (below). As with Steps 1 and 2 (above), the administrators of the programs must discuss the issues and reach agreement.

In many sport organizations the first three steps are often a "one time" activity. If the programs are ongoing they need only be checked from time to time to ensure they are still relevant. Only if there is a major shift in purpose, or clients, do administrators have to rethink these steps. They are, of course, essential for any new oranizational unit or program (cf. also with metavalue scrutiny in Chapter 9).

STEP 4: ASSESS THE SITUATION. Throughout the MBO process there should be an overlap of personnel between organizational hierarchical levels at each step. For example, higher administrators should include lower administrators or higher managers in their steps and so on down the scalar chain. The point of emphasizing this aspect here is that Step 4 is an obvious link stage between administration and management. (March and Simon [1958] call this process a means-end analysis: organizational goals are horizontal in nature whereas task-goals become vertical [i.e. protrude down the scalar chain].)

In Step 4, then, administrators or managers are asked to assess the present situation, based on the MIS (see below in Learning Design 10.2) information and personal observation, and decide what the status of the organization (or part of it) should be at a specific time in the future. This assessment should answer two questions in relation to each performance indicator: (1) Where are we now?, and (2) Where do we want to be? To identify the gap, the following questions are asked:

  (i) What was our past experience?
  (ii) What are the trends?
  (iii) What will be future demands?
  (iv) Based on this data, what assumptions can we make for planning purposes?
  (v) What are realistic expectations for improvement or advancement?

This assessment helps to identify what the task-goals (or

objectives) may be. As a further prelude to task-goal setting, the following further questions should be answered as part of this step:

(vi) What are the probable reasons for the gap identified in the assessment above?

(vii) What are the alternative ways to close the gap?

(viii) Considering the resources available, does filling this gap have a high, medium, or low priority?

STEP 5: SET TASK-GOALS (OR OBJECTIVES). Within task-goals are finer subdivisions that need to be identified and recognized. The subtypes are:

(i) Performance task-goals that relate to the organizational position assignment. They may be routine, problem solving, or innovative.

(ii) Personal development task-goals which relate to increasing the individual's skills, competence, or potential (cf. Tosi, Rizzo, and Carroll, 1970 and Odiorne, 1965:55-56). Note that these are not the same as "personal goals" (see above) but they are a key aspect of task-goal setting (see *Discussion* at the end of this section).

Returning specifically to the step-by-step process, task-goals are the objectives to be attained by individual managers or small organizational groups. They should only be set for significant (not trivial) objectives required to contribute to the organizational goal(s). Note that personal development task-goals would be doing so indirectly. Task-goals must have the following characteristics:

(i) Be specific (clear, concise, and unambiguous).

(ii) Be accurate (state the true end state sought).

(iii) Be controllable by an individual.

(iv) Have a completion date.

(v) Be consistent with the organization's philosophy, policies, plans, and organizational goals.

(vi) Be interesting, motivating, and/or challenging whenever possible (cf. Tosi, Rizzo, and Carroll, 1970).

Task-goal setting is a vehicle for getting individual managers (sometimes teachers, coaches, professors remember) to accept responsibility and accountability for specific results in support of organizational goals. It is the making of a social contract between a manager and his/her superiors in which there must be no unspoken doubts or reservations on either side. Reaching such a state of honesty and trust is the key to, and the biggest hurdle for, MBO. If honesty is missing, no real MBO exists.

STEP 6: MAKE THE ACTION PLAN. The action plan refers to the means which will lead to the end (the task-goal); it is a work plan outlining the way the manager intends to reach his or her goal. Also, it should indicate the resources required and the progress reporting procedures. When the action plan is accepted by the manager's supervisor, the manager has responsibility and is accountable for achieving the agreed upon results. If other task-goals are added later, or resources withdrawn, a new agreement (action plan) must be negotiated. If unexpected problems arise, an understanding must exist that the supervisor will be informed and, when necessary, the task-goal will be re-examined. On the other hand, if conditions at more senior organizational levels change, the employee must be told as soon as possible. Action planning has many of the characteristics of network planning (see Chapter 9) but is not so advanced a planning stage.

STEP 7: MEASUREMENT AND APPRAISAL. Sometimes this step is called "review" or "evaluation." In any event, it can serve these types of purposes at the completion of every task-goal when the following questions are asked by the manager and his superior:

    (i) How well did we do? (Quantitative aspects, qualitative aspects, deadline considerations, time allocation, creativity, efficient resource use, cooperative behavior, ethical practice.)

    (ii) How would we do things differently next time?

    (iii) What can we learn from this experience?

    (iv) Were our expectations realistic? Or too easy?

As was stated earlier, this is an ongoing process that requires regular, fairly frequent discussions between the involved individuals. MBO does not work if Step 7 activity only takes place at the year-end.

STEP 8: SET NEW TASK-GOALS. When a task-goal has been completed the administrator/manager and the subordinate employee reassess the situation (Step 4) and identify further task-goals in support of the organizational goal(s).

MBO Examples

Here are some examples, taken from actual sport applications, of parts of the MBO process steps. They are intended as a guide and do not claim to be flawless.

EXAMPLE ORGANIZATIONAL GOALS (STEP 1). These organizational goals were those of a city parks and recreation department and of an English regional sports council.

City Organizational Goals

Leisure Services

To provide by way of facilities, programs, and information the opportunity for all city residents to partake of those recreational experiences that they may choose. (This to be accomplished in cooperation with, but without overlap of the efforts and facilities provided by other agencies, private and/or commercial organizations, community leagues, or other public groups.) The above will include provision for athletic and fitness programs, cultural programs, interpretive programs (historical and scientific), special programs (senior citizens, disabled, other) and passive recreation and parkland environment-related pursuits (picnicking, hiking, informal play, other).

Environmental Services

To work towards the physical enhancement of the urban environment and the conservation and management of natural areas within the city. This will include programs for boulevard planting, ornamental landscaping and planting, weed control, mosquito control, erosion control, encroachment enforcement, conservation or natural area management, reforestation, and miscellaneous other areas related to physical enhancement of the urban environment (parkland sign control), roadway buffer design, walkway design, and environmental planning and design in general).

Other Services

To provide those services which fall under the responsibilities of the department as directed by city council. The operation of city cemeteries, trailer parks and campgrounds, and archives falls under this section.

Regional Sports Council's Organizational Goals

Programs of Work

Program 1*

THE DEVELOPMENT OF PARTICIPATION IN
SPECIFIC SPORTS AND RECREATIONS

I. The Council has established a regional policy stating the framework of relationships between the Southwestern Sports Council and the governing bodies of sport in the region and the principles on which resources are allocated to specific sports development.

II. The sports and recreations in membership of the Southwestern Sports Council are:

Angling	Movement	Sailing
Archery	Fencing	Shooting—small
Assoc. Football	Golf	and full bore
Athletics	Gliding	Shooting—
Auto sports—water,	Gymnastics	wildfowling,
land, air	Hockey	clay pigeon
Badminton	Judo	Skating
Basketball	Karate	Skiing
Bowls	Lacrosse	Squash
Boxing	Lawn Tennis	Sub Aqua
Canoeing	Modern	Surfing
Camping	Pentathalon	Swimming and
Caving	Mountaineering	Lifesaving
Cricket	Netball	Table Tennis
Cycling	Orienteering	Volleyball
Dance and Movement—	Parachuting	Water Skiing
keep fit, league	Rambling	Weight Lifting
of health and	Riding	Wrestling
beauty, Medau,	Rowing	
Margaret Morris	Rugby	

The council recognizes that there are many other forms of leisure activities that, though laudable in themselves, do not fit the generally held concepts of "sport and recreation."

III. The Southwestern Sports Council invites governing bodies to discuss their sports development programs in detail and on a partnership basis. The partnership will

---

*This is Program One of nine.

vary from one organization to another but, in principle, the council's contributions are:

A. The establishment of a program of development for a sport directed to the achievement of a number of objectives in specific areas, e.g.:

1. Organization of regional coaching and development schemes.

2. Assistance with administration through secretarial services, administrative assistance, and advice.

3. Administration of specific sports development events, including publicity, accounting, and use of facilities.

B. Contributing to the assessment of the success of sports development programs. The governing body's contribution to the partnership would include:

1. Responsibility for decisions on all matters of principle.

2. The active involvement in all stages of the formulation of the program of activities.

3. Agreement in detail of the extent of the participation in the program by the governing body and by the Sports Council.

4. Contributing to the assessment of the success of the development program.

IV. When allocating staff resources it is clearly impossible for the council to give identical services to all the sports and recreations listed above. Not only are there insufficient resources for a uniform service, there are also other factors that indicate a more specific approach to each activity. Work in specific sports is therefore undertaken on the basis of an assessment of eight factors. These taken together present a picture of the activity that shows the value of the contributions that the Southwestern Sports Council can make:

A. State of development of the activity and potential for development.

B. People within, or available to, the sport for development functions: (1) at present, (2) in the future.

C. Facilities available or likely to become available.

D. Influence of other agencies (e.g. local authorities,

local education authorities, governing bodies).

E. Contribution that the Sports Council, as an organization, can make.

F. Contribution that Sports Council members of staff can make.

G. People affected, numbers, ages: (1) at present, (2) in the future.

H. Value of Sports Council's contribution over time: (1) economic, (2) social, (3) environmental.

EXAMPLE TASK-GOALS (STEP 5). These are random task-goals taken from a city director of recreation's MBO sheets.

Formulated programs meet department policy standards and have the director's approval after director-district head consultation.

• • •

The dispositions of citizen suggestions and complaints to be effected within two weeks of receipt.

• • •

PPBS-approved programs to be implemented according to preset time schedule.

• • •

Budget proposals to be submitted to the superintendent by his established deadline.

• • •

Net current expenditures of the recreation branch do not exceed 100 percent nor fall below 90 percent of the annual allocation.

• • •

Capital budget funds under branch control must not be overexpended nor more than 5 percent under expended.

• • •

Revenue estimates to be 85 percent met.

• • •

1976 task-goals of district heads to be reviewed monthly.

• • •

Cooperative study with city social services to be completed by September 30, 1976.

• • •

Booking manual to be revised by August 1, 1976.

• • •

Fewer than 50 percent of commissioner reports require reminder slips.

The following are also task-goals that resulted from the Sports Council's organizational goal for volleyball (see above). They are those of one regional officer and constitute only part of his work load.

1. To train fifty coaches (governing body award).
2. To train sixty officials.
3. To arrange advanced coaching for twenty players.
4. To arrange introductory teaching for beginners in five cities.
5. To organize competitive leagues in three geographical areas.
6. To establish clear communication means with the SWAVA.
7. To increase clubs' affiliated to the SWAVA by 50 percent and player affiliations by 40 percent.

Note that task-goals have (or should have) at least two key components in addition to those characteristics stated earlier: they suggest an *area of activity* and a *performance level*. These components have clear implications for the measurement and appraisal to be done in Step 7.

EXAMPLE ACTION PLANS (STEP 6). This action plan is that associated with the Sports Council volleyball example (above.)

Action Plan (Volleyball)

1. Elementary Award Courses: (i) Poole (Oct. 70); (ii) Cheltenham (Nov. 70); (iii) Plymouth (April 71); (iv) Swindon (April 71).
2. Officials Courses: Bristol (Feb. 70) Exeter (Mar. 70)
   Weymouth Launceston
   (Oct. 70) (Feb. 71)
   Cheltenham Poole
   (Mar. 71) (Apr. 71)
   Plymouth Swindon
   (Oct. 71) (Oct. 71)
3. Advanced Coaching: Development of Area Squad System with regular coaching/ training sessions.

4. Intro. Teaching: Arrange one day courses at:
      (i) Cornwall—March 1970
      (ii) Poole—April 1970
      (iii) Taunton—October 1970
      (iv) Yeovil—February 1971
      (v) Blandford—Feb. 1971

5. League Development: Form new leagues in Poole (Sept. 1970), Plymouth (Sept. 70), and Cheltenham (Sept. 70) after holding one-day tournaments.
6. Improve communication: By making areas of responsibility clear within SWAVA executive and by developing area newsletter.
7. Increase affiliation to AVA (National)
    from 30 percent (Clubs) in 69/70 to 80 percent in 70/71
    from 20 percent (Players) in 69/70 to 60 percent in 70/71

Sports Council contribution

1. Full management of courses 1 (i), (ii), and 2 above.
2. Coordinate, arrange coaches for 1 (iii), (iv) above through PEOs.
3. Prepare outline plans for organizers of events in 4 and 5.
4. Provide secretariat for SWAVA until September 1970.
5. Edit newsletter until September 1970.

Contacts

AVA (secretary, fixtures' secretary, officials' secretary)
SWAVA (chairperson, squad managers, league secretaries)
Educational (PEOs, Exeter and Plymouth; Exeter University)

Discussion

Here some advantages and disadvantages of MBO are discussed and related research findings reported.

ADVANTAGES. The theoretical benefits of MBO may be summarized as identified by Carroll and Tosi (1973):

1. Directs work activity toward organization goals.
2. Forces and aids planning.
3. Provides clear standards for control.
4. Provides improved motivation among managers. (Note that Drucker (1973:439), himself, regards this as the greatest advantage of MBO because self-control is forced and this leads to higher motivation.)
5. Makes better use of human resources.

6. Reduces role conflict and ambiguity.
7. Provides more objective appraisal criteria.
8. Identifies problems more accurately.
9. Improves the development of personnel.
10. Integrates task and human orientation.

DISADVANTAGES. Clearly, if all this turned out to be the case in practice it would be an exceptional system. Unfortunately, it frequently does not for several major reasons. Firstly, MBO in many organizations does not have the full support or understanding of the administrators and/or top management. Secondly, it is not introduced into organizations by competent people and so the recipients quickly become very cynical. To work, it must be introduced to managers personally, patiently, and considerately. Thirdly, the "measurement and appraisal" step is often "ducked"; that is, appraisers do not appraise and the follow-up is weak. Fifthly, it is difficult to reach agreement on task-goals and on how to measure progress.

Finally a most notable attack on MBO, as it is usually applied, was made by Harvard Professor Harry Levinson (1970) in his article, "Management by whose objectives?" His main point of contention about MBO and its appraisal processes was that they ". . . are inherently self-defeating over the long run because they are based on a reward-punishment psychology. . . ." They fail to account for the deep emotional components of the worker's motivation and are ". . . rationalizations in the Taylor tradition. . . ." (cf. Chapter 5).

RESEARCH FINDINGS. Much of what is written about MBO is theoretical; it remains largely untested empirically. However, Steers and Porter (1975:443) cite nine field and laboratory studies which provide "strong and consistent evidence . . . that the act of setting clear goals on an individual's job does generally result in increased performance."

The above studies do not explain the why or what could be done to improve effectiveness. With such considerations in mind, Steers (1973) reviewed eighty empirical studies relating task-goal attributes to performance and isolated the following six relatively autonomous attributes by factor analytic techniques: (1) goal specificity; (2) participation in goal-setting; (3) feedback on goal progress; (4) peer competition for goal attainment; (5) goal difficulty; and, (6) goal acceptance (Steers and Porter, 1975:443).

From the review they concluded that goal specificity was consistently and positively related to performance (cf. above) and so was goal acceptance (but from fewer studies). With less consistency (but no definite relationships), goal difficulty, participation in goal-setting, and feedback on goal progress was positively related to performance. There was no consistent relationship between the degree of peer competition and performance. All the weak relationships suggest "important intervening variables which influence the relationships." (Steers and Porter, 1975:444).

Conclusions

As Steers and Porter (1975:444) point out, it would seem that successful goal-setting programs must identify those specific task-goal attributes that lead to performance and then load an employee's task goals with the attributes. Such is recommended in the prescriptive literature but Steers and Porter (1975:444) advise otherwise because of related psychological factors (cf. also Levinson, 1970).

They suggest, for example, theoretically analyzing how the various task-goal attributes would affect an individual's motivational force to perform. This they do with reference to the expectancy/valence model of motivation to work (see Chapter 5). Simply, the theory posits that the motivational force to perform is a multiplicative function of the individual's subjective probability assessment that effort will lead to certain rewards and the valence the individual places on those rewards. That is, for example, if the individual believes effort will lead to a pay increase (which is valued), his/her effort on the job would be high.

So, if, for example, goal specificity is considered in the expectancy/valence theory, a worker would know precisely what was expected of him and it would make it easy to see the relationship between effort and reward for performance; his level of expectations would be clear. Similarly, participation in goal setting is very likely to induce the worker to place a higher value on goal attainment; particularly if the worker had a high need for achievement (cf. Chapter 5). These are hypothetical examples of how goal-setting effects can be better understood if placed within a well-developed motivational framework. There are numerous other possibilities (Steers and Porter, 1975:445-446).

My recommendation for sport administrators who are concerned with these issues is twofold. Those involved in practice should theoretically test the task-goal attributes within their favored motivational model (perhaps selected from Chapter 5) as they would apply them in the cases of particular individual workers. If this is done skillfully, and in conjunction with the eight-step process I described here, MBO is a most effective administrative/managerial tool and does have the advantages listed above.

Sport administration research scholars, on the other hand, should carry out the theoretical tasks suggested for practitioners, but then develop testable propositions which may be empirically tested in sport situations.

Finally, in review, "performance under goal-setting conditions appears to be a function of . . . the nature of task-goals, additional situational-environmental factors, and individual differences" (Steers and Porter, 1975:448). And, "MBO does *not* succeed. However, men may succeed, using an MBO approach" (Humble, 1978:29). If so, managers have controls and administrators have control.

References

Carroll, Stephen J., and Tosi, Henry L.: *Management by Objectives*. New York, Macmillan, 1973.

Drucker, Peter F.: *The Practice of Management*. New York, Harper and Row, 1954.

Drucker, Peter F.: *Management: Tasks, Responsibilities, Practices*. New York, Harper and Row, 1973.

Humble, John W.: *How to Manage by Objectives*. New York, AMACOM, 1978.

Levinson, H.: Management by whose objectives. *Harvard Business Review*, 17-26, July-August, 1970.

March, J. G., and Simon, H. A.: *Organizations*. New York, Wiley, 1958.

Odiorne, G.: *Management by Objectives*. New York, Pitman, 1965.

Steers, R. M.: "Task Goals, Individual Need Strengths, and Supervisory Performance." Unpublished doctoral dissertation, University of California, Irvine, 1973.

Steers, Richard M., and Porter, Lyman W.: *Motivation and Work Behavior*. New York, McGraw-Hill, 1975.

Tarrant, John J.: *Drucker: The Man Who Invented the Corporate Society*. New York, Warner, 1976.

Tosi, Henry L., Rizzo, John R., and Carroll, Stephen J.: Setting Goals in Management by Objectives. *California Management Review, 12*: 70-78, 1970.

Supplementary Readings

Baldridge, J. Victor, and Tierney, Michael L.: *New Approaches to Management: Creating Practical Systems of Management Information and Management by Objectives.* San Francisco, Jossey-Bass, 1979.

Billings, C. David: MBO in the federal government. In Golembiewski, R. T., Gibson, F., and Cornog, G. Y. (Eds.): *Public Administration,* 3rd ed. Chicago, Rand McNally, 1976.

Cooper, J. D.: *How to Get More Done in Less Time,* rev. ed. New York, Doubleday, 1971.

Drucker, Peter F.: *Managing for Results.* New York, Harper and Row, 1964.

Etzioni, A. (Ed.): *A Sociological Reader on Complex Organizations,* 2nd ed. New York, Holt, Rinehart and Winston, 1969 (Section II, Organizational Goals)

Ivancevich, J. M.: A longitudinal assessment of management by objectives. *Administrative Science Quarterly, 16:*126-138, 1972.

Larkin, A.: *How to Get Control of Your Time.* New York, Peter H. Wyden, 1973.

Levinson, H.: *The Great Jackass Fallacy.* Cambridge, Massachusetts, Harvard University Press, 1973.

Locke, E. A., and Bryan, J. F.: The directing function of goals in task performance. *Organizational Behavior and Human Performance, 4:*35-42, 1969.

Loen, R. O.: *Manage More by Doing Less.* New York, McGraw-Hill, 1971.

MacKenzie, R. A.: *Time Trap.* New York, American Management Association, 1972.

Mali, P.: *Managing by Objectives.* New York, Wiley, 1972.

Mager, Robert F.: *Preparing Instructional Objectives,* 2nd ed. Belmont, California, Fearon, 1975.

Morrisey, George L.: *Appraisal and Development Through Objectives and Results.* Reading, Massachusetts, Addison-Wesley, 1972.

Raia, A. P.: Goal setting and self control. *Journal of Management Studies, 2:*34-53, 1965.

Raia, A. P.: A second look at goals and controls. *California Management Review, 8:*49-58, 1966.

Reddin, W. J.: *Effective Management by Objectives: The 3-D Method of MBO.* New York, McGraw-Hill, 1971.

Schein, E.: *Organizational Psychology,* 2nd ed. Englewood Cliffs, New Jersey, Prentice-Hall, 1972.

Simon, H. A.: On the concept of organizational goal. *Administrative Science Quarterly, 9:*1-22, 1964.

Vroom, V.: *Work and Motivation.* New York, Wiley, 1964.

Webber, R. A.: *Time and Management.* New York, Van Nostrand Reinhold, 1972.

Wikstrom, W. S.: *Managing by and with Objectives.* New York, National Industrial Conference Board, 1968.

Case 10.11

Off Target

George Burke was head of recreation programs in Southern City, which had just adopted MBO. The superintendent of parks and recreation, Bubba Watson, was at a convention when the scheme was first described to senior management but he was told by the city manager that he could adequately get the idea from Drucker's book *The Practice of Management.* Thus, in friendly consultation, Bubba and George set George's task-goals for 1972 and examples of them are here:

1. Develop recreation programs that will enable district units to meet their objective to improve the quality of citizens' lives by:
   (a) establishing objectives and procedures for programs;
   (b) updating program content and standards;
   (c) providing technical advice;
   (d) evaluating programs; and,
   (e) carrying out research projects to determine what people want.
2. Develop a union staff appraisal system in consultation with union representatives.
3. Operate the recreation budget according to the city-approved amounts per program.
4. Continue personal development by attending conferences and seminars; also by reading current literature.
5. Implement new programs for the underprivileged.

As part of the MBO adoption, Southern City initiated a "Performance Compensation Plan for Managerial Employees." Its purpose was: ". . . to encourage optimum performance of managerial personnel by enabling the city manager and department superintendents to reward their employees with salary and bonus awards which are directly related to their individual contributions and appraised levels of performance."

The compensation structure was tied to the "reference salary" which was defined as:

> The "reference salary" is the point of reference for comparison with rates prevailing outside the civic service and internal equity for comparable levels of responsibility. The minimum of the salary range

is 12.5 percent below the "reference salary" while the maximum is 2.5 percent above the "reference salary." The maximum *salary plus bonus*, however, is 12.5 percent above the "reference salary" for a total possible spread of 25 percent of the "reference salary." The basic concept is that an employee's development be rewarded with salary increases until he has achieved "fully satisfactory" performance level and such increases are thereafter retained by the employee while he remains in the position. The superior or outstanding performer remains in the "fully satisfactory" pay range but is rewarded on a "bonus" basis, which is awarded in a lump sum at the end of each "performance appraisal period" and depends entirely on his appraised level of performance.

To assist in selecting the appropriate performance rating, each category was defined as follows:

1. *The Outstanding Sector*—This sector may be achieved by employees about whose performance there are no reservations. They consistently exceed the requirements of performance targets of their positions to an exceptional degree.
2. *The Superior Sector*—This sector may be achieved by employees who exceed most of the major requirements and performance targets of their positions to a substantial degree and meet the balance in a completely satisfactory manner.
3. *The Fully Satisfactory Sector*—This sector may be achieved by employees, over a period of time, who fulfill all the requirements and performance targets of their positions in a completely satisfactory manner.
4. *The Acceptable Sector*—This sector may be achieved by employees who fulfill most of the major requirements and performance targets of their positions in a satisfactory manner and who have shown evidence of constructive effort to achieve the balance. The need for further training and development is recognized. This sector is also used as a "holding sector" for those employees that have been given adequate opportunity for further training and development, whose subsequent performance fails to improve from the "Acceptable" to the "Fully Satisfactory Sector" and who is appraised as having reached the limit of their performance.
5. *The Entry/Marginal Sector*—This sector is used for:
   (a) Recently appointed employees who are developing on the job (as mentioned in paragraph 4 this does not

include trainees for whom a developmental sector is provided).

(b) Employees whose expected results for most major requirements and performance targets indicate serious deficiencies in performance.

The Year-End Appraisal

Bubba Watson: "Come in George. Let's have a chat about your objectives. My, hasn't this year flown!

George Burke: Well, there are several new programs underway, they're of high standard, the staff seem quite happy, and we're well underspent in the budget.

Bubba Watson: (after about a 20-minute chat): That seems fine George. I have a meeting with the city manager and some other superintendents tomorrow when we'll review all lower managers' appraisals. I'll let you know what happens.

Two days later Bubba informed George that he had been rated "Fully Satisfactory" and asked him to sign his agreement on the appraisal form. George was livid. He felt he had worked really hard and substantially overachieved his targets; he thought he was at least "Superior." So, he indicated his dissent to Bubba and asked for his case to go to the Appraisal Review Board.

Case Analysis Method
CAM A or CAM B (see Chapter 1).

Case 10.12

Time Out

This is with reference to the organizational goals, task-goals, and action plan of the Sports Council regional officer mentioned earlier in this design. Jean Tiggot, the regional officer, substantially achieved her volleyball task-goals during 1970-71 when, in fact, MBO was first being introduced into the organization. However, during that year the organizational goals were printed and made public to all the sports governing bodies and to other agencies. Those organizational goals listed above referred to "Program One" but there were others and they are summarized here:

2. The development within local authorities, public bodies, and voluntary organizations of concepts relating to the development, provision, and management of recreation opportunities and facilities in the community.

3. Work with county and local sports councils in the development of their work.

4. Work with the collective group of governing bodies of sport in the region in the development of their activities. (Note: The region included six counties and approximately four million people; it was 250 miles from the SW to NE).

5. Examination of applications for grant aid for recommendations to The Sports Council (National).

6. Secretarial services to the sport governing bodies in the region.

7. Stating the views of the Southwestern Sports Council to government departments, local authorities, statutory and voluntary bodies, and sports organizations.

8. The development and improvement of relationships between the Southwestern Sports Council and the public who may benefit from its services.

9. Meetings of the Southwestern Sports Council.

Jean, then, in addition to involvements with programs two to nine and volleyball (program one), had responsibility for program one work with swimming, fitness, mountaineering, gymnastics, field hockey, badminton, sub-aqua, cycling, rambling, and lawn bowls. During 1971-72, several other sports began to demand similar actions to those volleyball received the previous year. Also, work in programs two and three escalated. Jean drove 40,000 miles in the year and worked seventy hours a week but still there was more to do. The principal regional officer, who was introducing MBO, realised what was happening with his five regional officers and called them all in for a series of meetings.

Case Analysis Method

CAM A or CAM B (see Chapter 1). Assume you are the principal regional officer when arriving at your solution.

Case 10.13

Early Goals

Brian Rogers had just completed his undergraduate physical education degree when he was appointed to teach and coach at newly opening Western World School. The department head, Roy Pound, invited him for a meeting early in July to discuss his assignments for September; explaining that the would-be students had virtually no previous physical education experiences. Pound told Rogers he would be coaching soccer and teaching physical education to boys in grades nine and ten (the most senior students for the first year); the school had excellent equipment and facilities. Pound continued by explaining that he believed in MBO and asked Rogers if he knew anything about the system. Rogers replied, "Yes, but in theory only."

"Well," replied Pound, "Now's your chance to put it into practice. This sheet (adapted from Fabricius, 1971:9-11) contains our department's organizational goals. I'd like you to bring me a draft of your task-goals one week from now."

The organizational goal statements for Western's students was:

1. *Physical Development*
    (a) To develop strength in the muscle groups of the shoulder area, trunk, legs and feet.
    (b) To develop aerobic endurance.
    (c) Through strength and endurance, to increase control of the body so that it will assure the individual's health and safety.
    (d) To understand the value of exercise to health.
2. *Physical Skills*
    (a) To learn the basic skills of walking, running, bending, lifting, climbing, dodging, falling, relaxation; for efficient, fatigueless, creative, and safe use of the body.
    (b) To learn sport and rhythmic or dance skills.
3. *Individual Emotional Development*
    (a) To gradually but consistently, improve in self-control, self-discipline, and self-direction; to do what is right and/or acceptable without threats or help from others; to control self in "stress" situations.

    (b) To play according to the rules, whether observed or not; to be honest.

    (c) To grow in self-confidence, courage, initiative, and poise.

4. *Social Development*

    (a) To learn to be a contributing group member; to listen to and follow directions; to cooperate with the group for the welfare of all; to carry responsibilities as a team member or a leader.

    (b) To begin to learn that life is governed and made more more pleasant and fruitful for all by adherence to certain unwritten social customs, rules, and traditions.

    (c) To try to be a good sport; to win without gloating; to lose without griping, arguing, or making alibis.

    (d) To be courteous to, and thoughtful of, one's playmates and peers.

    (e) To learn "to take it" gracefully.

5. *Fun*

    (a) To participate in physical activities with joy and enthusiasm.

    (b) To achieve release of physical and mental tension through activity.

    (c) By successful and enjoyable participation in activity, to use physical activities as after-school and leisure-activities.

    (d) To become aware of the role of sports in life, and to enjoy participating as a player and/or as a spectator.

Reference

Fabricius, H.: *Physical Education for the Classroom Teacher.* Dubuque, Iowa, William C. Brown, 1971.

Case Analysis Method

Assume you are Brian Rogers then comply with Roy Pound's directive.

LEARNING DESIGN 10.2

MANAGEMENT INFORMATION SYSTEMS

Definitions and Scope

Administrators and managers of sport organizations receive information from sources internal, and external, to their organizations. From this information they formulate strategy (or tactics), inform organizational members, and provide information to outsiders. In these ways, administrators and managers are information processors (cf. Mintzberg, 1972:93). A major problem faced by sport administrators and managers is that they receive more information than they need to do their jobs or the wrong information. It was because of the dysfunctional effects of information overload on administrators and managers that management information systems (MIS) were developed in business firms. Kennevan (1970:63) defines MIS as: ". . . an organized method of providing past, present, and projection information relating to internal operations and external intelligence. It supports the planning, control and operational functions of an organization by furnishing uniform information in the proper time-frame to assist the decision-making process." So, as Hodgetts (1975:395) also pointed out, MIS have a primary goal of "providing the manager with the necessary data for making intelligent decisions."

It should be noted, however, that there is a range of MIS—from very simple ones to very sophisticated ones; from no computer use through simple computer applications to sophisticated computer use. The simpler MIS, whether computer based or not, are really no more than data banks—they collect and store data then retrieve information for periodic reports. The systems, themselves, do not use the data but they provide data for administrators and managers to analyze before making human (non-programmed) decisions.

Advanced systems incorporate data banks but add the major component of "software to simulate the behavior of the institution by data manipulation" (Baldridge and Tierney, 1979:25-29).

That is, the system has the capability of answering the question, "What if?" So, it is not advanced systems that are being discussed in this design; it is the simpler MIS, which are more correctly described as "data banks." However, the term "MIS" is quite commonly used in many sport organizations so it is used here.

MIS Design

The two basic inputs for designing an effective MIS are called, (1) *major MIS determinants*; and, (2) *key success variables*. Major MIS determinants were identified by Zani (1970:96) for business firms but they are easily extrapolated for the more usual sport organizations. The determinants are opportunities and risks, company structure, management and decision-making processes, available technology, and available information sources. The key success variables are factors and tasks that determine success or failure.

When interrelated, the MIS determinants and the key success variables form the "blueprint" (Zani, 1970:96-97) for gathering the needed decision information. Of course, the type of information needed varies at different levels of an organization— general at the high administrative level to very specific at the lowest technical level.

MIS Checklist

It is impossible to specify here what should be included in every separate sport organization checklist, but the following list is sufficiently general to cover most eventualities. It interrelates major MIS determinants and key success variables.

1. Are departmental performance summaries available on at least a monthly basis?
2. Is there a hierarchy of back-up data available for the summary?
3. Are significant variances from budget or plans highlighted indicating responsibility and cause? (cf. Chapter 8).
4. Is information being generated that permits evaluation of (1) key activities, (2) of functions, and (3) of programs? (cf. Learning Design 10.1).
5. Are the costs of services provided to the department by

others included in the overall cost of the operations of the department under review? (cf. Chapter 8).

6. Are the costs of services and programs within the department compared to those of appropriate similar departments elsewhere?

7. Are exception-reporting principles followed?

8. Does the MIS allow concentration on the key results of (1) each manager, (2) each unit or branch, and (3) of each department?

9. Is the MIS based on responsibility accounting principles? (cf. Chapter 8).

10. Is maximum use made of performance measures such as unit costs, costs for level of service, cost-benefit relationships, ratios and comparisons? (cf. Chapter 8 and below).

11. Is one base of data used where possible to ensure reporting integrity, data consistency, and integration of the total system?

12. Is administrative/high managerial time spent on nonessential data review minimized by using recognized techniques of summarization, exception reporting, variance analysis, and graphic representations?

13. Are automated data processing techniques used where these contribute to faster, more accurate and improved data, and where the economics of data processing are justified?

14. Is the data provided to administrators/managers timely and reliable?

15. Is the data readily understood and oriented in such a way as to assist administrators/managers in effectively performing their tasks?

Possible Dysfunctions

Administrators and managers need to be aware that the introduction of a MIS into a sport organization is likely to have some dysfunctional consequences. The major reasons are similar to those referred to in Learning Design 10.1 when stating the case against MBO; they relate to "human" concerns.

Hodgetts (1975:399) has summarized these types of dysfunctions from the research of Dickson and Simmons (1970:59-71). They are: (1) MIS often causes redefinition of the formal organizational structure and, thus, makes changes for people which upset the status quo; (2) as for number one above but with reference to the informal organizational structure; (3) older people feel threatened and that they may lose their jobs; and (4) MIS is often introduced without proper consideration of opinions, fears, and anxieties of organizational members.

Common Complexities

There are many types of information that sport administrators and managers need to receive for processing before making various evaluation-type decisions. Some have been dealt with in the general form of this design; others were in the MBO design (10.1), PERT (Chapter 9), and budgeting and financial control (Chapter 8). Evaluation of mass sport programs was given attention in the diffusion of innovation section of Chapter 4 (Jackson, 1979) and another example of macro-evaluation was Pash's (1975:344-354) "Assessment of nonrevenue sports." The point is that there are too many to cover in detail, but the principles of this chapter are useful guides.

However, one persistent problem is given more attention here: evaluation of faculty teaching. The related evaluation of faculty scholarship is posed as a problem in Case 10.22.

Evaluation Of Sport Faculty Teaching

A particular problem for sport administrators and managers is knowing how to evaluate the teaching capabilities of their subordinates. The difficulty is present from low-level recreational instruction to high level university sport, recreation, and physical educational teaching. It is particularly sensitive at the university faculty level and is frequently a cause of intense job dissatisfaction.

Without claiming to have solved the problems, some colleagues and I drew up guidelines for the evaluation of faculty who claimed (for promotion and merit pay reasons) to be "meritorious" teachers (Mason, et al., 1977). Thus, executives who want information on faculty teaching should consider the protocols that follow for they are applicable below the meritorious standard as well as in other settings.

The measurement instruments, and their approaches, were decided on after an extensive literature review and finally included those for rating by students, rating by colleagues, and rating by chairperson. More complete information is obtained if all three are used but they should only be used at the request of the faculty member being evaluated. Self-rating, by the subject faculty member, is advocated by some but not by us.

RATING BY STUDENTS. The protocol described here must be used to gather the rating by students data on the rating by students instrument (see Figure 21).

Protocol:

1. A faculty member wishing to be rated by students should consult in private with the chairperson of the Committee on Meritorious Teaching.
2. Arrangements will be made for the chairperson, or his designate, to meet with the students and conduct the survey in the absence of the instructor. Respondents are to remain anonymous.
3. Respondents may choose to respond immediately or mail in the form to the chairperson of the committee.
4. Respondent are to be assured of the absolute confidentiality of the procedures and the impossibility of individual identification.
5. The chairperson of the committee will make a tally of the responses and mail a signed, confidential copy to the applicant.
6. The rating forms will be kept by the chairperson of the committee for one year and then destroyed.
7. The application to be rated must be considered a confidential matter between the chairperson of the committee (and his designate, if necessary) and the applicant. The chairperson of the committee shall under no circumstances disclose whether or not a faculty member has requested rating by students.

RATING BY COLLEAGUES. The protocol described here must be followed before the rating by colleagues form (Figure 22) is completed.

Protocol:

1. A faculty member wishing to be evaluated by colleagues

COURSE: _____ INSTRUCTOR'S NAME: _____

Based on your experience of university courses and instructors, rate each of the following items using the scale at the bottom of the page.

	A	B	C	D	E	N/A
1. Clarity of course objectives.						
2. Clarification of course concepts.						
3. Suitability of the pace of the class.						
4. Overall rating of course.						
5. Stimulation of my thinking.						
6. My increased knowledge and/or competence.						
7. My increased interest in the subject.						
8. Preparedness of instructor.						
9. Instructor's willingness to give help.						
10. Instructor's involvement and enthusiasm.						
11. Overall rating of instructor.						

SCALE TO BE USED

A	B	C	D	E		N/A
Top 10%	Next 20%	Middle 40%	Next 20%	Bottom 10%		N/A
Very Good One of the Most Effective	Good	About Average	Below Average	One of the Least Effective		Not Applicable for this Course

Figure 21. Rating of teaching by students

for meritorious teaching should first consult with the divisional chairperson to determine the appropriateness of various colleagues.

2. Those colleagues who will be requested to evaluate will be agreed upon jointly by the divisional chairperson and the applicant. The divisional chairperson will make the necessary arrangements for one or more class visits.

3. Before beginning the evaluation, the evaluators and the applicant shall discuss in detail the work to be presented, and examine any outlines, textbooks, notes, examination papers, etc., that the evaluators deem relevant to the evaluation.

4. The evaluators should work independently and not consult with each other.

5. Each evaluation must be treated as highly confidential and forwarded to the divisional chairperson.

6. The applicant may discuss the evaluations with the divisional chairperson. The name of the evaluator making any specific evaluation shall not be disclosed.

RATING BY CHAIRPERSON. The protocol described here must be followed before the rating by chairperson form (shown here) is completed.

Protocol:

1. A faculty member wishing to be evaluated by the chairperson for meritorious teaching shall so inform his divisional chairperson. The chairperson and the applicant will discuss the appropriateness of the chairperson conducting the evaluation.

2. The chairperson will make the necessary arrangements for one or more class visits.

3. Before visiting a class the chairperson shall discuss in detail the work to be presented and examine any outlines, textbooks, notes, examination papers, etc., that the chairperson deems to be relevant to the evaluation.

4. The applicant may discuss the evaluation with the divisional chairperson.

CONCLUSION. These three types of ratings were designed for a collegial bureaucracy (cf. Chapter 3) and provide a reasonably

---

RATING OF TEACHING BY CHAIRPERSON OR COLLEAGUE

COURSE NAME:_____ NAME OF INSTRUCTOR:_____

I. ASSESSMENT OF COURSE PLANNING:
(Course outline, objectives, evaluation procedures)

Very Good ( )   Good ( )   Average ( )   Weak ( )   Very Weak ( )

Comments are *required* to justify the above rating.

II. ASSESSMENT OF INDIVIDUAL LESSON(S): DATE(S): _____

    Preparation   (e.g. planning, materials, activities)
    Development   (e.g. introduction, development, pace, conclusion)
    Accomplishment   (e.g. objectives, concepts, emphasis)
    Tone   (e.g. interest, involvement, rapport)

Overall Assessment:

Very Good ( )   Good ( )   Average ( )   Weak ( )   Very Weak ( )

Comments are *required* to justify the above rating.

III. GENERAL LEVEL OF SCHOLARSHIP:

In your view, is the instructor abreast of the field?

A high order of scholarship ( )   Satisfactory ( )   Does not appear to be aware
of current developments ( )

Comments are *required* to justify the above rating.

                    NAME:_____ DATE: _____
                    Colleague/Chairperson

---

satisfactory method of gathering appropriate evaluative information for managers or administrators to use. The technique can be adapted for other teaching situations and, perhaps, incorporated within the sensitive type of goal setting I advocated at the end of Learning Design 10.1.

References

Baldridge, J. Victor, and Tierney, Michael L.: *New Approaches to Management: Creating Practical Systems of Management Information and Management by Objectives.* San Francisco, Jossey-Bass, 1979.

Dickson, G. W., and Simmons, J. K.: The behavioral side of MIS. *Business Horizons*, 59-71, August, 1970.

Hodgetts, Richard M.: *Management: Theory, Process, and Practice.* Philadelphia, W. B. Saunders, 1975.

Jackson, John J.: Promoting physical recreation in social systems. *Recreation Research Review*, 6:66-69, 1979.

Kennevan, Walter J.: MIS universe. *Data Management, 63*, September 1970.

Mason, G., Cawood, J., Goulson, C., Hodgkinson, C., and Jackson, J. J.: "Report of the Committee on the Evaluation of Meritorious Teaching." Unpublished, Faculty of Education, University of Victoria, Victoria, British Columbia, 1977.

Mintzberg, H.: The myths of MIS. *California Management Review, 93*, Fall, 1972.

Pash, K. Ladd: Assessment of nonrevenue sports. In Zeigler, Earle F., and Spaeth, Marcia J. (Eds.): *Administrative Theory and Practice in Physical Education and Athletics.* Englewood Cliffs, New Jersey, Prentice-Hall, 1975.

Zani, William M.: Blueprint for MIS. *Harvard Business Review*, November-December, 1970.

Supplementary Readings

Ackoff, R.: Management misinformation systems. *Management Science, 11:* 147-156, 1967.

Anthony, R. N.: *Planning and Control Systems: A Framework for Analysis.* Boston, Harvard University Graduate School of Business Administration, 1965.

Churchman, C. West: *The Systems Approach.* New York, Dell, 1968. (Delta Book edition, 1969, ch. 7, "Management Information Systems.")

Coleman, J. S., and Kerweit, N. L.: *Information Systems and Performance Measures in Schools.* Englewood Cliffs, New Jersey, Educational Technology Publications, 1972.

Gorry, G. A., and Morton, M. S. S.: A framework for management information systems. In Golembiewski, R. T., Gibson, F., and Cornog, G. Y. (Eds.): *Public Administration*, 3rd ed. Chicago, Rand McNally, 1976.

Hodgetts, *Management*, 1975, ch. 6, "*Management Information Systems and the Role of the Computer.*"

Simon, H. A.: *The New Science of Management Decision.* New York, Harper and Row, 1960.

Stoller, David S., and Van Horn, Richard L.: *Design of a Management Information System.* Santa Monica, California, Rand, 1958.

Taylor, J. W., and Dean, N. J.: Managing to manage the computer. *Harvard Business Review, 44:*98-110, 1966.

Theobald, William F.: *Evaluation of Recreation and Park Programs.* New York, Wiley, 1979.

Case 10.21

Good Shot, Wrong Goal!

The setting was Southern City in 1973 when Bubba Watson was superintendent of parks and recreation (cf. Case 10.11). After his experience with George Burke (described in Case 10.11), Bubba had some real concerns about the way his department was being managed and the sort of information his senior managers were receiving before making their decisions. So, he hired a firm of management consultants to study the management information needs of the department and to report back. Below is part of the consultant's report with reference to recreation programs and park maintenance.

Systems Findings and Evaluation

This section of the report presents our findings on the management information systems in existence within the parks and recreation department and our evaluation of the department's approach to management information systems. The comments that appear in the following subsections will tend to appear critical. Obviously one reason for this is that the study is oriented to identifying weaknesses and opportunities for improvement. Most members of management interviewed felt that this study was opportune and looked forward to assistance in achieving the required improvements.

Key findings for the department as a whole and then comments related specifically to the individual branches are presented below.

OVERALL DEPARTMENT MANAGEMENT INFORMATION SYSTEMS.

(a) Senior management are not provided with regular, summarized management control reports covering the key activities for which they are responsible.

(b) There is an overabundance of information supplied to senior management. Its quantity, lack of standardization, and lack of appropriate performance data means that valuable management time is wasted or that the data is not reviewed adequately.

(c) The major method used for management control is

dollars expended against budget. However, the inadequacies of the financial reporting systems, as noted later in subsections B and C, have resulted in numerous "bootleg" ledgers at lower levels in the organization. In addition, there is practically no correlation made between dollars expended and the amount of work performed.

(d) There is generally a lack of productivity data (e.g. units of work completed against standard, progress against schedule, amount of time spent on unproductive work, and amount of unused but available time within a facility).

(e) Significant variances from budget are not highlighted and reported upon in any consistent fashion. As noted later, the current structure of financial control reports inhibits the identification of the causes of variances.

RECREATION BRANCH.

(a) There is a lack of summarized management information to plan, coordinate, and control activities at the branch head level and the district head level.

(b) Generally, there is a lack of specific objectives, service levels, and performance criteria which would facilitate the reporting of management information. A program of developing objectives has been established to some extent. This system, which is embryonic, does not sufficiently address measures and the means by which performance will be reported.

(c) Although there is a multitude of reports prepared and submitted to the branch head, they lack standardization and do not generally provide comparisons to plans, deadlines, objectives, or indices, which would indicate that things are going well or not well.

(d) There appears to be little in the way of objectives or measures of cost-effectiveness in terms of comparison of time spent, resources, or facilities used against program use. This makes it particularly difficult to determine which programs should have higher priority in the allocation of resources.

(e) A great deal of information is prepared on attendance

at various programs and facilities. This seems to be the prime source of "hard" data on the branch's activities and effectiveness. With respect to attendance data and reports, a number of comments seem appropriate:

(i) little use seems to be made of the data in planning and controlling activities on a day-by-day or month-by-month basis. The data seems to be used more for overall, periodic review and to assist in supporting department recommendations for budget dollars.

(ii) oftentimes various types of attendees are added together inappropriately to arrive at total attendance. A more flagrant example is the addition of swimmers during public hours, participants in planned swimming programs, and spectators. Attendance, by itself, is an inadequate measure of program effectiveness. At present, there appears to be an overreliance on this type of measure. In addition, attendance figures, generally, are not compared to plan, analyzed in terms of unit cost, related to demographic coverage, or interpreted in terms of trend lines indicating increasing or decreasing popularity.

(f) In a number of programs the objective is for costs to be offset by revenues. As noted later, the current financial reporting system makes it difficult to identify and analyze this. Also, program or facility costs may rise with increased usage which is offset by increased revenue. Analysis of this is also complicated by the current financial reporting system.

MAINTENANCE AND CONSTRUCTION BRANCH.

(a) Overall branch control is dependent upon review of the financial data, meetings, visual inspection and limited written reports. Despite their reliance on the financial reporting system, senior managers indicate they cannot meaningfully use the PPB control reports or the cost summaries.

(b) Meaningful, summarized information on the branch's effectiveness or current position is not provided to the branch head or his subordinates. In fact, other than dollars expended, little information can be obtained readily.

(c) Current budgets and expenditures are not related meaningfully to volume of work completed. In most instances, it would be difficult to identify the amount of work that had been completed in relation to the dollars expended on that activity.

(d) Branch operations are highly labor intensive and make extensive use of casual labor. At present, there is little data generated on labor productivity or systems that would permit systematic determination of manpower requirements.

(e) There is generally considerable mistrust of financial and accounting data so that too much effort is expended by lower management levels in maintaining their own records.

(f) As management has recognized, there is an absence of anything resembling a complete inventory of physical facilities. Both this and agreed service levels are necessary ingredients for effective planning, budgeting, and control.

(g) Variances to meeting planned deadlines for project-oriented activities are not identified and reported in a meaningful fashion.

(h) There are not regular reports which compare the cost of equipment and the rental charged to user activities either by item of equipment, equipment type, or in total. Thus, it is difficult to monitor the appropriateness of rental rates used.

(i) In building maintenance, the reporting system does not provide for the accumulation of maintenance cost by facility being maintained and the supervisor has found it necessary to keep manual records of maintenance costs by trade and type of maintenance for each facility.

Case Analysis Method

CAM B (see Chapter 1) on the assumption that Southern City's

Parks and Recreation Department organizational goals are the same as those used as an example in Learning Design 10.1 (Step 1).

Case 10.22

Survival Of The Fittest

The faculty of human kinetics, sport, professional preparation, and leisure studies had a large faculty which, overall, had gradually developed lack of real trust between members. This dissatisfaction arose because of the reward structure; that is, the means by which faculty members received ongoing appointments, tenure, and promotion. The guidelines for evaluating the expected role performances of faculty members were:

Overall Function

Pursuit and dissemination of knowledge and understanding through research and teaching.

CRITERIA. Scholarship, professional achievement, leadership, and creative achievement.

Process of Prime Importance

TEACHING. University classes, supervision of student teachers, supervision of graduate students.

SCHOLARSHIP AND PROFESSIONAL ACHIEVEMENT. Research publications, scholarly papers, textbooks, original instructional materials, original contributions to in-service education, and other creative achievements relevant to the disciplines.

Process of Secondary Importance

University administrative assignments, university and faculty committee work, contributions to student life, contributions to the community, workshops, clinics, institutes, consultations, professional memberships, informal publications, awards, and fellowships.

Case Analysis Method

CAM B (see Chapter 1) on the assumption that you are dean of the faculty and have a major role to play in making final decisions on faculty appointments, tenure, and promotion.

Case 10.23

MIS Goals

Read Case 10.13, *"Early Goals."*

Case Analysis Method

Assume you have just been appointed to replace Roy Pound as department head, then design an MIS that you think would meet your needs in that position.

Summary

1. Controls are managerial means to control (which is what ought to be in the sport organization).
2. Goal setting is a dynamic process by which individuals and organizations determine their future aspirations within certain limitations.
3. Goals are of the following types: organizational, task (with subtypes of performance and personal development), and personal.
4. MBO process steps are: (1) set organizational goal(s), (2) identify major responsibility areas, (3) determine performance indicators, (4) assess the situation, (5) set task-goals, (6) make the action plan, (7) measure and appraise, and (8) set new task-goals.
5. Task-goals must suggest an area of activity and a performance level.
6. Goal specificity and goal acceptance are positively related to performance. Also, positively related but less strongly, are goal difficulty, participation in goal-setting, and feedback on goal progress.
7. It is important for practicing administrators and managers to try to analyze theoretically how the various task-goal attributes would affect an individual's motivational force to perform.
8. Sport research scholars should develop testable propositions based on a #7-type analysis.
9. A MIS is an organized method of providing past, present, and projection information relating to internal operations and external intelligence. It supports planning, control,

and operational functions of a sport organization by furnishing uniform information, which is timely, to assist in the decision-making process.

10. Simpler MIS are really data banks. Advanced systems incorporate software to simulate organizational behavior.
11. Basic inputs in MIS design are major MIS determinants and key success variables.
12. The MIS checklist contains fifteen items.
13. Information to evaluate teaching performance should come from students, colleagues, and the chairperson.

Concepts for Review

Control	Controls
MBO	MIS
Goals	Functions of goals
Organizational goals	Task-goals
Personal goals	MBO process steps
Major responsibility areas	Performance indicators
Situation assessing	Means-ends analysis
Performance task-goals	Personal development
(routine, problem-solving,	task-goals
innovative)	Action plan
Task-goal characteristics (6)	Performance level
Area of activity	MBO disadvantages
MBO advantages	Motivational frameworks
Task-goal attributes	(Chapter 5)
Data bank	Major MIS determinants
Key success variables	MIS checklist
MIS dysfunctions	Teaching evaluation protocols

Questions For Oral Or Written Discussion

1. CAM C (see Chapter 1) applied to instructor-specified topics taken from this chapter.
2. "Where expertise prevails, wisdom vanishes." Discuss in relation to this chapter's content.
3. Assume you have decided to use MBO in your sport organization, then outline the major problems you would expect to encounter and how you would overcome them.
4. What role does goal-setting play in equity theory (cf. Chapter 5)?

5. Think of three people in sport organizations who you think would be very difficult to supervise. Describe them, and then explain how you would use expectancy/valence theory in designing an MBO program for them if you were their manager.

6. What is a management information system? Are they needed in all sport organizations? Give reasons.

7. List the key success variables in two sport organizations you know.

Chapter 11

PUBLIC RELATIONS

PUBLIC RELATIONS (a singular term) is defined and its scope is explained with particular reference to the sport administration context. After superficially tracing its history, the process steps are described with reference to the "tools" to be used and the involved publics. Particular learning exercises are recommended in the design on *"Working With the Media."*

LEARNING DESIGN 11.1

PUBLIC RELATIONS: SCOPE AND PROCESS

Scope

Administrative Concept and Staff Function

As Cutlip and Center (1971:3) verify, "Distortions and disfavor cloud the term public relations." In forty-eight randomly selected news mentions of the field, only three were favorable; thus they advocate the need to "weed out the unethical and incompetent" (p. 4). So, what is public relations? It is often used synonymously with information, communications, and public affairs in the following three senses:

(1) relationships with individuals or groups which compose an institution's publics;

(2) the ways and means to achieve favorable relationships with these sub-publics;

(3) the quality or status of an institution's relationships (Cutlip and Center, 1971:4).

Thus, with one term for means *and* ends there is bound to be some confusion. A notable aspect of the ill definition is that

332

public relations is used as a synonym for "some of its functional parts, such as publicity, press-agentry, public affairs, propaganda, and institutional advertising" (Cutlip and Center, 1971:5). None of these parts equals the whole; public relations is an operating concept of administration and a specialized staff function which serves administrators and management (cf. Cutlip and Center, 1971:8).

ADMINISTRATIVE CONCEPT. All institutions, those of sport particularly here, have public responsibilities; they are accountable to the publics they serve. This to an ever-increasing extent, for today's public opinion may be tomorrow's legislation. So, as Cutlip and Center (1971:9) state: "Responsible performance on the part of a corporation, governmental agency, or non-profit organization is the foundation of sound public relationships." In sport organizations then, these broad public relationships are the responsibility of the administrators and not the specialist staff or line employees.

STAFF FUNCTION. For the reasons that "staff" are required in other specialist roles (cf. Chapter 3), so they are required in public relations. Chosen by administrators or top managers, the public relations officer has three major functions, namely: (1) To facilitate and insure an inflow of representative opinions from an organization's several publics so that its policies and operations may be kept compatible with the diverse needs and views of these publics; (2) To counsel administrators on ways and means of shaping an organization's policies and operations to gain maximum public acceptance; and (3) To devise and implement programs that will gain wide and favorable interpretations of an organization's policies and operations (Cutlip and Center, 1971: 9-10). This description of the staff function clearly demonstrates that it is a two-way process between the publics and the administrators.

Definitions

Webster's New Collegiate Dictionary (Toronto, Thomas Allen and Sons, 1979) defines public relations as: "The business of inducing the public to have understanding for and goodwill toward a person, firm, or institution; also: the degree of understanding and goodwill achieved." In the United Kingdom, the

Council of the Institute of Public Relations defines the practice as "the deliberate, planned, and sustained effort to establish and maintain mutual understanding between an organization and its public" (Black, 1970: 3-4). Cutlip and Center (1971: 5-7) cite the International Public Relations Association definition as: ". . . a management (administrative) function, of a continuing and planned character, through which public and private organizations and institutions seek to win and retain the understanding, sympathy and support of those with whom they are or may be concerned—by evaluating public opinion about themselves, in order to correlate, as far as possible, their own policies and procedures, to achieve by planned and widespread information more productive cooperation and more efficient fulfillment of their common interests."

Considering these definitions in conjunction with the earlier concept and function discussion, Cutlip's and Center's (1971:4-5) definition summarizes neatly: (Public relations is) ". . . the planned effort to influence opinion through socially responsible and acceptable performance, based on mutually satisfactory two-way communication." They further emphasize (p. 6) that "sound relationships with the public over time are compounded of performance that satisfies the public and communication of such satisfactory performance." So: X (the deed) plus Y (the way the deed is interpreted) = public attitudes.

History

No comprehensive history of public relations has been written but there is a fine account of the development in Cutlip and Center (1971:ch. 3-4). The force of people's opinions was recognized in ancient times; for example, information designed to influence behavior was found to have existed in Iraq in 1800 B.C., the ancient Greeks studied the importance of the public will, and in ancient India spies carried messages to the kings to keep them in touch with public opinion. "Propaganda" was first used in the seventeenth century Catholic church and the term *public opinion* was coined in the eighteenth century. Harvard College used public relations means to raise funds in 1641 and there are numerous other early examples of press agentry and advertising.

Though ancient in origin, public relations, as it is now known, had its definite beginnings in the early 1900s in what Cutlip and

Center (1971:70) call the "era of muckraking journalism countered by defensive publicity...." Ivy Ledbetter Lee was a key figure in that era; seeing that secrecy and silence in business was failing, the young reporter quit his newspaper reporting job in 1903 and entered business publicity. He advised corporations to "become articulate, open their books, and take their case directly to the people" (p. 75). So he laid the groundwork for today's practice by realizing the "fallacy of publicity unsupported by good works" and he reasoned that "performance determines the kind of publicity a client gets" (p. 78).

Social changes between 1917 and 1945 were great and these affected public relations practice. Post-1945 is called by Cutlip and Center (1971:70) "The mid-twentieth century era." It has been a boom period as mass communication methods have developed dramatically; extreme examples are the "making" of several United States presidents and *The Waste Makers*. In sports there has been parallel development; in the next section, recommended practices for the current situation are outlined.

Process

The sizes of public relations programs in sport organizations vary greatly; at least, from the one-person school physical education teacher-coach department to big city recreation departments with specialist staff. Nevertheless, the public relations process steps ought to be the same whatever the sport organization size; the difference should be in degree and emphasis.

The process steps that follow are closely allied with the administrative concept and staff functions that were described above. Within the "steps" are examples from sport situations and readers are advised to think of other instances from different sport organizations.

Step 1: Isolate The Problem

Cutlip and Center (1971:187) point out that it is "emphasis on fact-finding and planning (which) largely distinguishes public relations from straight publicity." At the highest organizational level, the organizational goal is considered and the administrator(s) must decide what is required to produce an end state of good public relations for the organization. The major general need will always be good programs. Factual information of various types should be available from the MIS (cf. Chapter 10) but, if it is not available, then steps must be taken to find out what the publics' attitudes to the sport organization are. The facts can be gathered by formal survey techniques, by informal methods, and by unobtrusive measuring (cf. Webb, et al., 1971).

In order to find important facts that have purpose for the sport organization, the administrators must specifically identify the various publics with which they want good public relations. For example, a school physical education and athletic department's publics include:

Curriculum class students	Athletes
Intramural sports students	Respective parent groups
Other subject teachers	Senior administration
School board members	Opponents
School non-teaching staffs	Outside sport agencies
Professional organizations	News media personnel
Former students	Community VIPs
Athletics supporters	Officials
Medical emergency services	Service clubs

A city recreation department's publics include:

Program participants	Would-be participants
Local recreation agencies	Schools
Sport governing bodies	Special groups (e.g. ethnic youth,
Governments	seniors, underprivileged)
Other cities' departments	Other city departments
Recreation board members	Professional organizations
News media personnel	

Private (profit) sport club's publics include:

Members	Prospective members (and their
Governments	likely locations such as
Sport governing bodies	schools, universities,
News media personnel	professions, other clubs)
Other clubs	

A university physical education or recreation department's graduate program's publics include:

Graduate students	Related departments
Librarians	Prospective students
Other universities	The graduate faculty
Grants agencies	Government agencies

The above is an incomplete list of sports organizations and each list of publics is incomplete. However, from the lists, it is clear that the publics do vary but the lists are easy to compile for any particular sport organization. Once the lists are compiled, the publics need to be ranked in order of importance to the sport organization. When this ranking is complete it is possible to allocate resources proportionately and appropriately.

For example, graduate students are most important in a graduate program so they must be given the best supervision by someone who understands the importance of the relationship from a public relations point of view. Remembering that it is a two-way relationship.

Step 2: Planning And Programming

Chapter Nine dealt particularly with planning, and the techniques recommended there need to be applied in the public relations process once the organizational public relations goals have been identified in Step 1. Similarly, if an MBO-type system (cf. Chapter 10) is used, public relations objectives should be incorporated into the task-goals. In this way the public relations tactics are developed from the administrative strategy.

Cutlip and Center (1971:223) identify a checklist for planning, which is a most useful guide. Well-planned public relations programs should be:

1. *Sincere* in purpose and execution.
2. *Durable* and in keeping with the organization's purpose.
3. *Firm* and positive in approach and appeals.
4. *Comprehensive* in scope and continuous in application.
5. *Clear and symbolic*, with simple messages.
6. *Beneficial* to both the sender and receiver of the messages.

TOOLS. For a public relations plan to become a program it must specify the tools to be used. Those commonly available in, or to, sport organizations include:

Newspapers	Journals
Television	Radio
Film	Slides
Photographs	Charts
Student newspapers	Bulletin boards
Demonstrations	Audio-recordings

Posters	Billboards
Information racks	Inserts, enclosures
Advertising	Meetings, conferences
Public speaking	Public address system
Closed-circuit television	Displays
Exhibits	Open days
Newsletters	Public recognition events

STAFF AND LINE. Everyone in sport organizations contributes to the public relations goals and this point should be remembered in the administrative and managerial planning stages. However, in those organizations that do not have specialist staff, it is advisable to give a capable person the task of overseeing the public relations coordination. The coordination is not only needed within the sport organization but, also, in the bigger organization; for example, the school or the university.

Step 3: Action

Having established the sport organization's public relations goals and planned their execution, the third step in the ongoing process is action. Public relations are affected by communication. To review what happens in the communication process, reread this section in Chapter Three. To further understand how the organization's different publics can be reached and how messages diffuse, read the *"Diffusion of Innovations"* part of Chapter Four.

Cutlip's and Center's (1971:260-261) *"Seven C's of Communication"* nicely summarize what has been written in the above chapters and what is needed in this step.

1. *Credibility*: Sound programs and the desire to serve the receiver.
2. *Context*: Sophisticated media only supplement words and deeds.
3. *Content*: The content determines the audience and must be compatible with the audience's values (cf. *Diffusion*, Chapter 4).
4. *Clarity*: Use simple terms and symbols which mean the same to the sender and receiver. The sport organization should speak with one voice.
5. *Continuity and Consistency*: Effective communication is

ongoing and sometimes repetition is required to achieve penetration.

6. *Channels*: Use channels of communication that the receiver uses and respects (cf. *Diffusion*, Chapter 4).
7. *Capability of Audience*: Must always be taken into account.

Step 4: Evaluation

In a systems fashion this step leads naturally back into Step 1; it involves fact finding by the same means suggested in the first step. With reference to particular sport public relations programs the evaluation data should provide answers to questions such as:

1. Was the public relations program adequately planned?
2. Did those responsible understand their task-goals?
3. Did appropriate people cooperate?
4. Was publicity adequate before, during, and after the program?
5. Was the program in budget?
6. What advance provisions were made for measuring results?
7. What percentage of the public(s) was aware of the sport program being offered?
8. What percentage responded?
9. What were receivers' attitudes?
10. What should be done to improve the public relations program?

Related Sport Research

Cantle and Soucie (1978:71) reviewed physical education, sport, and athletics public relations research literature and listed examples in the following groups:

1. Attitude surveys/opinion polls (Borcher, 1964; Bronzan, 1965; Dobson, 1970; Ziatz, 1973).
2. Organizational variables in sport administration studies (Healey, 1952; Swisher, 1959; Youngberg, 1971; Davis, 1972; Burelle, 1975).
3. Solely public relations in sport (Mackenzie, 1951; Colgate, 1967, Baskerville, 1975).

From the studies they concluded that public relations was not clearly defined, planned, or understood as a function even though sport managers rated the function as important.

References

Baskerville, Roger A.: "The Development of a Model for Public Relations Programs in the Iowa Intercollegiate Conference." Unpublished doctoral thesis, University of Nebraska, 1976.

Black, Sam: *Practical Public Relations*, 3rd ed. London, Pitman, 1970.

Borcher, William J.: "An Analysis of Public Opinion in Regard to Physical Education in Public Schools." Unpublished doctoral thesis, University of Oregon, 1964.

Bronzan, Robert T.: "Attitudes of University Publics Toward the Contributions of the Intercollegiate Football Program to General Education." Unpublished doctoral thesis, Stanford University, 1965.

Burelle, Jacques V.: "Qualifications of Athletic Directors of Member Institutions of the Canadian Intercollegiate Athletic Union." Unpublished doctoral thesis, Indiana State University, 1975.

Cantle, R., and Soucie, D.: Present versus preferred public relations practices of athletic departments in Canadian universities. In Lindsay, P., and Vallance, J. (Eds.): *Proceedings 6th Commonwealth Conference on Sport, Physical Education and Recreation, Vol II*. Edmonton, University of Alberta, 1978.

Colgate, Thomas P.: "An Evaluation of the Public Relations Programs of Physical Education Departments in Selected Colleges and Universities in the State of Iowa." Unpublished doctoral thesis, University of Iowa, 1967.

Cutlip, Scott M., and Center, Allen H.: *Effective Public Relations*, 4th ed. Englewood Cliffs, New Jersey, Prentice-Hall, 1971.

Davis, Charles C.: "An Analysis of the Duties Performed by the Administrative Head of Health, Physical Education and Recreation." Unpublished doctoral thesis, The Ohio State University, 1972.

Dobson, Max L.: "An Investigation of the Status of Physical Education and Intercollegiate Sports in Grades Four Through Six in the State of Oklahoma." Unpublished doctoral thesis, Oklahoma State University, 1970.

Healey, William A.: "An Analysis of the Administrative Practices in Competitive Athletics in Selected Colleges of the Midwest." Unpublished doctoral thesis, Indiana State University, 1952.

Mackenzie, Marlin M.: "Public Relations in College Physical Education." Unpublished doctoral thesis, Columbia University, 1951.

Swisher, Ivan W.: "Selected Criteria for the Evaluation of the Administration of College Physical Education." Unpublished doctoral thesis, University of California at Los Angeles, 1959.

Webb, Eugene J., et al.: *Unobtrusive Measures: Nonreactive Research in the Social Sciences*. Chicago, Rand McNally, 1971.

Youngberg, Richard A.: "A Comparative Analysis of the Qualifications Suggested for Intercollegiate Athletic Directors." Unpublished doctoral thesis, Indiana State University, 1971.

Ziatz, Daniel H.: "Effect of Public Relations Programs on Parental Attitudes Towards Physical Education." Unpublished doctoral thesis, University of Utah, 1973.

Supplementary Readings
Black, S.: *The Role of Public Relations in Management*. London, Pitman, 1972.
Blumenthal, L. Roy: *The Practice of Public Relations*. New York, Macmillan, 1972.
Bristol, Lee H. (Ed.): *Developing the Corporate Image*. New York, Scribner, 1960.
Canfield, Bertrand R.: *Public Relations: Principles, Cases, and Problems*, 4th ed. Homewood, Illinois, Richard D. Irwin, 1964.
Finn, D.: Struggle for ethics in public relations. *Harvard Business Review*, 37:30, 1959.
Heilbroner, R.: The invisible sell. *Harper's Magazine*, 214:23-31, June, 1957.
Hjelte, G., and Shivers, J. S.: *Public Administration of Recreational Services*. Philadelphia, Lea and Febiger, 1972, ch. 19.
Jefkins, F.: *Planned Public Relations*. London, International Textbook Co., 1969.
Markham, V.: *Planning the Corporate Reputation*. London, Allen and Unwin, 1972.

Case 11.11

P R Goals

Read Case 10.13, "*Early Goals*," and your analysis of Case 10.23, "*MIS Goals*."

Case Analysis Method

Assume you are Brian Rogers and that one of your new assignments is to be responsible for coordinating the public relations of the department. Begin by applying Steps 1 and 2 of this design to your task at Western World School.

Case 11.12

Once Bitten

Dr. Bill Toombs was a new professor of chemistry at State University; his manner was quiet and unobtrusive but he really enjoyed a tough game of racquetball. So, soon after his arrival at State, he set out for the gym after a class ended at 10:30 A.M.

On entering the building he saw an office with an open counter and a secretary was typing just behind it. He placed his bag on the counter and waited; the secretary kept on typing. Finally:

Secretary (sullenly): Yes?

Dr. Toombs: Can you direct me to the racquetball courts,

please, and tell me if there's a ladder competition?

Secretary: This is P.E., Recreation is further down the hall (as she quickly returned to typing).

Further along, Dr. Toombs noticed the equipment room so decided to by-pass secretaries.

Dr. Toombs: May I book a racquetball court for tomorrow, please, and borrow a towel now?

Attendant (sourly): All courts are booked; if you want one you need to be here at 8:30 A.M. the day before. What are you? Student? Faculty? Or what?

Dr. Toombs: Faculty.

Attendant: Got your faculty card?

Dr. Toombs: No, but. . . .

Attendant: Well you can't have a towel without handing your card in.

Dr. Toombs decided to go for a run then dry himself on a spare running shirt. He noticed that the changing room had a great deal of litter on the floor and the general odour was offensive. Next day he took out a membership in a private club and never set foot in State's gym again.

Case Analysis Method
CAM A or CAM B (see Chapter 1).

Case 11.13

Jack and Jill

Wendox was a city of 200,000 people and was quite well served with public and private recreational facilities. However, the only squash courts were at the university and at one small private club. As a business venture, Dick Jack decided to operate ten public squash courts with attractive ancillary facilities such as saunas, whirlpool, snackbar, and bar. He made a deal with the School Board; the ten courts would be in the grounds of Central High School (low-cost, long lease arrangement) and seven courts could be used by school p.e. class students anytime the school was open for regular daytime classes. There would be no charge made to the School Board for this use and three courts would be open to the public during school time. At all other times, the courts would be open to the general public on a "pay-as-you-play" basis. It was a big investment for Jack Enterprises Inc.

Jill McIntosh had almost completed her master's degree in Recreation Administration when she was appointed manager of the squash court complex; the courts would be ready to open in one month. Dick Jack told Jill that her first task was to publicize the courts and that she could spend $1,000 to do so.

Case Analysis Method

Assume you are Jill McIntosh and make a publicity plan that would be likely to succeed in helping to safeguard Dick Jack's investment and your new career.

LEARNING DESIGN 11.2

WORKING WITH THE MEDIA

Working with the media is emphasized for as Cutlip and Center (1971:407) point out, "the practitioner's standing with the media managers can shape and limit his accomplishments." In big sport departments, relations with the news media are important daily functions of the public relations officer but they are also important, less regularly, for small sport organizations. In this design the term press is used to include all news media.

Press Relations

There is always an underlying conflict of interest between the press and a sport organization that needs to be recognized by the sport administrator. Basically, the sport organization wants to promote itself, and the press wants news that will sell papers or be attractive on electronic media (cf. Cutlip and Center, 1971:407); the press represents the public point of view and may be at odds with that of the sport organization.

Cutlip and Center (1971:410) list the common complaints that each side has of the other and I have translated the complaints into the sport context. The press thinks that:

1. Sport organizations attempt to color and check the free flow

of legitimate news. For example, a player's injury is "hidden" or a recreation department does not disclose how it will cope with a budget cut of $200,000.

2. Sport organizations grab for "free advertising" with the consequent loss of revenue to the media; they want their events publicized but they do not want to pay for advertising. Hence, they flood the media with "news releases."

3. Sport organizations sometimes use pressure methods to get into news columns. For example, by bribing reporters or by saying, "We'll spend $30,000 on advertising this year if. . . ."

4. Sport organizations have no conception of what news is, how it should be written, and they are grossly ignorant of the media's editorial requirements.

To summarize the press' side and help sport administrators see their viewpoint, the following quote is helpful. It appears in Cutlip and Center (1971:409) where they cite a section of a loose-leaf manual of the Associated Press' Managing Editors:

> A flack is a person who makes all or part of his income by obtaining space in newspapers without cost to himself or his clients. Usually a professional . . . they are known formally as public relations men. The flack is the modern equivalent of the cavalier highwayman of old. . . . A flack is a flack. His job is to say kind things about his client. He will not lie very often, but much of the time he tells less than the whole story. You do not owe the P.R. man anything. The owner of the newspaper, not the flack, pays your salary. Your immediate job is to serve the readers, not the men who would raid your columns.

From the sport organizations' viewpoints the following are common countercharges laid against the press.

1. They do a poor job of reporting sports news and often employ poor reporters.

2. They emphasize sensationalism, conflict, and violence but do not report on socially constructive events.

3. Not all news is treated as news, only that which grabs money.

4. They do not discriminate between the honest, helpful, competent practitioner and the others.

With the battle lines drawn, the next section demonstrates how sport organizations can, and should, work with the press.

Publicity Principles

The headings here are taken from Cutlip's and Center's

(1971:410-416) authoritative book and sport instances have been added.

1. Shoot Squarely

Most press gatekeepers are shrewd, understanding, sophisticated, alert, intelligent, critical, and honest—"they can spot a phony or shady practice a mile off." So, to attain and maintain the support of the press, sport administrators must be honest, accurate, demonstrate integrity, and build their reputations by performance with all the appropriate press (no favourites). They must be candid and cooperative (cf. Cutlip and Center, 1971: 410-411). An extremely bad example surrounds the 1976 Montreal Olympic Games facilities construction, which is still being given adverse attention four years later for bad management practices that were "glossed over" at the time.

2. Give Service

Except for advertisements, the press does not want sport publicity; it wants news, and news very quickly perishes. So provide the press "with interesting, timely stories and pictures that they want when they want them and in the form in which they can readily use them" (Cutlip and Center, 1971:413). This does not mean the press will not publicize sport events, for they will; particularly local events that may be "news."

3. Don't Beg Or Carp

A quote used by Cutlip and Center (1971:414) explains this point beautifully: "Please, mister, if that's a handout in your hand, just give it to me. That's all there is to it. If we can use it, I'll ask a reporter to rewrite it. If we can't use it, I'll throw it away. Don't hold it under my nose and read it to me with your finger tracing every line. I can read. . . . And don't suggest that we have a little talk about it . I haven't got time for conferences. . . . No use standing there. There are sixteen more press agents waiting to see me" (McIntyre, 1962).

4. Don't Ask For Kills

"The way to keep unfavourable stories out of the press is to keep situations which produce such stories from taking place" (Cutlip and Center, 1971:415). To ask a newsperson to kill a story is a "crude insult" for the press works on "the unreserved acceptance that the public has a right to public information. *Good press relations must be earned*" (p. 415).

5. Don't Flood Media

Just as there are specific sport publics (cf. Learning Design 11.1) so there are right targets for sport news releases. Select them carefully for otherwise credibility is lost. "Flooding" shows the sport administrator is untrained, incompetent, and unreasonable.

6. Keep Lists Up To Date

Press personnel change frequently and media situations change so release lists must be dynamic. Keep them up-to-date and try to get to know people personally if only concerned with local press relations.

News Releases

The sample letter shown here (*News Release Example "A"*) contains some of the facts a news release should contain if it is being sent to the press. Other actual releases are illustrated here and in Figure 24.

Local minor sports should pay particular heed to these suggestions. They frequently complain that their sports get poor media coverage; usually, the fault is their own.

Photographs (matte-finish, four units long × three units of height for TV) and one- or two-minute film clips are welcomed by the press if they contain news for they are "an economical, effective means of reporting a story (Cutlip and Center, 1971:432) (see Figures 22 and 23).

News Conferences

News conferences should seldom be held but when they are be sure to invite only press people who will not leave disappointed. It should be a newsworthy event and not be confused with a press party or junket. They can be useful for giving news to all the media at one time (see *News Release Example "B"* and Figure 24) and for interaction; be sure experts are present to answer the press' questions. Provide working space, typewriters, paper, telephones and hand-out press kits; in the kit that accompanied the News

NEWS RELEASE EXAMPLE "A"

John J. Jackson   (I.D.: Upper left of 8½" x 11"
School of Physical Education   white paper)
University of Victoria
Victoria, B.C. V8W 2Y2
Phone: (604) 477-6911 (local 4510)

Immediate Release   (Release date)

(Leave 2" for headline—
Editor's job.)

Dr. Earle F. Zeigler (who), Lansdowne Visitor (how) and
one of the world's most distinguished physical education and
sport scholars will be lecturing (what) at the University
(where) during the week of February 25-29, 1980 (when)
on the Olympic boycott and other issues (why). (This is
called a "summary" lead.)

(Wide margins   Dr. Zeigler is the author or editor of sixteen books and
for editing)   over 300 articles. In recognition of his four decades of service
to physical education, he was awarded the Doctor of Laws   (all this should
degree, *honoris causa*, by the University of Windsor in 1975,   be double spaced
was the Alliance Scholar of the Year in the U.S.A. in 1978,   for print media
and has received the highest honors granted by numerous   and triple spaced
other professional and scholarly·organizations (including the   for electronic
Canadian Association for Health, Physical Education, and   media)
Recreation).

The University of Victoria and Victoria CAHPER is
sponsoring a lecture titled, "Soviet Sport and the Olympic
Ideal" which Dr. Zeigler will deliver in McKinnon 150 at
7:30 p.m. on Tuesday, *February 26, 1980.*

Full details of Professor Zeigler's program are available
from Dr. John Jackson of the School of Physical Education
(phone: 477-6911, local 4510).

(End)

(Try to get on one page. Be accurate and not too "pluggy."
Don't shout "NEWS," editors decide that: Proofread and
meet deadline.)

Release Example "B" (see below) for example, were Figures 22 and 23, details of local sports councils, and particulars of the Southwestern Sports Council.

NEWS RELEASE EXAMPLE "B"

Principal Regional Officer
The Sports Council
South-Western Regional Office
17 The Square
Crewkerne, Somerset
Telephone: Crewkerne (STD 0460 31)
3491/2

*EMBARGO 11:00 a.m. Monday, 2nd
October, 1972.*

Today the Southwestern Sports Council gave details of its part in the "Sport for All" campaign in the Southwest.

To help local authorities to recognise the recreation needs of the people the Council recommend a wide range of possible facilities. We have only to look within our own region to see that a number of authorities are already planning or building facilities. A number of authorities are already providing or planning multi-sports centres. There are also many examples of cooperation with local education authorities. The Bishops Cleeve centre shows what can be done when a parish council and an education authority jointly provide a school/community hall. At the other end of the scale the highly successful Poole Sports Centre is much bigger—as you would expect with a larger population. The opportunities for cooperation with the education authorities are endless from the very small provision in a local village primary school to the much larger complex in dense urban areas.

For people who want to learn something about a sport the Sports Council organises courses throughout the region. These range from climbing in Cornwall to Badminton in North Gloucestershire. Many courses are arranged locally by technical colleges and evening institutes so that there is usually somewhere that a budding player can learn or practice a game.

But just what are the chances of improving the sports opportunities in the region. The Sports Council recommend local authorities and local sportsmen to get together in local sports advisory councils. There are already many of these in operation and providing that they are imaginatively led and soundly based they are successful.

The Sports Council itself is already offering a service to local authorities and sports governing bodies in the region. It also encourages local authorities by offering grant aid on regional and sub-regional facilities. Three years ago there were no Sports Council grants of this nature, last year in the Southwest 60,000 of grant was offered. This year it is hoped that the figure will be up to 230,000. By helping with these regional and sub-regional grants the Sports Council hope the local councils will develop and assist participation at the local level.

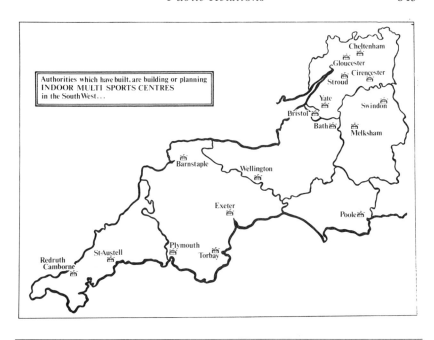

Authorities which have built, are building or planning
INDOOR MULTI SPORTS CENTRES
in the SouthWest...

THE XI COMMONWEALTH GAMES (CANADA 1978) FOUNDATION
P.O. BOX 1978, EDMONTON, ALBERTA, CANADA T5J 5J5 PHONE (403) 425-1978

FOR IMMEDIATE RELEASE:

EDMONTON 1978

KINSMEN PARK AQUATIC-FITNESS CENTRE
Sod-Turning Ceremony
April 1, 1976

Participants:

Government of Canada

Ian Howard, Regional Director, Sport Canada, representing the Minister of National Health & Welfare, The Honorable Marc LaLonde

Government of the Province of Alberta

The Minister of Recreation, Parks and Wildlife, the Honorable Allan Adair

City of Edmonton

His Worship, Mayor Terry Cavanagh

Commonwealth Games Canada (1978) Foundation

Dr. Maury Van Vliet, President

Kinsmen Club of Edmonton

Mr. Dave Starko, President

April 1, 1976

When the doors open to the Kinsmen Park Aquatic Centre in December of next year, visitors will find a roof over 1,300,000 gallons (U.S.) of water.

That's a lot of water.

Presuming an individual uses about 20 gallons for a bath, a person would need 178 years bathing once a day to use all that water.

To put it another way, that's enough to bath 65,000 people.

However, based on projected annual useage, more than half a million people will swim in that water before it's drained and the pools refilled. What makes it all possible is a system of filters which will reduce the need to change water to about once a year.

Comparing square feet of water surface, the Kinsmen Aquatic Centre is 25% larger than the Olympic Pool in Munich and just 544 square feet or 1% smaller than the water surface in the Olympic Pool at Montreal.

In all, the Aquatic Centre being developed for the XIth Commonwealth Games in 1978 will house four pools.

The competition pool will be 50 metres (164') long, 21 metres (69') wide and six feet deep.

The diving tank will be 25 metres (82') by 15.2 metres (50') and five metres or 16 feet in depth. There will be diving platforms at 3, 5, 7.5, and 10 metres and four springboards, two at one metre and two at three metres.

The facility will also house a warm-up pool 51 metres (167.32') in length and six lanes wide. That compares with eight lanes in the competition pool. However, the warm-up pool will only be one and one-half metres (just under five feet) in depth. It will employ a portable bulkhead allowing for division of the water surface into two 25 metre pools.

Finally, the Centre will include a teach pool 42' by 18' with a hydro-therapy capability. Water temperature in this pool will be maintained at about 85 degrees.

Aside from water, the facility will also contain permanent seating for 1,500 and space for 3,200 temporary seats during competitive meets.

Additional public facilities include four handball and two squash courts, a health club with two saunas, two showers, a massage table and an exercise room, change facilities with showers and more than 500 lockers for men and 400 for women, first aid and competition testing rooms, a classroom, four public restrooms, 2,000 square feet of space for a cafeteria, a multi-purpose meeting room, a pro shop, special facilities for the handicapped, and news media, timing and administration areas.

.....more

EDMONTON 1978

The entrance to the bi-level structure will provide access to the existing Kinsmen Fieldhouse at both levels, replacing the present entrance at the northwest corner of the building.

A total Sports Centre has long been a dream of the Kinsmen Club of Edmonton and has finally been realized through the selection of Canada and Edmonton as host for the 1978 Commonwealth Games.

As a result of the Kinsmen Club's presence, there are five partners participating in the financing of the project. They include the Government of Canada, the Government of the Province of Alberta, the City of Edmonton, the Commonwealth Games Canada (1978) Foundation and, of course, the Kinsmen Club of Edmonton, which has pledged $1,000,000 to the project, specifically the fitness area.

The Club is also maintaining an active role in the construction phase of the project. The Kinsmen's Aquatic-Fitness Centre committee, headed by Rod Tweddle, is Project Director and it has retained the services of Pete Peterson as Project Co-ordinator.

-o-

Figure 24. Press Release Example "C"

Note that the press prefers short, punchy sentences; if a second page is needed, "more" is typed at the bottom of the first page, and a paragraph should not run from one page to the next. The release should be written for a particular medium; "news stories for newspapers, . . . terse radio-style releases for radio; TV news scripts for TV" (Cutlip and Center, 1971:422).

With reference to the examples used in this design:
(1) News Release Example "A" (Zeigler) was for local papers and was used.
(2) News Release Example "B" (Sports Council) was part of a kit at a regional news conference attended by newspaper reporters and those from the electronic media. The long paragraphs are too long.
(3) Figure 24 (Aquatic Center) was intended for all media and much of the information was used. It was part of a kit.

Radio and Television Interviews

Sport administrators and managers are often called on to give interviews or "short spots" on radio or television; quite often radio interviews have to be given over the telephone with very little warning. This section presents some guidelines to help practitioners use these media to enhance their organization's public relations. Practical exercises are suggested which can be done in university/college classes or privately in any sport organization. Certainly, it is advisable to practice before doing a live performance. This section is based on my experience, which began with my receiving similar advice from John Wheatley; so I gratefully acknowledge his expertise here.

Notes For Interviewees
1. Give thought to your subject and particularly so if it is likely to be a probing interview. Think about the questions most likely to be asked and decide how they can be answered clearly and concisely. Pre-interview briefings are usually "scanty" to say the least.
2. Do not prepare answers word-for-word, as the broadcast outcome will be stilted and unnatural to the listener/viewer. An interviewer, who is doing his job properly, cannot just ask a string of prepared questions and, if he puts in an

extra one here or there, the "scripted" interviewee will be badly put off.

3. Check on facts and figures that might be asked about in relation to your subject. An interviewee is not expected to have all facts in his head but it is impressive to the listener if an interviewee can apparently spontaneously "rattle off" relevant and important figures. Equally it is off-putting to the listener if the interviewee is caught out and mumbles, "Well, I think it's probably 50 percent or maybe 75 percent."

4. In the exercise the time for the interview will only be three minutes, so you must be concise but be sure you make all the really important points; do not spend two-and-one-half minutes answering the introductory question. If called on in real life always check the time available with the producer.

5. Try to be yourself. Be natural and honest but also use elementary psychology. There is no use trying to "pull the wool" over the listener's eyes; 90 percent will see through the "phoney" and, in any case, viewers are generally more sympathetic to one who openly admits a mistake than one who tries to "plaster over the cracks." If there are certain facts you simply cannot reveal, you can possibly avoid the question about them by making sure you direct the conversation onto other interesting topics or be frank and say, for example, "I'm afraid at the moment it would be wrong for me to comment as our investigations aren't complete—ask me a week from now." This implies you have no objection to answering when the time is right.

6. If the interviewer starts the "needle" technique be quite firm and composed. Above all, do not allow yourself to become rattled or angry for that plays into his hands. A composed smile and a snappy, witty remark can send that type of interviewer reeling. Another technique is to push the ball back to his court by asking him a question.

7. When possible answer from personal experience rather than in the third person.

8. A sense of humor is a great asset, and an appropriate, short, witty remark or quickly related amusing incident helps to liven viewer's-listener's interest.

9. Do not try to oversell yourself; a more subtle approach is better.

10. Do not be overtechnical or pompous. Remember it is up to you to make the listener interested; few will be automatically interested.

11. In TV interviews, look at the interviewer only. Do not let your eyes stray to all the other activity in the studio or the viewer's attention will be attracted to the shift of eyes. "What's he looking at?" he wonders—he will probably never know (which is a bit frustrating) but the fact is that he may not have caught the point you were making. The same applies to overuse of hand movements, untidy appearance, and moving about in the chair.

12. Remember (on TV) that the producer will probably have you in a close-up shot for a substantial part of the interview so:
    (i) Every facial expression will be seen closely; a lively, animated, and interested face will appeal to the viewer more than a bored "dead pan" one.
    (ii) Do not move about in your chair or the camera will have to follow you and it looks bad. Get comfortable in a relaxed, upright position and stay that way. Don't slouch.

13. Put enthusiasm and vigor into your speech indicating that you have a genuine desire to communicate to others. Speak up and keep your voice level up. Don't try to make all your points at once in a list.

14. When the interview is over do not move until you are told to go.

Notes For Straight To Camera
Or Radio Short Spots

In the exercise that follows, the time for either is one minute; of course longer may be allowed in real situations but they are often short.

1. Make sure you know your main aim.
2. Decide the main points you want to make and write them down in note form (cf. "summary lead" in News Release Example "A").
3. Decide the order of priority these facts should be given—

how you can start and end the item to give it the necessary punch and vitality. Remember the listener/viewer can switch off.

4. Use down to earth conversational words, tone, and attitude. Be enthusiastic.
5. Gauge accurately what you can get into one minute. If you are precise you can give a lot of information. Have a few rehearsals (approximately 150 words).
6. Make sure you have a good, hard-hitting opening. Your first job is to get the listener's attention and your second is to keep it.
7. Speak as though you are talking to one person.
8. See number 12 in "Notes For Interviewees."
9. If there is more than one lens, ask the floor manager which is the right one to look at. Then look at it and don't let your eyes glance elsewhere. A pleasant smile is helpful.
10. Check that your appearance is tidy; television exaggerates untidiness.
11. When possible use the personal approach; e.g. "I don't know about you but. . . ."
12. The floor manager will "cue" you when he wants you to "wind up." He will get in your eyeline so don't begin eye-shifts to look where he is; also, don't nod that you've seen him!
13. Remember, one minute means one minute.

Practice Exercises

Do the following in order.

1. One minute "spot" for radio (use a tape recorder). Suggested topics:
   (a) Physical education teachers are underpaid.
   (b) More P.E. teachers are needed in elementary schools.
   (c) Recreation programs need public financial support.
   (d) The ugliness of sport.
   (e) The beauty of sport.
   (f) Fair play: The administrator's role.
2. One minute straight to camera for television (use VTR equipment). Topics as suggested in #1 above.
3. Prepare for a three-minute radio interview and then have a

colleague act as interviewer. Suggested topics:

(a) Sport plans for upcoming season.

(b) Vandalism in parks; the public wants to know what you are going to do about it.

(c) Three city open air swimming pools will be closed for economy reasons all summer. You must explain why without pointing fingers at politicians.

4. As for number 3 above but for television.

Evaluation Of Practice

Have class colleagues or work colleagues evaluate your performance using the following guidelines.

ONE-MINUTE SPOTS.

(a) Were the main points of the issue brought out?

(b) Did the beginning and the end have punch and vitality?

(c) Was the language suitably "down to earth?"

(d) Did you feel the speaker was talking to you?

(e) Were there any "uncomfortable" pauses?

(f) Was the speaker enthusiastic (or too enthusiastic?)

(g) Was the timing accurate?

(h) Give a grade out of seven.

INTERVIEWS.

(a) Was the interviewee well prepared?

(b) Did his answers appear "natural" (i.e. not prepared word for word)?

(c) Did he support his points by facts?

(d) Did he make the main points he should have made?

(e) Were there any uncomfortable pauses?

(f) Did he allow himself to be "needled?"

(g) Did he appear to answer honestly?

(h) Were there any witty or humorous responses?

(i) Did he try to "oversell" or was he suitably subtle?

(j) Was he over-technical or pompous?

(k) Did his tone of voice hold your interest?

(l) Give a grade out of eleven.

References

Cutlip, Scott M., and Center, Allen H.: *Effective Public Relations*, 4th ed. Englewood Cliffs, New Jersey, Prentice-Hall, 1971.

McIntyre, Robert B.: Good press relations is key to good PR. *Editor And Publisher*, May 26, 1962.

Supplementary Readings

Burger, C.: How to meet the press. *Harvard Business Review*, 62-70, July/August, 1975.

Klapper, J.: *The Effects of Mass Communication*. Glencoe, Illinois, The Free Press, 1960.

Schramm, W. (Ed.): *Mass Communications*. Urbana, Illinois, University of Illinois Press, 1960.

Case 11.21

Ghost's Goals

Read Case 10.13, *"Early Goals"* and your analysis of Case 11.11, *"PR Goals."*

Case Analysis Method

Assume you are Brian Rogers and, as the person responsible for the department's public relations, you must do the following:

1. Write a press release to publicize a speech Roy Pound will be making to the PTA about the proposed athletic policies. The policies will be in keeping with the organizational goals (see Learning Design 10.13).

2. Write a draft of Roy Pound's speech for him. It must last twenty minutes.

Case 11.22

Fair Exchange?

One hundred United States teachers and 100 British teachers were about to exchange jobs for a year and all of them gathered in a big New York hotel to exchange information before the year began. The hotel PR officer saw the potential of several "human interest" stories and invited the press to meet the incoming and outgoing teachers.

London grammar school physical education teacher Mike Rolling and his family were en route to Texas and were going to drive from New York with their two-year-old daughter and three-week-old son. The press mingled and chatted amiably over refreshments. Then, a reporter asked Mike about the differences he expected to find between the school systems—Texas and

London. The year was 1960 and, at that time in London, grammar schools existed that "creamed off" at age eleven those pupils who were supposed to be in the top 25 percent intelligence category for more intensive academic schooling. The majority received more vocational instruction and entered the work force at age fifteen. By contrast Mike commented, most of his Texas students would be at school until they were eighteen. Mike said to the reporter that he would not like to see some of the British 75 percent still in school at eighteen so he tended, presently, to favor the British system. Similarly, he preferred the less-intensive approach to athletics that was found in Britain compared with what he expected to find in Texas school football.

The conversation then turned to the baby and its British baby buggy before the group broke up. Next day a New York paper carried the headline "BRITISH TEACHER PANS U.S. EDUCATION." The story was picked up on wire services and given more extensive coverage in Mike Rolling's new Texas community.

Case Analysis Method
CAM A or CAM B (see Chapter 1).

Case 11.23

Mirror Image

Daily Mirror (London), September 20, 1972.
The Sports Council is setting up a fitness clinic in Cheltenham, especially for chubby businessmen.

But on the instructions of the council's regional officer, anyone wanting to take the course must pass a rigorous medical to prove he is fit enough to get fit.

Case Analysis Method
CAM B (see Chapter 1).

Case 11.24

The Grass Is Always Greener . . .

Headline: *Northern Journal*, March 30, 1976.
". . . AND THE GRASS GREW ALL AROUND."

A shortage of the green stuff in the northern parks department budget is going to mean a surplus of the green stuff on city boulevards.

Because city council trimmed $150,000 out of parks and recreation maintenance, Superintendent Boxer predicted Monday that his department will not be able to keep the grass trimmed on boulevards, parks, playing fields, and school grounds this summer.

And weeding out that money from five district maintenance budgets is going to lead to pruning staff. Boxer anticipates hiring 70 summer workers which is only 20 percent of last year's level (and that was half of 1974's total).

"We won't be doing as much cutting or field work as we should do," he said, explaining the department had hoped to spend $800,000 for 350 maintenance workers.

If the searing sun doesn't save the department, Boxer predicts his department will be scorched by complaints.

"The parks department will try to satisfy the complainers but other programs will have to suffer," explained Boxer. He declined to say which.

Letter to the Editor, April 4, 1976.

Something appears to be wrong with the mathematics of the article ". . . and the grass grew all around" (*Journal*, March 30). A cut of $150,000 from the budget represents approximately $500 for each of 255 people the parks and recreation department does not hire this summer. Perhaps Mr. Boxer might consider putting the entire maintenance operation out for tender—he would, unquestionably, find that not only would it be done for less money but also more efficiently.

It is about time the city got out of businesses it knows little or nothing about. Then we'll get things done better, cheaper.

P.J., Northern City.

Case Analysis Method
CAM A or CAM B (see Chapter 1).

Summary

1. Public relations, as a term, is used in the following three senses: a relationship, a means, and a status.

2. Public relations is an operating concept of administration and a specialized staff function. Administrators earn good public relations by ensuring responsible sport organizational performance. Staff facilitate inflow of information from relevant publics, advise administrators, and implement public relations programs.

3. Public relations is the planned effort to influence opinion through socially responsible and acceptable performance, based on mutually satisfactory two-way communication.

4. X (the deed) plus Y (the way the deed is interpreted) = public attitudes.

5. Public relations process steps are:
   (a) Isolate the problem;
   (b) Plan and program;
   (c) Action; and,
   (d) Evaluate.

6. The small amount of sport-related research indicates that public relations has not been clearly defined, planned, or understood as a concept or function.

7. The sport organization's standing with the press can shape and limit its accomplishments.

8. Sport organizations must earn good public relations and work with the media by:
   (a) Shooting squarely;
   (b) Giving service;
   (c) Not begging or carping;
   (d) Not asking for kills;
   (e) Not flooding the media; and,
   (f) Keeping release lists up to date.

9. See News Release Examples "A" and "B" and Figures 22, 23, and 24 for the key aspects of news releases and press kits given out at news conferences.

10. Radio and television performances should be prepared for carefully to earn good public relations.

Concepts For Review

Public relations (relationships, means, status)	Definitions
	Publics
PR Process Steps	Communication
Tools	Seven C's

Diffusion of innovations	Press complaints
Press	Publicity principles
Flack	News conferences
News releases	TV and Radio performances

Questions For Oral Or Written Discussion

1. CAM C (see Chapter 1) applied to instructor-specified topics taken from this chapter.

2. *The Harper Dictionary of Modern Thought* (New York, Harper and Row, 1977) defines public relations as:

> Euphemism for the professional organization of attempts to secure public understanding and support for the activities of bodies such as governments, political parties, commercial and industrial organizations, professional bodies, etc. Public relations thus include the winning of sympathy for the public activities of one state from the peoples of other countries. It includes, but is by no means confined to propaganda.

   Discuss and critique.

3. A former federal minister of sport was the athletic banquet guest speaker at the University of Victoria. She began by saying: "I would like to have a few words with the rugby players first. Ugh, Ugh, Ugh." Such is the image many athletes have with the public. How would you train such likely athletes to respond to short media interviews when they have, (a) done well/won; and (b) done badly/lost?

4.   "O wad some power the giftie gie us
      To see oursels as others see us!"   Robert Burns
   Discuss in relation to what you would do in your sport organization.

5. You have just been appointed director of leisure services for the city and have responsibility for the operation of a live theater. It loses money and MIS for the previous year reveals:
   (a) Box office takings dropped 40 percent.
   (b) Of the audience, 70 percent came from upper and upper-middle class sections of the community.
   (c) 40 percent attended every one or two weeks.
   (d) 60 percent of regulars think the performances were "a bit too highbrow."
   (e) 8 percent would pay more for seats.

Plan a detailed public relations program designed to make the theater financially self-supporting without losing previous regulars.

Chapter 12

THE BALL OF WAX NEVER WANES

$\mathbf{A}$ PURPOSE OF THIS final chapter is to make the point, symbolically, that sport administrative issues, problems, and challenges are ubiquitous and seem to gather disturbing momentum at times. Instead of the usual two learning designs, five short ones include new material while, in the final design, conclusions are made about the book's content.

LEARNING DESIGN 12.1

MEETINGS

Aye or No?

Counting back to my mid-teens as a sport participant, I have been attending sport meetings for over thirty years and the vast majority of the participants have disliked them; often hated them. The meetings were set in schools, colleges, universities, clubs, governing bodies, and various government agencies; the higher the level of administrative-managerial position I held, the more meetings I attended.

Citing common symptoms of poor organization, Drucker's (1973:548) prime one is *"too many meetings attended by too many people."* Parkinson (1957:50-62) has some delightfully irreverent things to say about big committees and concludes that "the whole organism begins to perish" when its "coefficient of inefficiency" of twenty-one members is reached.

Yet, in complex society of which sport is a part, we must recognize, as Thomas (1979:117) does, that "the work of committees can be a deadly serious business." The responsibilities that committees tackle are "not to be trusted to any single person; we have to do it together."

This design is written from the sport administrator's viewpoint and accepts Thomas' advice but attempts to take heed of the warnings given by Drucker, Parkinson, and my personal experience.

Meeting Planning

Before calling any meeting the sport administrator should carefully consider whether or not it is really necessary. Could the administrator properly do what the meeting would do? Or, could the same results be obtained more easily by other means of communication? However, if a meeting is needed, the following checklist, adapted from Lobingier (1969:14-25), is a useful guide for planning all meetings.

1. Decide, precisely, the meeting's purpose (cf. various goal types in Chapter 10). Once the reason is clear, it is obvious whom should be invited and when and where it should take place.
2. Analyse the participant's interests, needs, desires, knowledge, and sophistication.
3. Plan the agenda's sequence and emphasis in relation to the allocated time (which should be controlled and kept as short as possible). The agenda, with meeting participants' input, and supporting papers, if any, should be circulated well before the meeting.
4. Plan how the material is to be presented for maximum effective communication. Brief the proposed presenters and plan to encourage contributions from all participants (remember they ought not to be there if they are not important). Remember Murphy's Law, "If anything can go wrong it will," so be prepared.
5. Plan what to do regarding implementing the meeting's decisions. Keep records of what transpires (minutes).
6. Evaluate the meeting. This can be done by the sport administrator or by asking for participants' opinions; there is usually room for improvement.

Chairing

Having decided to have a meeting, the chairing sport administrator should demonstrate interest, enthusiasm, confidence, knowledge, good humor, empathy, mental agility, follow-through, and democratic procedures. The procedures need not be excessively formal for that is usually resented in most sport situations. Whatever the degree of informality, it is useful for those chairing meetings to be aware of some basic aspects of parliamentary procedure. They can then modify to further informality or learn more details by consulting *Robert's Rules Of Order.*

Order Of Business
1. The meeting is "called to order" by the chairperson.
2. The minutes of the preceding meeting are read by the secretary. They may be, (a) approved as read or, (b) approved with additions or corrections.
3. Monthly statement of the treasurer (if appropriate) is "Received as read and filed for audit" (chairperson so states.)
4. Reports of standing committees are called for by the chairperson.
5. Reports of special committees are called for by the chairperson.
6. Unfinished business.
7. New business.
8. The program (if any).
9. Adjournment.

Chairperson's Duties
1. To preside.
2. Keep calm at all times.
3. Talk no more than necessary while presiding.
4. Keep to the agenda in a businesslike manner.
5. Have a working knowledge of parliamentary procedure and a thorough understanding of the constitution and bylaws of the sport organization.
6. Keep a list of the organization's committees on the table while presiding.
7. Refrain from entering the debate of questions before the assembly. If it is necessary for the chairperson to debate, the vice-chairperson should assume the chair until a vote has been taken on the issue.

8. Extend every courtesy to the opponents of a motion even if the motion is favored by the chair.
9. Always be early at the rostrum and when the time arrives note whether a quorum is present; if so, call the meeting to order and declare "a quorum is present."

Common Terms

QUORUM. The number of members that must be present for business to be conducted legally. The actual number is usually stated in the bylaws but, if not, a simple majority is accepted.

MOTION. A motion is a call for action. When a motion has been made, seconded, and stated by the chair, the assembly is not at liberty to consider any other business and it may not be withdrawn.

TO AMEND. This motion is to change, add, or omit words in the original main motion and is debatable (majority vote).

TO AMEND THE AMENDMENT. This is a motion to change, add, or omit words in the first amendment (debatable, majority vote).

Voting method: The first vote is on changing words of the second amendment, the second vote (if the first vote adopts change) on the first amendment as changed; the third vote is on adopting the main motion as changed.

TO COMMIT. When a motion becomes involved through amendments or when it is wise to investigate a question more carefully, it may be moved to commit the motion to a committee for further consideration (debatable, amendable; committee must make a report).

TO LAY ON THE TABLE. The object of this motion is to postpone the subject under discussion in such a way that it can be taken up at some time in the near future when a motion "to take from the table" would be in order. These motions are not debatable or amendable (majority vote).

TO POSTPONE. A motion to postpone the question to some future time is in order except when a speaker has the floor (debatable, majority vote).

TO ADJOURN. This motion is always in order except:
   (a) When a speaker has the floor.
   (b) When a vote is being taken.

(c) After it has just been voted down.

(d) When the assembly is in the midst of some business which cannot be abruptly stopped.

If properly made and seconded, it is not debatable (majority vote). However, when a motion is made to adjourn to a definite place, and time, it is debatable.

TO RECONSIDER. The motion to reconsider a motion that was carried or lost is in order if made on the same day or the next calendar day, but must be made by one who voted with the prevailing side. No question can be twice reconsidered (debatable, majority vote). Requires two votes: first on whether it should be reconsidred then on the original motion after reconsideration.

THE PREVIOUS QUESTION. This is to close debate on the pending question. This motion may be made when debate becomes long and drawn out. It is not debatable. The form is "Mr./Madam Chairman, I move the previous question." The Chairman then asks, "Shall debate be closed and the question now be put?" If this be adopted by a two-thirds majority, the question before the assembly is immediately voted upon.

POINT OF ORDER. This motion is always in order, but can be used only to present an objection to a ruling of the chair or some method of parliamentary procedure. The form is "Mr./Madam Chairman, I rise to a point of order." The chairperson: "Please state your point of order." Answer: (a) "Your point of order is sustained," or (b) "Your point of order is denied." If any member is not satisfied, the decision may be appealed (debatable, majority vote).

TIE VOTE. On a tie vote a motion is lost. If there is a majority of one, the chair may vote with the minority and make it a tie. The chair votes in ballots.

The Delphi Technique

In the 1960s some Rand Corporation people were dissatisfied with meetings so they devised the Delphi technique (after Delphi which was Apollo's place and suggesting oracular prophetic function; see Thomas, 1979:118-119). Questionnaires are circulated to the group members who respond in writing. The responses are then circulated to all members who are asked to reconsider and complete the questionnaire again. Three cycles are usually enough to reach consensuses which are reported to be better than usual meeting outcomes. It is believed to be because everyone gets to "speak, think, and listen."

References and Supplementary Readings

Lobingier, John, Jr.: *Business Meetings That Make Business.* London, Collier, 1969.

Parkinson, C. Northcote: *Parkinson's Law and Other Studies in Adminis-tration.* New York, Ballantine, 1973. [First published in 1957.]

Robert, Henry M.: *Robert's Rules of Order.* New York, Pyramid, 1973.

Sturgis, Alice F.: *Sturgis Standard Code of Parliamentary Procedure.* New York, McGraw-Hill, 1950.

Thomas, L.: *The Medusa and the Snail.* New York, Viking, 1979.

Young, D.: "The Effectiveness of Temporary Adaptive Systems" [ad hoc committees]. Doctoral dissertation, the University of Alberta, 1979.

Questions

1. CAM C (see Chapter 1) applied to a sport meeting setting.
2. Use the Delphi technique in a group concerned with a sport issue. A case from this book could be the issue.

LEARNING DESIGN 12.2

OFFICE MANAGEMENT

Sport administrators' careers may take them through a wide range of "offices." It is not unusual for the sport administrator to have to perform nearly all office functions in addition to his/her major tasks. Conversely, the sport administrator may be employed where office space, personnel, and equipment is very sophisticated. Regardless of its position on this continuum, a sport office is likely to be concerned with most of the following functions; only the degree and emphasis will change. Ultimately, the responsibility for efficient office management rests with the sport administrator.

Telephone Calls

The people (usually secretaries) who make and receive tele-phone calls in sport offices are performing two key functions:

public relations and contributing to organizational efficiency. So, from the public relations viewpoint, they must behave according to the guidelines described in Learning Design 11.1. For efficiency purposes they must be knowledgeable about the organization's functions and the whereabouts of organizational personnel. Thus, other personnel must help secretaries to keep informed about programs and advise them of their own movements in and out of the office.

Given the choice then, it is not the most junior secretary who should do most of the telephone answering because a great deal of expertise is required that is not usually quickly gained.

Reception

If an extra-organizational person actually enters the sport organization's central office the purposes of a right reception are similar to the reasons for the correct telephone behavior described above; public relations and efficiency (cf. Learning Design 11.1).

Visual, auditory, and olfactory impressions are additionally important. If possible, the central office should be conveniently located to serve all its publics, be attractively decorated, and be as quiet as possible—indicating welcome and reassurance.

A visitor's first impression is likely to be a lasting one so, given good physical conditions, it remains for the secretary to perform the remainder of the important function. Skillful judgment is required to identify the "public" to which the visitor belongs: parent, student, faculty, client, press, alumni, or other. The initial cordial reception to all should be the same, but then the secretary must decide what to do next. Who can best serve the visitor? Is it a legitimate visitor? Has a prior appointment been made? Should the department head be interrupted? Or should an appointment be made for a later time? If the visitor has to wait, a comfortable seat should be available and the offer of a refreshing drink is always appreciated.

Appointments

Sport administrators have many appointments, are responsible for submitting frequent reports (particularly in governments where elected officials demand factual advice), and generally have to contend with varied, diverse activity. For the administrator to succeed, the scheduling of such activity cannot be left to chance or memory; the administrator must have an infallible system.

Assuming that division of work time is carefully planned, the sport administrator-secretary relationship should revolve around various forms of calendars. The following are recommended in big offices but numbers three and four are sufficient for those without a personal secretary.

1. A desk diary for the sport administrator in which all appointments and deadlines are written by either the secretary or the administrator. The secretary must check frequently to see if any new commitments have been added by the administrator (including all out-of-office time).
2. An appointment book on the secretary's desk into which the secretary puts appointments and deadlines made by the administrator in his/her desk diary and new secretary-made appointments.
3. A pocket diary carried everywhere by the administrator so that appointments and deadlines can be made when away from the office. Such commitments should, of course, be entered in the desk diary as soon as possible. This system can cause a little "double booking" at times but it rarely occurs if there is regular, close communication between the secretary and the administrator. In my experience, when difficulties have arisen, they have been easily rectified by rescheduling.
4. A tickler file on the secretary's desk and is carefully arranged to bring regular and irregular commitments to timely attention. These often consist of 3 by 5-inch cards on a cylinder; allowing regular checks and easy amendment.

Correspondence

The basic principles applicable in telephoning and receiving visitors apply in dealing with correspondence. It should receive prompt attention and be written in concise yet cordial style. The English should be good, it should be proofread by the secretary and the administrator, and the address should be checked.

It is appropriate to use form letters for some purposes and for the administrator to refer some letters for the action of others. When correspondence is referred, the secretary must keep a referral book to follow-up on the actions. If a typing pool system is in use, there needs to be a priority work list, but correspondence should receive top priority in most situations.

Secretaries, generally, do not like too much impersonal use of dictaphones. They are sometimes necessary, considering administrators' long hours of work, but an attempt should be made to dictate letters regularly for the secretary to take down in shorthand. To further enlarge the secretary's job, it is advisable to ask her/him to compose letters occasionally for the administrator's signature.

Filing

An efficient filing system is an important requirement; secretaries and administrators must be able to retrieve any item quickly. Various systems exist: for example, alphabetical by name, subject, combined name/subject; by number; and/or by letters and numbers combined. Sometimes, the above may be subdivided by file drawer; for example, athletics, intramurals, physical education, and students. Cross-referencing systems sometimes help retrieval as do "out" cards which indicate where they are. Also, periodic clearouts are necessary.

Various elaborate mechanized electronic systems exist in big offices. For example, incoming mail is machine opened, a microcopy is made of the correspondence, and a number added. A photocopy of the numbered original then goes to the person to whom the letter is directed. The receiver then answers the letter and the answer is similarly copied for the micro-filing system. Originals are also centrally filed for a period, but no files need be kept in satellite offices. Correspondence can be retrieved by number, person, subject, or other designated references.

Such systems work well to a point. The principal drawbacks are that people tend not to trust the system and keep their own files anyway! Also, opening mail causes problems at times; particularly if personal mail is opened in error. Except where there is a very high volume of mail, my preference is to let addressees open their own mail.

Controls

The secretary is a very important member of the administrator's team and must develop certain efficient control devices without too much irritating "red tape." Thus, the secretary and administrator must have working policies for such things as the allocation of keys, stationery, and the supervising of photocopying. Without proper controls, budgets can be destroyed and other dysfunctions occur.

Supervision Of Secretaries

Nothing very special needs to be recorded here because supervision of workers was dealt with in Chapter Five. Secretaries are people who work and they require the same supervision and consideration that any other worker is given; review Chapter Five.

Questions

1. CAM C (see Chapter 1) applied to a sport office setting.
2. Describe the working arrangements of a sport office you know and critique its practices.

Recommended Reference

Eckersley-Johnson, Anna L. (Ed.): *Webster's Secretarial Handbook*. Springfield, Massachusetts, Merriam, 1976.

LEARNING DESIGN 12.3

EXECUTIVE DISTRESS

What Is Stress?

To conform to common understanding of the word *stress*, this learning design would have been titled "Executive Stress." However, the interpretation of one who has studied the phenomenon more than most is preferred. Selye (1975:14) states, "Stress is the nonspecific response of the body to any demand made upon it." So, though stresses are specific (e.g. heat, cold, exercise, distressing information, joyful news) and produce various physiological, psychological, and social derangements, they also produce a "demand for readjustment," which is nonspecific. That is, the human being tries to readjust to a homeostatic condition or normalcy. Selye (1975:15) describes this nonspecific demand for homeostasis-seeking activity as "the essence of stress" and what "counts is the intensity of the demand for readjustment or adaptation." So, "stress is not merely nervous tension" (p. 17).

What Is Distress?

Selye's (1975:26) general adaptation syndrome (GAS) provides a framework within which this question can be answered. It has the following three stages: (1) the alarm reaction, (2) the stage of resistance, and (3) the stage of exhaustion. Thus, a stressor first causes biological adaptation to begin and the second stage ensues, so long as the initial stress is not too severe. If the stressor is compatible with adaptation, the body's resistance can rise above normal levels for a time (Stage 2). Eventually, however, "adaptation energy is exhausted" (Stage 3) and irreversible signs of the alarm reaction reappear; the individual then dies.

With it being possible for stress to be pain or pleasure, how can it be decided what is harmful stress at work or leisure? Harmful stress for one may be optimal stress for another; without stressors a person is dead. So, for living at work or leisure, a person must seek some stressors to motivate life (cf. Frankl, 1959). Therefore, as Selye wrote in his foreword to Albrecht's (1979:vi) *Stress and the Manager*, "(harmful) stress is perception." So distress is what is perceived as harmful or unpleasant stress and that is what people are usually referring to when talking about executive stress.

Reference back to Chapter Two, and the description of the nature of executives' work, hints at why such activity may be distressing. The suggested readings that follow this design deal with this large topic fully but, here, some research by Rogers (1977:265-273) pinpoints the issue. After studying 113 "upper-middle managers" he found the following factors contributed to distress: work load, organization structure and design, management responsibility, and communication and interpersonal interaction. Furthermore, the managers' perceptions of the distress "were not significantly related to age, level of education, or type of industry."

If this sort of executive activity is distress, what are the dysfunctional outcomes in executives and organizations? Selye (in Albrecht, 1971:vi) elaborates: ". . . it can contribute to coronary heart disease, peptic ulcers, suicide, nervous disorders, migraine headaches, insomnia, pill popping, cocktail hangups, marital disorder, child abuse, self-abuse, lack of confidence, allergies, strikes, picketing, and labor violence."

In my experience of sport situations, I have seen very nearly all of these symptoms, plus a few others, and am willing to believe that they all exist. Of course there are other contributory factors, and the degree of distress varies with each executive.

Develop PACE

Assuming that each sport executive is bound to encounter some degree of distress, what strategy and tactics ought to be adopted to ameliorate the condition? My answer is that the sport executive must develop and control his/her own **PACE**. Pace is well understood by sports people; here it is meant to have its usual meaning but also it is used as the acronym: **P**revent, **A**void, **C**reate, and **E**xpect.

Prevent

Rogers' (1977:265-273) empirical study identified distress factors as workload, structure, responsibility, and interpersonal interaction. There may be others, but my point here is that much of the distress can be prevented if competent administration/management is practiced. In earlier chapters it has been suggested how such prevention may be achieved, so a review is urged on students and would-be executives. That is, prevent potential distress factors occurring.

Avoid

Distress scholars (e.g. Selye, Albrecht) point out that executives need to know themselves; they need to know which work (or leisure) situations cause them to feel distressed. Once the distressors are known, they should be avoided whenever possible. Executives can take such avoiding actions much more often than they usually do. Thus, some distress which cannot be prevented, can be avoided.

Create

This aspect should be easier for sport executives than others; it refers to creating a physical, psychological, and social personal environment that can cope with distress. This is what sport can do for people anyway so, "Sports executive, heal thyself!" Engage in diversions from work, eat and drink wisely, do not smoke, do not take drugs, learn to relax (cf. Jacobson, 1976) and do regular stretching and aerobic exercises. Here, then, it is recognized that some distress cannot be prevented or avoided, but fit people can beat it!

Expect

The final word in the acronym re-emphasizes the point immediately above; sport executives must expect to encounter some distress in their jobs. Knowing there will be distress, they should regularly take quiet time to view their organization, and themselves, in appropriate perspective. Such perspective can usually make the distressor seem to be trivial.

References and Recommended Readings

Albrecht, K.: *Stress and the Manager: Making it Work for You.* Englewood Cliffs, New Jersey, Prentice-Hall, 1979.

Cooper, Cary L., and Payne, R. (Eds.): *Stress at Work.* New York, Wiley, 1978.

Frankl, Victor E.: *Man's Search for Meaning: An Introduction to Logotherapy.* Boston, Beacon Press, 1959. (New York, Pocket Books, 1976).

Greenwood, James W., III, and Greenwood, James W., Jr.: *Managing Executive Stress: A Sytems Approach.* New York, Wiley, 1979.

Jacobson, E.: *You Must Relax,* 5th ed. New York, McGraw-Hill, 1976.

Levinson, H.: *Executive Stress.* New York, Harper and Row, 1970.

Rogers, Rolf E.: Components of organizational stress among Canadian managers. *The Journal of Psychology, 95*:265-273, 1977.

Selye, H.: *Stress Without Distress.* New York, Signet, 1974.

Wolff, H. G.: *Stress and Disease.* Springfield, Illinois, Thomas, 1968.

Questions

1. CAM C (see Chapter 1) applied to sport executive distress.
2. Briefly describe a distressed sport executive known to you and outline specifics of what he/she should do to develop appropriate PACE.

LEARNING DESIGN 12.4

UNION-MANAGEMENT RELATIONS

The purpose of this design is to sensitize would-be administrators and managers to the basic concepts of union-management relations. In fact, the topic is closely allied with the final conclusions that were reached in the earlier chapter on the supervision of workers.

Fundamental Issues

In the distant past there was a small elite class and most people were "lower participants." There was a steep slope between the center of society and the periphery (cf. Shils, 1975). With the advent of mass society, the slope from the center of society to the periphery has become much less steep, the center is larger, and the periphery is smaller (in Western industrialized societies). Because of technology, those in the periphery learned how the elite lived so, of course, experienced the inequity. They fought a battle and made the slope less steep partly through the means of organized labor (after conflict).

Mass society also brought large work organizations that led to extreme divisions of labor, and the work was much less satisfying than it was when people did a variety of jobs in small, local organizations; hence, more conflict.

Consider, also, the pool lifeguard who is told that he is to receive a salary increase of $400 for exceptional service and his co-workers are to get $300. Likely, he would be pleased. Then, let him imagine he will receive $700 instead but, also, that his colleagues will get $800. Even though he is given much more money, his feelings are morose and he is aggrieved. But why? Because he perceives it as unfair; there is no equity so this situation also causes conflict. And, note that it is not just a money issue; lower participants are not just "money grabbing country wreckers."

So, inequity, which may arise in a multitude of ways, and the ensuing conflict is the fundamental reason for the need for union-management relations.

Procedures

Union-management relations procedures provide an opportunity for frank and free discussion on issues confronting union and management. The basis for such discussion is the establishment of a collective bargaining agreement between the employer and a bona fide recognized union. The initial impetus for such an agreement may come from either side but both sides must state in advance that they want an agreement.

The local union executive and top administrative/management must be equally represented numerically, and meetings must be held whenever union-management discussions could help solve problems of mutual concern. Such dialogue enables management to really understand the union's points of view *and* the union to properly appreciate the very different difficulties that management faces. If they can meet cordially under these conditions, and not *only* under pressure to reach a new collective agreement, there is much less likely to be outright hostility. Labour Canada reports: "Documented evidence shows that where union and management are honestly endeavouring to solve their problems as they arise, there are not only reductions in formal grievances but also faster settlements of collective agreements. In some instances, negotiations which previously took up to eight months of bitter wrangling were settled next time round after only four to eight meetings."

Many sport administrators do not have much involvement in union-management relations but, if they do, they should remember the fundamental issues at stake and follow the procedures recommended here. When union and management representatives openly discuss their day-to-day problems they learn to respect each others' positions and to *trust* each other. My experience is that union personnel want their workers to be good and expect them to be.

References

Canada, Labour Canada, Union-Management Services Branch: *Coming to Terms With Conflict.* Ottawa, Information Canada, 1974.

Canada, Labour Canada, Union-Management Services Branch: *Introducing Union-Management Relations Procedures.* Ottawa, n.d.

Shils, E.: *Center and Periphery: Essays in Macrosociology.* Chicago, University of Chicago Press, 1975.

Case 12.41

The Deep End

The city of Xion had fifteen indoor swimming pools and five

open air ones and were only open for three summer months each year. All pool staff were members of a local branch of a union, which had a special section in the collective agreement devoted to pool staff.

Key positions in each indoor pool were manager, lifeguard II (assistant manager), and Lifeguard I. The major qualification for lifeguard was a current lifesaving certificate and they were usually appointed after having experience as part-time swimming instructors. The collective agreement stated that pool managers would be appointed according to lifeguard II seniority from those who applied for vacant positions.

Wendy Rix had a recreation administration degree, was a keen lifeguard II, and had successfully managed an outdoor pool one summer. Her lifeguard II seniority was just under two years. Based on her potential and demonstrated expertise, Superintendent Jones appointed her manager to fill the vacancy at Westview pool.

However, another applicant was George Potts. Potts had been a lifeguard II for ten years, was unreliable, and had never tried for promotion previously. Superintendent Jones simply discarded Potts' application when he saw that Rix had applied.

The day after the appointment of Rix was announced, Jones received an angry call from the union local officer demanding an early meeting with management.

Case Analysis Method
CAM A or CAM B (see Chapter 1).

Question

1. CAM C (see Chapter 1) applied to a sport union-management issue.

LEARNING DESIGN 12.5

ROLE PLAYS

In-Tray Play

To supplement the purposes and advantages of the case method in sport administration (see Chapter 1), it is suggested in this design that useful vicarious experience can be obtained by students of sport administration through in-tray (or in-basket) and role-playing exercises. It is recommended that instructors develop some of their own for class use but several examples are provided below. For class use, the book can be used as it is but, for instructor-prepared in-trays, a duplicated set of tray items for each class member is best.

A Physical Education Teacher's In-Tray

School:	Rural junior high with 440 students.
P.E. Staff:	You (in your first month at the school) and a colleague of the other sex with ten years of service.
Principal:	Retreats to managerialism.
Other Staff:	Several will coach and sponsor trips if you treat them properly.
Dates:	Monday, September 21 to Tuesday, September 29.
Time:	10:00-10:30 A.M. on September 21 (i.e. you must answer all the items yourself or write a draft for the school secretary to type in this, your "free" period. The secretary will only type for you in exceptional circumstances. You are leaving for a five-day outdoor recreation field trip on September 25.
Guidelines:	Exhibit right administrative behavior.
Place:	An empty staff room.

Item 1

Dear Teacher:

Superintendent Mitchell was to have spoken at the PTA banquet on September 28 but finds he is unable to attend and has suggested you may speak in his place. Ideally we would like you to speak for twenty minutes on "The parent and physical education." I look forward to a positive reply and to meeting you.

> Sincerely,
> N. West
> Secretary, PTA

Item 2

Dear Teacher:

We are pleased to offer you soccer fixtures for grades seven and eight on November 1 (Saturday) at 10:00 A.M. here.

Sincerely,
M. Brown
P.E. Teacher
Westmington School

(This can be accepted.)

Item 3

To: P.E. Teacher

From: Drama Teacher

Re: Use of assembly hall for badminton on September 23.

I regret that I cannot let you use the hall for your match against Westmington because I simply must have a final play practice.

(The phone rings and you must answer. The science teacher's wife asks you to get him out of class for an urgent message. Time loss: three minutes.)

Item 4

A very dirty roller towel with a scribbled note pinned on. "I am disgusted with this. It comes from your p.e. students' changing room."

Janitor

Item 5

Dear Teacher:

I regret I must cancel the basketball game arranged for November 10.

Sincerely,
G. Garbut
Extere School

(This was the final pre-conference scrimmage.)

Item 6

Dear Teacher:

Why do you make Jane have showers? It's not good for her

to get cold and is no use anyway. She says you want her to smell good but what do you know about that. I've had five kids and like the body smells of my man. Don't make her have one again.

Angry Mother

(The history teacher enters and tells a joke. Time loss: three minutes.)

Item 7

To: P.E. Teacher
From: President, Students' Union
Re: Student Paper

Will you write a short (200 words) article on the five-day outdoor recreation field trip for the school paper. It must be in tomorrow to meet the deadline. Sorry!

Item 8

To: P.E. Teacher
From: Principal

I understand the superintendent wants you to speak in his place at the PTA. This would be a wise move for you, and I'm not sure our funds can stand the field trip anyway.

Item 9

Dear P.E. Teacher:

I am told that you are a good badminton player so wondered if you would give us some help with the junior program at the club. Our planning meeting is on September 25 at 8:00 A.M., so I could give you full particulars then.

Sincerely,
Jane Greer
Secretary, Badminton club

Item 10

Dear P.E. Teacher:

Welcome to our community!

I have been selling sports equipment and supplies to the school for ten years and always provide quality goods and repair services. So, I look forward to meeting you and hope we'll be able to continue our excellent relationship. For your information, I am the only sports goods retailer within twenty miles of the school. With your approval, I'll call to see you on September 28 at noon.

> Yours truly,
> Arthur Dyson
> Dyson Sports Goods

Item 11

Zodiac Sports Inc.
Big City

Dear P.E. Teacher:

Our bulk buying capability enables us to offer you phenomenal savings on sports equipment and supplies. We'll guarantee to beat the prices of any competitor by at least 7 percent (often considerably more).

I'll call to see you on September 28 to fully describe the services we can offer.

> Yours truly,
> Mike Henshaw
> Sales Manager

A Recreation Director's In-Tray

The Setting:	Smithville (see Case 2.23)
Recreation Director:	You, and you have held the position five months.
Other Personnel and Programs:	See Case 2.23.
Dates:	Sunday September 20 to Monday September 28.
Time:	6:00-6:30 P.M. on September 20 (i.e. you must either write complete resolutions of the item issues, or write directions for your secretary).
Guidelines:	Exhibit right administrative behavior.
Place:	Your empty office on Sunday, September 20. You have been out of town for a

week so have gone into the office to
make a start on the accumulated work.
Your secretary has left one file marked
"immediate attention" and another "look
at later." This exercise includes the contents of the first file.

Item 1

To: Director
From: Secretary
Re: District 6 Pool Manager (on maternity leave)
  Jan had twin boys on September 18; all are well.

Item 2

To: Director
From: Secretary
Re: Senior Citizens' Center Secretary
  Mrs. Joseph was knocked down by a car as she left work
on September 17; she's in the county infirmary, room 804.
(Both legs broken plus other injuries; stable now.)

Item 3

Dear Director:
  Your District 2 manager has applied for a senior position
in our city and given your name as a reference. Will you
comment on his likely suitability to supervise a much larger
staff and budget than he is doing currently. Any other
comments you think may be helpful would be appreciated
and should reach me by September 23.
                    Yours truly,
                    Personnel Director
(A very good reference is deserved.)

Item 4

To: Recreation Director
From: City Manager
Re: Closure Of Open Air Pools in July Next Year
  Council wishes to consider the possibility of closing six
outdoor pools next July to save money. Send me a report

containing your recommendations and alternatives by September 25.

Item 5

To: Recreation Director
From: City P.R. Director
Re: Oktoberfest Procession

Will you drive the mayor in an open 1910 car, please? You would have to wear period costume and hat. Please reply by September 21.

Item 6

Dear Director:

I was horrified to see your night watchman at the zoo with his savage guard dog. I very much doubt if he can control it, so what happens if he can't and our children are playing near the open field? This is an urgent request to have it removed.

Yours truly,
J. Goodyear
Secretary
Residents' Association

(You did not know there was a guard dog.)

Item 7

To: Director
From: Secretary
Re: School Visits to Planetarium

The Principal of St. Mark's School called on Friday to complain. Twenty-five of his students booked to visit the planetarium on September 17 only to find it full; they had travelled thirty miles each way!

(The planetarium curator reported to the manager of district 2.)

Item 8

Dear Director:

My daughter Mary is one of the most promising figure skaters in the country and yet, in this city of twenty public rinks, I can only get practice time for her at 5:00 A.M. or 1:00 A.M. I realize that everyone is hockey-mad but surely you can do something to improve this situation.

Yours sincerely,

Petra Pendagest

(The city skating programmer coordinated programs for 2,000 young players, "old-timers," communities, and free public skating. Ice time was too scarce to give Mary Pendagest more attractive hours.)

Item 9

To: Director

From: Secretary

Re: Local Service Club Lunch on September 21 (noon).

The Mayor wants you to go and receive a $50,000 cheque on behalf of the city's disabled citizens. The money is towards the recreation center for the disabled. A "very short" speech is needed and the mayor wants to see a draft before you go.

(The phone rings; it is your spouse. Two youths were speeding round and round the drop-off circle outside Westforce swimming pool, lost control, and crashed through the plate glass doors and into the play kiosk. It happened ten minutes ago [District 4].)

Item 10

To: Director

From: Secretary

My mother died on Friday afternoon so I have to be with Dad at least until September 29. City personnel couldn't get a regular high level secretary for you at least until September 24, but *you* may be able to get some help on Monday morning.

Role Playing

The simulation technique of role playing in case-like situations is another way of vicariously gaining sport administrative "experience." Two examples explain how it may be done, and the suggestion is made that other cases from earlier in the book are suitable for such dramatization.

The Park Play

Big City had a large park very close to downtown, which had a mainly "natural" appearance and many big trees. However, some "business interests," through the chamber of commerce, convinced city council to reconsider the land use. The council agreed and asked for specific proposals to be presented for mayor and council members to hear.

(At this point, the teacher assigns the following roles and instructions before allowing a five-minute preparation period for the principal "actors" to prepare their positions. Each initial statement may take five minutes.)

Actor A: Wants to build a shopping center in the park.

Actor B: Proposes to build several good quality, adult-only, twelve-story apartment buildings.

Actor C: Wants the park to remain as is or have its natural qualities enhanced.

Mayor: Chairs the presentation, says council members (other class members) may wish to ask brief questions, explains that each presenter will be allowed a one-minute final statement after the questions, and that council (the class) will then vote on the park's future.

Fair Play

Fairfield High School had poor physical education facilities that had to be shared by the boys and girls. A domineering male department head had for years over-favored boys in all resource allocation respects. Finally, a new principal appointed a young female as physical education department *head* and asked her to make appropriate changes so that the girls would be treated equally. She called a meeting to which the following were invited.

(At this point the instructor should assign roles in a fashion similar to that used in "The Park Play.")

Principal: Expects changes.

Department Head: Wants to implement changes.

Ex-Department Head: Wants the status quo.
Football Captain: Wants the status quo.

Case Casts

The following cases lend themselves for easy adaptation into role playing simulations.

Case 2.11:   The Donkey
Case 2.21:   The End's In Sight
Case 2.22:   Field House Blues
Case 2.23:   Where There's Smoke
Case 4.03:   The Hired Gun
Case 5.11:   Jack's A Dull Boy
Case 5.13:   Summer Follies
Case 6.12:   A Few Too Many
Case 6.13:   The Bounty Hunters
Case 6.14:   The Lesson
Case 6.15:   The Silly Season
Case 6.24:   Pot Hunting
Case 6.26:   Flunk Flunks
Case 10.11: Off Target
Case 12.41: The Deep End

LEARNING DESIGN 12.6

BOOK CONCLUSION

Efforts throughout this book have been directed towards the preparation of sport administrators; with the intention of leading them through general theories to sport particular situations. So that they would have as sound a theoretical base, as is possible at present, upon which to develop their practice.

Those who have persevered to here will know that, despite numerous administrative-managerial texts and journals, there is "no universally accepted theory which is substantiated by a body of tested behavioral hypotheses" (Hodgkinson, 1978:157). And, particularly so in sport situations. Those theories we do have, have been described in the earlier chapters and it is not the intention to try to summarize here. They are very useful, but sport administrators/managers and their organizations are also saturated with a variety of pathologies (cf. Hodgkinson, 1978:151-170).

The sport administration-sport management continuum is one of the most important concepts of the book. Through an understanding of this, the new sport administrator is, at least, pointing in the right direction towards eliminating some of the pathologies which have been demonstrated in numerous cases.

The sport administrator is the sport philosopher in action so it is hoped that *right* sport administrators are chosen. Some would argue that administrators do not set policy but that politicians do. In his book, Hodgkinson (1978:158) refers to administration as "a subset of politics." However, in discussion, we agree that politics is administration at an extreme end of the continuum. This does not mean that only politicians make broad policies; they do not for they are tremendously influenced by high-level administrators who possess many of the qualities and skills recommended in earlier chapters. It is no surprise, then, that some top civil servants are paid more money than their country's top elected politician. A fine discussion of the roles of high-level administrators and politicians is in Self's (1972) *Administrative Theories and Politics*. Of course, Self was not trying to say that politics was administration, he was merely describing the functions of senior administrators and their relationships with politicians.

Hopefully, student readers will have really tried hard to resolve the book's cases by adopting "right" stances. I do not want to discourage such action now but offer a word of caution: With the sport organization world being an inferred "ball of wax," the insistence on right moral actions all the time can cause more sport organizational dysfunction than it is worth. So, the sport administrator is advised always to work towards Type I values but to save making big issues with antagonists for really important occasions. That is, be satisfied at times with the rational Type II values; IIA "Consequences" or IIB "Consensus" (see Chapter 2). On this point, Hodgkinson (1978:219) developed a proposition from Broudy (1965) which states: "The essence of leadership is to know when to raise and when to avoid a moral issue." Certainly, in all its facets, administrative leadership is an exciting challenge for the young sport professional.

References

Broudy, Harry S.: Conflicts in values. In Ohm, R. E., and Monahan, W. G. (Eds.): *Educational Administration: Philosophy in Action.* University of Oklahoma Press, 1965.

Hodgkinson, C.: *Towards a Philosophy of Administration.* Oxford, Basil Blackwell, 1978.

Self, P.: *Administrative Theories and Politics.* London, George Allen and Unwin, 1972.

INDEX